The Revelation Commentary
A Unique Prewrath Perspective

Dennis James Woods

LIFE TO LEGACY
ACADEMIC

The Revelation Commentary
A Unique Prewrath Perspective
Dennis James Woods, Copyright ©2025

ISBN-13: 978-1-947288-75-1

Life To Legacy Academic is an imprint of Life To Legacy, LLC

Produced with the assistance of Peachtree Publishing Services.

Typesetting provided by The Livingstone Corporation.

Library of Congress Control Number: 2024934363

Printed in the United States

10 9 8 7 6 5 4 3 2 1

TABLE OF CONTENTS

TABLE OF CONTENTS

ACKNOWLEDGMENTS

I would like to express my deepest and sincerest gratitude to the following individuals who have directly or indirectly contributed to this great work. Without the help of the Lord and your prayers and support, I never would have seen this project through to the end.

To my wonderful and precious wife, Chantia, you are a constant encourager and prayer partner and supporter who stuck by me through thick and thin. Thank you for being committed to Christ and me. You are a pearl of great price and precious to many.

Thank you to Elder James Gordon, whom I shared with at the very beginning of this project and who has been a source of encouragement as a friend and fellow minister to this day. To Benito Olivas and Nate Spate, my first students at the Milwaukee Rescue Mission, you have been a source of encouragement along this glorious path.

A special thanks to all the Victory Apostolic Church family for their love and support shown toward me and my wife. To Pastor Andrew D. Singleton Jr., M.Div., CPA, you are solid in doctrine, unmovable in faith, but not afraid to hear a different perspective. Thank you for your wisdom, encouragement, and support.

To all the followers and supporters of the Revelation Revolution Podcast and PHD Ministries' Radio Bible Class in Chicago, thank you for your support, and God bless you!

To all the individuals who will be blessed by this commentary, this work is for you, so you may be better equipped to inform family, friends, associates, and those who are in Christ to be prepared for the glorious coming of our Lord.

ACKNOWLEDGMENTS

THE REVIEW COMMITTEE

Special thanks to the following individuals who served on the commentary review committee from the beginning to the end. You encouraged and challenged me to help perfect this work. Your prayers and expertise were of great value to the completion of this work. As iron sharpens iron, so have your thoughtful input help sharpen this commentary.

Rev. Henry S. Roberts, MA, Northern Baptist Theological Seminary

Martin Stratton, Pastor of Christian Education,
Victory Apostolic Church, Matteson, Ill.

Sloan J. Luckie, CPA, MBA
Victory Apostolic Church, Matteson, Ill.

Deacon Mark Daniels
Victory Apostolic Church, Matteson, Ill.

ABBREVIATIONS

1 Chr	1 Chronicles
1 Cor	1 Corinthians
1 Kgs	1 Kings
1 Macc	1 Maccabees
1 Pet	1 Peter
1 Thess	1 Thessalonians
1 Tim	1 Timothy
2 Chr	2 Chronicles
2 Cor	2 Corinthians
2 Kgs	2 Kings
2 Pet	2 Peter
2 Thess	2 Thessalonians
2 Tim	2 Timothy
AD	*anno Domini*; "in the year of [our] Lord"
Ap. Lit.	Apocalyptic Literature
BC	before Christ
BDAG	Bauer, Danker, Arndt, and Gingrich (*Greek-English Lexicon of the New Testament*)

bk.	book
cf.	compare
chap(s).	chapter(s)
CJB	Complete Jewish Bible
Col	Colossians
CSB	Christian Standard Bible
Dan	Daniel
Deut	Deuteronomy
ed(s).	editor(s)
e.g.	*exempli gratia*; "for example"
Eph	Ephesians
ESV	English Standard Version
et al.	*et alia, et alii*; "and others"
etc.	*et cetera*; "and other things"
Exod	Exodus
Ezek	Ezekiel
ff.	folio; "and the following [pages]"
Gal	Galatians
Gen	Genesis
Gk.	Greek
Hab	Habakkuk
Heb	Hebrews

Heb.	Hebrew
Hos	Hosea
i.e.	*id est,* "that is"
Isa	Isaiah
Jas	James
Jer	Jeremiah
Josh	Joshua
Judg	Judges
KJV	King James Version
Lev	Leviticus
Mal	Malachi
Matt	Matthew
Mic	Micah
Midtrib	Midtribulational(ist)
NA	*Novum Testamentum Graece*
NASB	New American Standard Bible (1995 update)
Neh	Nehemiah
NET1	New English Translation First Edition
NIV	New International Version
NT	New Testament
Num	Numbers
OT	Old Testament

ABBREVIATIONS

p.	page
Phil	Philippians
Posttrib	Posttribulational(ist)
pp.	pages
Pretrib	Pretribulational(ist)
Prov	Proverbs
Ps(s)	Psalm(s)
Rev	Revelation
Rom	Romans
s.v.	*sub verbo*; "under the word"
s.vv.	*sub verbis*; "under the words"
trans.	translator
v.	verse
vv.	verses
Zech	Zechariah
Zeph	Zephaniah
*	Glossary reference

✝

INTRODUCTION

One of the many advantages that believers have today that Christians in centuries past did not have is access to a wide range of biblical information. We have at our disposal Bible software containing countless resources for historical data and smartphones programmed with multiple Bible versions and commentaries. Technology has put learning and research right at our fingertips. While sitting in a pew, a layperson can effortlessly fact-check a minister's sermon points with a simple Google search. However, with so much knowledge at our disposal, the question is, Why are so many Christians ignorant of the book of Revelation?

If you ask Christians if they read the book of Revelation, the responses will vary. Many will claim, "Our pastor tells us to stay away from Revelation because it's too mysterious." Others will say, "It's too frightening with all its cryptic symbols and metaphors." Others will claim they cannot understand it. Still others will say most of Revelation has already been fulfilled, and therefore it is not necessary to read it. However, among the many objections to reading Revelation, the most significant and troubling response is probably the most common—that Revelation does not apply to the church.

The question is, How are people reaching that conclusion? The answer is simple. For almost two hundred years, dispensational eschatology has been a dominant influence on how the book of Revelation has been interpreted. In the dispensational system, Israel and the church are two distinct programs and God deals with both separately. After the Jews rejected Christ during His earthly ministry, Israel as a nation fell into a state of spiritual blindness or hardness (Rom 11:25). God then turned His salvific attention to "the church," consisting of Jews and *Gentiles*,* which began on the Day of Pentecost (Acts 2) and has been running for two thousand years and counting. However, once the full number of souls is reached, God will rapture the church to heaven. After the church is gone, God will pour out His wrath on *Israel** to bring them to national repentance after they enter into a seven-year covenant with the Antichrist. Subsequently, Israel will then accept Jesus as the Messiah upon His return. Therefore, according to dispensational thought, most of Revelation deals with the wrath of God specifically appointed for Israel and the wicked secular world, but not the church. This is the primary reason that those who embrace a dispensational understanding of eschatology (end times prophecy) believe in a Pretribulation rapture, seeing most of Revelation as not applying to the church (also see "Dispensationalism Comes to the United States").

In the West, particularly in the United States, most Christians have been taught or influenced by the *Pretribulation Rapture Theory**(Pretrib). When believers are asked about end-times prophecy and the events contained in the book of Revelation, their overwhelming response is that we're not going to be here for these events. This almost dismissive attitude has been fostered by the tenets of the Pretrib position, which has emphatically insisted that the church will not be on earth during most of the events contained in the book of Revelation. In many church organizations, this position is so passionately held that lay people can be disfellowshipped and ministers can be stripped of ministerial responsibilities. The Pretrib rapture is part of many churches' statements of faith, and compliance is expected and enforced. If they teach otherwise (though some quietly have reservations), they can be declared heretics. For some, it has even become a salvific issue.

However, after approaching Revelation with an open mind, without any doctrinal constraints, many people are discovering that Revelation does apply to the church, and they are beginning to question the validity of Pretrib. Unfortunately, pastors and laypeople who have second thoughts concerning Pretrib may sometimes feel pressured into silence; speaking up could lead to their ostracization. Yet just because a doctrine is traditional or is a staple of denominational dogma, that does not make it true. The Scriptures warned against the pitfalls of tradition. Jesus stated, "Thus you nullify the word of God by your tradition that you have handed down. And you do many things like that" (Mark 7:13 NIV). The question is, Has the book of Revelation been nullified by Pretrib because of its insistence that most of this divinely inspired book does not apply to the very church it was given to?

Let's be clear: The purpose of this commentary is not to attack those who believe in a Pretrib rapture. In fact, if the Pretrib rapture theory is correct and the church is raptured before the *tribulation period*,* that's great news. Glory be to God! That means the church will not be on earth during all the events that occur in Revelation between chapters 6 and 19. The church will also not be on earth during the signing of the *peace covenant*,* the building of the third temple in Israel, the revealing of the Antichrist, or the challenges associated with the mark of *the beast*.* If Pretrib is correct, then the book of Revelation is merely informational because it has no application to the church. Those who believe in a Midtrib, Prewrath, or Posttrib rapture will receive the benefit of being caught up sooner than they expected. Of course, those who support Pretrib will get the benefit of having it right. This is a win-win situation for everyone.

However, what if the Pretrib rapture theory is wrong? Would there still be a win-win situation for everyone? The answer is an emphatic no. There would be no win-win because millions of unsuspecting Christians would still be on earth for a time of tribulation that their pastors, commentaries, scholars, family, and friends have all insisted the church would not be here to experience. Christians would be caught flat-footed while facing the reality of persecution, imprisonment, death, and financial disenfranchisement. Though none of these trials can separate us from the love of Christ (Rom 8:35–39), those who believe in a Pretrib rapture see facing these tribulations as being under the wrath of God, which contradicts the position that the church cannot be on earth during the tribulation period. However, that would simply mean that modern-day Christians would face conditions that the early Christians lived with daily. To some Pretribulationists, that is simply unacceptable.

INTRODUCTION

This is a serious weakness. Pretrib does not leave room for the "what if" scenario. It offers no alternative to those who embrace it. It can cause current adherents to stick their heads in the sand and not consider anything else. A better perspective for Pretribbers would be "This is how we hope it will turn out, but if it doesn't, the book of Revelation gives instructions for that coming time." If Pretrib was presented like that, people would at least be exposed to the possibility of an alternate outcome. However, many Pretribulationists do not allow that. They present no options that circumstances could turn out differently. That's unfortunate because no human being can assure that the rapture will be Pretrib. We can speculate, we can hope, we can believe, but we cannot guarantee.

Another problem is that many Pretrib adherents *are not* told that this position is a theoretical proposition. In the celebrated dispensational reference work *Things to Come*, author J. Dwight Pentecost correctly refers to it as the "Pretribulation Rapture Theory."[1] However, the word *theory* has long been dropped when teaching this position because a theory implies some areas of uncertainty—something people do not want when it comes to the future. But since the rapture has not occurred, there are many unknowns about what is to come. No human being is an expert on future events; no one knows what will happen tomorrow, let alone what events will lead up to a prophecy's fulfillment. Neither exposition nor exegesis of any prophetic verses can reveal *how* or *when* a prophecy will be fulfilled. God can tell us exactly *what* He is going to do, but we will not know *how* or *when* He is going to do it unless He reveals it. Consequently, there are no interpretive tools available to humankind that can extract the *how* and *when* from a prophetic text. Despite this, millions of Christians are putting all their eggs in a Pretrib basket because they have received human assurances that no person has the authority to give.

---

[1] J. Dwight Pentecost, *Things to Come: A Study in Biblical Eschatology* (Grand Rapids, MI: Zondervan Publishing House, 1965), 193.

Finally, Pretrib has taught Christians that there is no comfort in being persecuted by the Antichrist. Therefore, the believers' desire for comfort becomes the framework for their selection of an eschatological view. Comfort becomes the mold into which Pretrib's acceptance is shaped. However, that is inconsistent with historical Christianity, which has been drenched in the blood of the saints. Tertullian, an early Christian writer, wrote, "The oftener we are mown down by you, the more in number we grow; *the blood of Christians is seed.*"[2] The apostle Paul stated, "For to me, to live is Christ and to die is gain" (Phil 1:21). Paul was comforted by the fact that, though he would be martyred, he would be present with the Lord. Therefore, he saw dying for the faith as gain, not loss. Another example of comfort in action during dire times was the martyrdom of Stephen when he was about to be stoned to death. Stephen was so filled with the Holy Spirit, the Comforter Himself, that he asked the Lord to forgive those who were stoning him (Acts 7:54–60). That's comfort under fire. Comfort and tribulation are not mutually exclusive. However, many Pretribulationists embrace a concept of comfort that avoids suffering in the end times. For Christians, the concept of comfort is not so much about being comforted in this world as it is about being comforted by the assurance of eternal life. Jesus stated, "These things I have spoken to you, so that in Me you may have peace. In the world you have tribulation, but take courage; I have overcome the world" (John 16:33).

When considering early Christians' view on tribulation, another important point is that they believed they would see the arrival of the Antichrist (1 John 2:18). The following church fathers make this point clear. Tertullian writes, "Heresies, at the present time, will no less rend the church by their perversion of doctrine, than will Antichrist persecute her at that day by the cruelty of his attacks."[3] Tertullian held to

---

[2] Tertullian, "The Apology," in *Latin Christianity: Its Founder, Tertullian,* ed. Alexander Roberts, James Donaldson, and A. Cleveland Coxe, trans. S. Thelwall, vol. 3, *The Ante-Nicene Fathers* (Buffalo, NY: Christian Literature Company, 1885), 55.

[3] Allan Menzies, *Latin Christianity: Its Founder Tertullian,* vol. 3, chap. 4, "Ante-Nicene Fathers: The Writings of the Fathers Down to AD 325" (Edinburgh, Scotland: 1867), 245.

*historic premillennialism,** the position that argues that the church will endure the great tribulation but will not be the object of God's wrath poured out on the wicked.[4]

*Cyprian,** bishop of Carthage, states, "For even Antichrist, when he shall begin to come, shall not enter into the Church because he threatens; neither shall we yield to his arms and violence, because he declares that he will destroy us if we resist."[5] If Christians in the early centuries expected to see the Antichrist, that means they were not Pretrib in the contemporary dispensational sense, but closer to today's Posttrib position.

St. Augustine, bishop of Hippo, asserts, "I do not think, indeed, that what some have thought or may think is rashly said or believed, that until the time of Antichrist the Church of Christ is not to suffer any persecutions besides those she has already suffered,—that is, *ten,*—and that the eleventh and last shall be inflicted by Antichrist."[6]

Unfortunately, many Christians in the West, especially in the United States, see the rapture through the lens of comfort and believe a rapture position that teaches the church is rescued from the persecution of the Antichrist. When looking at Revelation through a lens of comfort, much of Revelation would not qualify as comforting. The typical mindset of Christians is *Why would God let us go through that? Being martyred by the beast is not comforting.* Therefore, they believe the Pretrib rapture position must be the right one. With that position, believers can maintain their concept of comfort.

The "comfort" issue is primarily taken from 1 Thessalonians 4:18 where Paul tells the Thessalonians to "comfort one another with these words."

---

[4] *Holman Illustrated Bible Dictionary* (Nashville, TN: Holman Bible Publishers, 2003), s.v. "eschatology," "Posttribulationism."

[5] Cyprian of Carthage, "The Epistles of Cyprian," in *Fathers of the Third Century: Hippolytus, Cyprian, Novatian, Appendix*, eds. Alexander Roberts, James Donaldson, and A. Cleveland Coxe, trans. Robert Ernest Wallis, vol. 5 of *The Ante-Nicene Fathers: The Writings of the Fathers Down to AD 325* (Buffalo, NY: The Christian Literature Company, 1886), 346.

[6] Augustine of Hippo, "St. Augustin's City of God," vol. 2, bk. 18, chap. 52, *Nicene and Post-Nicene Fathers of the Christian Church*, ed. Philip Schaff, trans. Marcus Dods (Edinburgh, Scotland: The Christian Literature Company, 1886).

Pretrib emphasizes the word "comfort" while not considering the context in which "comfort" is being used. In 1 Thessalonians 4:18, "comfort" is used in contrast to the *sorrow or grief* the Thessalonians were experiencing due to their concern for the eternal position of their dead loved ones upon Christ's return (1 Thess 4:13–14). First and foremost, the Thessalonians, like many in churches during the first century, experienced severe persecution. They fully embraced the fact that they were suffering on behalf of the kingdom of God (2 Thess 1:4–7). Their dilemma was concerning their loved ones who had already passed away. This was the issue that caused them to grieve, not the persecution they were facing. In response to their concern, Paul said, "[we do] not grieve as do the rest who have no hope" (1 Thess 4:13). In other words, the Christians' comfort is to be tied to the fact that we have eternal life and a blessed hope in Christ. On this basis, we do not grieve as others who do not have the blessed hope.

In the 1 Thessalonians 4 text, the idea of *comfort* was to counter the saints' uncertainty as to the state of their loved ones who had died before the Lord's return. Paul was not teaching that the comfort he offered should be the lens through which they saw future events. Unfortunately, many who hold to a Pretrib rapture interpret 1 Thessalonians 4 in this way. They use v. 18 as a basis to determine which rapture position is acceptable and to reinforce the idea that comfort should trump suffering. Remaining faithful to Jesus during the time of the beast will cause imprisonment, loss of life, and loss of livelihood, none of which is comforting, especially for the person focused on human concerns.

This is the reason Jesus rebuked Peter when He disclosed His coming sufferings. Peter responded, "Never, Lord! This shall never happen to you" (Matt 16:22 NIV). Then Jesus rebuked him sharply and said, "Get behind me, Satan! You are a stumbling block to me; you do not have in mind the concerns of God, but merely human concerns" (Matt 16:23 NIV). Placing human concerns, like maintaining one's comfort, above God's concerns is a narrative inspired by the devil. Peter thought he was saying the right thing. He did not want his Lord to experience suffering. However, he didn't realize that he was being inspired by Satan to exalt human concerns over God's. The comfort of self-preservation reigns supreme in the human heart.

What is reaffirming and comforting to the flesh gives priority to the individual's preferences, not to Jesus'—the one who has called for us to suffer for His name's sake (Phil 1:29). Whether we accept it or not, God has a purpose for our suffering. He uses it to bring glory to His name and to serve as a reason to testify about our faith in Christ. Jesus stated,

> But before all these things, they will lay their hands on you and will persecute you, delivering you to the synagogues and prisons, bringing you before kings and governors for My name's sake. It will lead to an opportunity for your testimony. (Luke 21:12–13)

This is a powerful statement because it gives the reason why the Lord would allow His disciples to go through suffering: so that they could testify about the goodness and greatness of God to those who were persecuting them. This fact is affirmed in Revelation 12:11 where it states, "They overcame [Satan] because of the blood of the Lamb and because of the word of their testimony." Another important point to consider is that Jesus has the keys of death and hell (Rev 1:18) and declared, "Do not fear those who kill the body but are unable to kill the soul; but rather fear Him who is able to destroy both soul and body in hell" (Matt 10:28). Those who die for being faithful to Christ unto the point of death are exalted in heaven. Believing this is the source of true comfort. It's not avoiding suffering that counts but participating in it that fulfills God's purpose for it. Paul declared,

> For this light momentary affliction is preparing for us an eternal weight of glory beyond all comparison, as we look not to the things that are seen but to the things that are unseen. For the things that are seen are transient, but the things that are unseen are eternal. (2 Cor 4:17–18 ESV)

He also said,

> The Spirit Himself testifies with our spirit that we are chil-
> dren of God, and if children, heirs also, heirs of God and
> fellow heirs with Christ, if indeed we suffer with Him so that
> we may also be glorified with Him. (Rom 8:16–17)

One day, the righteous will see the final end of the wicked, including the judgment of Satan, the Antichrist, the false prophet, and all those who took the mark of the beast and worshiped the Antichrist. It is the ulti-mate comfort to know that no Christian's service, sacrifice, and suffering will go unrewarded and that no evil deed perpetrated against them will go unpunished. This is the enduring message and comfort that the book of Revelation provides to Christians of every generation, from the first century until today and forward. In the end, God will certainly settle all accounts based on the veracity of His infallible Word.

> For God is not unjust so as to forget your work and the love
> which you have shown toward His name, in having min-
> istered and in still ministering to the saints. And we desire
> that each one of you show the same diligence so as to realize
> the full assurance of hope until the end, so that you will not
> be sluggish, but imitators of those who through faith and
> patience inherit the promises. (Heb 6:10–12)

It is undeniable that Revelation 13:7 explicitly states the beast will "make war with *the saints*"*(emphasis added). It is indisputable that these saints are saved, have eternal life, and are in heaven before the throne of God. Salvific status is not the issue. So, what then is the prob-lem? The answer is simple: suffering. Because the Revelation 13 saints are on earth during the time of the Antichrist and suffer imprisonment and martyrdom, Pretrib separates the Revelation 13 saints from the body of Christ, making them a secondary group of believers that has no relationship to the church. However, this is a doctrinal distinction, not a biblical one.

Dispensationalism Comes to the United States

Most evangelical, Pentecostal, charismatic, and nondenominational congregations teach a Pretrib rapture of the church, which is a prominent feature of what is known as dispensationalism. Many of those who do not know the technical aspects of Pretrib are familiar with the series of books and movies titled *Left Behind*. This fictional storyline has influenced what many believe about the rapture. And when it comes to defending the Pretrib rapture theory, people will often say clichés like, "We're not going to be here," "The church is not in most of the book of Revelation," "If you want to be here, fine; I'll be gone," or "Jesus would not beat up His bride right before the wedding." These are just a few of the rhetorical responses you hear defending a Pretrib rapture.

Dispensationalism, the theological system from which Pretrib proceeds, has deep roots in the United States. However, since dispensationalism did not become embedded in US eschatology until the mid-1800s, there's the question of what *eschatology** was embraced beforehand. In the 1800s, several ecclesiastical and theological movements emerged in America. One of these was the *Restorationist Movement*, where restoring Christian unity and the commitment to the authority of the Scriptures were of primary emphasis. During this movement, various groups focused on the coming millennium.[7] Chief among these millennial perspectives was the postmillennial view, whose most influential advocate was Puritan scholar Jonathan Edwards. Postmillennialism had a very optimistic view that the spread of the gospel through revival and missionary endeavors would realize a golden age of the church to prepare for Christ to return.[8] However, there were other groups that emphasized various millennial perspectives that differed from postmillennialism. On April 6, 1830, Joseph Smith started The Church of Jesus Christ of Latter-day Saints,

---

[7] James B. North, "Restorationist Movement," in *Dictionary of Christianity in America*, eds. Daniel G. Reid, Robert D. Linder, Bruce L. Shelley, and Harry S. Stout, (Downers Grove, IL: InterVarsity Press, 1990), 1005.

[8] Robert G. Clause, "Postmillennialism," in *Dictionary of Christianity in America*, 919.

later known as the Mormon Church.[9] A few years later, an influential Baptist preacher named William Miller convinced a vast group of his followers, called *Millerites*,* that the Lord would return in 1844. From the Millerites came the Seventh-day Adventist Church.[10] In 1870, a more doctrinally radical Adventist adherent, Charles Taze Russell, started the Watch Tower Bible and Tract Society, which was renamed Jehovah's Witnesses in 1956.[11]

The expansion of millennial thought and theology during this period was the perfect theological environment for an Anglican minister named *John Nelson Darby** to bring dispensationalism to America. Dispensationalism's focus is expansive, extending back to the garden of Eden and forward to the New Heaven and New earth, identifying seven dispensations that determined the method in which God dealt with humankind (see "Millennial Views" later in this introduction). Its primary tenets maintain a strict separation between Israel and the church and assert an *imminent return of Christ** for the church by a Pretribulational rapture (more on Darby later).

However, the Restorationist Movement was not the only trend that brought change and challenge to the United States. There were many ideological, sociological, political, and theological challenges that vied for prominence in the population's consciousness. Two other pressing issues were the *abolitionist movement** and the fight against *theological liberalism*.* The South was a battleground against both movements.

In the slaveholding states, many Christians embraced chattel slavery and found biblical justification for maintaining the institution. Church leaders in those states mounted vehement defenses for the institution of slavery on biblical grounds and despised the abolitionists who stood against it. J. Albert Harrill observes, "The proslavery, plain sense of all

---

9   Irving Hexham, "Joseph Smith," in *Dictionary of Christianity in America*, 1097.
10   Gary G. Land, "William Miller," in *Dictionary of Christianity in America*, 740.
11   Irving Hexham, "Charles T. Russell," in *Dictionary of Christianity in America*, 1032.

these sacred texts had remained undisturbed throughout their history of interpretation until, [quoting Albert Bledsoe], 'abolitionists set its cloven foot upon the Bible.' "[12] However, the abolitionists also used the Bible to argue their side against slavery, but it was bitterly opposed. "The hermeneutics of plain sense took priority in proslavery argumentation to attack the infidel antislavery abolitionist hermeneutics."[13]

Though Southerners defended the institution of slavery, the inhumanity associated with the institution was indefensible. Maddex observes, "In the 1830s, southern Presbyterian theologians studied the question intensively and arrived at a pro slavery consensus. Dealing with slavery's future incidentally rather than as a central issue they nevertheless considered it in a millennial perspective."[14] In 1858, Thomas R. R. Cobb wrote an expansive treatise in defense of slavery titled *An Inquiry into the Law of Negro Slavery, In the United States of America*, of which Maddex notes, "Cobb interpreted references to slaves in the Book of Revelations as indications that slavery would continue until the Second Coming. It not only might, but must, exist in the millennium."[15] However, there were many other prominent advocates for slavery. "In their controversy with northern abolitionists, southern Presbyterian theologians insisted that the Bible recognized slavery as a legitimate system without hinting that it was bad or transient."[16] "[James] Thornwell, the foremost Southern Presbyterian thinker, regarded slavery and other coercive institutions as instruments in God's long-term program to perfect humanity... God might intend slavery to continue as long as mortality itself—until the

---

[12] J. Albert Harrill, "The Use of the New Testament in the American Slave Controversy: A Case History in the Hermeneutical Tension Between Biblical Criticism and Christian Moral Debate," *Religion and American Culture: A Journal of Interpretation* 10, no. 2 (Summer 2000): 171 (quoting Bledsoe, Albert T., *Liberty and Slavery*, J. B. Lippincott & Co., 1856, Philadelphia, 377), https://www.jstor.org/stable/1123945.

[13] Harrill, "The Use of the New Testament," 171.

[14] Jack P. Maddex, "Proslavery Millennialism: Social Eschatology in Antebellum Southern Calvinism." *American Quarterly* 31, no. 1 (1979): 49–62, https://doi.org/10.2307/2712486.

[15] Maddex, "Proslavery Millennialism," 55, quoting Cobb Inquiry, Chap. 2, p. 64.

[16] Maddex, "Proslavery Millennialism," 49.

end of the Millennium."[17] This ideology weds postmillennial beliefs with the institution of slavery and reflects the optimism embraced by postmillennialists that slavery fits naturally into the scheme of "perfecting humanity." Maddex sees this as a basis for the concept called *proslavery millennialism.** Contemporary dispensational scholar Thomas Ice observed, "Postmillennialism was the popular view of eschatology, but increasingly things did not appear to be following its optimistic script.... Americans had difficulty retaining postmillennial optimism in view of the Civil War."[18]

It was during this turbulent period that dispensationalism came to the shores of the United States. "The premillennialists [dispensationalists] gained popularity during the *postbellum** period, accepting the Bible as an infallible guide for understanding both history and the future."[19] They also embraced *inerrancy** and the literal interpretation of the Scriptures. On the other hand, liberal beliefs about the millennium were reinterpreted as metaphorical and figurative."[20] At this time, dispensationalism featured the hope for an imminent return of Christ for the church, judgment and wrath for the wicked, and the establishment of God's kingdom on earth during the *millennium.**

English Bible teacher and leader of the original *Plymouth Brethren,** John Nelson Darby was born in London in 1800 and later *systematized* and introduced dispensationalism to the United States. After a disruptive clash with fellow Brethren leader and evangelist B. W. Newton in 1845 over the doctrine of the secret rapture, Darby developed his distinctive views through prophetic conferences and Bible study. He shaped the

---

[17] Maddex, "Proslavery Millennialism," 50, quoting Thornwell, Writings, 4:419-22

[18] Thomas D. Ice, "A Short History of Dispensationalism," *Article Archives* (2009): 37, https://digitalcommons.liberty.edu/pretrib_arch/37.

[19] W. Michael Ashcraft, "Progressive Millennialism," in *The Oxford Handbook of Millennialism*, ed. Catherine Wessinger (Oxford: Oxford University Press, 2011), 54, quoted in James H. Moorehead, *World Without End: Mainstream American Protestant Visions of the Last Things, 1880–1925* (Bloomington: Indiana University Press, 1999).

[20] Ashcraft, *The Oxford Handbook of Millennialism*, 54.

prophetic perspective and outlook on eschatology for the Brethren.[21] "Between 1859 and 1874, he [Darby] made several trips to the United States and Canada."[22] In the year 1818, before Darby's trips to the US, William Miller predicted that Christ would return between 1843 and 1844. Miller taught his view fervently, but it led to a predictive debacle that came to be known as the *great embarrassment*.*[23] In the wake of Miller's public humiliation, Darby's dispensationalism was more attractive because it taught that Christ could return at any moment but did not propose a specific date for His return, which Miller and others previously insisted on in their similar predictions.

Some opponents of the dispensational Pretrib rapture assert that Darby developed dispensationalism in the nineteenth century. They disregard dispensationalism because they see it as a more recent doctrine that was not widely taught in the first centuries. However, supporters of dispensationalism, like author and prophecy teacher Grant Jeffrey, have long disputed this point. In addition, William C. Watson's book *Dispensationalism Before Darby: Seventeenth-Century and Eighteenth-Century English Apocalypticism* makes the case that dispensationalism was not from Darby but that it preceded him. Pretribulationists such as Lee Brainard, Ken Johnson, Thomas Ice, and many others have picked up this mantle.

Though many embrace the early-church dispensational evidence, others have disputed and refuted those findings. Joel Richardson of the *Maranatha Global Bible Study* podcast, in the series titled *The Rapture and the Endurance of the Saints* (2023), conducts a thorough refutation of the claims that dispensationalism and Pretribulationism are found in the writings of *Victorinus,* *Pseudo-Ephraem,* *Aspringius,* *Oceumenius,* and others. Though it is true that some concepts of dispensationalism can be *found* in early writings, the system we call dispensationalism today

---

[21] John D. Hannah, "John Nelson Darby," in *Dictionary of Christianity in America*, 339.

[22] John D. Hannah, "John Nelson Darby," in *Dictionary of Christianity in America*.

[23] Gary G. Land, "William Miller," in *Dictionary of Christianity in America*, 740.

was an expansion on Darby's work by Brookes, Scofield and others. Some suggest the term dispensationalism was coined later in the 1920s.

Though historic premillennialism (Posttrib) and amillennialism were common, postmillennialism was the dominant view. (See "Millennial Views" later in this introduction.) During the nineteenth century, dispensationalism and conservative coalitions became galvanized in their stance against theological liberalism. The threat of a civil war that sought to change the way of life in the *antebellum** South was seen by Southerners as an unwarranted incursion by liberal Northerners. The confluence of ideological, sociological, political, and theological ideas of the time facilitated dispensationalism's becoming entrenched in the thinking and theology of Southerners. From this perspective, we can see that today's dispensationalism and Pretribulationism are not merely doctrinal positions but closely align with the traditions, psychological and economic roots, and political and religious ideology of many Christians in the South. Though it was not as popular in Europe from which it came, dispensationalism spread throughout the United States, Canada, and eventually around the world once its roots were well established, reaching the prominence that it has today.

However, after the defeat and fall of the Confederacy, many of the Southern Christians who embraced the perpetuity of slavery—an obviously failed ideology and theology—shifted to a premillennialist view, which had already made its way onto the US theological landscape. The failure of the Confederacy was also the failure of proslavery millennialism and undermined the optimism of postmillennialism. Subsequently, many Southerners were attracted to the imminent and soon-coming of the Lord espoused in premillennialism, featuring a Pretrib rapture. From their perspective, the soon-coming and imminent return of the Lord to rapture them and bring judgment upon the wicked world that ensued in the wake of the South's devastating defeat was desirable. The *American Quarterly* states the following:

In the 1860's Southern Presbyterians underwent confusion about eschatology. Some embraced the premillennialist belief that humanity was plunging into an orgy of evil which only the impending advent could halt. . . . Conservative Presbyterians in the border states, most of whom joined the Southern branch of the denomination after 1865, showed similar tendencies. Protesting against Unionist civil religion, they championed "spirituality" and showed an interest in premillennialism. The St. Louis minister James H. Brookes, disgusted with the direction of the church and society, adopted the "dispensational" idea that Christ would soon remove his true followers from the irredeemable world.[24]

James Hall Brookes*—a Presbyterian pastor as well—became a key proponent of dispensationalism. The fall of the Confederacy meant the hopes of an eschatology that projected slavery into the millennium were now destroyed. The emancipation of the slaves, Reconstruction, and the upending of life in the South were significant factors for the discontentment and confusion about a postmillennial eschatology. Many Southern Christians were disillusioned in the aftermath of losing to the North. "The downfall of slavery and the Confederacy crushed the very structure of their hopes and plunged them into a crisis of faith. They recalled in anguish their wartime anticipation of a perfected slaveholding society, nation, and church."[25]

As Maddex cites, "Brookes . . . adopted the dispensational idea that Christ would soon remove his true followers from the irredeemable world."[26] This was an especially attractive position that gave hope to those who despised the world they inherited in the aftermath of the Civil War and the emancipation of slaves.

---

[24] Maddex, "Proslavery Millennialism," 60–61.

[25] Maddex, "Proslavery Millennialism," 59.

[26] Maddex, "Proslavery Millennialism," 59–61.

After pivoting to premillennialism, Brookes became a driving force in the spread of dispensationalism in the US and "was instrumental in promoting the *doctrine of imminence** that Christ might return at any moment."[27] Brookes was one of the first to teach a Pretrib rapture" and "he hosted [the] British Brethren leader . . . at his church on multiple occasions."[28] Brookes was prominently featured at the *Niagara Bible Conferences** held at Niagara-on-the-Lake, Ontario (1883–1897).[29] The conference, originally called "Believers' Meeting for Bible Study," was organized by James Inglis and George Needham[30] and was later presided over by Brookes. Brookes was a prolific writer who wrote seventeen books, released more than 250 tracts, published numerous articles, and widely distributed his magazine, *The Truth.*

One of Brookes's most influential students was *C. I. Scofield,** who served as a Confederate infantryman of the Seventh Regiment of Tennessee[31] and who later became a lawyer and legislator. Scofield edited the immensely popular *Scofield Reference Bible,** published by Oxford Press in 1909. Its content spread dispensationalism and Pretrib rapture theology throughout the United States and around the world. In this groundbreaking reference Bible, Scofield's notes and commentaries were so closely intertwined with the Scriptures that many accepted Scofield's notes with the same veracity as the Scriptures, further validating the dispensational view. The Scofield Bible promoted several dispensational tenets: (a) holding to a literal interpretation of the Scriptures, (b) accepting that

---

[27] P. C. Wilts, *Dictionary of Christianity in America*, eds. Daniel G. Reid, Robert D. Linder, Bruce L. Shelley, and Harry S. Stout (Downers Grove, IL: InterVarsity Press, 1990), s.v. "Brookes, James H." 191.

[28] Thomas D. Ice, "James Hall Brookes: Early Pretribulational Rapture Pioneer —Tom's Perspectives," Pre-Trib Research Center, 3, https://www.pre-trib.org/pretribfiles/pdfs/Ice-James-HallBrookes.pdf.

[29] Stephen Spencer, *The Encyclopedia of Christianity*, eds. Eriwin Fahlbusch, Jan Milic Lochman, John Mbiti, Jaroslav Jan Pelikan, Lukas Vischer, and David B. Barrett, trans. Geoffrey W. Bromiley, vol. 1, *A–D* (Grand Rapids, MI: Eerdmans–Brill, 1998), s.v. "Dispensationalism," 854.

[30] W. V. Trollinger, "Niagara Conferences," in *Dictionary of Christianity in America*, eds. Daniel G. Reid, Robert D. Linder, Bruce L. Shelley, and Harry S. Stout (Downers Grove, IL: InterVarsity Press, 1990), 824.

[31] John D. Hannah, "Scofield, C.I.," in *Dictionary of Christianity in America*, 1057.

God has administered successive dispensations over history along with an accompanying covenant (i.e., the terms governing the dispensation), e.g., the dispensation of Law under the Mosaic covenant, (c) adhering to a strict distinction between Israel and the church, (d) believing in an imminent return of Christ, and (e) waiting for a Pretrib rapture before the seven-year tribulation, which will coincide with the beginning of *Daniel's Seventieth Week.** The Scofield Bible had an enormous impact on the acceptance of dispensationalism throughout the world because it made this doctrine accessible to everyday Christians.

Other luminaries responsible for the spread of dispensationalism and the Pretrib rapture doctrine were James Inglis, through his monthly magazine titled *Waymarks in the Wilderness;*[32] A. J. Gordon; Arno Gaebelein, a consulting editor for the *Scofield Reference Bible* (1939) and advocate for the Jews' role in the second coming of Christ;[33] William E. Blackstone; James M. Gray; and Clarence Larkin, best known for his vivid, detailed dispensational charts and celebrated books, *Dispensational Truth, The Book of Daniel,* and *The Book of Revelation.*

Dwight L. Moody* was the first major American revivalist to adopt premillennialist views,[34] which he avidly promoted. His powerful revivals, which attracted thousands, made him well-known. Moody also conducted revivals in the UK and met many of the Brethren—including their most influential member, John Nelson Darby. Though he had only a fifth grade education and was never ordained,[35] that did not hinder Moody's influence as a top revivalist. Because of his influence, many others embraced dispensationalism. Moody was the founder of Moody Memorial Church of Chicago and was also the president of the Chicago YMCA. The institutions

---

[32] James Inglis, *Waymarks in the Wilderness,* (New York: n.p., 1857), 2, https://archive.org/details/waymarksinwilder00ingl/page/2/mode/2up.

[33] T. P. Weber, *Dictionary of Christianity in America,* eds. Daniel G. Reid, Robert D. Linder, Bruce L. Shelley, and Harry S. Stout (Downers Grove, IL: InterVarsity Press, 1990), s.v. "Arno Gaebelein," 471.

[34] *Dictionary of Christianity in America,* s.v., "Dwight L. Moody."

[35] *Dictionary of Christianity in America,* s.v., "Dwight L. Moody."

founded in his name include Moody Bible Institute, Moody Publishers, and Moody Bible Institute radio network (WMBI).

Another dispensational giant was *Lewis Sperry Chafer*,* a Presbyterian minister and soloist who served in Moody's music ministry. After meeting Scofield in 1901, Chafer worked closely with him, becoming an extension teacher at Scofield's correspondence school. In 1924, he established the Evangelical Theological College, which in 1936 was renamed *Dallas Theological Seminary**(DTS). DTS became the flagship seminary that promoted dispensationalism. Chafer served there as president and professor of systematic theology until his death in 1952 and published several books, including his highly regarded four-volume work, *Systematic Theology*.[36] Some of Chafer's prominent students were Walvoord, Pentecost, Ryrie, and J. Vernon McGee. John Walvoord (probably the foremost authority on dispensationalism in the twentieth century) took over as president after Chafer's death. Pentecost, known for his celebrated reference book, *Things to Come*, a comprehensive defense of dispensationalism; and Ryrie, author of *The Ryrie Study Bible*, both taught at DTS and made significant modifications to classical dispensational thought.[37]

The names of influential dispensational pastors and scholars trained at DTS are too numerous to list here. However, one individual, who was a defender of Pretrib and who popularized end-times prophecy by linking it to current world events and geopolitical alignments, was Hal Lindsey. As Christopher C. Rowland observes, "Although thoroughly influenced by the particular fears of the late 20th century, most influential in this tradition has been Hal Lindsey's [*The*] *Late Great Planet Earth*,* according to *U.S. News and World Report* (December 13, 1997). This book and its sequels have phenomenal sales: 40 million copies."[38] Lindsey's books inspired a whole new pop cultural perspective on the end times,

---

[36] John D. Hannah, "Lewis Sperry Chafer," in *Dictionary of Christianity in America*, 237.

[37] Spencer, *The Encyclopedia of Christianity*, s.v. "Dispensationalism."

[38] Christopher C. Rowland, "The Book of Revelation," in *The New Interpreter's Bible Commentary* (Nashville, TN: Abingdon Press, 2015), 946.

which fueled its immense popularity. In addition, twice as successful as Lindsey were Tim LaHaye and Jerry Jenkins, though not DTS graduates, who wrote the fictional end-times book series *Left Behind,** which sold more than 80 million copies and led to movies of the same name.[39] Referencing the series, the late Moral Majority coalition leader Jerry Falwell Sr. reportedly said, "In terms of its impact on Christianity, it's probably greater than that of any other book in modern times, outside the Bible."[40] Lindsey and LaHaye and many others have made significant contributions to the spread of Pretrib. However, as other rapture views have developed and challenged the validity of the Pretrib rapture, modifications to this position have been made over time and are still ongoing. The latest dispensational approach is *progressive dispensationalism,** which attempts to soften the rigidity of classical dispensationalism by not insisting on strict boundaries between the dispensations. This system allows more fluidity and the overlapping of dispensations. It also examines how prophecies related to Israel apply to the church, instead of insisting on a strict separation of the two.

In conclusion, it is not being asserted that the events that led to the Civil War are the only factors in the acceptance of dispensationalism in America. However, the fall of the Confederacy forced those who embraced a pro-slavery millennial view fostered by postmillennial optimism to rethink their eschatology. In the aftermath of the Confederacy's demise, the pioneers of dispensationalism found comfort in this doctrine because it asserted an expectation of an imminent coming of the Lord, not in the distant future but at any moment. From this tumultuous yet transitional era, dispensationalism emerged as a glorious beacon of hope. It was from these roots that dispensationalism and the Pretrib rapture doctrine flour-

---

[39] Ann Byle, "LaHaye, Co-Author of Left Behind Series, Leaves a Lasting Impact," *Publishers Weekly,* July 27, 2016, News, Religion, https://www.publishersweekly.com/pw/by-topic/industry-news/religion/article/71026-lahaye-co-author-of-left-behind-series-leaves-a-lasting-impact.html.

[40] Mark Wingfield, "What's Wrong with 'Left Behind'?" Baptist News Global, August 12, 2021, Analysis, https://baptistnews.com/article/whats-wrong-with-left-behind/.

ished into the twentieth century, aided by the publication of the Scofield Reference Bible in 1909. Though amillennialism, postmillennialism, and preterism have considerable audiences, dispensationalism continues to enjoy wide acceptance and popularity among several Protestant denominations, particularly among fundamentalists and evangelicals.

HISTORIC METHODS OF INTERPRETATION OF REVELATION

No book in the *canon of Scripture** has solicited as much controversy and debate as the book of Revelation. No matter whose literature you read, pastors, commentators, and authors have their own opinion about this highly symbolic, *apocalyptic** book. However, throughout history, there have been systems of interpretation that Christians have embraced. Four of the main interpretive camps follow.

(1) **The Preterist Interpretation** sees Revelation as a book that addresses historic events contemporary to the first century. This camp asserts that most of these events occurred around AD 70 and that they are in no way predictive or futuristic. Those who hold this view prefer an early date of authorship for Revelation, between AD 54 and 68. Preterist emphasize that events in Revelation are "the things which must soon take place" (1:1) and that "the time is near" (1:3), meaning they were fulfilled during the first century. They also assert that Jesus' declaration that "this generation will not pass away until all these things take place" (Matt 24:34) is further evidence that these prophecies are historic and were fulfilled during the destruction of the temple in AD 70. Many hold to this or variations of this view today, distinguished as full or partial preterist.

(2) **The Historicist Interpretation** considers the book through the lens of Christian history and sees the church from John's time to the consummation of the ages. The seals, trumpets, and bowls are viewed as chronologically successive and

coinciding with chief phases of the church's development and struggle, all the way to its final victory being set forth in a panoramic view of church history. This interpretation sees Revelation's imagery as applying to the Roman Empire, the Roman Catholic Church, the Protestant Reformation, the French Revolution, and as the means for the spread of Christianity.

(3) **The Futurist Interpretation** sees the book of Revelation as primarily prophetic, having prophecies yet to be fulfilled. Many cite a weakness with the futurist interpretation in that the book would have had no significance to first-century Christians if it were primarily futuristic. However, that reason alone is insufficient to negate the overwhelming futuristic character of the Apocalypse. God has given Revelation from His eternal now perspective, where all time is before Him. The preterist assertion that Revelation is primarily concerned with first-century Christians is an overreach similar to futurists' claiming the book is only futuristic. The reality is the Revelation of Jesus Christ has the entire span of the church in sight, from congregational encouragement and rebukes of the seven churches in *Asia Minor** to the first resurrection, the marriage supper of the Lamb, and the New Heaven and the New Earth.

Regarding the NT, apostolic authorship was necessary for a book or letter to meet the criteria for inclusion in the canon of Scriptures. This alone would require that Revelation be written during the first century because all the original apostles were dead by the beginning of the second century. Therefore, the argument that first-century Christians would have had no benefit from futuristic prophecies places the argument in the wrong court. An apocalyptic book that benefited first-century Christians would not have been the uppermost priority. Prophecies related to the end times were all written well in advance of their actual fulfillment. This is explicitly demonstrated in Daniel where the prophet writes, "I heard this, but I couldn't understand what it meant; so I asked, 'Lord, what will be the outcome of all this?' But he said, 'Go your way, Daniel; for these words are to remain secret and sealed until the time of the end' " (Dan 12:8–9 CJB).

In this passage, God's priority was not focused on the people of Daniel's day having understanding or benefiting from this prophecy. The details contained in Daniel's prophecy were "to remain secret and sealed until the time of the end." The prophecy was sealed because it had nothing to do with anyone in Daniel's generation, and it could not be comprehended because it was to be fulfilled thousands of years into the future. So it is with the book of Revelation. The futuristic aspects of the book had nothing to do with first-century Christians. However, looking forward to the resurrection and reward of the righteous, the defeat of Satan and the beast, the damnation of the wicked, the coming of the New Heaven and earth, and the bliss of eternity would be encouragement for first-century Christians and all successive church generations.

A widely accepted futurist interpretation today is *dispensationalism.** "At the heart of dispensationalism is the dividing of all time into distinguishable economies (or dispensations) which are seen as different stages in God's progressive revelation."[41] Seven dispensations were delineated by Scofield: *Innocence, Conscience, Human Government, Promise, Law, Grace,* and *Kingdom.* Another aspect of the dispensational view sees chapters 2 and 3 of Revelation as representative of the entire *church** age. Dispensationalists assert that the church, including the very word, is not found in Revelation after chapter 3 until it is mentioned again in chapter 22, which supports their assertion that

---

[41] Timothy P. Weber, "Dispensationalism," in *Dictionary of Christianity in America,"* 358.

the church is not on earth during any of the chapters following chapter 3. Dispensationalism, though popular, is problematic, which will be discussed throughout this commentary.

This commentary is in the futurist camp of interpretation, seeing much of Revelation as yet to be fulfilled. However, the Pretrib rapture *is not* taught in this commentary. Dispensationalists hold to a seven-year tribulation period consistent with Daniel's Seventieth Week, the seven-year period described in Daniel 9:27. From a Pretrib perspective, the rapture occurs before the Seventieth Week of Daniel arrives. The Midtrib position would assert that the rapture will happen in the middle of the seven years. The Prewrath view is that the rapture happens between the middle and the end of the week. Finally, with Posttrib, the rapture happens at the end of the Seventieth Week, when the church goes up to meet the Lord in the air and then immediately returns with Him, almost in simultaneous fashion.

The rapture position that a person espouses has an impact on how he or she interprets the book of Revelation. If you are Pretrib, you see the church as having no part in the vast majority of the book. All the other positions (Midtrib, Prewrath, Posttrib) see the church as being present on earth during the events described in Revelation, being here either partly or all the way through Daniel's Seventieth Week.

(4) **The Idealist/Spiritualist Interpretation** assumes that the visions of the Apocalypse are neither literal nor prophetic and are only representing the common conflict between good and evil under the form of the symbols and figures that would have been familiar to Jews and Christians in the first century. Therefore, the information contained in Revelation applies to all church ages without any concrete interpretations as to the

fulfillment of past or future events. This view separates the symbolism of the book from any historical events but regards the book as having pictorial representations of great principles of divine government for an all-time application. This is the preferred view taught in liberal seminaries.

MILLENNIAL VIEWS

Historic Premillennialism This is a view that was held by many in the early centuries of the church. It is similar to Posttribulationism that we have today. Its basic tenets are that Christ will return at the end of the tribulation period and will institute His thousand-year reign. The church will experience the tyranny of the Antichrist but will find ultimate victory during the start of the millennium after the *first resurrection.**

Premillennialism This view teaches that when Christ returns in His second advent, He inaugurates the millennium and rules the earth from *Jerusalem** for a literal thousand years. Satan will be imprisoned in the *abyss** during this period, and the earth will be restored to an Edenic state. Millennial citizens will experience a cessation of the evils from the former age. People will live much longer, and infant mortality for God's people will be no more. The nature of ferocious carnivorous animals will be changed so that the lion will lie down with the lamb and eat straw like an ox. During this age, the church will rule and reign with Christ. The main premillennial rapture views are based upon when the rapture occurs in relation to Daniel's Seventieth Week. The views are Pretrib, Midtrib, Prewrath, and Posttrib.

Amillennialism *Amillennial* means "no millennium." This position does not accept a literal thousand-year earthly reign of Christ. "It suggests that references to a millennium for the period between Christ's ascension and second coming are figurative."[42] Amillennialism contends

---

[42] Douglas Mangum, *The Lexham Glossary of Theology*, s.v., "Amillennialism" (Bellingham, WA: Lexham Press, 2014).

that the millennial reign of Christ already began with his first advent and will continue through this present church age. This view also asserts that Satan is currently bound during this present age. Unlike Postmillennialists, Amillennialists believe Christians will have an impact on the wicked world but will not transform it. Evil will culminate with the great tribulation, where the Antichrist will emerge and be destroyed when Christ returns. After which, Christ will usher in the eternal state. Amillennialism is a widely accepted eschatological view held by Lutherans, Anglicans, Reformed, Methodist, and other churches.

Postmillennialism This view asserts that the millennium is not a literal thousand-year period but a nonspecific extended period that began with Christ's first advent. During this millennial period, which has extended two thousand years and running, evil and wickedness in the earth will be overcome by the spread of righteousness through the preaching of the gospel. Through the influence and growth of the church, peace and prosperity will result, thus paving the way for Christ to return at the end of this nonspecific period. In this system, there is no reign of Christ for a literal thousand years, as a premillennialist would assert. Movements having postmillennial eschatology would be dominion theology, the *New Apostolic Reformation** (NAR) movement, and the more recent *Seven Mountain Mandate.** Postmillennialism, dominion theology, and NAR would have little or no interest in end times prophecy themes and events as emphasized by premillennialists.

SOME DISTINCTIONS BETWEEN THIS COMMENTARY AND OTHER PREWRATH PROPONENTS

This commentary holds to a Prewrath rapture position but differs in many aspects from others who also espouse Prewrath. This commentary's position is that the Scriptures declare that the church is not appointed to the wrath of God. This conclusion is based upon 1 Thessalonians 1:10 and 5:9. Ironically, these verses are central to all the positions. However, this commentary is not aligned with others who hold to a Prewrath position, such as Marvin Rosenthal (2022), Robert D. Van Kampen (1999), Alan Kurschner, and others. The earliest version of the Prewrath positions this author and this commentary espouse began with his book titled *Unlocking the Door: A Key to Biblical Prophecy* (1994).

Though there are similarities between the Prewrath espoused in this commentary and the traditional Prewrath views, there are also major differences. This commentary does not hold that the rapture occurs between the sixth and seventh seal. Neither is it asserted that Revelation 7:13–14 is the rapture. The author does not hold that the sixth and seventh seals occur in the last half of the Seventieth Week (as do other Prewrath and some Pretrib proponents). It is not espoused that *Michael the archangel** is the restrainer of 2 Thessalonians 2:6–7. This author does not hold, as some Prewrath proponents do, that *Armageddon** and the *second coming* occur at least thirty or more days after the end of the Seventieth Week. However, it is agreed that the Pretrib rapture has the most potential to be harmful if end-times events do not unfold as dispensationalists have scripted. A full disclosure of the positions held will be taken up in the entirety of this commentary.

The What, When, and How of Prophetic Fulfillment

The primary emphasis behind this commentary is to focus on a very practical question: *What happens if the Pretrib rapture theory is wrong?* To this question, Pretrib proponents rarely, if ever, offer an answer or entertain its possibility. However, that is a mistake because there are no experts on how God will fulfill events in the future. As much as we think we know, there is just as much or even more that we do not know. For example, in Revelation 10:4, John heard the seven thunders speak. When he was about to write down what they said, God forbade him. The sequence of sevens would have been the seven seals, the seven trumpets, *the seven thunders*, and the seven bowls, but the seven thunders were kept secret. God, in no uncertain terms, explicitly informs the readers of Revelation that, by divine order, the seven thunders' portion was intentionally left undisclosed. This means none of us has a complete picture of Revelation. We only know what God has chosen to reveal. For other examples of nondisclosure, see Mark 13:33 and Acts 1:6–7.

Though God declares the *what* of prophecy, no one knows *when* or *how* a prophecy will be fulfilled. Indeed, the rapture is a fact. The Lord's second coming is a fact. But when these events will be fulfilled is unknown. Therefore, scholars used to refer to all the rapture positions, regarding their timing, as theories.[43] The word *theory* means something has yet to be proven; a level of uncertainty exists. But that's not what people want to hear when it comes to their futures. People want answers and assurances. Thomas Ice, formerly of Liberty University, wrote an article titled "A Short History of Dispensationalism," which states, "Dispensationalism had a tailor-made answer to a growing technological society. As life became more complicated, so did explanations of God's plan for history in dispensational charts. This era appreciated complicated and logical explanations. . . . Dispensationalism allowed a layman to answer liberal ministers thru Scofield's notes."[44]

This is an insightful assessment of dispensationalism. In view of Revelation's content, people wanted answers about whether the church would be present for the events it describes or whether it would be raptured before these events occur. If given a choice, the church not being here easily wins, but there is a problem. The eschatological system that provides the most sophisticated answers and that is accepted by the masses can still be wrong. The interpretation of prophecy is not a contest where whoever comes up with the most acceptable answer wins. Scholars and the masses can be wrong. The winner of a debate can still be wrong.

---

[43] J. Dwight Pentecost, "The Pretribulation Rapture Theory," in *Things to Come: A Study in Biblical Eschatology,* (Grand Rapids, MI: Zondervan, 1964), 193.
[44] Ice, "A Short History of Dispensationalism."

None of us have been to heaven, seen the future, or have any idea how God is going to fulfill futuristic prophecy. The best we can do is use the tools that are available to us. When it comes to *how* and *when* futuristic prophetic events will come to pass, no exegetical tool or technique can help us. Those answers cannot be found in the grammar, the syntax, the etymology, or by analyzing what other scholars have written throughout church history.

No matter what hermeneutical, theological, philosophical, historical, scientific, or etymological tools are used to extract meaning from a literary text, there are limits to what is accessible to humans as they use these methods. For example, Jesus' birthplace was prophesied in the following verse: "But as for you, Bethlehem Ephrathah, too little to be among the clans of Judah, from you One will go forth for Me to be ruler in Israel. His goings forth are from long ago, from the days of eternity" (Mic 5:2). No matter which interpretive tool one used at the time Micah was written, there was nothing in this text that could have revealed that seven hundred years after this prophecy was given, God was going to use Augustus Caesar to declare a census requiring people to return to the city of their ancestry. Nothing in the text mentioned that Mary, who was pregnant with Jesus at the time, and Joseph, her espoused husband, would live away from Bethlehem in Nazareth and at the precise time would be required to return to Bethlehem, with Jesus being born while there (Luke 2:1–7).

No interpretive tool available could have possibly revealed these circumstances from Micah's prophecy. This is why exegesis cannot always help you with futuristic prophecy. *How* a prophetic event is going to be fulfilled is not contained in the words of the prophecy itself nor can it be extracted by exegetical means. No method of human inquiry could have disclosed the specific circumstances around Jesus' birth beforehand. And when it was fulfilled, the scholars at the time still didn't recognize what had been fulfilled. In retrospect, we know the details.

It was only after Jesus started His public ministry, some thirty years after His birth, that He came to the scholars' attention in a very significant way. When this happened, some scholars rejected Jesus because they did not realize Micah's words "from you One will go forth" (5:2) meant that Jesus *would be born* in Bethlehem. They expected His *ministry* would come forth from Bethlehem. It is probable that many rejected the Lord because of a misunderstanding of Micah 5:2 and because Jesus' ministry started from His hometown of Nazareth. One scholar, Nicodemus, tried reasoning with others concerning Jesus, and their response to him was a stinging rebuke: "They replied, 'Are you from Galilee, too? Look into it, and you will find that a prophet does not come out of Galilee' " (John 7:52 NIV). They were saying Jesus could not be a prophet and the Messiah because they assumed He was a Galilean from Nazareth, since His ministry started there. They knew Micah's prophecy distinctly indicated the Messiah would come from Bethlehem.

Today, on the other side of fulfillment, we know Micah's phrase meant *where Jesus was to be born*. Had those who confronted Nicodemus understood the passage to mean the Messiah would be born in Bethlehem, they may have asked about His birthplace rather than being concerned about where He launched His ministry. Though Micah 5:2 is not cited in the John 7:52 narrative, the fact that the scholars told Nicodemus, a ruler and teacher of Israel, to "look into it, and [he would] find that a prophet does not come out of Galilee" implies they were aware of Micah 5:2. They determined that Jesus being from Nazareth disqualified Him from being *the prophet*. The prophecy they missed was Isaiah 9:1–2, which prophesied concerning Galilee, but this prophecy is quite veiled. However, Matthew, citing Isaiah 9:1–2, confirmed the prophecy's connection to the Lord (Matt 4:14–17). Though the chief priests had it right about Bethlehem at the time of Jesus' birth (Matt 2:4–5), thirty years later, some were confused when Jesus' ministry came out of Nazareth. This is one example of how humans can be limited in their understanding and interpretation of prophecy.

It is also vital to understand that the way a prophecy appears in a given passage often does not reveal a clear marker for fulfillment. A fulfilled prophecy does not come with neon signs and bright lights. Fulfillment is often obscured by events occurring at the time, meaning a prophecy can be fulfilled right in the midst of people, and they still will not know it. This is why Jesus had to *open the eyes* of His disciples so they could comprehend what was contained in the books of Moses, the Prophets, and the Psalms concerning Him (Luke 24:44–45). None of us knows *how* or *when* God is going to fulfill a prophecy unless God reveals it. The best we can do is develop theories.

In this regard, there are no experts on how God will bring to pass a prophetic word. We can know the *what* of prophecy, but the *when* and *how* no one ever knows. God can use anything in all creation to bring about prophetic fulfillment, none of which are predictable. Our best theological and interpretive tools are very limited when it concerns things to come, unless God makes them known. Therefore, we must all approach this great subject with humility, because in the final analysis, we are just human beings who have no clue as to what tomorrow brings.

The Period with No Equal

The book of Revelation is absolutely essential for a Christian's life and is not to be marginalized by the preferences of popular eschatological theories. It is God's disclosure of a period that has no equal or no prior earthly occurrence. Of these times, Jesus stated, "There will be a great tribulation, such as has not occurred since the beginning of the world until now, nor ever will" (Matt 24:21). As Jesus emphatically states, there is nothing to compare with what is coming on this world. Therefore, the book of Revelation compensates for the unique severity of the time by revealing eschatological specifics in advance. Though there has never been a time like it, through the book of Revelation, we know what that time entails.

In God's divine love and concern for the redeemed, in a great act of love and awesome power, He allowed a human being to see events thousands of years into the future, even though these events were beyond the apostle's ability to fully comprehend. In this way, God accommodates the redeemed in a divine act of compassion and gives us a play-by-play prophetic view into future events that have no parallel in history. Therefore, from the beginning of the church, God has revealed the events that will occur at the close of this age and beyond. Only God can reveal the end from the beginning (Isa 46:8–10).

What Happens If Pretrib Is Wrong?

Those who support dispensationalism have had a profound impact on how Revelation is interpreted by insisting the church has no presence in Revelation between chapters 6 and 19. According to that tenet, the church will not be here to see the reconstructed temple, the seven-year covenant, the beast's rising to power, etc. However, as promising as it sounds to miss some of these events, this is where the problem lies. Pretrib leaves Christians with no way out, or no alternative in the event their theories do not turn out as promised. While God has given the church vital information concerning the events covered in Revelation, it is not being heeded by many because the Pretrib doctrine has undercut the message God intended for the church. Many Christians do not read the book of Revelation because they have been told that, for the most part, it doesn't apply to the church. This may be an unintended consequence of Pretrib teaching, and it runs contrary to the reason God placed Revelation in the NT.

If the Pretrib rapture position is correct, and the church is raptured before the events found in the book of Revelation between chapters 6–19 occur, that is great news. No one gets hurt by being raptured early. What the other positions (Midtrib, Prewrath, Posttrib) espouse would not make a difference. However, what happens if the Pretrib theory is wrong? To that question, some may respond, "You cannot base your eschatology on fear." Though it's true that one's eschatology should not be motivated by fear, however, it should be based on what is true. What happens if Pretrib is wrong is not a matter of evoking fear but seeking truth. Therefore, what's at stake if there is no Pretrib rapture?

Millions of Christians who thought they would be raptured before the Seventieth Week (the seven-year period) would still be here. If that happens, history will repeat itself and set in motion a modern-day Thessalonians situation. Why? Because Pretrib teaches that the entire Seventieth Week is *the day of the Lord* and *the wrath of God.* The Thessalonians believed, albeit erroneously, that they had entered the day of the Lord, and their faith was seriously shaken. (See "The Imminent Return" essay.)

Today's church is potentially being positioned for a similar but much worse situation because Pretrib assures us that the church will not be here for any part of Daniel's Seventieth Week. If the Seventieth Week starts and the rapture hasn't occurred, people would think they, too, have entered the day of the Lord, just as the Thessalonians did. In that event, millions of Christians who thought they should have been raptured already will face circumstances they have not prepared themselves for. This same group could factor into those who fall away just as prophesied by Jesus and the apostle Paul in Matthew 13:20–21, 24:9–10, and 2 Thessalonians 2:3, especially once persecution and martyrdom begin.

WHAT THE READER SHOULD KNOW GOING FORWARD

Throughout the history of the church, Revelation has been a source of encouragement and intrigue while inspiring faith in the trustworthiness of God's Word. The God who sent His Son into the world is the same God who writes history in advance and brings to pass His plans in accordance with the counsel of His own will. God is sovereign. All creation yields to and obeys Him. As recorded in Daniel's prophecy,

I blessed the Most High and praised and honored Him who

> lives forever; for His dominion is an everlasting dominion, and His kingdom endures from generation to generation. All the inhabitants of the earth are accounted as nothing, but He does according to His will in the host of heaven and among the inhabitants of earth; and no one can ward off His hand or say to Him, "What have You done?" (Dan 4:34–35)

Though the early church was far from seeing the fulfillment of the Lord's coming, they rejoiced in knowing the final victory predestined for the saints was sure. Therefore, no matter how vehemently the enemy resists the Word of God, the gospel message, and the people of God, the Lord will build His church, and the gates of hell will not prevail against it. Just as God has written it in the book of Revelation, Satan and his angels, along with all the wicked who follow them, will stand in judgment and have a certain end in the lake of fire. God's people will be victorious, and the wicked will be judged. This certainty has been a source of comfort throughout the history of the church.

Tenets That Make This Commentary Unique

Since dispensationalism came to the United States in the mid-1800s, to a great extent, the Pretrib rapture theory has shaped how the book of Revelation is interpreted and how eschatology is understood. Dispensational theology's influence has been so pervasive that, by default, its terminology that defines Daniel's Seventieth Week is used across the board by people who hold to other positions in end-times theology. Pretrib asserts the Seventieth Week in its entirety is the *tribulation period*, the day of the Lord, and the wrath of God. However, these are not precepts that are used in this commentary. To avoid confusion, this commentary will refer not to the "tribulation period" but to Daniel's Seventieth Week or the seven-year period in which the last three and a half years is *the great tribulation.**

This commentary asserts the following tenets, which differentiate it from other eschatological positions.

1. This commentary emphasizes that Revelation was written to the church and much of it is about the church. Dispensationalists have removed the church from Revelation in chapters 4–19. However, Revelation works better with the church in it, not out of it. This inspired prophecy was given to the church as an infallible proof of God's absolute, providential control of all things in heaven and on earth. Revelation is not merely fodder for scholarly and doctrinal debate but is a necessity and a lamp for the path of those who will be alive during the time of the Apocalypse. Revelation's contents are so important that it contains both a divine blessing for those who read it and heed its prophecies and a warning for those who tamper with it. By no means was this book to be marginalized by anyone declaring that it does not concern the very church to whom it was given.

2. Since we acknowledge the church's presence in Revelation, it is necessary where applicable to harmonize Revelation with the NT, just as the NT is often harmonized with the OT.

3. This commentary does not interpret Revelation 1:19 as an outline to guide how Revelation is to be interpreted. Dispensationalists assert the following parameters: *The things which you have seen* are the events in chapter 1. *The things which are* would be the church age found in chapters 2–3, and *the things which will take place after these things* are chapters 4–22, which take place on earth after the church is raptured. Dispensationalists support this outline because it is used to reinforce the concept of a Pretribulational rapture. The net effect of this interpretation is that it shuts out the church from much of Revelation. Daniel was told, "Go your way, Daniel, because the words are rolled up and sealed until the time of the end" (Dan 12:9 NIV). However, the Lamb of God prevailed to unseal the scroll and opened the visions it contained (Rev 5:6–14). Unfortunately, in the minds of many, and because of the traditions of men, Revelation has been closed in a sense because many believe that it does not apply to today's Christians, consequently sealing the book to the church.

4. This commentary does not interpret the messages to the seven churches as representing the entire church age from Pentecost to the rapture. Additionally, many Pretribbers insist that the rapture is pictured in the message to the church of Philadelphia in 3:10, even though there is nothing characteristic of the rapture in the passage. Furthermore, many interpret the call for John to "come up here" in 4:1 as a representation of the rapture of the church. Neither view is supported in this commentary. Though dispensationalists claim to hold to a literal interpretation of Revelation, they spiritualize the meaning of the seven churches to be periods of church development down through the centuries. However, Pretribulationists vary on how these ages apply in history. (See the "3:10: The Hour of Testing Dilemma" essay.)

5. This commentary does not support the concept that the lack of the word *church* in the book after chapter 3 is equivalent to the church not being on earth. (A refutation on this point is covered in the "What Happened to the Church?" excursus.)

6. This commentary does not accept that the *tribulation saints* * are a different group of Christians consisting of the "left behinds" who will fail to be caught up in the rapture. Contrarily, this will be the last and greatest group of Christians the church has ever known. These saints will be celebrated in heaven because they will come out of the most difficult period in human history, remaining faithful to Christ even though it cost them their lives. One of the major themes of Revelation is the faithfulness and fortitude of the tribulation saints in their resolute refusal to bow to the Antichrist, as they lay down their lives for the Lord. Truly, "they loved not their lives unto the death" (12:11 KJV) does not describe a group of backslidden Christians who failed to make the rapture cut. (See "The Mischaracterization of the Tribulation Saints" excursus.)

7. This commentary does not accept that the Holy Spirit and the church will be removed as the *restrainer* * of sin from the earth. The Holy Spirit is fully active in the lives of the saints during the reign of the Antichrist. It

is noteworthy that the Scriptures declare, "And no one can say, 'Jesus is Lord,' except by the Holy Spirit" (1 Cor 12:3b). If it takes the indwelling Spirit to confess that Jesus is Lord, then how much more of the Spirit would it take for one to die because of that confession? The concept that the Holy Spirit is to be taken from the earth comes from the Pretrib interpretation that the Holy Spirit is the person who is currently restraining the revealing of the Antichrist. (See "The Threefold Reality of the Beast" essay.)

8. This commentary recognizes the threefold reality of the beast as *a man, a kingdom,* and *the demonic principality** that ascends from the abyss or *bottomless pit.** (See "The Threefold Reality of the Beast" essay.)

9. This commentary recognizes the restraining ministry of angels in their role regarding the revealing of the Antichrist. The human aspect of the beast cannot be revealed until his demonic-principality counterpart is released from the abyss, the prison in which he is currently incarcerated. It is the restraining angel that has the key and the means (the great chain) to restrain the inmates of the abyss. The angel is the "he" and the abyss, the place of restraint, is the neuter "what" (2 Thess 2:6-7).

10. This commentary asserts that the entire book of Revelation should be embraced by the church, not only because it is part of the NT but because its message is about the church. Before *dispensationalism** reshaped how Revelation is interpreted, the church embraced Revelation as being about Christians and the church. What other group in church history has made the claim that the church is not on earth in Revelation chapters 4–19? If there were some who held to this view in previous centuries, it was not widespread. This idea is largely a post-dispensational interpretation. By claiming the church is not on earth from Revelation 4–19, dispensationalists have given the false impression to Christians that the events contained in Revelation have no impact on the body of Christ. However, the simple fact that Revelation is in the NT should necessarily mean that *it is* for and about the church.

About the Book of Revelation

Authorship

There are basically three options to consider for authorship: *the apostle John, another John,* or an *unknown author* using John's name as a pseudonym. Many agree that John, the beloved apostle of Jesus Christ and the author of the gospel bearing his name, as well as the three epistles, is the same author of Revelation. However, this is contested by both historic and contemporary scholars on the grounds of the difference between the style of Greek used in John's gospel and epistles and the Apocalypse. Another reason to contest Johannine authorship is that John does not identify himself as an *apostle* but *as a bondservant of the Lord.* This argument seems to originate with Dionysius, bishop of Alexandria in the third century. However, there were others who affirmed that John was the author. Concerning John's authorship, the early historian *Eusebius** quoted the second-century Christian apologist Justin Martyr, writing, "He mentioned also, the Revelation of John plainly calling it the work of the apostle and recorded also certain prophetic declarations in his discussion."[45] Others who affirmed Johannine authorship are *Irenaeus,** *Tertullian,** *Clement of Alexandria,** and *Origen.** The fact that the author simply calls himself John, without any appellations, may have been because he was well known to his readers.[46]

Another consideration is that this is not John's revelation but the revelation of Jesus Christ. John is not the prominent figure but is the mere observer and recorder of the Apocalypse. John clearly understood that he was not the source of the apocalyptic material he was recording. The Lord appeared to him and translated him into heaven by God's divine prerogative. John was merely the bondservant of the Lord. In view of

---

[45] Eusebius, "The Books of Justin That Have Come Down to Us," in *Eusebius' Ecclesiastical History,* bk. 4, chap. 18.8, trans. C. F. Cruse (Peabody, MA: Hendrickson Publishers, 1998), 132.

[46] D. A. Carson, Douglas J. Moo, and Leon Morris, "Revelation," in *An Introduction to the New Testament* (Grand Rapids, MI: Zondervan Publishing House), 469.

his participation in such a tremendous divine experience, John had no consideration for any inappropriate self-aggrandizement.

An interesting consistency found in John's gospel, the epistles bearing his name, and Revelation is in none of these did John refer to himself as an apostle. Therefore, no one should be put off and reject Johannine authorship of Revelation because John did not refer to himself as an apostle. Silence on John's apostolic office is a point that actually affirms unity of authorship by an individual who intentionally shuns any personal appellations in all his writings.

Even so, John's use of the word *commandment(s)* (Gk. *entolē*) throughout his writings is interesting. For example, in the *thirteen* epistles attributed to Paul, he used the word *entolē* twenty-three times. However, John brought to us only *four* books, and the word is used thirty-two times. Additionally, Paul's use of the term is most cases, by way of reference. John's use of the word, especially in his epistles and Revelation, is overwhelmingly functional. He emphasized *keeping* the commandments of God. John's use of the term "Lamb of God" as a divine title is introduced in John 1:29 and 36 but is used twenty-five times in Revelation. Paul does not use this term once in any of his letters. John's reference to Christ as being the "Word" of God is used in John 1:1 and 14 and 1 John 1:1. Both passages are introductory and are closely phrased. Similarly, "The Word of God" is in Revelation 19:13 and is a divine name. In conclusion, authorship cannot be determined based upon the usage of particular words and phrases, but these similarities are noteworthy and support arguments for common Johannine authorship of several biblical books.

DATE

The date of authorship that is mostly supported is AD 96, toward the end of the reign of the Roman emperor Domitian, who ruled from AD 81–96. This date of authorship was also supported by Irenaeus. It was *Domitian**who banished John to the *island of Patmos*,* where Revelation was written. However, one of the primary reasons cited by those who support an earlier date, AD 64–69, is because of the reference to the temple in 11:1–2. The Jewish temple in Jerusalem was destroyed in 70 AD. Therefore, according to the early date view, Revelation was written when the temple was still standing. Those who support the later date see the reference to the temple as the future temple that will be the place where the *Antichrist** commits the *abomination of desolation,** spoken of by Jesus, Daniel, and Paul (Dan 9:27; Matt 24:15; 2 Thess 2:4).

ACCEPTANCE INTO THE CANON

In order for a book to have been considered for inclusion into the NT, church leaders considered some important factors, such as works having apostolic authorship or authorship by direct associates of an apostle, such as Mark and Luke. After laborious scrutiny and lengthy debate, Revelation met the criteria for inclusion in the canon. Full acceptance was documented in the *Festal Letter of Athanasius* in 367. In the West, Revelation was included in the list of NT Scriptures finalized at the *Council of Carthage** in 397. However, in the Eastern church, it was accepted much later.[47] Ironically, if it had been up to *Martin Luther,** Revelation would not be in the canon. In his preface to *The German New Testament*, also known as the *September Testament*, in 1522, Luther "expressed a strong aversion to the book, declaring that to him it had every mark of being neither Apostolic nor prophetic. Apostles spoke clearly, without figure or vision, of Christ and his deeds; and no prophet of the OT, to say nothing of the NT, deals so entirely with visions and figures."[48] Thank God that Luther and all the other Revelation detractors got it wrong.

GENRE

Revelation is classified as prophecy and is the only such book in the NT to receive that designation. Revelation would also be classified as

---

[47] D. J. Wiseman, *The Zondervan Pictorial Encyclopedia of the Bible,* trans. Merrill C. Tenney, 5 vols. (Grand Rapids, MI: Zondervan Publishing House), 94.

[48] James Hastings, *Hastings' Dictionary of the Bible* (Peabody, MA: Hendrickson Publishers, 1988), 241.

*apocalyptic literature.** Some understand it to be either/or, while others would see it as both.

PURPOSE

The purpose of Revelation is stated in the first verse: "The Revelation of Jesus Christ, which God gave Him to show to His *bond-servants,** the things which must soon take place" (1:1). Many object to a futuristic characterization of Revelation on the grounds that first-century Christians would not have been familiar with futuristic content. However, consider the fact that Isaiah prophesied about Jesus seven hundred years before His birth and earthly ministry (Isa 9:6; 53:1–12). Messianic prophecies about Christ appeared in several Psalms (e.g., 2, 8, 22, 23) eight hundred years before they were fulfilled. Micah prophesied about Jesus' birthplace seven hundred years before fulfillment (Mic 5:2). Also, consider the eschatological prophecies of Ezekiel and Daniel, written in the sixth century BC, that still await fulfillment 2,500 years later and counting (Ezek 38–39; Dan 9:27; 12). When these prophecies were written, they had nothing to do with the people of that time. They were not understood by contemporaries because their fulfillment was too far in the future (Dan 12:8). Today, we know that events recorded in Revelation were not only about first-century Christians who looked for Jesus to return during their lifetime. Twenty centuries later, we still await His coming.

Now that we have reached the twenty-first century, Revelation's purpose is coming into greater clarity, particularly with the establishment of modern-day Israel in 1948. There cannot be a final Antichrist until the Jews are back in Israel and Jerusalem is under their control. Then, the Antichrist must enact a covenant with many for a seven-year period. The third temple must be constructed for the Antichrist to commit *the abomination of desolation,* spoken of by Daniel the prophet. Revelation, therefore, gives the details on that seven-year period, along with the second coming of the Lord, His millennial reign, the judgment of the righteous and wicked, and the manifestation of the New Heaven and

New Earth. Therefore, Revelation is essential in giving us details in advance of events that are yet to come.

Finally, Jesus stated, "For then there will be great suffering unlike anything that has happened from the beginning of the world until now, or ever will happen" (Matt 24:21 NET). The time of which Jesus spoke will be unequaled in all human history. There is nothing in the past nor will there be anything in the future to compare with this time. Herein is the purpose of Revelation. God has provided an equally unique book to fill in the blanks on a period that has no parallel. Revelation is absolutely indispensable for Christians and provides details about the future contained in no other book in the canon of Scripture nor any other literature in the world. Without Revelation, no human being would know about the seven seals, the seven trumpets, or the seven bowls. We would know nothing about the two witnesses, the mark of the beast, the actions of the *false prophet*,* the battle of Armageddon, the imprisonment of Satan, the great white throne judgment, the *second death*,* and all the other unique details found only in Revelation. Due to the importance of this divinely inspired book, John gave a special blessing for anyone who would read and take to heart the words of its prophecy.

The Final Seven Years of This Age

During the *Mount Olivet Discourse*,* Jesus, speaking of the end of the age, listed several things that would occur before His return: wars and rumors of wars; nation (Gk. *ethnos*, meaning "a body of persons united by kinship, culture, and common traditions, nation, people"[49]) rising against nation; kingdoms against kingdoms; famines; pestilences (KJV); and earthquakes in various places. In Matthew 24:8, Jesus said, "But all these things are merely the beginning of birth pangs." The term "birth pangs" is a good analogy because it comes from the Greek word *odin*, which refers to "the 'Messianic woes,' the terrors and torments tradition-

---

[49] Walter Bauer et al., *A Greek-English Lexicon of the New Testament and Other Early Christian Literature* (Chicago: University of Chicago Press, 2000), s.v. "nation."

ally viewed as the prelude to the coming of the Messianic Age."[50] Just as a pregnant woman's birth pangs increase in severity and frequency as the baby's birthdate approaches, so will the signs of the Lord's second coming increase in frequency and intensity.

After listing these preliminary signs, He announced the most pivotal sign yet: "Therefore, when you see the abomination of desolation which was spoken of through Daniel the prophet, standing in the holy place (let the reader understand)" (Matt 24:15). The parenthetical statement "let the reader understand" alerts us to the fact that *understanding* will only come for the one who comprehends Daniel's prophecies, which are *the key* that *unlocks understanding* concerning these culminating events of the *end of the age* or the end of *this current world system.*

The *abomination of desolation,* or the *abomination that causes desolation,* is taken up in Daniel 9:27, 11:31, and 12:11 and occurs in the middle of a period called *Daniel's Seventieth Week.* Daniel's Seventieth Week is the final prophetic period that will close out the end of the age, when the Lord will return as King of Kings and Lord of Lords (Rev 19:11–21).

In the NT, the word *abomination* comes from the Greek word *bdelygma* (bdel'-oog-mah), meaning "that which causes revulsion or extreme disgust, a loathsome, detestable thing," in reference to what is detested by God.[51] The word *desolation* comes from the Greek word *erēmōsis,* meaning "state of being made uninhabitable, devastation, destruction, depopulation."[52] Together, these words mean "a desolating sacrifice." The abomination will occur when the Antichrist walks into the *holy place* of the temple in Jerusalem (which is yet to be built) and declares himself to be God. He then will erect an image of himself and demand that the world worship the image as God (2 Thess 2:3–4; Rev 13:14–15).

---

[50] Bauer, *Greek-English Lexicon,* s.v. "birth pangs."
[51] Bauer, s.v. "abomination."
[52] Bauer, s.v. "desolation."

In 2 Thessalonians 2:4, speaking of the *abomination of desolation*, Paul declared that the Antichrist, the man of lawlessness, will be one "who opposes and exalts himself above every so-called god or object of worship, so that he [will take] his seat in the temple of God, displaying himself as being God."

THE TIMELINE—THE SEVENTY WEEKS OF DANIEL

This *abomination of desolation* will occur in the middle of a seven-year period called Daniel's Seventieth Week, which is the last prophetic week (seven years) waiting to be fulfilled. The Seventieth Week is mentioned in the following verses:

> Seventy weeks have been decreed for your people and your holy city, to finish the transgression, to make an end of sin, to make atonement for iniquity, to bring in everlasting righteousness, to seal up vision and prophecy and to anoint the most holy place. So you are to know and discern that from the issuing of a decree to restore and rebuild Jerusalem until Messiah the Prince there will be seven weeks and sixty-two weeks; it will be built again, with plaza and moat, even in times of distress. Then after the sixty-two weeks the Messiah will be cut off and have nothing, and the people of the prince who is to come will destroy the city and the sanctuary. And its end will come with a flood; even to the end there will be war; desolations are determined. And he will make a firm covenant with the many for one week, but in the middle of the week he will put a stop to sacrifice and grain offering; and on the wing of abominations will come one who makes desolate, even until a complete destruction, one that is decreed, is poured out on the one who makes desolate. (Dan 9:24–27)

The word "week[s]" is translated from the Hebrew word *shâbûa*, a masculine noun meaning "seven; a week, a group of seven days or years (a heptad) of years."[53] In this passage, the "week" *consists of seven years* as opposed to seven days. An example of *week* being used as *seven years* can be found in Genesis 29:27–29.

In Daniel 9:24, the prophetic agenda is set forth as follows: *"to finish the transgression, to make an end of sin, to make atonement for iniquity, to bring in everlasting righteousness, to seal up vision and prophecy and to anoint the most holy place"* (emphasis added). God will accomplish this in *seventy weeks** of years (70 x 7), or in 490 years.

It should be noted that the agenda items listed in v. 24 are concerning *your people* (the Jews) and *your holy city* (Jerusalem). This means that all eschatological fulfillments will be centered around the Jews—and by extension, all Israel's tribes and the land of Israel reestablished in the modern era in 1948—with Jerusalem as the central focus. However, this *does not* exclude the church because when Daniel was written, the church was yet a mystery and had not been revealed. The church was hidden in OT texts such as Joel 2:28–32, which Peter linked to the beginning of the church on the *day of Pentecost.**

THE SIX-POINT PROPHETIC AGENDA

1. *To finish the transgression.* That is, to finish Israel's national *rebellion** against Christ. Due to their rejection of the Lord, Israel has been *partly* hardened ("blindness," KJV) until "the fullness of the Gentiles" is completed and the rapture has occurred (Rom 11:25). When the Lord returns at His second coming and Israel gazes upon Him whom they pierced, they will repent for their transgressions, particularly for their alliance with the Antichrist, who in time will turn on them (Zech 12:10; Rev 1:7).

2. *To make an end of sin.* The cessation of transgression is not enough; sin must also be forgiven, which can only occur through the shed

---

[53] Warren Baker and Eugene Carpenter, eds., *The Complete Word Study Dictionary: Old Testament* (Chattanooga, TN: AMG Publishers, 2003), s.v. "week."

blood of the Lamb. Israel will stop transgression, turn to the Lord, and their sins will be forgiven.

3. *To make atonement for iniquity.* "Atonement for iniquity" carries the concept of the mercy seat, where God is propitiated or satisfied. Ultimately, all sin is against God and His righteousness, authority, and rule. Therefore, iniquity must be atoned, which is only possible through the shed blood of the Lamb of God.

4. *To bring in everlasting righteousness.* Once the Lord returns and sets up His kingdom, it will be an everlasting kingdom of righteousness that has no end, described in the following passage:

> I kept looking in the night visions, and behold, with the clouds of heaven One like a Son of Man was coming, and He came up to the Ancient of Days and was presented before Him. And to Him was given dominion, Glory and a kingdom, that all the peoples, nations and men of every language might serve Him. His dominion is an everlasting dominion which will not pass away; and His kingdom is one which will not be destroyed. (Dan 7:13–14)

5. *To seal up vision and prophecy.* All prophetic visions and revelations concerning this age will be completed, the last of which is detailed in the book of Revelation. As Paul declared, "Prophecies, they will cease" (1 Cor 13:8 NIV).

6. To anoint the most holy place. Most translations have "holy place," and a few refer to the Holy One. If it is "place," this could be a reference to the future dedication of the temple after the *Antichrist** desecrates it. Historically, after Antiochus Epiphanes committed the abomination of desolation (prophesied in Dan 11:31) that triggered the *Maccabean revolt,** the temple was rededicated and continues to be celebrated each year during *Hanukkah.** If "place" is correct, then the temple reference in Revelation 11:1–2 could fit. Most prefer that it is a refer-

ence to the millennial temple of Ezekiel 40–44. Finally, if translated holy "One," it could be a reference to the Lord and His exaltation and coronation as the King of Kings and Lord of Lords, who will rule with the rod of iron through the millennium and forever more.

The Sixty-Ninth and Seventieth Week

So you are to know and discern that from the issuing of a decree to restore and rebuild Jerusalem until Messiah the Prince there will be seven weeks and sixty-two weeks; it will be built again, with plaza and moat, even in times of distress. Then after the sixty-two weeks the Messiah will be cut off and have nothing, and the people of the prince who is to come will destroy the city and the sanctuary. And its end will come with a flood; even to the end there will be war; desolations are determined. And he will make a firm covenant with the many for one week, but in the middle of the week he will put a stop to sacrifice and grain offering; and on the wing of abominations will come one who makes desolate, even until a complete destruction, one that is decreed, is poured out on the one who makes desolate. (Dan 9:25–27).

Verse 25 says, "From the issuing of a decree to restore and rebuild Jerusalem until Messiah the Prince there will be seven weeks." The first seven weeks equal forty-nine years. Most agree that the "decree" was issued by King Artaxerxes in March 444 BC (Neh 2:1–8). On that occasion, Artaxerxes granted the Jews permission to rebuild Jerusalem's city walls.

The next period of sevens continues after the first forty-nine years. *Gabriel** said, "And sixty-two weeks; it will be built again, with plaza and moat, even in times of distress. Then after the sixty-two weeks the Messiah will be cut off and have nothing, and the people of the prince who is to come will destroy the city and the sanctuary. And its end will come with a flood; even to the end there will be war; desolations are determined" (Dan 9:25–26). Artaxerxes's issuing of the decree to rebuild Jerusalem in troublesome times accounts for the first forty-nine years, or seven weeks. Then the words "after the sixty-two weeks [434 years] the Messiah will be cut off" begin the next period. Here, *the Messiah*, or *the Anointed One*, is Christ who was crucified, or *cut off*. The KJV renders, "Shall Messiah be cut off, but not for himself." The emphasis, *but not for himself*, is in line with Isaiah 53:5 (KJV): "But he *was wounded for our transgressions, he was bruised for our iniquities*: the chastisement of our peace *was* upon him; and with his stripes we are healed" (emphasis added).

In AD 70, some thirty-seven years after Christ was crucified and resurrected, the Roman general Titus destroyed Jerusalem. Daniel 9:26, the prophecy details this: "*And the people of the prince who is to come will destroy the city and the sanctuary. And its end will come with a flood; even to the end there will be war; desolations are determined*" (emphasis added). However, between Christ being crucified and Jerusalem being destroyed in AD 70, the church was born. Though it is silent in the text, the church's birth on Pentecost screamed loudly and was the fulfillment of what Jesus prophesied in Matthew 16:18 when He said, "Upon this rock I will build My church; and the gates of Hades will not overpower it." It was not necessary for Gabriel to include something about the church in his message to Daniel because Daniel's prophecy focused on Israel. The church was hidden but not excluded. It was not Daniel's place to mention the church because it was Jesus' church.

Between these two points, *the Messiah being cut off* and *Jerusalem being destroyed in AD 70*, the church began on Pentecost, fifty days after Jesus' crucifixion on Passover. Additionally, during the period between these two events, there were many occurrences of the church's growth and persecution. Paul completed his three missionary journeys, wrote all his epistles, and established several churches. James was martyred in AD 45, Peter in AD 64, and Matthew between AD 60 and 70. Luke wrote his gospel around AD 61 and the book of Acts about AD 63. Therefore, between the crucifixion and the destruction of Jerusalem, there was monumental and foundational activity in *the church*.* Daniel may not have known about the church, but God, who gave Daniel his prophecy, knew exactly what would occur between *the Messiah's crucifixion* (AD 33) and *Jerusalem's destruction* (AD 70)—the beginning of Jesus' church on the day of Pentecost.

THE FINAL SEVEN YEARS—DANIEL'S SEVENTIETH WEEK

> And he will make a firm covenant with the many *for one week*, but in the middle of the week he will put a stop to sacrifice and grain offering; and on the wing of abominations will come one who makes desolate, even until a complete destruction, one that is decreed, is poured out on the one who makes desolate. (Dan 9:27, emphasis added)

This final prophetic week has been on hold now since AD 70, spanning almost two thousand years. During this period, the church has gone from a regional, fledgling entity to a worldwide phenomenon with more than two billion members today.[54] When this final week begins, a person identified as "he" will make a firm covenant with many (nations) for one week, or a seven-year period. It is the same person who, three and a half years later, will become the *Antichrist* or, as Revelation 13 depicts him, "the beast." Many believe the covenant will be a *Middle Eastern* peace treaty between Israel and the surrounding nations that have been hostile to Israel since the Jews reestablished the nation of Israel on May 14, 1948. The conditions of the covenant will allow Israel to become a land of peace and safety and to reinstitute animal sacrifice and daily grain offerings. These activities will require a temple to be built in Jerusalem. Today, there is an organization called the *Temple Institute**in Jerusalem that is working toward making the temple a reality. They are training priests. They are making utensils and have already drawn plans for the new temple.

When will this temple be built? That is unknown. Some say it won't be

---

[54] WorldData.info, a project of eglitis-media, accessed February 16, 2023, https://www.world-data.info.

built until Daniel's Seventieth Week arrives. However, no one knows for sure. What we do know is that a temple must be in place for the abomination of desolation to occur. Jesus referred to the temple when He spoke of the abomination of desolation. He said, "Standing in the holy place," meaning "the most holy place" of the temple sanctuary (Matt 24:15). The apostle Paul also referred to this when he described the "*man of sin... the son of perdition** [who] *sitteth in the temple of God,* [showing] *himself that he is God*" (2 Thess 2:3–4 KJV, emphasis added). All of this will occur in the middle of the seven-year period. Once the abomination of desolation is in place, that's when the "great tribulation" will occur, a time of trouble that has never been, since the beginning of the world until now, nor will ever be again (Matt 24:21).

The debate concerning the rapture of the church centers on this controversial seven years. If you hold to a Pretrib rapture, your contention is the rapture will happen before the Seventieth Week of Daniel arrives. If you ascribe to Midtrib, your position would be the rapture will happen in the middle of the Seventieth Week. If you are a proponent of Prewrath, you contend the rapture will happen between the middle and the end of the week. And if you are Posttrib, you believe the rapture will happen at the end of the Seventieth Week, at the same time as the Lord returns (see chart 1).

Rapture Position Chart

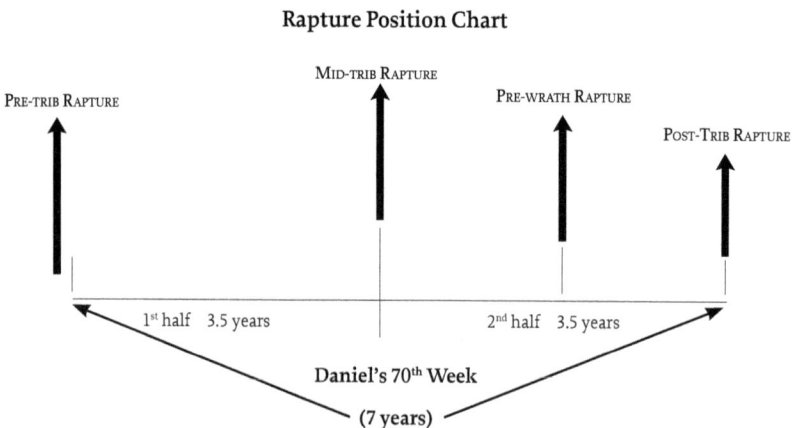

MID-TRIB RAPTURE

PRE-TRIB RAPTURE

PRE-WRATH RAPTURE

POST-TRIB RAPTURE

1st half   3.5 years

2nd half   3.5 years

Daniel's 70th Week

(7 years)

REVELATION 1:1–7

THE REVELATION OF JESUS CHRIST

¹ The Revelation of Jesus Christ, which God gave Him to show to His bond-servants, the things which must soon take place; and He sent and communicated it by His angel to His bond-servant John, ² who testified to the word of God and to the testimony of Jesus Christ, even to all that he saw. ³ Blessed is he who reads and those who hear the words of the prophecy, and heed the things which are written in it; for the time is near.

⁴ John to the seven churches that are in Asia: Grace to you and peace, from Him who is and who was and who is to come, and from the seven Spirits who are before His throne, ⁵ and from Jesus Christ, the faithful witness, the firstborn of the dead, and the ruler of the kings of the earth. To Him who loves us and released us from our sins by His blood—⁶ and He has made us to be a kingdom, priests to His God and Father—to Him be the glory and the dominion forever and ever. Amen. ⁷ Behold, He is coming with the clouds, and every eye will see Him, even those who pierced Him; and all the tribes of the earth will mourn over Him. So it is to be. Amen.

(1) At the very outset, this divine book is set apart from all others found in the NT. Without a doubt, this is *the Revelation of Jesus Christ,* which God (the Father) gave to Jesus. It is essential not to confuse this very important fact because this *is not* the revelation of the beloved apostle John.

Many commentators approach this inspired book as if John was writing under his own literary discretion. However, this phrase explicitly destroys that concept. Here, the word "Revelation" is translated from the Greek word *apokalypsis*, meaning "making fully known, revelation, disclosure."[55] This disclosure reveals Jesus' divine counsel and plan. It shows this is not merely His observation of the events contained in this book, but that He is sovereign over their activity and fulfillment. All things must conform to His divine will in history and in the *eschaton** (the fulfillment of final things to come). Thus, we should understand this book to be "His" (possessive) revelation in which He has total control. Revelation is not a news reporter's observation of what happens, but John's record of events is the predetermined counsel of God, who is in complete control of every aspect of the fulfillment of His divine plan. All things are under His authority and conform to His will. It is He who executes judgment on the righteous and the wicked of humankind and the angelic host.

(a) For the benefit of those who serve Him, Revelation was given to **His bond-servants,** *doulos,* meaning "being under someone's total control, slavish, servile, subject."[56] Here, the term *servant,* or *slave,* is not being used in a pejorative sense but is a confirmation that all believers *were bought with a price.* Peter informs us that we "were not redeemed with perishable [NASB, NIV; "corruptible" KJV] things like silver or gold . . . but with precious blood, as of a lamb" (1 Pet 1:18–19). Indeed, we were "bought with a price" (1 Cor 6:20). We are not our own; our spirits, souls, and bodies are God's (see 1 Cor 6:19–20).

(b) The messages and visions of Revelation concern **the things which must soon take place,** a statement that has stumped commentators and students alike. What today's Christians have that first-century Christians did not have is two thousand years of hindsight. Now it is clear that their expectations that things would "soon take place" did not mean

---

[55] Bauer, *Greek-English Lexicon*, s.v. apokalypsis, "revelation."

[56] Bauer, s.v. *doulos*, "servant."

they were to be fulfilled in their lifetime. First-century Christians who believed that Christ's return was imminent discovered that there would be what R. C. Sproul and others refer to as the *parousia* delay*[57] (a long delay in Christ's second coming), which has spanned over two thousand years now. Robert H. Mounce also asserts, "With the passing of that generation and the apparent failure of the book's eschatological promises to find fulfillment, confusion began to set in."[58]

Peter referred to the mockers who capitalized on this. They said, "Where is the promise of His coming?" (2 Pet 3:4). He encouraged his readers, "But do not let this one fact escape your notice, beloved, that with the Lord one day is like a thousand years, and a thousand years like one day" (v. 8; see also Ps 90:4). God was fully aware that no Christians of the past centuries had any chance of being alive when Christ returned. However, of course, God would not have disclosed that in explicit terms to them because the revelation is to all Christians in all church ages, given from His *eternal now* perspective.

The passing of two thousand years has given us a perspective that was not available to first-century Christians. Therefore, we must understand that "soon take place" is from His perspective, not ours. However, our expectation of His coming must never wane, no matter how many years pass before He comes. We must understand it in the context of "the Lord is not slow about His promise, as some count slowness, but is patient toward [us], not wishing for any to perish but for all to come to repentance" (2 Pet 3:9). Giving humankind time to repent means allowing humans to be born so that they may be "born again." So far, His grace, mercy, and long-suffering have extended into the twenty-first century. Thank God that He didn't come in the first century, or else all the generations of the church after that point would have never had the opportunity to

---

[57] R. C. Sproul, *1–2 Peter, End of All Things: St. Andrew's Expositional Commentary* (Wheaton, IL: Crossway, 2011), 150.

[58] Robert H. Mounce, *The Book of Revelation: The New International Commentary on the New Testament* (Grand Rapids, MI: Wm. B. Eerdmans Publishing Co., 1997), 24.

share in the eternal bliss prepared for those who love Him.

(c) *by His angel*: The Greek *angelos* means "messenger." Angels are created, immensely powerful, immortal, supernatural beings, all created holy, but a third rebelled with Satan and are forever wicked. Throughout Revelation, as typical of apocalyptic literature in general, angels play a major role in executing God's plan: they blow the trumpets (8:6), they pour out the wrath of God (16:2), they restrain Satan (20:1–3), they give warning to the world not to get the mark of the beast (14:9–11), they preach the everlasting gospel (14:6), they reveal mysteries (17:7), they give instruction (17:9–18), they exert control over heavenly bodies and weather (7:1; 16:8), they speak to wildlife (19:17–19), they harvest and cast into the winepress of the wrath of God (14:18–19), they identify themselves to be "fellow servant[s]" and "brethren" (22:9), they refuse worship (19:10), and they are extremely numerous (5:11).

(2) *who testified to the word of God and to the testimony of Jesus Christ*: This is typical of John, the only Gospel writer who records Jesus as being the Word of God manifested in the flesh (see John 1:1, 14): "What was from the beginning, what we have heard, what we have seen with our eyes, what we have looked at and touched with our hands, concerning the Word of Life" (1 John 1:1). John declares that "the testimony of Jesus is the spirit of prophecy" (Rev 19:10). The testimony of Jesus Christ, though liberating, is also the cause for persecution and martyrdom and yet ultimate victory.

(3) *Blessed is he who reads and those who hear the words of the prophecy, and heed the things which are written in it*: This is the first of *seven beatitudes** or *blessings* (1:3; 14:13; 16:15; 19:9; 20:6; 22:7, 14) found in Revelation. All of God's Word is blessed; however, the explicit blessing gives additional weight to the importance of this book. During the early centuries, the Western church accepted Revelation as *canonical* (the accepted books of the Bible), but this was not the case in the Eastern

4

church.[59] However, God's providential hand guided the church fathers in the acceptance of this book, which was given to and is about the church. By divine appointment, God assured that Revelation was included in the canon of Scripture during the era when the Bible was finalized and the canon was closed. There would have been no other chance to include it after that point. Revelation is so critical that it gives a specific blessing to all who "read," "hear," and "heed" the "words of the prophecy." Additionally, this book concludes with a solemn warning: "I testify to everyone who hears the words of the prophecy of this book: if anyone adds to them, God will add to him the plagues which are written in this book; and if anyone takes away from the words of the book of this prophecy, God will take away his part from the tree of life" (22:18–19). Therefore, the book opens with a *blessing* but ends with a *curse*. Certainly, down through the centuries, Revelation has been a blessing to all who read and heed the words of this prophecy, and it will especially bless those who will be living during the time these things come to pass.

(4) *from Him who is and who was and who is to come*: This three-part repetition is one of many found in Revelation. It speaks of God in His eternal *self-existence*. God is not a *contingent being** but the Supreme Being, the creator of all things. All creation depends upon Him for existence and is therefore contingent on Him. However, God is self-existent, depending upon nothing and no one. He is God, "from everlasting to everlasting" (Ps 90:2), and He "is the same yesterday and today and forever" (Heb 13:8). "And who is to come" anticipates the coming and institution of God's glorious kingdom that shall have no end.

(a) *and from the seven Spirits who are before His throne*: "Seven" is a prominent number in Revelation, appearing over fifty times. Some emphasize "seven" to mean "completeness" or "perfection." Its use here is mysterious, but most agree it is in reference to the Holy Spirit (5:6). Others assign it to

[59] D. A. Carson, Douglas Moo, and Leon Morris, *An Introduction to the New Testament* (Grand Rapids, MI: Zondervan, 1992), 480.

seven archangels, or the angels of the seven trumpets. However, it could be a reference to Isaiah 11:2, implying a *sevenfold* Spirit. See also Zechariah 4:1–10.

(5) *and from Jesus Christ, the faithful witness*: Certainly Jesus is "faithful," meaning a "trustworthy witness," in His life, death, and resurrection; His power to keep the saints and redeem the lost; His exaltation; His anticipated return; and so many other facets of His eternal work. He told His disciples, "Let not your heart be troubled: ye believe in God, believe also in me" (John 14:1 KJV). Since He is God, He is trustworthy, and therefore a "faithful witness."

(a) *the firstborn of the dead*: * This statement is packed with golden nuggets of truth. Jesus is the first begotten of the dead. The Greek *prōtotokos* "signifies not only priority in time but also the primacy of rank that accrues to Jesus with his resurrection."[60] Unfortunately, many commentators identify "firstborn" only in the context of Christ being preeminent. Certainly, *He is* preeminent, but He is more than that. Christ is "firstborn of a new humanity which is to be glorified."[61] This concept goes back to Psalm 2. In Acts 13:30–33, Paul makes a compelling argument about the resurrection of Christ partly stated in v. 33: "That God has fulfilled this promise to our children in that He raised up Jesus, as it is also written in the second Psalm, 'You are My Son; Today I have begotten You.'" The English word "begotten" comes from the Hebrew word *yalad*, which means "to bear young, to be born."[62] Colossians also picks up on this same concept: "And he is the head of the body, the church; he is the beginning and the firstborn from among the dead" (Col 1:18 NIV). In these passages, "firstborn" is also in reference to Christ's resurrection. However, He is not the first to be *raised* from the dead (see John 11:33–34) but is the first to be born from the dead, or raised

---

[60] Geoffrey W. Bromiley, *Theological Dictionary of the New Testament: Abridged in One Volume*, eds. Gerhard Kittel and Gerhard Friedrich (Grand Rapids, MI: Wm. B. Eerdmans Publishing Co., 1985), s.v. *prōtotokos*, "firstborn."

[61] Bauer, *Greek-English Lexicon*, s.v. *prōtotokos*, "firstborn."

[62] *Strong's Hebrew Dictionary*, s.v. *yālad*, 3205.

in a *glorified body*, never to die again. During Christ's earthly ministry, all those raised from the dead were raised in their *natural* bodies and eventually succumbed to death once again. To be *born from the dead* is a greater eternal reality in which Christ was *the first*, not *the only*, as all the redeemed will follow in the likeness of His resurrection.

(b) *the ruler of the kings of the earth*: Christ exercises rule over all the earth as Nebuchadnezzar declared:

> But at the end of that period, I, Nebuchadnezzar, raised my eyes toward heaven and my reason returned to me, and I blessed the Most High and praised and honored Him who lives forever;
>
>> For His dominion is an everlasting dominion,
>> And His kingdom endures from generation to generation.
>> "All the inhabitants of the earth are accounted as nothing,
>> But He does according to His will in the host of heaven
>> And among the inhabitants of earth;
>> And no one can ward off His hand
>> Or say to Him, 'What have You done?'" (Dan 4:34–35)

Christ is the "King of kings, and the Lord of lords" (Rev 19:16), and the government will be upon His shoulders (see Isa 9:6), as will be all world affairs.

(c) *and released us from our sins by His blood*: ("washed us from our sins in his own blood," KJV). One of the great salvific benefits the redeemed receives is the forgiveness of sins, the result of being washed in His blood (see Eph 1:7; Col 1:14).

(6) *and He has made us to be a kingdom, priests*: The saints are a *royal priesthood*. Priests serve God in His temple. Peter states, "You also, as living stones, are being built up as a spiritual house for a holy priesthood, to offer up spiritual sacrifices acceptable to God through Jesus Christ" (1 Pet 2:5). Also, "But you are a chosen race, a royal priesthood, a holy nation, a people for God's own possession" (v. 9). Where the Levites were a *tribe of priests* under the old covenant (the law), the church fulfills that earthly role now. However, in eternity we are also "a kingdom and priests" (Rev 1:6 NIV) or a *kingdom of priests*. This text speaks of an eternal role of the redeemed in heaven. "Therefore, 'they are before the throne of God and serve him day and night in his temple; and he who sits on the throne will shelter them with his presence'" (7:15). Priests function in God's presence. The heavenly priesthood will not only serve God in His temple but also have the honor and right to be in His glorious presence.

(7) *Behold, He is coming with the clouds*: is a reference to the OT prophecy found in Daniel: "I kept looking in the night visions, and behold, with the clouds of heaven One like a Son of Man was coming, and He came up to the *Ancient of Days** and was presented before Him" (7:13). Clouds are typically associated with the coming of Christ (see Matt 24:30; 26:64; Mark 13:26; 14:63; 1 Thess 4:17; Rev 14:14–15). Clouds are also associated with Christ's ascension: "And after He had said these things, He was lifted up while they were looking on, and a cloud received Him out of their sight" (Acts 1:9).

(a) *and every eye will see Him*: Jesus' second coming will be unmistakable; every eye throughout the world will see Him. "And then the sign of the Son of Man will appear in the sky, and then all the tribes of the earth will mourn, and they will see the Son of Man coming on the clouds of the sky with power and great glory" (Matt 24:30). Whenever Halley's Comet appears, the entire world can see the awesome comet passing as the earth rotates. This could also be true of the coming of the Lord. As He approaches, all the world will see Him. Or He could simply circle the earth in a powerful train of glory. Whatever method of display, when He comes, all who dwell on the earth will see Him.

(b) *even those who pierced Him*: This phrase looks back to Christ's crucifixion, "They will look on the one they have pierced" (John 19:37 NIV), but it also looks forward to His second coming in glory. Though it is true that the Jews cried out, "Crucify Him!" (Luke 23:21), all of us, both Jew and Gentile, pierced Him. Isaiah prophesied, "He was pierced through for our transgressions, He was crushed for our iniquities; the chastening for our well-being fell upon Him, and by His scourging we are healed" (Isa 53:5). More importantly, this passage depicts the scene during the Lord's second coming. John references Zechariah 12:10:

> I will pour out on the house of David and on the inhabitants of Jerusalem, the Spirit of grace and of supplication, so that they will look on Me whom they have pierced; and they will mourn for Him, as one mourns for an only son, and they will weep bitterly over Him like the bitter weeping over a firstborn.

Imagine the horror of those who mocked His coming and denied His very existence when they see the Lord coming in great power and glory, followed by the armies of heaven.

(c) *and all the tribes of the earth will mourn over Him*: Not only will the inhabitants of the earth be dumbfounded, terrified, and dismayed, *but then they will lament.* Imagine the Jews who rejected Jesus and the world who doubted Him now coming to the shocking reality that Jesus is real and that He has returned in a stunning display of power and glory. Not as a *lamb* but as a *lion*, the King of kings and Lord of lords who will rule the nations with a rod of iron. However, for the remnant of Israel, *the Lord will pour out the spirit of grace*, and those left among the Gentile nations will all mourn.

REVELATION 1:8–16

Write in a Book What You See

[8] "I am the Alpha and the Omega," says the Lord God, "who is and who was and who is to come, the Almighty."

[9] I, John, your brother and fellow partaker in the tribulation and kingdom and perseverance which are in Jesus, was on the island called Patmos because of the word of God and the testimony of Jesus. [10] I was in the Spirit on the Lord's day, and I heard behind me a loud voice like the sound of a trumpet, [11] saying, "Write in a book what you see, and send it to the seven churches: to Ephesus and to Smyrna and to Pergamum and to Thyatira and to Sardis and to Philadelphia and to Laodicea."

[12] Then I turned to see the voice that was speaking with me. And having turned I saw seven golden lampstands; [13] and in the middle of the lampstands I saw one like a son of man, clothed in a robe reaching to the feet, and girded across His chest with a golden sash. [14] His head and His hair were white like white wool, like snow; and His eyes were like a flame of fire. [15] His feet were like burnished bronze, when it has been made to glow in a furnace, and His voice was like the sound of many waters. [16] In His right hand He held seven stars, and out of His mouth came a sharp two-edged sword; and His face was like the sun shining in its strength.

(8) *"I am the Alpha and the Omega," says the Lord God:* This is an awesome introduction. To encapsulate the Lord's omnipotence, omniscience, and omnipresence, plus His sovereignty over all things, a figure of speech called a *merism,** "a statement of polar opposites in order to highlight everything between the opposites,"[63] is used. The merisms *the Alpha and the Omega** (the first and last letters of the Greek alphabet) and "the beginning and the end" (Rev 21:6) emphasize the Lord's *preeminence.** Compare these with Isaiah 41:4, "Who has performed and accomplished it, calling forth the generations from the beginning? 'I, the Lord, am the first, and with the last. I am He,'" and Isaiah 44:6, "Thus says the Lord, the King of Israel and his Redeemer, the Lord of hosts: 'I am the first and I am the last, and there is no God besides Me.'" Therefore, *first and last, Alpha and Omega,* are to say not only that the Lord is *first and last** in line or succession but that there is none like Him. Jesus is totally unique, the "only," as in "the only begotten from the Father" (John 1:14), the only God-man—a *hypostatic union,** meaning "fully God and fully man."

(a) The merism is followed by the three-part repetition *who is and who was and who is to come:* "Who is" confirms God is self-sufficient, "who was" demonstrates He has no beginning because He is from everlasting to everlasting, and "who is to come," as in "Your kingdom come" (Matt 6:10), shows that no matter how long the delay, it is certain the Lord shall come. He shall come in power and glory to usher in everlasting righteousness in a kingdom that shall never end (see Dan 7:13–14). After the three-part repetition comes the divine punctuation, *the Almighty:* He is sovereign and all-powerful.

(9) *I, John, your brother and fellow partaker in the tribulation and kingdom:* John does not appeal to his readers through an exalted apostolic position but in humility calls himself "your brother" and a companion (co-participant) "in the tribulation." Here, John does not grasp for glory

---

[63]   G. K. Beale, *The New International Greek Testament Commentary: The Book of Revelation* (Grand Rapids, MI: Wm. B. Eerdmans Publishing Co., 1998), s.v. "merism," 199.

or earthly adulation. He closely identifies with the tribulation that walking with the Lord inevitably brings. He does not hide, deny, or shirk from it; instead, he embraces it, thereby uniting himself with the sufferings of Christ. Jesus stated, "If anyone wishes to come after Me, he must deny himself, and take up his cross and follow Me. For whoever wishes to save his life will lose it; but whoever loses his life for My sake will find it" (Matt 16:24–25). In today's highly materialistic and self-indulgent Christianity, especially in the United States, suffering is a message that has been rejected by most, not embraced.

(a) *was on the island called Patmos because of the word of God and the testimony of Jesus:* In approximately AD 95, John was banished to Patmos by the Roman emperor Domitian. Patmos is a small volcanic island in the Aegean Sea, southwest of Ephesus and between Asia Minor and Greece. John was banished there "because of the word of God and the testimony of Jesus," the reality that puts believers in direct opposition to the world. John repeats this phrase in 1:2, 9; 6:9; 20:4. Today, Patmos has a small population of three thousand. Many tourists visit Patmos for its rich religious history—it's the place where John penned the Apocalypse. Patmos was designated as "Holy Island" by the Greek Parliament in 1981.[64]

(10) *I was in the Spirit:* It was necessary for John to be "in the Spirit" because to be in God's direct presence is too traumatic for a human being. God warned Moses, "Thou canst not see my face: for there shall no man see me, and live" (Exod 33:20 KJV). Therefore, to communicate directly to us, God circumvents our frailties and limitations by moving us beyond the sensory realm. Though we can be led by the Holy Spirit while in the body, what John experienced is beyond the earthly realm. Throughout the Bible, God appears and communicates to select humans through a *trance*, "a state of being in which consciousness is wholly or partially

---

[64] Maximina Triantafillidou, "Patmos," Grecias Vision, accessed May 6, 2024, https://grecias-vision.com/patmos/.

suspended, frequently associated with divine action, *trance, ecstasy*"[65] (see Acts 10:10), a *dream* (see 1 Kgs 3:5; Matt 1:20), or in John's case, *in the Spirit* or possibly *out of the body*, akin to Paul's experience (cf. 2 Cor 12:2–3). As a result of being *in the Spirit*, John could experience the heavenly realm and see, hear, and record mostly everything he encountered.

On the Lord's day: is a phrase found only here in the NT. Three views have been put forth by various scholars: (1) *The day of the Lord*, or the period of wrath. Some Pretribulationists, such as John F. Walvoord, see this as being the *day of the Lord*,[66] that fits the Pretrib narrative. However, other Pretrib proponents, such as John MacArthur, would disagree.[67] (2) *Easter Sunday*. (3) *The first day of the week*. Sunday, *the first day of the week*, is preferred by most because early Christians began commemorating Christ's resurrection on the first day of the week (see Mark 16:1–2). For us today, it is the day of worship analogous to the Jewish Sabbath.

(11) *Write in a book what you see*: The command to "write in a book what you see" is the first directive to John to make a written record of all he would see and experience. At this early juncture, John has no idea of the totality of what awaits him in the Apocalypse. The directive to make a written record is emphasized again in v. 19. The instruction to make a written record stresses that the message is to be enduring. Other prophets had been told the same: "Then the LORD said to Moses, 'Write this in a book as a memorial and recite it to Joshua'" (Exod 17:14). "Record the vision and inscribe it on tablets" (Hab 2:2). "Now go, write it on a tablet before them and inscribe it on a scroll, that it may serve in the time to come as a witness forever" (Isa 30:8). Information recorded in books is a powerful witness—including what is recorded in the books written in heaven (e.g., the book of Life; Rev 3:5; 20:15).

---

[65] Bauer, *Greek-English Lexicon*, s.v. *ekstasis*, "trance."

[66] John F. Walvoord, "Revelation," in *The Bible Knowledge Commentary: An Exposition of the Scriptures*, eds. J. F. Walvoord and R. B. Zuck, vol. 2 (Wheaton, IL: Victor Books, 1985), 930.

[67] John MacArthur, *The MacArthur New Testament Commentary, Revelation 1-11* (Chicago: Moody Publishers, 1999), 41.

(a) *and send it to the seven churches: to Ephesus and to Smyrna and to Pergamum and to Thyatira and to Sardis and to Philadelphia and to Laodicea:* *Asia Minor* is meant here, which today is the nation of Turkey. John was directed to distribute this divine book to seven *actual churches* in the various cities listed here. There is no mystery as to their order. Starting at Ephesus, one could follow the route to all the cities along the way, ending up in Laodicea.

(12) *Then I turned to see the voice that was speaking with me:* This statement is very interesting. John does not write, "I turned to see *who* spoke to me." Rather, he says he turned to see "the voice" that spoke to him. This is interesting because it is from John's Gospel that we understand that "in the beginning was the Word, and the Word was with God, and the Word was God" (John 1:1). The voice was not mere words but "the Word." *I saw seven golden lampstands.** Revelation 1:21 informs us that the seven lampstands represent the seven churches to whom the book is addressed.

(13) *and in the middle of the lampstands I saw one like a son of man:* The voice is now identified as the "son of man," who is in the midst of the lampstands. This means Christ, the Son of Man, is integrally observant of the functioning and well-being of the church, which by extension is His body. The most important OT use of the title Son of Man is found in Daniel 7:13. In the Gospels, Son of Man was Christ's preferred title for Himself; it is used over eighty times and speaks of His messianic mission and full humanity. In Revelation, the term is only used twice, in 1:13 and 14:14.

(a) *clothed in a robe reaching to the feet, and girded across His chest with a golden sash:* Long robes reaching down to His feet were symbols of a high official, a person of dignity and distinction.

(14–15) *His head and His hair were white like white wool, like snow; and His eyes were like a flame of fire. His feet were like burnished bronze, when it has been made to glow in a furnace, and His voice was like the sound of* *many waters*: The description of Jesus' appearance in divine glory is far removed from His earthly humanity. Paul emphasizes this point when he states, "Therefore from now on we recognize no one according to the flesh; even though we have known Christ according to the flesh, yet now we know Him in this way no longer" (2 Cor 5:16). Here Christ is exalted and glorified; however, we should not try to interpret too literally. If one makes too much of His head and hair being white like wool, one must also account for a two-edged sword proceeding from His mouth in Revelation 1:16, which is symbolic of judgment (Rev 19:15, 21). Apocalyptic literature communicates in symbolic and literal terms. Care must be taken to distinguish between the two.

(16) *In His right hand*: In the Gospel of John, Jesus, speaking of His sheep, declares, "No one will snatch them out of My hand. My Father, who has given them to Me, is greater than all; and no one is able to snatch them out of the Father's hand" (John 10:28–29). The right hand is the symbol of authority, power, and strength. In His powerful hand, *He held seven stars* (see Rev 1:20), *and out of His mouth came a sharp two-edged sword*. Often, the two-edged sword is a symbol of the Word of God. The author of Hebrews declares,

> For the word of God is living and active and sharper than any two-edged sword, and piercing as far as the division of soul and spirit, of both joints and marrow, and able to judge the thoughts and intentions of the heart. (4:12)

In Revelation, it is also a symbol of the Lord's judgment (see 2:16, 19:15, 21). *His face was like the sun shining in its strength*: The Lord, in His heavenly glory, shines in incomprehensible brilliance, which Paul describes as "unapproachable light" (1 Tim 6:16). In his first epistle, John describes God as being light. The sun's light on earth is at its full strength at high noon, when it shines in its highest radiance and intensity. In the OT, Moses was exposed to God's light. This encounter caused his face to shine in such a manner that he had to put a veil over his face because the people were afraid to look at him (see Exod 34:29–35).

†

REVELATION 1:17–20

THE FIRST AND THE LAST

¹⁷ When I saw Him, I fell at His feet like a dead man. And He placed His right hand on me, saying, "Do not be afraid; I am the first and the last, ¹⁸ and the living One; and I was dead, and behold, I am alive forevermore, and I have the keys of death and of Hades. ¹⁹ Therefore write the things which you have seen, and the things which are, and the things which will take place after these things. ²⁰ As for the mystery of the seven stars which you saw in My right hand, and the seven golden lampstands: the seven stars are the angels of the seven churches, and the seven lampstands are the seven churches.

(17) *I fell at His feet like a dead man:* Even though John was "in the Spirit," seeing Jesus in an exalted, glorified state was so overwhelming that he fell at the Lord's feet as a dead man. *And He placed His right hand on me, saying, "Do not be afraid; I am the first and the last":* Not only did the Lord say, "Do not be afraid," but first He *touched* John. The touch of a compassionate, loving Lord conveys safety and security, dispelling John's anxiety. Like Daniel's encounter with the angel in Daniel 10, a touch was required to strengthen, revive, and arrest fear.

(18) *and the living One; and I was dead, and behold, I am alive forevermore:* This is another three-part repetition. Christ is the "living One," speaking of His preincarnate existence, His death and burial, and His

16

triumphal resurrection to live forevermore. The other three-part repetitions occur in 1:4, 8, 17; 4:8; 11:17; 17:8. "The frequent use of 3 in Revelation; the description of God as 'who is and who was and who is to come' (1:4); and 'the Father, the Son, and the Holy Spirit' (Matt 28:19), and 'holy, holy, holy' (Isa 6:3) are noteworthy. In some of these cases, three-fold repetition is a mode of expressing the superlative."[68]

(a) *and I have* ("I hold," NIV) *the keys of death and of Hades*: Keys* represent the authority to open and close, lock and unlock. Hebrews 9:27 says, "It is appointed for men to die once and after this comes judgment." Job observes that a person's life and death are *appointed*: "Since his days are determined, the number of his months is with You; and his limits You have set so that he cannot pass" (Job 14:5). Jesus exercises power (holds the keys) over death and hell regarding humans and angelic principalities, particularly the latter since hell (hades) and by extension, *the lake of fire*— "was prepared for the devil and his angels" (Matt 25:41).

(19) *Therefore write the things which you have seen, and the things which are, and the things which will take place after these things*: Those who espouse a dispensational Pretrib rapture position see this passage as an outline on how the book is to be interpreted. They assert "the things which you have seen" concern chapter 1, "the things which are" cover chapters 2–3 (with the seven churches representing the church age to the rapture), and "the things which will take place after these things" appear in chapters 4–22 and point to future events after the church has been raptured. However, these divisions along chapter lines were not John's intent but were imposed upon the text. Chapters and verses were not added to the Bible for over fifteen centuries after John wrote Revelation. This is another threefold repetition that conveys the idea of *write the vision in its totality*. On this, G. K. Beale observes, "John is to

---

68   Geoffrey W. Bromiley, ed., *The International Standard Bible Encyclopedia*, vol. 4 (Grand Rapids, MI: Eerdmans, 1995), s.v. "three."

write down the entire vision that he saw."[69] H. D. M. Spence-Jones asserts, "The threefold division of things probably refers to past, present, and future *visions*, not to the past, present, and future in history."[70] George R. Beasley-Murray upholds that "it is commonly thought to indicate the divisions of Revelation.... It is best to see [v 19] as a command to write the entire Revelation, rather than as an analysis of the book itself."[71]

EXCURSUS—PROGRAMMATIC PROBLEMS WITH 1:19

Dispensationalists have determined that the entire church age is represented in chapters 2 and 3. However, that forces an allegorical interpretation on those two chapters that is inconsistent with the typical dispensational claim to employ a literal interpretation of Revelation. Though there are always similarities that can be drawn from one congregation to the next, these were seven literal congregations in Asia Minor during the first century. To employ a *church age* interpretation to these historic churches to give credence to a dispensational structuring of the book is a stretch. The most respected dispensational scholar of the twentieth century, Walvoord, states, "Ephesus seems to characterize the apostolic church as a whole, and Smyrna seems to depict the church in its early persecutions. However, the Scriptures do not expressly authorize this interpretation."[72] Walvoord's assertion is correct. The Scriptures do not authorize this interpretation. Such structuring has been imposed doctrinally, not by God. Churches throughout history have had similar issues because the common denominators have

---

[69]   G. K. Beale, *The Book of Revelation: A Commentary on the Greek Text* (Grand Rapids, MI; Wm. B. Eerdmans Publishing Co.; Paternoster Press, 1999), 216.

[70]   H. D. M. Spence-Jones, ed., *The Pulpit Commentary,* vol. 23, *Revelation* (London; New York: Funk & Wagnalls Company, 1909), 8.

[71]   George R. Beasley-Murray, "Revelation," in *New Bible Commentary: 21st Century Edition*, eds. D. A. Carson et al., 4th ed. (Leicester, England; Downers Grove, IL: Inter-Varsity Press, 1994), 1427.

[72]   John F. Walvoord, "Revelation," in *The Bible Knowledge Commentary: An Exposition of the Scriptures,* eds. J. F. Walvoord and R. B. Zuck, vol. 2 (Wheaton, IL: Victor Books, 1985), 932–33.

been Satan and human nature, which haven't changed since the fall of Adam. Additionally, if the Lord intended these churches to represent the age of the church or to become seven church templates, then why would He include cryptic references to specific deeds and individuals (see 2:10, 13) and doctrines of the Nicolaitans (see 2:14–15, 20) without disclosing those specific errors so future churches could avoid those heresies, which the Lord hates? And why only these seven churches? There were other churches (in the areas of Antioch, Galatia, Thessalonica, Corinth, Rome, etc.).

Pretribulationists typically see "the things which are" as the entire age of the church, which has spanned for almost two thousand years. They claim Philadelphia is the church of the rapture. Under this dispensational structure, Philadelphia is the sixth of seven church ages. The five preceding churches, or church ages, must pass to get to Philadelphia. That being the case, the rapture could not have occurred before the age of Philadelphia, because Pretribulationists insist the rapture is described at 3:10. How then can the rapture be imminent if the church must first pass through the Ephesian, Smyrnaean, Pergamene, Thyatirean, and Sardian ages before it gets to the Philadelphian age?

Some dispensationalists would assert that we are the Philadelphian church today. Others insist that we are the Laodicean church. Here is the necessary question that must follow: When did we exit the Sardian age and enter the Philadelphian age? Of course, there would be no answer to that question because the entire structure is contrived. Warren W. Wiersbe also reaches a similar conclusion as does this commentator when he states, "If this sequence is a 'prophetic history' of the church, then Jesus could not return for His people until the era of the Laodicean church; and this would make His imminent return impossible."[73] Dispensationalists make this a necessary structure, not the Scriptures, be-

[73] Warren W. Wiersbe, *Wiersbe's Expository Outlines on the New Testament* (Wheaton, IL: Victor Books, 1992), 798.

cause they need this interpretation to back the premise that the church is not on earth after chapter 3. They associate the missing word *church* with the missing church on earth. When one embraces the premise that all Revelation is for and concerns the church, there is no doctrinal imperative to program the church out of Revelation beyond chapter 3. (See additional comments in "The Imminent Return Problem" essay and "What Happened to the Church?" excursus.)

(20) One of the great features of Revelation is that it interprets itself, and v. 20 is a clear example of this. The ***seven stars are the angels of the seven churches:*** Most interpret this as referring to the pastors of those congregations because here the word "angels" (Gk. *angelos*) can mean "human or angelic messengers." ***The seven lampstands*** represent the seven churches of Asia Minor. However, by this time, several churches had been established, exceeding seven. Therefore, many interpret the seven churches to represent all churches, an interpretation that relies on a symbolic understanding of seven to indicate the completion of the church age far beyond the first century. However, this interpretation unnecessarily projects pretribulationism on the text. The verse-by-verse commentary continues on page 46.

ESSAY:
THE IMMINENT RETURN
PROBLEM

Though the doctrine of imminence insists that there are no signs, or that nothing must occur before the rapture happens, here are some important things to consider. The first-century Christians would have fared far better if they had known specifically what signs indicate Christ's return for His church. Though it is true no one knows *the day or the hour* (the specific timing) of His return, we can know the season when it is near. Jesus Himself said,

> Now learn the parable from the fig tree: when its branch has already become tender and puts forth its leaves, you know that summer is near; so, you too, when you see all these things, recognize that He is near, right at the door. (Matt 24:32–33)

Since the first-century Christians did not have a better grasp of eschatology, they concluded that the rapture was going to occur in their lifetime. However, today, we know this was a serious miscalculation. We have two thousand years of history to prove that they got this issue wrong. The fact is, there was no chance they would live to see the rapture. God was fully aware of this even if they were not. So, what was God to do? Tell them, "You will never live to see the rapture because it will be at least two thousand years away"? Of course not. Christ would not have said that, even though it would have been true.

The NT had to be written in the first century because the primary sources (the apostles and their associates) were still alive. And though it was written during the first century, the NT message was and is for all Christians so that the entire body has the same canon (standard) of Scripture. However, the timing of the writing did not mean any generation of Christians prior to the twenty-first century would be alive when the rapture occurred. Eschatology had to be placed in the NT from the first century to ensure that the message reaches those to whom it will most likely apply. To be clear, there were many things the early church got right. However, the arrival of the end of the age was not one of them—it was too far away, and none of them comprehended that.

The Long Journey

How eschatology was meant to play out over time can be likened to a father taking his son on a long, two-thousand-mile journey. The child has no concept of the distance or how much time it will take to reach their destination. Every few miles the child is asking, "Are we there yet?" The father does not take time to explain what a mile is. Nor does he try to explain to a child who cannot count past ten that the destination is two thousand miles. He doesn't explain all the details about why they are taking the trip. The father gives no information as to how many miles they have already traveled or how many miles remain. He does not explain how much time it will take or why it takes that amount of time. None of these details will benefit a young child because his comprehension is limited. However, with patience, the father looks back and says to his son, "We will get there soon," with no explanation of what *soon* means. The child gets excited because to him *soon* means "in the next few minutes." However, the father knows that *soon* will be in terms of days, not minutes.

The father has not deceived the child by saying they will reach the destination soon. From the adult's perspective, a couple of days is soon. But for an anxious child, that's forever. The father is aware that the child lacks the ability to comprehend what it means to take a long trip. Therefore, the best and most comforting message is "I'm going to be with you, and I will never leave you. I'm going to get you there safely, and we will be there soon."

The first-century Christians had no idea that millions more Christians would come to Christ in the following twenty centuries and counting. It wasn't about them and their immediate circumstances. Christ loved future Christians just as much as those of the first century. Had they thought about the world beyond their immediate time frame—which mortals, without divine help, cannot do—they may have realized that Christ's plans included Christians thousands of years in the future. They simply had no idea of how expansive a project building the Lord's church would be. Had they known all of what the Lord was going to do and all those who were going to come to Christ after them, they would have behaved like Job, placed their hands over their mouths, and not said another word. However, the Lord lovingly encouraged the fledgling church by saying, "I am coming quickly" (Rev 3:11; 22:7, 12, 20). That's all they needed to know. When His disciples asked, "Lord, is it at this time You are restoring the kingdom to Israel?" (Acts 1:6), Jesus told His disciples, "It is not for you to know times or epochs which the Father has fixed by His own authority" (v. 7). In other words, "That's none of your business, but your job is to be My witnesses throughout the ends of the earth." Whether they understood it or not, this was going to be a long journey.

One of the most fundamental tenets of the Pretrib rapture theory is the doctrine of the imminent return of Christ. This doctrine states that there are no signs given, or that nothing needs to occur, before the Lord raptures the church. His coming for the church can happen at any time. Concerning this doctrine, Paul N. Benware states,

> The word *imminent* is not found in the Bible but has become the word to express the theological idea of the "any-moment"

coming of the Lord Jesus Christ. The word itself speaks of something that is about to happen.[74]

Benware is correct; the word *imminent* is not found in the Bible. However, this fact does not mitigate the significance of this teaching. Imminence is a *theological* and *doctrinal* concept on which Pretribulationists place great reliance. It becomes a self-imposed boundary that dispensationalists consider impassable regarding the *any-moment* rapture. Imminence would consider no futuristic prophecy found in Scripture as having to occur before the rapture.

Benware further asserts,

> It is difficult to get around the conclusion that the early church really did anticipate the Lord's return at any moment. They were eagerly looking for the Savior, but clearly they were not looking for signs. They were motivated to godliness because they believed that Jesus could return at any moment. If they thought that the Lord's return was far off, their tendency would be toward sinful, careless living— just as Jesus Himself taught (Matt. 24:48–49). The concept of imminency is a strong argument for the pretribulational rapture of the church.[75]

Let's unpack these assertions. An important question is, "Why were early Christians looking for the Lord to come at any moment?" It is true that first-century Christians believed that the Lord would come during their lifetime. However, Christ's plan to build His church extended far beyond what first-century Christians could have possibly comprehended. Indeed, it has been a long journey. What is clear to us today that was not evident to them back then is the Lord had no intention of returning during the first century or any other century before the twenty-first

---

[74] Paul N. Benware, *Understanding End Times Prophecy: A Comprehensive Approach* (Chicago: Moody Publishers, 2006), 248.

[75] Benware, 253.

century. Spence notes, "The primitive Church had not yet found its true perspective, and, in common with all Christians of the first age, the apostles believed that Christ would return soon, possibly within the lifetime of some then living. 'Yea, I come quickly' (Rev. 22:20) was by them understood in the most literal sense of Ταχύ (come quickly)." [76]

The apostles were not infallible. Just like any other human being, they made mistakes and got things wrong. However, when the Holy Spirit moved upon them to record Scripture, that's where inerrancy existed. Whatever God did not reveal, they did not know. When Jesus completed His forty days with His disciples, He was taken up into heaven and disappeared in a cloud (see Acts 1:9). After this, the angels said something that could give us insight into why the apostles thought Jesus' return would be so soon.

> They also said, "Men of Galilee, why do you stand looking into the sky? This Jesus, who has been taken up from you into heaven, will come in just the same way as you have watched Him go into heaven." (Acts 1:11)

It is understandable how the apostles thought as they did. The angels said the Lord would return "in just the same way as [they had] watched Him go." It is easy to misconstrue this to mean that *they* would see the Lord return just as *they* saw Him go into heaven. Therefore, it is plausible that the idea of a soon-returning Christ *could* have originated with the apostles. But at this point in Acts, the apostles would have had in mind the return of the Lord from the perspective of Daniel 7:13–14 or Zechariah 14:3–8. They would not have had the rapture of the church in mind because the church had not yet started. Paul had not yet been converted, and no revelations concerning the church or the rapture had yet been revealed.

---

[76] H. D. M. Spence-Jones, ed., *The Pulpit Commentary,* vol. 22, *1 John* (London; New York: Funk & Wagnalls Company, 1909), 25.

THE IMMINENT RETURN PROBLEM

The contemporary doctrine of imminence that Pretrib relies on has its roots in a first-century error. The rapture did not occur in their lifetime as they expected. Since the NT was written during the first century, the encouragements to "look for Christ" and "wait for Christ" and affirmations like "I'm coming quickly" applied to first-century believers as well as to us today. This way, whenever Christ comes, it remains an active hope for the living or those who have fallen asleep. However, as history has borne out, it certainly did not mean the Lord would come by the end of the first century. Certainly, this has turned out to be a very long delay between Christ's two advents.

What Benware asserts—"If they thought that the Lord's return was far off, their tendency would be toward sinful, careless living—just as Jesus Himself taught (Matt. 24:48–49)"—is misguided. His assertion here is far off because Jesus' return in the rapture was at least two thousand years away. Secondly, Jesus' not returning in the first century, which became clear by the beginning of the second century, did not lead to sinful and careless living. Benware's assertion on this point comes from misapplying his proof text to all Christians. The Matthew 24:48–49 text speaks not about righteous Christians but about those with evil hearts:

> Who then is the faithful and sensible slave whom his master put in charge of his household to give them their food at the proper time? Blessed is that slave whom his master finds so doing when he comes. Truly I say to you that he will put him in charge of all his possessions. *But if that evil slave says in his heart, 'My master is not coming for a long time,'* and begins to beat his fellow slaves and eat and drink with drunkards; the master of that slave will come on a day when he does not expect him and at an hour which he does not know. (Matt 24:45–50, emphasis added)

Plainly it is the evil slave that says, "My master is not coming for a long time," and then starts to act evilly. The righteous do not have this

26

mindset. They are not concerned as much about when the master comes as they are about pleasing the master by completing the work he has given them to do. A slothful employee only works when the boss is present. He's the one constantly watching the clock. The good employee does their job regardless of whether the boss is looking, simply because it is the right thing to do. Therefore, Benware's assertion does not fit the meaning of the passage he uses to promote imminence. Those who love Christ serve Him because He saved and redeemed them, not because He's coming back soon. For the righteous, if Christ comes tomorrow or does not come for another thousand years, it doesn't make a difference. They see Christ's long delay as having more time to serve the God of their salvation, not as an extended opportunity to sin.

WAITING DOES NOT AUTOMATICALLY SUPPORT IMMINENCE

Benware also asserts, "They were eagerly looking for the Savior, but clearly they were not looking for signs." This statement is problematic because the Bible is full of signs concerning the end times. Jesus was the one who said, "But when these things begin to take place, straighten up and lift up your heads, because your redemption is drawing near" (Luke 21:28).

Just because someone is eagerly looking or waiting for something does not mean that it could happen at any time. A sixteen-year-old can eagerly await their eighteenth birthday, but that does not mean that their eighteenth birthday can come at any time. Eagerly waiting for something has no influence on when the expected event will occur. *Eagerness* does not equate to *imminence.*

NO SIGNS GIVEN BEFORE THE RAPTURE?

The NT gives many end-time signs. So, why are some people insisting that no signs were given to the church? In each of the passages used to support imminence (1 Cor 1:7; 16:22–24; Phil 3:20–21; 1 Thess 1:10; 4:15; Titus 2:13; Jas 5:7–9), there is nothing explicit in the texts identifying any accompanying sign. Since nothing is explicitly stated connecting a specific sign, Pretribulationists take that to mean that *there are no signs*, even though the NT records many signs. This reasoning is not tenable. For example, Paul speaks of the perilous times that shall come in the last days (see 2 Tim 3:1). Peter speaks of the scoffers/mockers who will come—those who will mock believers who are looking for the Lord to return (2 Pet 3:3–10). Both Paul and Peter are speaking to the body of Christ, saying these conditions will be experienced by the church of the last days.

These are just two of the many signs of the end times given in the NT. Among them is the Mount Olivet Discourse of Matthew 24; Mark 13; and Luke 21. Jesus also prophesied, "Because of the increase of wickedness, the love of most will grow cold" (Matt 24:12 NIV). In the twenty-first-century United States and around the world, wickedness is so prevalent socially, politically, religiously, economically, and geo-politically that people have become desensitized and indifferent to lawlessness and have grown cold.

The Pretrib assertion that no signs precede the rapture and, therefore, it can occur at any moment is based not on Scripture declaring *there are no signs* but on a conclusion reached by Pretribulationists. A conclusion reached is not the same as an explicit biblical fact. Applying a similar line of reasoning, it could be concluded that Paul walked from one place to the next during his missionary journeys. Why? Because there is no mention of Paul riding a horse. From that assumption, it could also be argued that since Paul never mentions horses, he could have been afraid of horses. Do you see what nonsense can proceed from a conclusion that's based upon something not being mentioned in a text? If a parent writes about their child's birthday celebration and focuses on the fun and excitement their child had, that does not mean the child didn't endure excruciating pain the week before the birthday due to breaking their arm. The fact that the parent does not mention the broken arm cannot be interpreted as meaning their child has never had a broken arm. If the Scriptures hold commandments not to look for the signs Christ gave concerning His own return, then the Pretrib argument would be substantiated. But of course, those Scriptures do not exist.

THE MOUNT OLIVET DISCOURSE

The Mount Olivet Discourse (Matt 24; Mark 13; Luke 21) presents problems for the doctrine of imminence. Pretribulationists assert that the signs mentioned here are for the Jews and not for the church, and for the coming kingdom age of the millennium, not for the church.[77] In order to maintain fidelity to the doctrine of imminence, Pretribulationists must hold to disallowing the signs given in the Mount Olivet Discourse as signs that will occur before the rapture. Renald Showers, author of *Maranatha, Our Lord, Come!*, declares,

> An imminent event is one that is always hanging over-
> head, is constantly ready to befall or overtake a person, is
> always close at hand in the sense that it could happen at any
> moment. Other things *may* happen before the imminent
> event, but nothing else *must* take place before it happens. If
> something else must take place before an event can happen,
> that event is not imminent. The necessity of something
> else taking place first destroys the concept of imminency.[78]

Here the Pretribulationists get to have it both ways. They emphatically assert that prophetic events *may happen* before the rapture, but nothing *must happen* before the rapture can occur. But this amounts to double-talk. If a prophecy comes to pass before the rapture occurs, how can someone claim—after the fact—that it didn't have to happen before the rapture? This allows the Pretribulationists to acknowledge prophetic fulfillment while remaining faithful to the doctrine of imminence. This allows them to sidestep prophetic events by saying *it is*

---

77 Walvoord, *The Bible Knowledge Commentary*, 76.

78 Renald Showers, *Maranatha: Our Lord, Come!: A Definitive Study of the Rapture of the Church* (Bellmawr, NJ: Friends of Israel, 1995), 195.

a sign but *not a sign* for the rapture, while the proverbial clock is still ticking. Dispensational authors such as Hal Lindsey and many others have sold millions of books and touted prophetic fulfillment while remaining faithful to the doctrine of imminence.

In the twenty-first century, we see the Mount Olivet Discourse birth pangs occurring all around us. No one can deny that. But when it comes to the rapture, that's exactly what the Pretrib view does: it acknowledges the signs but does not apply them in any regard to the closeness of the rapture. Even if we do not know what day the rapture will occur, with the passing of each day, we are still getting closer to it. The Pretrib argument would say these are signs that precede the Lord's second coming but not the rapture. However, my position would be that the signs for the second coming are signs for rapture, too, because they occur at the end of the age.

Even if there is a seven-year gap between the second coming and the rapture, in comparison to the passing of two thousand years, that gap is small. Both happen at the end of the age and are in close proximity to each other. Therefore, the signs for one should be considered as the signs for the other as well. For example, traveling through Chicago on the expressway, there is a sign on I-57 that says "Memphis." However, that Memphis sign is also the sign for a town called Kankakee, because to get to Kankakee, you must take I-57 Memphis. Therefore, Memphis, is the sign for Kankakee, too, because Kankakee is on the route to Memphis even though they are two different cities in two different states. The sign for one is also the sign for the other.

All the signs of the end are from God's Word, not the ramblings of some mystic soothsayer. Since they are the Word of God, they must be heeded. Trying to parse which signs apply to the rapture and which signs apply to the second coming misses the point. All the end-time signs indicate the coming of the Lord. That is the most salient point. The church needs to watch as well as pray. For a continuation of the argument, see "The Day of the Lord Dilemma" portion of this essay.

The Mystery of Israel's Blindness

One of the major prophecies that presents a problem for imminence is found in Romans 11:25:

> For I do not want you, brethren, to be uninformed of this mystery—so that you will not be wise in your own estimation—that a partial hardening has happened to Israel until the fullness of the Gentiles has come in.

The key word here is "until," Greek *achri*, which means a "marker of continuous extent of time up to a point, until."[79] It is not merely *after*, as in sequence, but *until*. What this passage declares is that the removal of Israel's hardness or blindness is conditioned upon the full number of Gentiles being reached first.

Concerning this, Charles Ryrie comments:

> Israel's *hardening* is partial (Jews are being saved today) and temporary (*until* they acknowledge Jesus at His second coming). *the fulness of the Gentiles.* I.e., the full number of Gentiles who will be saved (Acts 15:14). After that, God will turn again to the Jews and will save "all Israel" at the Lord's return (v. 26).[80]

Arno Gaebelein asserts:

> The fulness of the Gentiles means, the full number of the saved, gathered out from among the Gentiles, who constitute the church, the body of Christ.[81]

Both of these dispensational scholars agree that Paul is teaching that Israel will remain in *partial blindness* (KJV, NKJV) or hardening *until* (conditioned

---

79 Bauer, *Greek-English Lexicon, achri*, "until."
80 Charles Caldwell Ryrie, *Ryrie Study Bible: New American Standard Bible*, 1995 Updated, Expanded ed. (Chicago: Moody Press, 1995), 1808.
81 Arno C. Gaebelein, *The Annotated Bible: Romans to Ephesians*, vol. 7 (Bellingham, WA: Logos Bible Software, 2009), 68–69.

upon) the full number of Gentiles that is to be saved is reached. Once the fullness of the Gentiles is reached, the rapture can take place. This by itself is a condition that must be reached *before* the rapture can occur. The full number of Gentiles being saved and Israel's blindness being lifted meet at the same prophetic juncture. One coincides with the other, leaving this question: When will Israel's blindness be lifted? Paul declares,

> And so all Israel will be saved; just as it is written,
>
> > "The deliverer will come from Zion,
> > He will remove ungodliness from Jacob."
> > "This is My covenant with them,
> > When I take away their sins." (Rom 11:26–27)

Concerning this passage, Bruce Barton asserts,

> To confirm his statement, Paul quotes from Isaiah, first from 59:20–21. Jesus Christ is the Deliverer who will come from Jerusalem. For the first and only time in this letter, Paul speaks of the second coming of Christ.[82]

Here we have confirmation that Israel's blindness is lifted during the second coming of Christ, which happens after the abomination of desolation is in place and the beast has begun his forty-two-month reign. The Lord returns near the end of the Seventieth Week. At this point, Israel will look upon Him whom they have pierced, and they will mourn (see Rev 1:7). At no point in Israel's history after being scattered in AD 70 (see Luke 21:24) has Israel been in a position to have her hardness or blindness removed. Too many prophetic milestones have had to be reached first. We know this to be true because we are in the twenty-first century and the rapture has not occurred and Israel's hardness has not been removed. The timing for the church to reach fullness is indeterminable; however, Israel's prophetic milestones are determinable.

---

[82] Bruce Barton et al., *Life Application New Testament Commentary* (Wheaton, IL: Tyndale, 2001), 621.

(1) In the Gospel of Luke, Jesus prophesied that Israel would be "led captive into all the nations" and Jerusalem would be "trampled under foot by the Gentiles until the times of the Gentiles are fulfilled" (Luke 21:24). This is a double-reference prophecy that applies to the temple being destroyed (see Matt 24:1–2). Luke says "trampled under foot by the Gentiles until the times of the Gentiles are fulfilled," which was partly fulfilled in AD 70 when Jerusalem and the temple were destroyed by the Roman general Titus and the Jews were scattered. However, Luke's account also looks forward to the Gentile domination of Jerusalem by the Antichrist during Daniel's Seventieth Week. The beast will set up the abomination of desolation and declare himself to be God from the temple that is yet to be built (see Matt 24:15; 2 Thess 2:4; Rev 11:2). The fact that Israel enters into a covenant with the Antichrist proves they are still experiencing hardness or blindness. Since Israel is still blind by this point, it necessarily means the fullness of the Gentiles has not yet been reached. Israel's blindness cannot be removed "until" the fullness of the Gentiles is reached. Israel's blindness must extend at least to the abomination of desolation, which for all practical purposes is the end of the age.

(2) After being scattered among all nations (see Luke 21:24) in AD 70, Israel was to be "gathered . . . to the mountains of Israel" (indicating the land of Israel) during what the Scriptures identify as "the latter years" and "the last days" (Ezek 38:8, 16). This gathering occurred when Israel was reestablished as a nation on May 14, 1948, which puts the mid-twentieth century and forward in a period of what the Scriptures call "the latter years." For more on Ezekiel's prophecy, see the following section.

(3) Israel will need control of Jerusalem to eventually build a temple and to reinstitute the sacrifices and offerings identified in Daniel 9:27. However, after returning in 1948, Israel did not get control of Jerusalem until the Six-Day War of 1967.

(4) Israel will need to become a land of peace. This will most likely occur when the covenant of peace is put in place (Dan 9:27). Near the

end of the Antichrist's reign, the nations will gather and surround Jerusalem, leading to the battle of Armageddon (see Zech 14:1–5; Rev 16:16).

(5) The lifting of Israel's blindness or hardness has not yet occurred. It could not have occurred before Israel was reestablished as a nation because Israel's being back in the land is necessary to accommodate the prophetic chain of events recorded in the Scriptures. Israel's blindness will be lifted during the time the Lord will "come from Zion" (Rom 11:26), which Paul confirms by quoting Isaiah 59:18–21; this is a "second coming" event.

(6) As for the church, the entire church age fits between the two bookends given by Peter on the day of Pentecost. The church began on the *day of Pentecost* * and will continue "before the great and glorious day of the Lord shall come" (Acts 2:20). The "day of the Lord" here is the wrath of God that the church is not appointed to. Therefore, the church is *filling up* during this extended period that has lasted two thousand years now. Israel has been back in the land for over seventy years, and their *blindness or hardness* toward Jesus continues, excluding those Jews who have come to Christ. Israel's blindness cannot be removed "until" the fullness of the Gentiles comes in. Both are interdependent upon one another, and to this day, the church and Israel are contemporaneous entities on earth. Therefore, the rebirth of Israel and the subsequent prophecies that follow have to occur before the rapture can occur. History has borne this out.

The fulfillment of the prophecy concerning Israel's regathering to the land (see Ezek 38:8) is required before "the covenant with the many," which is backed by the Antichrist, can be enacted (Dan 9:27). The Antichrist will desecrate the temple that is yet to be built, committing the abomination of desolation (see Matt 24:15; 2 Thess 2:4). Before the temple can be rebuilt, Israel must be in control of Jerusalem, and this occurred in 1967 after the Six-Day War. Israel will not receive the Antichrist unless they are still in a state of hardness or blindness. Israel, who rejected Christ, will receive the Antichrist (see John 5:43), which is something they would not do unless they were hardened and spiritually blind. Therefore, Israel's hardness (toward Christ) must continue into the Seventieth Week. While Israel is in the condition of hardness, the church has not reached fullness. Israel's hardness continues "until" the fullness of the Gentiles is reached. Obviously, the exact date of the fullness of the Gentiles is indeterminable. However, the continuance of Israel's blindness is a key indicator, which must extend to the revealing of the Antichrist, which is the abomination of desolation (see 2 Thess 2:3–4).

Finally, there are those who claim "the fullness of the Gentiles" in Romans 11:25 is not the fullness of the church at all but is "the times of the Gentiles" (Luke 21:24). They draw from Daniel 7 imagery where Gentile kingdoms were seen as wild animals—the lion (Babylon), the bear (Medo-Persia), the leopard (Greece), and the monstrous beast (Rome), from which the final Gentile kingdom of the last days, having ten horns, is the kingdom of the beast (the Antichrist, Rev 11:1–2). However, considering the immediate context of Romans 11:11–13, Paul is speaking about the Gentiles who are saved during the church age, not the succession of wicked Gentile nations.

The Imminence Inconsistency

The question is, Should we be maintaining fidelity to the Scriptures or to the doctrine of imminence? Was it God's intention to disregard all end-time prophecy in order to remain loyal to a doctrine created by dispensational scholars? Do they regard all of Jesus' sayings as applying only to the Jews, or do they pick and choose where it benefits their position?

For example, most Pretribulationists assert that the Mount Olivet Discourse does not apply to the church because Jesus is speaking of events that will affect the Jews after the rapture has already occurred. However, when it comes to Jesus' Sermon on the Mount, He declared, "You are the salt of the earth.... You are the light of the world" (Matt 5:13–14), a passage Pretribulationists use to support the rapture, in connection with the removal of the Holy Spirit restrainer. The *Believer's Bible Commentary* asserts,

THE IMMINENT RETURN PROBLEM

> It is by the indwelling Spirit that believers are the salt of the
> earth (Matt. 5:13) and the light of the world (Matt. 5:14). Salt
> is a preservative, but it also hinders the spread of corruption.
> Light dispels darkness, the sphere in which men love to per-
> form their evil deeds (John 3:19). When the Holy Spirit leaves
> the world as the permanent Indweller of the church (1 Cor.
> 3:16) and of individual believers (1 Cor. 6:19), the restraint of
> lawlessness will be gone.[83]

In this passage, "salt of the earth" and "light of the world" are applied to
the presence of the church in the world. It should be noted that here,
too, Jesus is speaking to the Jews. However, the *Believer's Commentary*,
as well as other dispensational/Pretrib commentaries, applies this to
Christians and the church. Therefore, Pretribulationists are inconsistent
in interpreting Scripture. They see Jesus' comments to the Jews as applying sometimes to the church and other times to the Jews. Such is
the case with the Mount Olivet Discourse, which concerns the birth
pangs.

Another key passage where Pretribulationists selectively ignore that
Jesus is only talking to the Jews is John 3:7, where it states, "You must
be born again." Undoubtedly, Jesus is talking to a Pharisee (a Jew)
named Nicodemus. Pretribulationists don't apply the *Jesus was just
talking to the Jews* concept here. What about John 14:1–3, which is
one of the main passages used to support the rapture of the church?
Jesus says, "I go to prepare a place for you." Here, Jesus is talking to
the Jews (His Jewish disciples). Pretribulationists never say, "Jesus is
only talking about the Jews here," even though these are the same
disciples He was talking to in Matthew 24 when He was declaring the
signs of the end. The Pretrib view claims this message in Matthew 24
is for the Jews and not the church.

---

[83] William MacDonald, *Believer's Bible Commentary: A Complete Bible Commentary in One Volume!* (Nashville, TN: Thomas Nelson Publishers, 1995), 2054.

During His earthly ministry, Jesus, a Jew, declared many things to Jewish people, primarily because He was in Israel, where Jews lived. Indeed, Jesus "came to His own" as He should have (John 1:11). Dispensationalism tends to focus more on the significance of whom He was speaking to than on the message itself. It's almost like saying the book of Timothy only applied to Timothy, the book of Titus to only Titus, or the book of James to only James. When we interpret the Bible that way, we miss the point of the message that applies to those who have ears (see Matt 13:9). Jesus understood that thousands of years later, Christians would be reading the Gospels and the Epistles.

A better way to understand prophecy is not to let the doctrine of imminence influence interpretation. Any prophecy that is fulfilled while the church is still on earth is by default a prophecy given to the church, even though it may not be specifically about the church. For example, consider the reestablishment of the nation of Israel in 1948. The church was on earth to see this fulfillment and has acknowledged its importance to God's prophetic plan. Therefore, all the Word of God, from cover to cover, is given to the saints for our benefit, edification, and instruction, whether it specially addresses the church or not. When we try to force the Scriptures to conform to our doctrinal tenets, we create unnecessary problems.

THE DAY OF THE LORD DILEMMA

Since the mid-nineteenth century, dispensational scholars have touted that there are no signs given to the church indicating that the rapture is near. However, a text that presents a problem for that assertion is found in 2 Thessalonians 2:

> Now we request you, brethren, with regard to the coming of our Lord Jesus Christ and our gathering together to Him, that you not be quickly shaken from your composure or be disturbed either by a spirit or a message or a letter as if from us, to the effect that the day of the Lord has come. Let

no one in any way deceive you, for it will not come unless the apostasy comes first, and the man of lawlessness is revealed, the son of destruction. (vv. 1–3)

If it were Paul's intention to emphasize a Pretrib rapture, why wouldn't he make the obvious point to the Thessalonians? That is, *they could not be in the day of the Lord because the rapture hadn't happened yet. The rapture will happen before the day of the Lord comes*, which is the point of view regularly claimed by today's Pretribulationists. The problem is, Paul *is not* making that claim here. The question is, why doesn't he?

Paul begins his instruction by identifying the subject matter, which is "with regard to the coming of our Lord Jesus Christ and our gathering together to Him." Some see two separate events: "the coming of our Lord" (the parousia), meaning the actual day He returns (see Zech 14:1–8; Rev 19:11–21), and "our gathering . . . to Him," meaning the rapture (see 1 Thess 4:13–18). But some Pretribulationists would see both the "coming" and the "gathering" as the rapture. And Posttribulationists would see this as one event occurring at the end of Daniel's Seventieth Week. However, in this examination, we will not be taking sides in this debate but will focus on Paul's use of the term "day of the Lord" in this context.

Paul places both events, the parousia and "our gathering . . . to Him," under the heading of the "day of the Lord." Whether Paul is addressing this issue from the perspective of the Thessalonians' being shaken because they thought they missed the rapture or because they thought they were in the day of the Lord, the timing of God's wrath is not where the controversy lies. These are two sides of the same coin. One would mean the other. However, the text is better understood by how Paul uses the term "day of the Lord" here.

Sometimes Paul uses the term "day of the Lord"—normally used in connection with the wrath of God—interchangeably with the "day of Christ," the day of reward for the church. This is shown in the following verses:

So that you are not lacking in any gift, awaiting eagerly the revelation of our Lord Jesus Christ, who will also confirm you to the end, blameless in the *day of our Lord* Jesus Christ. (1 Cor 1:7–8, emphasis added)

You are to deliver this man to Satan for the destruction of the flesh, so that his spirit may be saved in the *day of the Lord.* (1 Cor 5:5 ESV, emphasis added)

For we do not write you anything you cannot read or understand. And I hope that, as you have understood us in part, you will come to understand fully that you can boast of us just as we will boast of you in the *day of the Lord Jesus.* (2 Cor 1:13–14 NIV, emphasis added)

In none of these passages is the "day of the Lord" referring to the wrath of God as we typically see it used in the OT (e.g., Joel 2:30–32) or in 1 Thessalonians 5:2, 9. In these three verses, the day of the Lord is the day of reward, also known as the *day of Christ**(Phil 1:6). Perhaps the King James translators recognized the nuance from "our gathering together to Him" and translated it as "the day of Christ." The Geneva Bible translates it, "That ye be not suddenly moved from your mind, nor troubled neither by spirit, nor by word, nor by letter, as it were from us, as though the day of Christ were at hand." The Tyndale Bible, 1526–1535, also translates it as the "day of Christ." In these translations the "day of Christ" rendering would not be incorrect because it emphasizes "our gathering together to Him," which is the rapture. Additionally, the manuscripts from which some English translations derived (Textus Receptus, or Authorized Text) would also be a determining factor in whether *christos* (Christ) was used. Modern translations like the NASB used the *Novum Testamentum Graece* (NA) and translate it "day of the Lord" because Greek *kurios* is used.

Understanding "the day of the Lord" as either *the wrath of God* or *the day of Christ* is supported in this passage. "Our gathering together to

Him" supports the rapture and *the day of Christ*. And "the day of the Lord," as in "wrath," is supported by 2 Thessalonians 2:8: "Whom the Lord will slay with the breath of His mouth and bring to an end by the appearance of His coming" (parousia).

The background to this controversy involves the Thessalonians' apparently receiving a teaching that may have come as a forged letter claiming apostolic authority or as a false prophecy that the "day of the Lord" (or *day of Christ*) had already come. This caused the saints at Thessalonica to be shaken up and disturbed. Paul dispelled their anxiety and consternation by sharing two specific signs that must occur first[84] (Gk. *protos*, "to be first in a sequence"):

> Let no one in any way deceive you, for it will not come unless the apostasy *comes first*, and the man of lawlessness is revealed, the son of destruction, who opposes and exalts himself above every so-called god or object of worship, so that he takes his seat in the temple of God, displaying himself as being God. (2 Thess 2:3–4, emphasis added)

Paul is explicitly teaching that the *day of the Lord*, which in this context is both the *parousia* and *the rapture*, cannot come unless two events precede it: first, the *apostasy*, or *rebellion*, and second, *the revealing of the man of sin*. The *apostasy* is the defection from the faith, which was also prophesied by Jesus as coming because of persecution (see Matt 13:21; 24:9–10). If the church is already raptured, who then is apostatizing? Sinners and unbelievers cannot fall away from a faith they never possessed. The church is still on earth at this point, underscoring the reason for this instruction.

The revealing, or the uncovering, of the Antichrist (the beast) will occur when he walks into the rebuilt temple in Jerusalem and declares himself to be God. This is the abomination of desolation spoken of by Daniel the prophet (Dan 9:27). Jesus refers to this in Mark 13:14—"the

---

84   Bauer, *Greek-English Lexicon*, s.v. *protos*, "first."

abomination of desolation standing where it should not be"—and in Matthew 24:15. The abomination of desolation will require a temple to be built, which is another sign or event that must take place before the abomination of desolation occurs.

As Paul says in 2 Thessalonians 2:2, he did not want the Thessalonians to become "soon shaken in mind" (KJV; "quickly shaken in mind or alarmed" [ESV], "easily upset in mind or troubled" [HCSB], "easily unsettled or alarmed" [NIV]) that "the day of the Lord [NASB; "the day of Christ" (KJV)] has come." Paul emphatically states that day ("with regard to the coming of our Lord Jesus Christ and our gathering together to Him," v. 1) cannot happen "unless the apostasy comes first, and the man of lawlessness is revealed" (v. 3). Verse 3 is a tremendous problem for the Pretrib doctrine of imminence because it includes two events, *the apostasy* and *the revealing of the Antichrist,* that must come before the *parousia* or *the rapture* can occur, referred to as "the day of the Lord" in v. 2.

To reiterate what Showers has stated, "If something else must take place before an event can happen, that event is not imminent. The necessity of something else taking place first destroys the concept of imminency."[85] I certainly agree with Showers here, because the 2 Thessalonians 2:1 text destroys the doctrine of imminence.

The position in this commentary is that the church is still on earth during the reign of the Antichrist but is raptured before the bowl judgments of Revelation 16. Therefore, I agree with Paul that *the apostasy* and *the abomination of desolation* must come before *the day of the Lord,* which in this context is *the gathering together to Him.*

What always remains imminent is when the Lord comes for us individually. That can occur at any moment. Therefore, we should always be ready to meet our Maker. Certainly, there is only one generation of Christians who will be raptured and never taste death. Everyone else

---

85   Renald Showers, *Maranatha: Our Lord, Come!,* 195.

will die. The day we make our transition to be present with the Lord is always imminent. Our focus should always be on being ready when it's our time. If today is your day to leave this world, are you ready to meet Jesus? That is what's important, not which rapture position is correct.

THE RIGHTEOUS LIVING ARGUMENT

Pretrib proponents insist that the Pretrib rapture is the best position to support righteous living. This is asserted because the Lord could come at any time and catch us in the act of sinning. Though one can make that argument, the imminent return of Christ is not the practical way to curtail or prevent sinning. The chance of being caught is not the best motivation to prevent sin. Sinning against Christ should be repulsive to us because we love Him. We should be in a committed relationship with the One who died for us. A husband's motivation to remain faithful to his wife should not rest upon the possibility of her catching him in an act of adultery. Rather, it should be because he loves her, is in a committed relationship with her, and wouldn't dare violate their wedding vows whether she knows it or not. If you love someone, you don't want to violate their trust or break their heart.

The fact is, all humans sin, and that includes Christians. Before responding sinfully in a moment of weakness, no one goes outside to see if the Lord is coming. How we overcome the enticement to sin is through the presence of the Holy Spirit dwelling within us. Therefore, it is not so much the *imminence* of Christ's return that stops us but the *intimacy* with Christ that we have through His indwelling Spirit that does. His presence constrains and convicts us so we do not "grieve" or "quench" His precious Holy Spirit (Eph 4:30; 1 Thess 5:19). Righteous living should be the result of an *intimate* relationship with Him, regardless of when He returns.

In the following verses, Paul admonishes Christians not to sin because of the reality of the indwelling Spirit, not because Christ could return at any moment.

> Do you not know that your bodies are members of Christ?
> Shall I then take away the members of Christ and make them
> members of a prostitute? May it never be! . . . Or do you not
> know that your body is a temple of the Holy Spirit who is in
> you, whom you have from God, and that you are not your
> own? For you have been bought with a price: therefore glorify
> God in your body. (1 Cor 6:15, 19–20)

Paul's argument here is based on a relationship with Christ, because our bodies are the temple in which the Holy Spirit dwells. That's intimacy. Our desire should always be not to put Him to open shame by living a life that is contrary to the faith and the standard of holiness. Whereas the shame of being caught is a deterrent, the greater virtue is choosing righteousness over sin and remaining unspotted from sin. By the time a person commits an act of sin, something deeper has already gone wrong within their heart. Guarding your relationship with Christ is a much greater deterrent to sinning than the idea that Christ could return at any moment. A common Pretrib talking point is that righteous living is the result of anticipating the Pretrib rapture, but it is weak in practical application.

THE "LOOKING FOR CHRIST, NOT SIGNS" ARGUMENT

One of the main defenses of the Pretrib rapture is that Christians should be looking not for signs but for Christ. Emphasizing that point, Benware asserts,

> As far as end-time prophetic events are concerned, the rapture of the church is the first to take place. *It is an event to which no signs or indicators are attached.* We are not told to look for certain signs in order to correctly anticipate the time of the rapture. There are no signs; the rapture event itself is what is to be anticipated.[86]

This is an interesting argument because it ignores the fact that, in the

---

[86] Benware, *Understanding End Times Prophecy* (emphasis added), 230.

Mount Olivet Discourse, Jesus gives the signs of His own return. Here is what He declares:

> But keep on the alert at all times, praying that you may have strength to escape all these things that are about to take place, and to stand before the Son of Man. (Luke 21:36)

It should be noted that Christ admonishes us to "keep on the alert." The NKJV translates it "watch therefore," and in the NIV it is "be always on the watch." The question is, *What are we to be on the watch for?* The answer is "all these things that are about to take place." What things are about to take place? Wars and rumors of wars, nation rising against nation, kingdom rising against kingdom, plagues and famines, earthquakes in various places, cosmic disturbances and fearful signs in the heavens (the sky and outer space), roaring waves, and more. In Luke 21:7, a specific question was asked: "What will be the sign when these things are about to take place?" The very thing that Pretribulationists tell us we should not be looking for is exactly what the disciples asked about. The signs are the things for which we are to "keep on the alert." Why else would we be told to be on the alert? Why would Jesus give signs concerning His return if, according to the Pretrib view, we are not supposed to look for them? The signs the Lord gave are the signs for His return.

However, Benware asserts that we are to look for Christ and not for signs. Jesus is the One who gave the signs. Watching for the signs Jesus said would precede His coming is the very essence of looking for Christ. Aren't these signs part of the Scriptures? Are we not to take heed to the Scriptures that give the signs? Jesus further emphasizes this point when He says, "Behold the fig tree and all the trees; as soon as they put forth leaves, *you see it and know for yourselves* that summer is now near. So you also, when you see these things happening, recognize that the kingdom of God is near" (Luke 21:29–31, emphasis added). Jesus' use of a budding tree to indicate summer approaching is a perfect analogy for His coming. However, the Pretrib doctrine of imminence would interpret the budding tree analogy this way: "The summer will come with no signs preceding it. However, the trees *may* start budding, but they don't *have* to start budding before the summer comes. But if they do bud, that is not a sign that summer is near because summer is a signless event that could happen at any time" (humor intended).

Today, we are well into the twenty-first century. The rapture has not occurred. Israel has been reestablished as a nation. The political alignment of nations mentioned in Ezekiel 38–39 (Russia, Iran, Libya, Ethiopia, Sudan, and Turkey) is in place, and the time is identified as "the latter years" (Ezek 38:8) or "the last days" (v. 16). The kings of the east, primarily China, are all threatening global instability. We see extreme weather, fires, floods, and earthquakes, not to mention wars all over the world and the rumors of a global World War III. There are heightened global tensions, uncertain financial markets and crushing national debt, social unrest and racial tensions, and economic systems that are teetering on collapse. Murder racks our inner cities, and mass shootings threaten our schools and workplaces. These are certainly the perilous times that Jesus predicted. The stage is being set for the Antichrist to come with answers to bring peace and stability to a chaotic world.

Jesus declared, "When these things begin to take place, straighten up and lift up your heads, because your redemption is drawing near" (Luke 21:28). Wouldn't it be prudent to take these prophecies to heart? Are they not the Word of God? What harm could possibly be caused by looking for the things the Lord declared would occur before His return? Since the rapture and the second coming (parousia) are so closely related to events of the end of the age, the signs for one should be understood as signs for the other. If we approach it that way, we will continue to be watchful and alert and not distracted with the cares of this life so that neither day catches us by surprise (see Luke 21:34–35).

MESSAGES TO THE SEVEN CHURCHES

The messages to the seven churches of Asia Minor follow a similar format. Each begins with a salutation, addressed to the angel (or pastor) of the church. Each presents Jesus in a descriptive role (e.g., the one who has, the one who holds) regarding the respective church. Except for Laodicea, an affirmation of positive actions and works is given, usually followed by a rebuke (except for Smyrna and Philadelphia). What follows is a declaration for correction and repentance, along with a warning. Finally, there is an encouragement to the overcomers, punctuated with the call to heed the message. Another interesting aspect of the letters to the seven churches is there is a nexus between characteristics of the respective cities and characteristics that manifested in the churches. In some respects, as it was with the city, so it was also with that local church.

Many dispensationalists interpret the messages to the churches as representing seven church ages. An example of this can be found in the *Scofield Reference Bible* study notes, which identify the following: *Ephesus* represents Christians of the first century; *Smyrna* is the age of persecution; *Pergamum* is the church settled down in the world "where Satan's throne is" (Rev 2:13); *Thyatira* is the papacy, developed out of the state: Balaamism (worldliness) and Nicolaitanism (priestly assumption); *Sardis* is the Protestant Reformation, whose works were not "fulfilled"; *Philadelphia* is whatever bears clear testimony to the Word; and Laodicea represents the time of self-satisfied profession.[87] Others such as J. B. Smith, author of *A Revelation of Jesus Christ*, promote a similar scheme. Though this is neatly packaged, there is absolutely nothing in this text to justify interpreting these individual congregations as being specific ages as delineated by the Scofield Bible. Though others have developed similar proposals, they are unwarranted. The one thing they have in common is they are highly speculative.

---

[87]   *Scofield Reference Bible* study notes, "Message to the Seven Churches," 1332.

REVELATION 2:1–7

[1] "To the angel of the church in Ephesus write:

The One who holds the seven stars in His right hand, the One who walks among the seven golden lampstands, says this:

[2] 'I know your deeds and your toil and perseverance, and that you cannot tolerate evil men, and you put to the test those who call themselves apostles, and they are not, and you found them to be false; [3] and you have perseverance and have endured for My name's sake, and have not grown weary. [4] But I have this against you, that you have left your first love. [5] Therefore remember from where you have fallen, and repent and do the deeds you did at first; or else I am coming to you and will remove your lampstand out of its place—unless you repent. [6] Yet this you do have, that you hate the deeds of the Nicolaitans, which I also hate. [7] He who has an ear, let him hear what the Spirit says to the churches. To him who overcomes, I will grant to eat of the tree of life which is in the Paradise of God.'"

History Note: Ephesus was one of the great cities of the ancient world. It was known for its pagan worship and was the home of the goddess Artemis or Diana (Acts 19:28), whose magnificent temple was one of the seven wonders of the world. The city was also a bustling center of trade and commerce with a very active harbor. However, as the harbor began to silt (become shallow from sediment), ships could not dock there. With a decline in commerce, Ephesus began to fade from glory. Similarly, the church of Ephesus also began to decline in its fervor for its "first love," the Lord. Paul's disciple Timothy was the first pastor of this church.

(1) *To the angel of the church in Ephesus:* Each of these letters is tailored specifically to a respective congregation and addressed to the angel (messenger) of the church, which is widely accepted to mean the pastor. Just as individuals have unique attributes and characteristics, there are differences in churches and their members. Congregations reflect their pastor's personality, leadership, and ecclesiastical abilities, which influence the congregation for better or worse.

(a) *who walks among the seven golden lampstands:* The Lord, speaking of His ever-abiding presence to evaluate and scrutinize any church, is never hindered. All things are open to Him as He walks among the lampstands.

(2) *I know your deeds and your toil and perseverance, and that you cannot tolerate evil men:* That is, God knows their good works, steadfastness, and struggles. Evidently, the Ephesians did not tolerate evil people. Today, churches still struggle with having evil people in their midst. Too often, churches are quick to tolerate the wickedness introduced by individuals who are wolves in sheep's clothing. Some of these people could be rich, making large contributions to the church, and because of their influence, they curry favor. Others promote loose and sinful lifestyles. No matter who they are, evil people who refuse to repent should not be tolerated because sin spreads. The church at Ephesus was commended for standing against evil.

(a) *and you put to the test those who call themselves apostles, and they are not, and you found them to be false:* As this text reveals, the intrusion of counterfeits into the apostolic office goes all the way back to the first century, when at least one of the original apostles was still alive. The apostles and prophets were the foundation of the church, with Jesus being the chief "corner stone" (Eph 2:20). Their writings were considered Scripture (2 Pet 3:16) and inspired by God (2 Tim 3:16), and their ministry through the Scriptures will never stop (John 17:20). They also possessed miracle-working power (2 Cor 12:12). A requirement for holding the apostolic office was having been a witness of Christ's ministry and resurrection (Acts 1:22). Only one instance is recorded in Scripture that demonstrates replacing an original apostle who died, and that was for Judas. If this office was to be expanding, why wouldn't the apostles have chosen Barsabbas (also known as Justus) and Matthias, who both met the criteria to replace Judas? According to Psalm 108:9, only one person was to fill the office vacated by Judas (see Acts 1:20; see also Ps 69:25).

In Paul's day, false apostles encroached upon the apostolic office (2 Cor 11:13). We still see this today as countless individuals carry the title of *apostle*. The contemporary apostles are, in fact, in title only and do not meet any of the criteria set forth in the Scriptures for the official office. In today's church, people sometimes give themselves whatever title they want. Present-day apostles are made by men (Gal 1:1).

(3) *you have perseverance and have endured for My name's sake, and have not grown weary*: In the face of adversity, the Ephesian church persevered and showed endurance for standing up against persecution and ridicule without growing weary.

(4) *But I have this against you:* Jesus started by being supportive and gave compliments before confrontation. Good counselors understand this principle: be supportive before addressing shortcomings.

(a) *you have left your first love:* How easy it is for Christians, individually and as congregations, to drift away from being Christ-centered and sensitive to the leading of the Spirit. We are distracted with good works, social programming, and political and economic concerns that cause us to lose focus and drift away from the Great Commission to go and make disciples. Though we are not sure of the specifics of this rebuke as it relates to the church in Ephesus, we do know that we must always maintain our first love.

(5) *remember from where you have fallen:* The Ephesians were to remember what it was that pleased the Lord before their fervor began to fade. Repentance must begin at the point of infraction and must address sin at its root.

(a) *repent and do the deeds you did at first:* Many times we are looking for the new, bigger, or better thing we must do to grow as a Christian. But knowing how to grow in Christ is not a mystery; do what you did at first—be faithful, love, and serve Christ.

(b) *or else I am coming to you and will remove your lampstand out of its place—unless you repent:* From this warning, it is clear Christ was not speaking metaphorically of Ephesus representing a church era (the universal church of the first century) as some dispensationalists assert. This probably means that Christ would remove His presence from this church, as represented by "removing their lampstand." So many churches today are dead in spirit. No matter how much programming a church has, if God's presence is not in the midst, it's dead or dying (cf. Rev 3:1).

(6) *Yet this you do have, that you hate the deeds of the Nicolaitans, which I also hate:* After the warning, the Lord added a departing positive: "You hate the deeds of the Nicolaitans" (the doctrine of v. 15). The *Nicolaitans** were a heretical sect thought to be followers of Nicolaus of Antioch, a Gentile convert to the Jewish faith. It is believed that he was a former member of the church at Antioch and was chosen as one of seven deacons there (Acts 6:5). Both Irenaeus and Hippolytus believed he was an apostate, and his followers became known as the Nicolaitans. The Lord rebuked the churches of Ephesus and Pergamum for allowing his teachings in their respective churches. Other church fathers—for example, Clement—asserted the Nicolaitans were not actual followers of

Nicolaus but falsely claimed him as their teacher. However, very little is known about the origin and development of this ancient sect.[88]

Because of the lack of specifics, there is no shortage of controversy and speculation concerning the Nicolaitans. Whoever they were, their deeds and doctrine were detested by the Ephesians and the Lord. Whatever name it goes by, false doctrine cannot be tolerated in the church. It leads to sin and wicked lifestyles that destroy congregations.

(7) *He who has an ear, let him hear what the Spirit says to the churches* is a similar phrase (minus "what the Spirit says to the churches") to the Lord's words recorded in the Gospels (Matt 11:15; 13:9, 43; Mark 4:9, 23; 7:16), after each address to the seven churches in Revelation, and in 13:9. The phrase "who has an ear, let him hear" indicates the importance and universality of the message—that is, whoever will listen, let them heed what has been spoken. At the end of each message to the churches, an admonition is given to the one who **overcomes**—Greek *nikaō* (from which the sports brand name Nike is derived), meaning "Christians who prevail in Christ have the ultimate victory" (see 13:9 note).

(a) *I will grant to eat of the tree of life which is in the Paradise of God*: Adam and Eve were given full access to the tree of life, which was first mentioned in Genesis 2:9. However, there was an important reason why they were forbidden to partake of the tree after they fell into sin. "Then the LORD God said, 'Behold, the man has become like one of Us, knowing good and evil; and now, he might stretch out his hand, and take also from the tree of life, and eat, and live forever'—therefore the LORD God sent him out from the garden of Eden, to cultivate the ground from which he was taken" (Gen 3:22–23). Had they eaten from the tree of life after falling into sin, Adam and Eve would have been locked into an unredeemable state forever, like fallen angels, who cannot die. Therefore, God denied them access to the tree so that death could occur. "So He drove the man

---

[88] Walter A. Elwell and Philip W. Comfort, *Tyndale Bible Dictionary* (Wheaton, IL: Tyndale House Publishers, 2001), 950.

out; and at the east of the garden of Eden He stationed the cherubim and the flaming sword which turned every direction to guard the way to the tree of life" (Gen 3:24). Though death is the consequence of disobedience and sin (Gen 2:17), it is also the way in which salvation ultimately came through Christ. Once we enter the eternal state, we will once again have access to "the tree of life … in the Paradise of God" (heaven).

✝

REVELATION 2:8–11

MESSAGE TO SMYRNA

[8] "And to the angel of the church in Smyrna write:

The first and the last, who was dead, and has come to life, says this:

[9] 'I know your tribulation and your poverty (but you are rich), and the blasphemy by those who say they are Jews and are not, but are a synagogue of Satan. [10] Do not fear what you are about to suffer. Behold, the devil is about to cast some of you into prison, so that you will be tested, and you will have tribulation for ten days. Be faithful until death, and I will give you the crown of life. [11] He who has an ear, let him hear what the Spirit says to the churches. He who overcomes will not be hurt by the second death.'"

History Note: Ancient writers have commented on the beauty of Smyrna. It was a flourishing center of trade and business on the west coast of Asia Minor. "Smyrna" means "myrrh," a perfume and ointment used for embalming.[89] The city was known for its loyalty to Rome and was the center for the imperial cult of emperor worship. In the midst of a city

---

[89]   Bauer, *Greek-English Lexicon*, *Smyrna*, "myrrh."

with great material wealth, the church of Smyrna was apparently impoverished. It was in this city that *Polycarp*,* the bishop of the church of Smyrna, was burnt at the stake for refusing to denounce Christ and call Caesar "Lord." Smyrna is one of two churches that received no rebuke.

(8) *who was dead, and has come to life*: This is a reference to Christ's sacrificial death and resurrection. However, it could also be linked to the fact that Smyrna was a city that had died and now lived once more. Smyrna was destroyed in 580 BC, but in 290 BC Lysimachus rebuilt it.[90] Like Ephesus and its church, the life of the city of Smyrna coincided with the message to its church.

(9) *I know your tribulation and your poverty (but you are rich)*: So often wealth is seen as a measure of blessing. And certainly, God is good and takes pleasure in blessing His children in a number of ways. However, in a fallen world system controlled by Satan, wealth may not be the best indicator of one's spiritual standing with God. Though the Smyrnaeans were materially impoverished, the Lord declared, "But you are rich." Being rich in spiritual graces such as faith, love, and righteousness is more important to God than an amount in a bank account or the number of material possessions one owns.

(a) *the blasphemy by those who say they are Jews and are not, but are a synagogue of Satan*: During the first century, Christians were persecuted by certain Jews who were hostile toward those who followed Christ,[91] also called "the Way" (Act 9:2; 19:9, 23; 22:4; 24:14, 22). Paul, before his conversion, was one of these persecutors (Acts 9:1–2). On the Damascus road, Jesus confronted Saul, saying, "Saul, Saul, why are you persecuting Me?" (Acts 9:4). Persecuting Christians is the same as persecuting Christ. Jesus said to the Pharisees, "But as it is, you are seeking to kill Me.... This

---

[90] Leon L. Morris, ed., *Tyndale New Testament Commentaries: Revelation* (Wheaton, IL: Tyndale House Publishers, 1987), 67.

[91] Alexander Roberts, James Donaldson, and Arthur Cleveland Coxe, eds., "The Martyrdom of Polycarp," in *The Ante-Nicene Fathers* (Buffalo, NY: Christian Literature Company, 1885), vol. 1, chap. 12.

Abraham did not do. . . . You are of your father the devil, and you want to do the desires of your father. He was a murderer from the beginning" (John 8:40, 44). Satan is the one who inspires killing and persecuting Christians. Though the Jews may have been the natural descendants of Abraham, since they followed Satan to persecute the church, they were in reality "a synagogue of Satan."

(10) *Do not fear what you are about to suffer. Behold, the devil is about to cast some of you into prison:* Jesus did not say, "I will not let the devil cast you into prison" or "I will deliver you once you are incarcerated." No, the Lord foretold what they would endure. As Christians, we should expect persecution. In Philippians we are told, "For to you it has been granted for Christ's sake, not only to believe in Him, but also to suffer for His sake" (Phil 1:29). Suffering for Christ, while commonplace in many parts of the world, is foreign and rejected in the West, particularly in the United States. *You will have tribulation for ten days:* Though it is not known exactly what the "ten days" refer to, we can be assured that trouble does not last forever. Though the Lord allows tribulation, there is a limit to its endurance. "Ten days" could mean "a predetermined period set by the Lord," who is in sovereign control of what the devil can do.

(a) *Be faithful until death, and I will give you the crown of life:* Jesus said to His disciples, "If anyone wishes to come after Me, he must deny himself, and take up his cross and follow Me. For whoever wishes to save his life will lose it; but whoever loses his life for My sake will find it" (Matt 16:24–25). Jesus was brutally crucified, and all the apostles except John followed Christ to the grave through martyrdom, along with countless others. Here Christ is calling for the Smyrnaeans to "be faithful until death," not *up to death.* There is more to be considered than in this life only. Jesus reassured the church in Smyrna that faithfulness will be rewarded with the crown of life eternal. Those who are concerned only with this life fall short.

(11) *not be hurt by the second death*: It is interesting that the first mention of "the second death" is here in the message to Smyrna. By far, the second death is infinitely worse than any of the seal, trumpet, or bowl judgments that come later in Revelation. Many expositors cite the seal, trumpet, and bowl judgments that occur during Daniel's Seventieth Week to be the sum total of the wrath of God. However, this is incorrect. The suffering during the last half of the Seventieth Week, called the great tribulation, only lasts three and a half years. The worst judgment in Revelation that can "hurt" someone is the second death, which is eternal and the ultimate form of the wrath of God. (For more on this, see "3:10: The Hour of Testing Dilemma" at Rev 3:10.)

REVELATION 2:12–17

[12] "And to the angel of the church in Pergamum write:

The One who has the sharp two-edged sword says this:

[13] 'I know where you dwell, where Satan's throne is; and you hold fast My name, and did not deny My faith even in the days of Antipas, My witness, My faithful one, who was killed among you, where Satan dwells. [14] But I have a few things against you, because you have there some who hold the teaching of Balaam, who kept teaching Balak to put a stumbling block before the sons of Israel, to eat things sacrificed to idols and to commit acts of immorality. [15] So you also have some who in the same way hold the teaching of the Nicolaitans. [16] Therefore repent; or else I am coming to you quickly, and I will make war against them with the sword of My mouth. [17] He who has an ear, let him hear what the Spirit says to the churches. To him who overcomes, to him I will give some of the hidden manna, and I will give him a white stone, and a new name written on the stone which no one knows but he who receives it.'"

History Note: Unlike Ephesus and Smyrna, Pergamum was located approximately fifteen miles inland and, therefore, was not a center of commerce or trade. However, it was of administrative significance and was the home of a great library, having over two hundred thousand parchment scrolls, the ancient books of that day, and a famed medical school. People came from all over the world to seek healing from the *Asclepius** (the Greek and Roman god of medicine and healing), whose symbol was a physician's staff with a snake wrapped around it. Pergamum was a center of emperor worship and was the home of many pagan cults such as Athena, Asclepius, Dionysus, and Zeus. Behind the city arose a huge conical hill, one thousand feet high, covered with heathen temples and altars. Along with all its attributions to pagan gods, Pergamum was also known as a university town and a place of royal residences.

(13) *I know where you dwell, where Satan's throne is:* Pergamum was infested with pagan cults. People who worship humans or idols are worshiping demons and, by extension, Satan (1 Cor 10:20–21). The meaning of the phrase "where Satan's throne is" cannot be easily determined. Whatever it was, it was wickedness that came forth from the kingdom of darkness and the seat of Satan's authority that manifested itself in a wide array of idol and emperor worship in Pergamum. This could be the reason why the Lord said that Satan had his throne there. Another possibility is that "where Satan's throne is" referred to the city's being the official cult center of emperor worship, where several altars were built to facilitate the worship of Roman emperors. There is also a possible connection to the symbol of the serpent, which is reported to have been everywhere. The symbol of the serpent represented both Satan and Asclepius, one of the chief deities of the city. The *caduceus** symbol (a staff with two snakes and two wings, which is today's medical symbol) could have originated with the symbol of Asclepius, which consists of a single rod with one snake wrapped around it. Though many cities in the ancient world were infested with pagan cults, this city was wholly given over to them. The phrase "where Satan's throne is" could also be in reference to the throne or the altar of Zeus, which was much more than a mere altar. It was a colonnaded, horseshoe-shaped court that was 120 by 112 feet, with the podium of the altar standing at a height of 18 feet. The *Gigantomachy* *(the frieze depicting the war of the gods) was also featured in this structure.[92] Finally, it is possible that in the spirit realm Satan had a throne in Pergamum.

(a) *did not deny My faith even in the days of Antipas, My witness, My faithful one, who was killed among you:* Though steeped in pagan and Caesar worship, Pergamum had faithful Christians who refused to deny Christ, like Antipas, who was martyred for his steadfastness and faith. As legend has it, he was roasted in a brazen bowl at Domitian's request. This was an exceptionally horrendous way to die.[93] The Lord memorialized Antipas's faith under fire; even until the very end, he never wavered.

(14) *But I have a few things against you, because you have there some who hold the teaching of Balaam:* "The teaching of Balaam" represents any false teacher or false prophet who leads God's people to compromise. Balaam's counsel to the king of Moab was that the Israelites would forfeit God's protection and blessing if he could induce them to worship idols (Num 31:16). In the city where Satan had his throne, there were many who seduced the Christians through false doctrine. Though Balaam had long been off the scene, the evil spirit that influenced him was referenced here because this spirit exalted itself against the knowledge and word of God. It did so with Balaam and was doing so again in the church in Pergamum.

(15) *So you also have some who in the same way hold the teaching of the Nicolaitans:* Another strike against Pergamum was the doctrine of the Nicolaitans (see 2:6 note). No matter what name it goes by, all false doctrine is to be rejected, but somehow the church in Pergamum em-

---

[92] Edwin Yamauchi, *New Testament Cities in Western Asia Minor* (Grand Rapids, MI: Baker, 1980), 35–36.

[93] Brand, Chad, Charles Draper, and Archie England, eds., *Holman Illustrated Bible Dictionary* (Nashville: Holman Bible Publishers, 2003), s.v. "Antipas."

braced it. In Galatians 3:1, Paul leveled this stinging rebuke: "You foolish Galatians, who has bewitched you?" Unfortunately, foolish Christians are too easily duped by false doctrine, as was the case in Pergamum.

(16) *Therefore repent; or else I am coming to you quickly, and I will make war against them with the sword of My mouth:* No one should want the Lord to oppose them. If Satan is your problem, you can turn to the Lord. But if the Lord is your problem, then you have a serious problem. The only way to turn that circumstance around is to repent so you can take part in His favor, not His fury. "The sword of My mouth" is in reference to judgment.

(17) *To him who overcomes, to him I will give some of the hidden manna, and I will give him a white stone, and a new name written on the stone which no one knows but he who receives it:* To twenty-first-century Christians, *hidden manna** and "a white stone [with] a new name written on [it]" for the recipient might sound rather mundane. In the OT, manna was the life-sustaining heavenly food miraculously provided for the Israelites in the wilderness for forty years. The word "manna" implies the question "What is it?" because they didn't know what it was (Exod 16:15). Other significant passages about manna are Exodus 16:14–36; Numbers 11:7–9; Deuteronomy 8:3; Joshua 5:12; Psalm 78:24–25. After some time, the people of Israel grew tired of manna and complained about it (Num 11:4). This "hidden manna," however, must be sustenance beyond comprehension. Though there are several theories about them, no one on earth knows with any certainty what these gifts of manna and a stone will actually be in eternity. However, we do believe that whatever will come from the Lord in eternity will be beyond good. Paul summed it up well when he quoted the words of Isaiah 64:4: "'What no eye has seen, what no ear has heard, and what no human mind has conceived'—the things God has prepared for those who love him" (1 Cor 2:9 NIV).

✝

REVELATION 2:18–28

MESSAGE TO THYATIRA

[18] "And to the angel of the church in Thyatira write:

The Son of God, who has eyes like a flame of fire, and His feet are like burnished bronze, says this:

[19] 'I know your deeds, and your love and faith and service and perseverance, and that your deeds of late are greater than at first. [20] But I have this against you, that you tolerate the woman Jezebel, who calls herself a prophetess, and she teaches and leads My bond-servants astray so that they commit acts of immorality and eat things sacrificed to idols. [21] I gave her time to repent, and she does not want to repent of her immorality. [22] Behold, I will throw her on a bed of sickness, and those who commit adultery with her into great tribulation, unless they repent of her deeds. [23] And I will kill her children with pestilence, and all the churches will know that I am He who searches the minds and hearts; and I will give to each one of you according to your deeds. [24] But I say to you, the rest who are in Thyatira, who do not hold this teaching, who have not known the deep things of Satan, as they call them—I place no other burden on you. [25] Nevertheless what you have, hold fast until I come. [26] He who overcomes, and he who keeps My deeds until the end, to him I will give authority over the nations; [27] and he shall rule them

61

with a rod of iron, as the vessels of the potter are broken to pieces, as I also have received authority from My Father; [28] and I will give him the morning star.'"

History Note: Thyatira was a city in Lydia about forty miles southeast of Pergamum. It was known for its large number of trade guilds, such as dyers, leatherworkers, tanners, wool workers, linen workers, potters, bakers, slave dealers, and bronzesmiths. It was the city where Lydia, "a seller of purple fabrics" (Acts 16:14), was from. Though significant in size, it was a much smaller city than the others. Ironically, the smallest city of the seven was the recipient of the lengthiest letter, which included piercing rebukes.

(19) *I know your deeds, and your love and faith and service and perseverance, and that your deeds of late are greater than at first:* Once again, the Lord first accentuated the positives. As opposed to the church at Ephesus, Thyatira's later works were greater than its first.

(20) The positives give way to some harsh rebukes that begin with this statement: *But I have this against you.*

(a) *you tolerate the woman Jezebel, who calls herself a prophetess, and she teaches and leads My bond-servants astray so that they commit acts of immorality and eat things sacrificed to idols:* These rebukes are in line with how the Lord appears at the beginning of this message to the church in Thyatira. He is "the Son of God, who has eyes like a flame of fire, and His feet are like burnished bronze" (v. 18). The Lord's piercing gaze with angry eyes accentuates the tone of the message He gave, and the bronze for His feet represents His judgment. Whoever this *Jezebel** was, she was a false prophetess who taught and seduced the people to sin. Her encouragement toward "acts of immorality" ("fornication," KJV; "sexual immorality," NIV) and spiritual compromise by eating "things sacrificed to idols" was repugnant to the Lord. Because of her actions, she is certainly reminiscent of King Ahab's wicked wife (1 Kgs 16:31; 21:25). Thyatira's Jezebel was responsible for the same type of iniquity as the

Jezebel of old, committing witchcraft and whoredoms (2 Kgs 9:22). Yes, Jezebel was wicked, but the fact that those at Thyatira tolerated her is even worse. People tolerate what they enjoy.

(21) *I gave her time to repent, and she does not want to repent of her immorality:* This would suggest that this prophetess was warned about her wicked ways and given an unknown amount of time to repent. Though the Lord is merciful and gives people time to turn from sin, false prophets may not. They can be addicted to the control they exert over others and not want to give up their power.

(22) *Behold, I will throw her on a bed of sickness, and those who commit adultery with her into great tribulation, unless they repent of her deeds:* The Lord declared punishment not only for Jezebel but also for those in Thyatira who were in league with her and followed her lascivious ways. The "bed of sickness," "great tribulation," and death of "her children with pestilence" (v. 23) are the consequences for allowing false doctrine and sin to persist in a congregation. One of the punishments for rebellious Christians is to be thrown into "great tribulation," which G. K. Beale asserts "is probably identical to the great tribulation."[94] However, John MacArthur asserts that this "great tribulation" is "not the eschatological tribulation described in Revelation 4–19, but distress or trouble."[95] Pretribulationists such as MacArthur are forced to claim that "great tribulation" in this text does not mean the great tribulation to come because it provides a good argument against a Pretrib rapture. Other dispensationalists such as John F. Walvoord and others (Ladd, MacDonald, Luter) are surprisingly silent concerning the use of "great tribulation" in this text.[96]

---

[94] G. K. Beale, *The Book of Revelation: A Commentary on the Greek Text* (Grand Rapids, MI; Wm. B. Eerdmans Publishing Co.; Paternoster Press, 1999), 263.

[95] John MacArthur, *The MacArthur New Testament Commentary: Revelation 1–11* (Chicago: Moody Press, 1999), 102.

[96] John F. Walvoord, "Revelation," in *The Bible Knowledge Commentary: An Exposition of the Scriptures*, ed. J. F. Walvoord and R. B. Zuck, vol. 2 (Wheaton, IL: Victor Books, 1985), 937.

(23) *all the churches will know that I am He who searches the minds and hearts; and I will give to each one of you according to your deeds*: This explains the purpose for the judgment. The Lord, in His divine *sagacity,** is the One who searches the heart (Ps 139:1; Luke 16:15; Rom 8:27) and is the same One who will administer rewards when He returns (Matt 16:27; Rev 22:12).

(24) *who have not known the deep things of Satan, as they call them*: So often people are seduced by "deep things." Most *esoteric** groups, cults, and the occult are shrouded and built upon secret knowledge that only the chosen few, or those who excel among their ranks, can know. But this wickedly seductive knowledge is really inspired by Satan, who transforms himself into an angel of light (2 Cor 11:14). Satanically inspired knowledge should be considered never as "deep" but as poison bait alluring people to destruction. "As they call them" is intentional sarcasm. Today there is a fascination with the romanticized version of Satan in music, movies, and weekly television programming. Still others worship Satan by seeking empowerment through bizarre rituals and liturgies, all to probe his *so-called* depths. No matter how enticing, attractive, interesting, fascinating, or deep, it's all wicked. Even more tragic is when satanic things cross the threshold of the local church. Jezebel introduced wickedness to the church in Thyatira, apparently through false prophecy and heresy, causing many to stumble. Her teaching led to immorality and eating things sacrificed to idols (Rev 2:20), behind which were demons (1 Cor 10:20). In this way, they participated in the "deep things of Satan."

(26–27) *he who keeps My deeds until the end, to him I will give authority over the nations; and he shall rule them with a rod of iron, as the vessels of the potter are broken to pieces*: The faithful who endure to the end in this life will rule and reign with Christ. This emphasizes the fact that he who keeps Christ's "deeds" will have glorious authority in heaven.

(27–28) *as I also have received authority from My Father; and I will give him the morning star*: For as many commentaries as there are questioning the meaning of *morning star*,* referenced here, there are as many answers. It is clear that Christ, speaking of Himself in first person, is the One who will give "the morning star." Before this, the Lord stated, "I also have received authority from My Father." Undoubtedly, "authority" is the subject here. Therefore, it is possible that Christ will give "the morning star"—that is, messianic authority to rule the nations with a rod of iron—to those who overcome (vv. 26–27), which is *possibly* a reference to Numbers 24:17. However, in Revelation 22:16, Christ Himself is "the bright morning star" (NIV, NKJV capitalize "Morning Star"), meaning Christ is the brightest among the stars (among the heavenly authorities). Speaking of heavenly authorities, Paul declared, "So that the manifold wisdom of God might now be made known through the church *to the rulers and the authorities in the heavenly places*" (Eph 3:10, emphasis added). Certainly, Christ is higher than all (cf. Col 1:14–20).

REVELATION 3:1–5

MESSAGE TO SARDIS

[1] "To the angel of the church in Sardis write:

He who has the seven Spirits of God and the seven stars, says this: 'I know your deeds, that you have a name that you are alive, but you are dead. [2] Wake up, and strengthen the things that remain, which were about to die; for I have not found your deeds completed in the sight of My God. [3] So remember what you have received and heard; and keep it, and repent. Therefore if you do not wake up, I will come like a thief, and you will not know at what hour I will come to you. [4] But you have a few people in Sardis who have not soiled their garments; and they will walk with Me in white, for they are worthy. [5] He who overcomes will thus be clothed in white garments; and I will not erase his name from the book of life, and I will confess his name before My Father and before His angels.'"

History Note: Sardis was located approximately thirty miles southeast of Thyatira and was on a major trade route that ran east and west through the kingdom of Lydia. As a thriving commercial city and center for commerce, its industries included jewelry, dye, and textiles. It also had gold that was found in the sand of the river Pactolus. All these factors contributed to the city's considerable wealth. As typical of cities located in Asia Minor, it was a hub of pagan worship known for its temple of Artemis, the goddess of fertility, and for its temple of the goddess Cybele, who was worshiped in a similar manner to Diana of Ephesus. While Sardis was once lively and had a great reputation, by the time John's message from Jesus was written, the city's vibrancy was dying. This characteristic of the city mirrored the spiritual condition of the church.

(1) *I know your deeds, that you have a name that you are alive, but you are dead:* No matter what people said about the church in Sardis, the Lord retorted, "I know your deeds ... you are dead." It is so easy for us to get by on a past reputation or by what others think about our outward appearance. Apparently, the church of Sardis had "a name" ("a reputation," NIV) for being "alive," but the fact was they were really "dead." Today, churches are judged on how "lively" they are. A church may appear alive if it has stage props, dynamic preaching, loud music, jumping, and shouting, but having these things does not mean a church is alive. If a church's activity is not Christ-centered and Spirit-led, the church is really dead.

(2) *Wake up, and strengthen the things that remain, which were about to die; for I have not found your deeds completed in the sight of My God:* The Lord admonished them to "wake up" from their spirit of slumber and complacency and "strengthen" or revive that which was dying. Complacency kills, but revival heals.

(3) *So remember what you have received and heard; and keep it, and repent. Therefore if you do not wake up, I will come like a thief, and you will not know at what hour I will come to you:* The church at Sardis was to remember this message, heed it, and repent. Next is the warning that if they did not wake up, Jesus would come while they were not watching, at a time they would not expect. Sleeping people have no awareness or expectation. Those who are spiritually asleep are dulled and unaware and cannot detect Christ's presence; they are driven by emotion and sensuality.

(4) *But you have a few people in Sardis who have not soiled their garments; and they will walk with Me in white, for they are worthy:* There were a few who did not succumb to the spiritual lethargy in Sardis. We never have to cave in to what others are doing. We do not have to be part of the "in crowd." No matter what anyone else is doing, we can do what is right so our garments are not soiled. Even if our faithfulness is not acknowledged by others, the Lord sees it, and we will walk with Him in white. Our faithfulness will be rewarded.

(5) *He who overcomes will thus be clothed in white garments; and I will not erase his name from the book of life:* White garments are part of the reward in heaven, representing purity and righteousness (19:8). "I will not erase his name from the book of life" has sparked much controversy. Those who believe in *eternal security* (Calvinism) tiptoe around this passage. Those who believe in *probationary salvation* (Arminianism) harp on this passage. However, the text actually affirms security because if someone is an overcomer, He "will not erase his name." Want to settle the issue? Be an overcomer. So when it comes to *your* name, Christ won't need an eraser.

REVELATION 3:7–12

MESSAGE TO PHILADELPHIA

[7] "And to the angel of the church in Philadelphia write:

He who is holy, who is true, who has the key of David, who opens and no one will shut, and who shuts and no one opens, says this:

[8] 'I know your deeds. Behold, I have put before you an open door which no one can shut, because you have a little power, and have kept My word, and have not denied My name. [9] Behold, I will cause those of the synagogue of Satan, who say that they are Jews and are not, but lie—I will make them come and bow down at your feet, and make them know that I have loved you. [10] Because you have kept the word of My perseverance, I also will keep you from the hour of testing, that hour which is about to come upon the whole world, to test those who dwell on the earth. [11] I am coming quickly; hold fast what you have, so that no one will take your crown. [12] He who overcomes, I will make him a pillar in the temple of My God, and he will not go out from it anymore; and I will write on him the name of My God, and the name of the city of My God, the new Jerusalem, which comes down out of heaven from My God, and My new name.'"

History Note: Philadelphia, meaning "brotherly love," was 105 miles from Smyrna and just under 30 miles southeast of Sardis. The city was founded in 140 BC by Attalus II Philadelphus of Pergamum, for whom the city was named. It was approximately 650 feet above sea level, and much of the land there was very fertile, producing its famed fine wine. It was located on the route of the Imperial Post from Rome to the east. Due to the many pagan gods worshiped in Philadelphia, it was referred to as "little Athens," but its primary deity was the god Dionysus, not Athena. In this environment, the Philadelphian church faced persecution from pagan worshipers and Jews hostile to Christianity. It is believed the church in Philadelphia was small, and like Smyrna, it was in good standing, receiving no rebuke from the Lord.

(7) *who has the key of David, who opens and no one will shut, and who shuts and no one opens:* This seems to be a reference to Isaiah 22:22, which says, "Then I will set the key of the house of David on his shoulder, when he opens no one will shut, when he shuts no one will open." It is the Lord's sovereign providence to exercise divine authority to "open" or "shut" doors to direct His people. This is an enduring encouragement that whatever the Lord opens, no one can close. But it must be accepted, too, that whatever He closes, no one can open. His will is done in Heaven and on earth.

(8) *you have a little power, and have kept My word, and have not denied My name:* Though many claim to wield the power of God, the truth is we have "little power" and are depending upon God. The church in Philadelphia had not denied His name; therefore, their faithfulness would be rewarded (vv. 10–12).

(9) *Behold, I will cause those of the synagogue of Satan, who say that they are Jews and are not, but lie—I will make them come and bow down at your feet, and make them know that I have loved you:* Once again, the Jews who persecuted Christians were called "the synagogue of Satan" (cf. 2:9). The Lord said He would make these Jews humble themselves and worship at the Philadelphians' feet so that the Jews would know that the Lord loved the Philadelphians.

(10) *Because you have kept the word of My perseverance, I also will keep you from the hour of testing, that hour which is about to come upon the whole world, to test those who dwell on the earth:* No one is sure what "the word of [His] perseverance" means, whether it was a specific word given through prophecy as encouragement to endure the persecution they were undergoing or it was the gospel message in general. Whatever the meaning, they were commended for holding fast to it. In addition, there is controversy centered around "I also will keep you from the hour of testing... which is about to come upon the whole world." Those who hold to a Pretrib rapture (dispensationalist) see the rapture here as being emphasized by "I also will keep you from the hour of testing." The typical Pretrib assertion sees the Philadelphian church as representative of the body of Christ at the time of the rapture (with the rapture being at least some two thousand years removed from the Philadelphian church that is addressed in the text). They also see "the hour of testing" as representing the tribulation, which is the period that follows in the subsequent chapters of Revelation. MacArthur asserts, "This verse promises that the church will be delivered from the Tribulation, thus supporting a pretribulation Rapture.... The hour of testing is Daniel's Seventieth Week (Dan 9:25–27), the time of Jacob's trouble (Jer 30:7), the seven-year tribulation period."[97]

The Beacon Bible Commentary says, "The primary reference is to the so-called Great Tribulation period at the time of the Second Coming. But there is perhaps a secondary application to the Roman persecutions of Christianity, which extended throughout the then known earth—the Roman Empire."[98]

---

[97] MacArthur, *The MacArthur New Testament Commentary: Revelation 1–11*, 123.

[98] Ralph Earle, The Book of Revelation, *Beacon Bible Commentary* vol.10 (Beacon Hill Press: Kansas City, 1967).

Though Pretribulationists insist on a Pretrib rapture here, it should be noted that none of the elements that occur during the rapture—such as the Lord descending from heaven, the sound of the trumpet, the change from mortal to immortal, the catching away, and meeting the Lord in the air—are mentioned or even implied in this text. The Lord made a promise to the church of Philadelphia to "keep [them] from the hour of testing, that hour which is about to come upon the whole world," which He literally intends to keep. For a more detailed refutation of the Pretrib interpretation of this text, please see the "3:10: The Hour of Testing Dilemma" essay.

(11) *I am coming quickly:* Obviously, "coming quickly" did not mean "quickly" in the passing of time from the human perspective. See 1:1 note and "The Imminent Return Problem."

(a) *hold fast what you have, so that no one will take your crown:* Crowns are symbols for eternal rewards. In the Epistles, crowns are used to convey honor and special recognition: 1 Thessalonians 2:19: "of exultation"; 2 Timothy 4:8: "of righteousness"; James 1:12: "of life"; and 1 Peter 5:4: "of glory." However, this is not to suggest that crowns are the benefit of competitive achievement, where someone can be outplayed, or that the crowns can be stolen by another competitor. This is to show that eternal rewards can be lost or be forfeited by being tainted with sin or wrong motives (see 1 Cor 3:12–15).

(12) *I will make him a pillar in the temple of My God, and he will not go out from it anymore:* There seems to be a contradiction here because 21:22 states that in the new Jerusalem *there is no need for an actual temple* (see 21:22 note). This can be reconciled by understanding that the promise to make believers "a pillar in the temple" in this text is from John's perspective as he saw a vision of the throne room in heaven, where there would still be a heavenly temple along with the associated activity (e.g., chap. 5). Revelation 21:22 is after the conclusion of the earthly millennial kingdom and the great white throne judgment. Revelation 21:1 states, "Then

I saw a *new heaven* and a *new earth*; for the *first heaven and the first earth passed away*, and there is no longer any sea" (emphasis added). From this we can conclude that up to the occurrence of the "new heaven," where God reorders everything and where He declares, "Behold, I am making all things new" (21:5), there still is a temple in heaven (see 15:5). However, as it relates to a glorified believer being "a pillar in the temple" of God, "pillar" represents *permanent status* in heaven and the honor of serving God, hence the affirmation "and he will not go out from it anymore." On earth, when we say a person is a pillar of the community, we mean they have a well-established, upstanding reputation and are respected and honored. The verse-by-verse commentary continues on page 91.

ESSAY:
3:10: THE HOUR OF TESTING DILEMMA

One of the most important passages of Scripture used to back a Pretrib rapture is Revelation 3:10. To some, it is the most definitive affirmation. The text reads, "Because you have kept the word of My perseverance, I also will keep you from the hour of testing, that hour which is about to come upon the whole world, to test those who dwell on the earth." Tony Evans asserts, "This verse suggests a pre-tribulational rapture because it says, 'I will also keep you from the hour of testing that is going to come on the whole earth.' Jesus will not merely keep them from the test but from the period of the test—that is, the tribulation period."[99] Walvoord also asserts, "It is difficult to see how Christ could have made this promise to this local church if it were God's intention for the entire church to go through the Tribulation that will come on the entire world."[100] Robert H. Gundry, supporting a Posttribulation interpretation, writes, "Here in Revelation 3:10 'keep you from' doesn't mean 'take you out.' It means 'protect you from the hour of the test while you're in the world' just as John 17:15 means 'keep them from the evil one while they're in the world.'"[101]

---

[99] Tony Evans, *The Tony Evans Bible Commentary* (Nashville, TN: Holman Bible Publishers, 2019), 1400.

[100] Walvoord, "Revelation," in *The Bible Knowledge Commentary*, 939.

[101] Robert H. Gundry, *Commentary on Revelation* (Grand Rapids, MI: Baker Academic, 2010), Rev 3:10.

To begin, let's state the obvious: there is nothing in this passage that contains any elements associated with the rapture. There is no trumpet, no mention of the Lord descending from heaven on a cloud, no voice of the archangel, no dead people rising in incorruptible bodies, no living people being changed in the twinkling of an eye, and no one being caught up to meet the Lord in the air. There's not a single aspect of saints being translated in this text. Nor does the Lord say, "I will come take you out" or "I will come receive you to Myself." Yet without any explicit connection to the rapture and with a total reliance on interpretation, this passage is considered the go-to Scripture that best supports a Pretrib rapture.

Where many do agree is in understanding "the hour of testing" as representing the events in Revelation that are contained in chapters 6–19 and as being synonymous with Daniel's Seventieth Week. The point of contention is focused on the phrase "keep you from [Gk. *tereo ek*] the hour of testing." The Pretrib position argues that this phrase should be interpreted as "keep you from all the events in chapters 6–19," which means that the church will not be on earth during any of the tribulation period. The other side argues that the phrase "keep you from" means the church would still be on earth during the events of Revelation 6–19 but would be kept safe through the hour of testing. From the Pretrib perspective, MacArthur makes the following points:

> First, the test is yet future. Second, the test is for a definite, limited time; Jesus described it as the hour of testing. Third, it is a test or trial that will expose people for what they really are. Fourth, the test is worldwide in scope, since it will come upon the whole world. Finally, and most significantly, its purpose is to test those who dwell on the earth—a phrase used as a technical term in the book of Revelation for unbelievers (cf. 6:10; 8:13; 11:10; 13:8, 12, 14; 14:6; 17:2, 8). The hour of testing is Daniel's Seventieth Week (Dan. 9:25–27), the time of Jacob's trouble (Jer. 30:7), the seven-year tribu-

lation period. The Lord promises to keep His church out of the future time of testing that will come on unbelievers.[102]

The above points, as well as others, will serve later in this essay as a framework to present counterarguments to the Pretrib interpretation of this passage. However, some important groundwork must first be covered. This commentary does not support the position that the church passes through the tribulation. My assertion is that the church is raptured sometime after the middle of the week but before the bowl judgments of chapter 16. I also disagree with other proponents of the Prewrath position who place the rapture between the sixth and seventh seals.

THE TEMPORARY AND ETERNAL ASPECTS OF GOD'S WRATH

The passage of Scripture that is key to all the positions is found in 1 Thessalonians 5:9, where Paul stated, "For God has not destined us for wrath, but for obtaining salvation through our Lord Jesus Christ." There are important questions to be considered here. First, who is the "us" the apostle spoke of? Second, who are those "destined [or "appointed"] . . . for wrath"? Third, what is the "wrath" of God? There is probably little doubt that the "us" in this case is the church, the body of Christ, which is not destined to experience the wrath of God. However, this begs another important question: If the church is not destined for the wrath of God, then who is? Once again, the obvious answer to this question is the unredeemed, or the wicked, who are not saved. However, if the wrath of God is considered to be "the hour of testing," or "the tribulation period" as Pretribulationists would assert, then only the wicked living during that time of the tribulation would experience God's wrath. All the other wicked, from Adam's time to those who lived and died right before the Seventieth Week started, would not be alive to experience the events of Daniel's Seventieth Week,

---

[102] MacArthur, *The MacArthur New Testament Commentary: Revelation 1–11*, 124.

which Pretribulationists insist are the tribulation events detailed in Revelation 6–19.

Therefore, MacArthur, speaking of the wrath of God in 1 Thessalonians 5:9, observes:

> *Orgē* (**wrath**) does not refer to a momentary outburst of rage, but to "an abiding and settled habit of mind" (Richard C. Trench, *Synonyms of the NT* [reprint; Grand Rapids: Eerdmans, 1983], 131). It is a general reference to the final judgment, when God's wrath will be poured out on the wicked (Matt. 3:7; John 3:36; Rom. 1:18; 2:5, 8; 3:5; 4:15; 5:9; 9:22; 12:19; Eph. 5:6; Col. 3:6; Rev. 14:9–11). But God's **wrath** here must also include the Day of the Lord, since that was the Thessalonians' primary concern. Paul assured them that they would face neither temporal **wrath** on the Day of the Lord (cf. Rev. 6:17), nor eternal **wrath** in hell.[103]

MacArthur is correct here. The wrath of God can be considered not only as the *tribulation period* but also as *eternal damnation*. Therefore, there is a *temporary* aspect and an *eternal* aspect of the wrath of God. This is why Paul stated it the way he did, that "God has not destined" the church to wrath "but [to] obtaining salvation." The Christians at the church of Thessalonica were already saved, so what salvation was left for them to obtain? The answer is the final act of the salvific process, which is *glorification*, something no one in the body of Christ has yet experienced. This is the salvation we are destined to, which has yet to be obtained and which happens when the resurrection/rapture occurs.

The same is true for the wrath of God and those appointed to it. God's wrath will be experienced not only during Daniel's Seventieth Week, which coincides with chapters 6–19, but also during eternal

---

[103]   John MacArthur, *The MacArthur New Testament Commentary: 1 & 2 Thessalonians* (Chicago: Moody Press, 2002), 163.

destruction, where everyone appointed to it will experience God's everlasting wrath. Paul explicitly spoke of the punishment of the wicked when he wrote, "These will pay the penalty of *eternal destruction*, away from the presence of the Lord and from the glory of His power" (2 Thess 1:9, emphasis added). Jesus also spoke of hell in an everlasting sense: "Where their worm does not die, and the fire is not quenched" (Mark 9:47–48).

We also get a picture of the *temporary* and the *eternal* aspects of the wrath of God in Revelation 14:

> Then another angel, a third one, followed them, saying with a loud voice, "If anyone worships the beast and his image, and receives a mark on his forehead or on his hand, he also will drink of the wine of the wrath of God, which is mixed in full strength in the cup of His anger; and he will be tormented with fire and brimstone in the presence of the holy angels and in the presence of the Lamb. And the smoke of their torment goes up forever and ever; they have no rest day and night, those who worship the beast and his image, and whoever receives the mark of his name." (vv. 9–11)

Verse 10 is key. The first part of the verse speaks of the *temporary* aspect of the wrath of God: "He also will drink of the wine of the wrath of God, which is mixed in full strength in the cup of His anger." Those receiving the mark of the beast will experience the wrath of God in the bowl judgments of chapter 16. These bowl judgments will occur near the end of Daniel's Seventieth Week. The second part of v. 10 through v. 11 indicates *everlasting* torment by emphasizing that whoever receives the mark of the beast "will be tormented with fire and brimstone in the presence of the holy angels and in the presence of the Lamb. And the smoke of [his] torment [will go] up forever and ever; [he will] have no rest day and night." The *temporary* aspect of the wrath of God is exhibited in the bowl judgments, and the *eternal* aspect is consigned to the lake of fire (Rev 20:14). These are two separate events but are aspects of the same wrath of God.

Let's turn our attention back to the letters to the seven churches, particularly to Smyrna, a church that has similarities to the church of Philadelphia. As Philadelphia was undergoing persecution, so was Smyrna. As Philadelphia was of a good, moral character, so was Smyrna. Just as Philadelphia received no rebuke, neither did Smyrna. However, the Lord says something only to Smyrna that is extremely significant:

> Do not fear what you are about to suffer. Behold, the devil is about to cast some of you into prison, so that *you will be tested*, and *you will have tribulation for ten days*. Be faithful until death, and I will give you the crown of life. He who has an ear, let him hear what the Spirit says to the churches. He who overcomes will not be *hurt by the second death*. (Rev 2:10–11, emphasis added)

For the first time in the Scriptures, the term "second death" is used in the context of a message given to the churches. It should not be lost on today's readers that it is Jesus Himself who was the One who introduced this term without any elaboration or explanation. It is used before any mention of judgments in the seals, the trumpets, or the bowls. The significance of the *second death* is noteworthy because this is the penalty for those whose names will not be found in the Lamb's book of life during the great white throne judgment. By far, this is the worst judgment in Revelation—more horrific than the seals, trumpets, and bowls combined—and is the result of being found guilty before the tribunal of the great white throne judgment. Revelation records this judgment in the following passage:

> And I saw the dead, the great and the small, standing before the throne, and books were opened; and another book was

opened, which is the book of life; and the dead were judged from the things which were written in the books, according to their deeds. And the sea gave up the dead which were in it, and death and Hades gave up the dead which were in them; and they were judged, every one of them according to their deeds. Then death and Hades were thrown into the lake of fire. *This is the second death, the lake of fire.* And if anyone's name was not found written in the book of life, he was thrown into the lake of fire. (20:12–15, emphasis added)

Chapter 14 amplifies the horror of the second death:

He also will drink of the wine of the wrath of God, which is mixed in full strength in the cup of His anger; and he will be tormented with fire and brimstone in the presence of the holy angels and in the presence of the Lamb. And the smoke of their torment goes up forever and ever; they have no rest day and night, those who worship the beast and his image, and whoever receives the mark of his name. (vv. 10–11)

A LITTLE HELP FROM PAUL

Therefore, the second death is by far the worst judgment in the book of Revelation, far worse than the seals, the trumpets, and the bowls that will occur during Daniel's Seventieth Week, which will last only seven years. The second death is forever and ever. The judgments occurring under Daniel's Seventieth Week are the *temporary* aspects of the wrath of God; the second death in the lake of fire is the *everlasting* aspect of the wrath of God. Understood from this perspective, we can connect the Pauline teaching that the church is "not destined . . . for wrath, but for obtaining salvation" (1 Thess 5:9) and see that it means more than just the church's absence during the tribulation. This verse anticipates and includes the second death. This means that the second death will have *no power* over the redeemed. As stated specifically to Smyrna, they "will not be *hurt* by the second death" (Rev 2:11, emphasis added).

It is important to understand that 1 Thessalonians 5:9 exempts the church from both the *temporary* wrath experienced in the bowl judgments of Revelation 16 and the second death, which Jesus first announced to the church in Smyrna. Again, Paul addressed this issue when he wrote,

> Therefore, we ourselves speak proudly of you among the churches of God for your perseverance and faith in the midst of all your persecutions and afflictions which you endure. This is a plain indication of God's righteous judgment so that you will be considered worthy of the kingdom of God, for which indeed you are suffering. For after all it is only just for God to repay with affliction those who afflict you, *and to give relief to you who are afflicted and to us as well when the Lord Jesus will be revealed from heaven with His mighty angels in flaming fire, dealing out retribution to those who do not know God and to those who do not obey the gospel of our Lord Jesus.... When He comes to be glorified in His saints on that day,* and to be marveled at among all who have believed—for our testimony to you was believed. (2 Thess 1:4–8, 10, emphasis added)

The above passage corresponds to the Revelation 19:11–16 scenario that occurs during the Lord's second coming at the end of Daniel's Seventieth Week. This is temporary. However, the eternal aspect of punishment is referenced in 2 Thessalonians 1:9, where the apostle declares,

> These will pay the penalty of *eternal destruction*, away from the presence of the Lord and from the glory of His power. (emphasis added)

Therefore, when considering the wrath of God and what the church is not appointed to, the *temporary* and *eternal* aspects of wrath must be factored in. It is at this point where most Pretribulationists/dispensationalists are shortsighted. They typically focus on the *temporary* aspects of wrath encompassing Daniel's Seventieth Week. However, when dealing with "the hour of testing" (Rev 3:10), both *temporary* and *eternal* aspects should be considered.

Again, it must be emphasized that before any other judgments were announced or delineated, Jesus was the One who introduced "the second death" when addressing the church of Smyrna (Rev 2:11). Since the Lord Himself put in play the second death as a wrath-of-God judgment to be avoided by the church, we, too, must follow suit and make it part of our calculus. However, Pretribulationists fail to do so.

BACK TO THE PRETRIB ARGUMENT

The Philadelphian church was to be kept from "the hour of testing" (Rev 3:10). The Greek word *peirasmos* is translated into English as "testing" (NASB, CSB, NRSV, NET), "temptation" (KJV), and "trial" (NJKV, NIV, ESV) and means "an attempt to learn the nature or character of something, test, trial."[104] On the basis of this definition, let's reexamine the points MacArthur, as well as most Pretribulationists, makes concerning this hour of testing.

(1) *The test is yet future.*

Response: It is agreed that the hour of testing is yet future.

(2) *The test is for a definite, limited time; Jesus described it as the hour of testing.*

Response: It is agreed that the hour of testing is for a limited time.

(3) *It is a test or trial that will expose people for what they really are.*

Response: It is agreed that the hour of testing will determine who people really are.

(4) *The test is worldwide in scope since it will come upon the whole world.*

---

[104] Bauer, *Greek-English Lexicon, peirasmos,* "testing."

82

Response: It is agreed that the scope is the entire world.

> (5) *The hour of testing is Daniel's Seventieth Week (Dan 9:25–27),*
> *the time of Jacob's trouble (Jer 30:7), the seven-year period.*

Response: Here is where the problem starts. MacArthur and other Pretrib-ulationists have only considered the temporary aspect of the wrath of God contained in Daniel's Seventieth Week. They have acknowledged the calamities of the seals, trumpets, and bowls, but they have not looked far enough to include the penalty of the great white throne judgment, the second death, which is the worst judgment and the worst aspect of the wrath of God. To not consider the second death, the very judgment Jesus introduced to Smyrna, which He said the overcomers "will not be hurt by," is shortsighted and has led to the wrong conclusion—that Daniel's Seventieth Week is the hour of testing. Though the events of the Seventieth Week will be bad, they are nothing compared to the judgment that will bring the greatest hurt, and that is the second death.

> (6) *Its purpose is "to test those who dwell on the earth"—a phrase*
> *used as a technical term in the book of Revelation for unbelievers.*

Response: It is agreed that the test is for the wicked because the great white throne judgment is only for all the wicked who ever lived on the earth, going all the way back to the days of Adam. However, the one hundred and forty-four thousand sealed during this period, and the saints who refused the mark of the beast, all dwell on earth too, but they are not the wicked.

As we look again, the definition of the word "testing" (*peirasmos*) is "an attempt to learn the nature or character of something, test, trial" (*BDAG**). Therefore, the purpose of this testing is to discover the nature, or character, of something. MacArthur explains it this way:

> Unbelievers will either pass the test by repenting, or fail it
> by refusing to repent. Revelation 6:9–11; 7:9–10, 14; 14:4;
> and 17:14 describe those who repent during the Tribulation

and are saved, thus passing the test; Revelation 6:15–17; 9:20; 16:11; and 19:17–18 describe those who refuse to repent, thus failing the test, and are damned.[105]

MacArthur is limiting the period of testing to the seals, trumpets, and bowls and states that these judgments are what is being used to "expose people for what they really are" (point 3). He then says that unbelievers will either pass or fail the test based on *whether they repent*. On the outset, this reasoning is faulty. God will be pouring out wrath on the world during this testing, but He will not be executing wrath to cause people to repent. For example, those who have taken the mark of the beast at this point are already hellbound. Even if they did repent at this point, it would be useless because their names are not written in the Lamb's book of life (Rev 13:8; 17:8). No one whose name is not written in the Lamb's book of life will enter heaven. Instead they will be thrown in the lake of fire, the second death (20:15). The time to repent is before taking the mark of the beast, not after it.

Chastisement seeks repentance; the eschatological wrath of God does not. The passages that describe how people will refuse to repent during the judgments, such as 16:9, emphasize how incredibly hardened their hearts will be. It seems that they would repent under such intense judgments. However, the purpose of these judgments is not to solicit repentance. These people will be "haters of God" (Rom 1:30), so they will refuse to repent. The wicked will grow even harder rather than repent during the judgments due to the hardness of their hearts. This will expose how deeply reprobate these individuals are. The same type of situation occurred with Pharaoh: each plague hardened his heart even more (Exod 9:34–35). Second Thessalonians 2:11–12 says God Himself will turn these people over to a "deluding influence" so they will believe a lie and be condemned. Therefore, God will not send these judgments in expectation of anyone's repenting.

---

[105] MacArthur, *The MacArthur New Testament Commentary: Revelation 1–11*, 124.

In addition, forces of nature like hailstones, fire, plagues, or man-made calamities such as war cannot "expose people for what they really are" (point 3). Though calamities can solicit fear and can kill, they cannot go into the past and scrutinize a person's words, thoughts, deeds, and motivations or weigh out anyone's circumstances to determine right or wrong actions. A hailstone or an earthquake cannot uncover a liar's deception, a sexual pervert's deviant proclivities, or the extent of a swindler's thefts. The seals, trumpets, and bowls do not come to expose wickedness, but they will come in response to it. As Paul declares,

> For the wrath of God is revealed from heaven against all ungodliness and unrighteousness of men who suppress the truth in unrighteousness, because that which is known about God is evident within them; for God made it evident to them. (Rom 1:18–19)

Therefore, the wrath of God is not about exposing wickedness to bring repentance. The wicked will already be exposed because God will see them. The wrath of God will come in response to wickedness.

However, there will be an appointed time for God to scrutinize and uncover all the secret and hidden things of wicked people's hearts (1 Cor 4:5). The place and time to examine the nature or character of someone will be at the great white throne judgment.

> Then I saw a great white throne and Him who sat upon it, from whose presence earth and heaven fled away, and no place was found for them. And I saw the dead, the great and the small, standing before the throne, and books were opened; and another book was opened, which is the book of life; and the dead were judged from the things which were written in the books, according to their deeds. And the sea gave up the dead which were in it, and death and Hades gave

up the dead which were in them; and they were judged, every one of them according to their deeds. Then death and Hades were thrown into the lake of fire. This is the second death, the lake of fire. And if anyone's name was not found written in the book of life, he was thrown into the lake of fire. (Rev 20:11–15)

This is the event that will expose what *sort* people are, based upon the evidence that is recorded in the books in heaven. MacArthur states that "*the hour of testing* is Daniel's Seventieth Week" (emphasis added). However, Pretribulationists do not look far enough into Revelation to the worst judgment of them all, the great white throne judgment, and its penalty, the second death. Another problem is that MacArthur, citing the hour of testing as being "Daniel's Seventieth Week," limits the wrath of God to those living at the time of the Seventieth Week. What about all the other wicked people who have lived on earth who have been dead for thousands of years? This creates a problem with determining "the hour of testing" as being the Seventieth Week because it doesn't include all those who lived and died before the tribulation period arrives. However, this cosmic court for the great white throne judgment truly brings forth all the wicked who ever dwelled on the earth, going back to the beginning of time. Characteristically, the great white throne judgment is for the wicked and only lasts for a period of time ("the hour of testing"). However, the penalty of the great white throne judgment is the second death, and that's everlasting torment, making it the worst consequence for wickedness in Revelation.

A Promise Kept or Not Kept?

The promise that Jesus made to keep the Philadelphian church from the hour of testing is one He intends to keep literally. However, with the way the Pretribulationists interpret Revelation 3:10, the Lord made a promise to the church in Philadelphia that He *isn't* going to keep literally. Why? Because Pretrib claims "the hour of testing" is Daniel's

Seventieth Week. The Philadelphian church was a first-century church that has long been off the scene. Therefore, in this regard, Pretrib concludes that the Lord wasn't focusing on the members of the Philadelphian church per se, who would never live to see the tribulation or the rapture. It suggests He was speaking to Christians two thousand years into the future. We are now in the twenty-first century, and the rapture has not occurred. This Pretrib interpretation is awkward because there is no transition in this passage to indicate that Christ was looking beyond the first-century Philadelphian church to Christians in a very distant future.

This problem is caused by identifying "the hour of testing" as Daniel's Seventieth Week. By doing so, it forces the problem of the Lord making a promise to a church that He knew would never live to see these eschatological events. It forces the Lord to be speaking beyond that local congregation in ancient Asia Minor to Christians thousands of years later. It forces Jesus into making a promise that He did not intend to keep. And it forces a Pretrib rapture narrative onto a text where it does not belong. However, when we consider that the Lord told the church in Smyrna that they "will not be hurt by the second death" (Rev 2:11), we can now come to the understanding that this has been the missing link that's been here all along. The Lord was emphasizing the fact that He has appointed the church in Smyrna to salvation and not to be hurt by the second death, which is the fullest expression of God's wrath.

The first resurrection (the resurrection of the righteous) will occur at least one thousand years before the second resurrection (the resurrection of damnation). All the redeemed will be resurrected, including those saints of the ancient church of Philadelphia. And just as Jesus promised Philadelphia, Smyrna, and all Christians, we will be kept from the hour of testing because none of the redeemed will experience the penalty of the great white throne judgment, the second death. We are not appointed to wrath; we are appointed to obtain salvation in the resurrection of the righteous, where we will be glorified. The wicked who are appointed to wrath will have their own resurrection a thousand years later. They will stand before God and be judged for who they really are, which is the definition of the word "testing" (Gk. *peirasmos*; Rev 3:10). In Revelation, Jesus spoke of the "hour of testing," and in the Gospel of John, He also declared "an hour is coming" in reference to the two resurrections:

> Truly, truly, I say to you, *an hour* is coming and now is, when the dead will hear the voice of the Son of God, and those who hear will live. For just as the Father has life in Himself, even so He gave to the Son also to have life in Himself; and He gave Him authority to execute judgment, because He is the Son of Man. Do not marvel at this; for *an hour* is coming, in which all who are in the tombs will hear His voice, and will come forth; those who did the good deeds to a resurrection of life, those who committed the evil deeds to a resurrection of judgment. (5:25–29, emphasis added)

According to this passage, the righteous and the wicked will be appointed to their own respective resurrections. It is certain that the church "will not be hurt by the second death" (Rev 2:11). This means the church and the redeemed of all ages will not be in the court call for the unrighteous. Nor is the second death applicable to any of the redeemed. In this way, God keeps us from the hour of the testing, the great white throne judgment, and second death.

Just as Jesus spoke of "the hour of testing" in Revelation, He also referenced the resurrection in the context of *an hour* that is coming. In the Gospel of John, Jesus characterized the events of both resurrections as "an hour" where the righteous and the wicked will face judgment after being resurrected. Without a doubt, the great white throne judgment will be that event for the wicked only. However, Christians will be at the trial of the great white throne judgment, in some capacity, as judges. Paul writes,

> Or do you not know that the saints will judge the world? If the world is judged by you, are you not competent to constitute the smallest law courts? Do you not know that we will judge angels? How much more matters of this life? (1 Cor 6:2–3)

The saints will judge both people and angels. But, as for the second death, it will not hurt the church.

THE WHOLE WORLD

Finally, in Revelation 3:10, the hour of testing affects the "whole world" (Gr. *holos oikoumenê*). *Holos* means "whole, entire, complete,"[106] and *oikoumenê* means "the inhabited earth."[107] Many have interpreted "whole world" to mean "worldwide," spanning the entire globe at the time of Daniel's Seventieth Week (the tribulation period). Whereas the events of chapters 6–19 will be global in scope, concerning the "hour of testing," it may be necessary to move beyond restricting it to the tribulation period. The "whole world" can also mean "all who have ever lived on the earth," not only those living throughout the earth during the tribulation. For example, 12:9 states, "And the great dragon was thrown down, the serpent of old who is called the devil and Satan, who deceives the *whole world*" (emphasis added, *holos oikoumenê*). In this context, "whole world" should be understood as the span of the world's entire history. Satan's deception will cover every inch of the earth during the Seventieth Week, but it has also spanned the entirety of world history (see also 1 John 5:19). To emphasize this point, Satan is called "the serpent of old," a reference to his activity in the garden of Eden (Gen 3:1–15).

---

106 Bauer, *Greek-English Lexicon*, "whole, *holos*."
107 Bauer, *Greek–English Lexicon*, "world, *oikoumenê*."

First John 2:2 has similar wording: "He Himself is the propitiation for our sins; and not for ours only, but also for those of the *whole world*" (emphasis added). In this verse, the Greek words for "whole world" are *holos kosmos*. *Holos* (meaning "whole, entire, complete") has the same meaning as it does in Revelation 3:10, but *kosmos* means "humanity in general, the world."[108] Jesus' sacrifice was efficacious enough to save every soul that ever lived on the earth, but unfortunately, all do not access the gift of salvation by faith. In 1 John 2:2, "whole world" refers to all humanity from the beginning of time to the end. Therefore, the term "whole world" can have a much wider application than insisted on by Pretribulationists. It has been asserted in this essay that *the second death* should be connected to the "hour of testing" because Jesus introduces it in His message to Smyrna. Though typically overlooked, it is the severest judgment in Revelation, worse than anything found in chapters 6–19, which Pretrib prefers. The great white throne judgment is the platform where the nature of each of the unredeemed is determined, where those found guilty are sentenced to the second death. The second death is for all the wicked that have ever lived, from the beginning to the end of the world, representing the truest meaning of "whole world." The *hour of testing* occurs at the great white throne judgment. However, the word "testing" in 3:10 does not refer to a courtroom trial. It refers to an attempt to learn the nature or character of something, which will ultimately occur when the books are opened in 20:11–13. The final arbiter is the Lamb's book of life: "If anyone's name was not found written in the book of life, he was thrown into the lake of fire" (v. 15), which burns forever and is the second death—God's eternal wrath. When understood from this perspective, 3:10 does not support a Pretribulation rapture. It is a promise that the church is not appointed to the ultimate wrath of God, which is the second death, and does not suggest the church will avoid the temporary judgments of chapters 6–19.

---

[108] Bauer, *Greek-English Lexicon*, "world, *kosmos*."

REVELATION 3:14–21

[14] "To the angel of the church in Laodicea write:

The Amen, the faithful and true Witness, the Beginning of the creation of God, says this:

[15] 'I know your deeds, that you are neither cold nor hot; I wish that you were cold or hot. [16] So because you are lukewarm, and neither hot nor cold, I will spit you out of My mouth. [17] Because you say, "I am rich, and have become wealthy, and have need of nothing," and you do not know that you are wretched and miserable and poor and blind and naked, [18] I advise you to buy from Me gold refined by fire so that you may become rich, and white garments so that you may clothe yourself, and that the shame of your nakedness will not be revealed; and eye salve to anoint your eyes so that you may see. [19] Those whom I love, I reprove and discipline; therefore be zealous and repent. [20] Behold, I stand at the door and knock; if anyone hears My voice and opens the door, I will come in to him and will dine with him, and he with Me. [21] He who overcomes, I will grant to him to sit down with Me on My throne, as I also overcame and sat down with My Father on His throne.'"

History Note: Laodicea was located about forty miles southeast of Philadelphia. It was one of the richest commercial centers in the world.

Laodicea was known for its banking and for manufacturing clothing made from black wool. The city also had a renowned medical school. In AD 60, a devastating earthquake almost destroyed the entire city. Due to its enormous wealth, the citizens declined aid from Rome and financed the rebuilding themselves. Laodicea also had a large population of Jews, which may have been a contributing factor to the early establishment of the church there. As for its water, it was lukewarm because it reached Laodicea through a system of aqueducts. Lukewarm water is often nauseating, not refreshing, and so it was with the lukewarm Laodicean church.

(14) *The Amen,* meaning "a strong affirmation of what is stated, as expression of faith, let it be so, truly,"[109] is amplified by the next phrases, *the faithful and true Witness, the Beginning of the creation of God.* Jesus is the divine affirmation of God's Word, being the Word of God manifested in the flesh. Jesus fulfills what God has said. "For as many as are the promises of God, in Him they are yes; therefore also through Him is our Amen to the glory of God through us" (2 Cor 1:20).

(15–16) *I know your deeds, that you are neither cold nor hot; I wish that you were cold or hot. So because you are lukewarm, and neither hot nor cold, I will spit you out of My mouth:* Of the seven churches, Laodicea received the sharpest rebuke. Once again, we see that the rebuke here of being "neither hot nor cold" aligns with the topographic characteristics of the city. Laodicea did not have its own water resources. "This need was met by bringing water six miles north from Denizli through a system of stone pipes."[110] By the time the water made its way to Laodicea, it was "neither hot nor cold" but a nauseating "lukewarm," unworthy of digestion. The thought here is dramatic. To "spit out" something is bad. But to "vomit" (NKJV) out something is worse because it must be swallowed in order to cause nausea. That which

---

109   Bauer, *Greek-English Lexicon,* 53.

110   *Holman Illustrated Bible Dictionary,* s.v. "Laodicea."

makes one sick cannot be tolerated. What was the church doing that required such an explicit analogy?

(17) *Because you say, "I am rich, and have become wealthy, and have need of nothing," and you do not know that you are wretched and miserable and poor and blind and naked:* Apparently the Laodiceans were stricken with a condition that many Christians and churches struggle with today: materialism and the pursuit of wealth. Many have been blinded by the so-called prosperity gospel, where wealth is the principal measure of spirituality. Their rationale is the more wealth Christians have, the more proof there is that they have God's favor and blessing. The thinking goes, if Christians have wealth, they can pay more tithes and offerings. The more money in the church's coffers, the more the kingdom can expand through ministry broadcasts, outreach programs, and missions. The more the kingdom can expand, the more people can come to Christ.

However, what often happens in prosperity gospel churches is the pastors get richer and the people become increasingly poorer. This approach to so-called kingdom work often leads to corruption, where the only kingdom that's expanding is theirs, not God's. However, true kingdom expansion depends not on dollars but on the power of God to transform lives from the inside out. To let some of these deceivers tell it, God wants every believer to be dollar rich. But Jesus said we should "seek first His kingdom and His righteousness, and all things will be added to [us]" (Matt 6:33). What others end up seeking is teachers to tell them what their itching ears want to hear (2 Tim 4:3). However, they will not receive from God because they "ask with wrong motives" in order to "spend it on [their] pleasures" (Jas 4:3), and they don't realize that "those who want to get rich fall into temptation and a snare and many foolish and harmful desires which plunge men into ruin and destruction" (1 Tim 6:9–10). Once wealth is obtained, they believe they are secure because they "have need of nothing." But this delusion has them spiritually bankrupt because they "do not know that [they] are wretched and miserable and poor and blind and naked." There are dirt poor Christians in the world today who are filled with the Spirit of God and the joy of the Lord. This is why the Lord said to Smyrna, "I know your tribulation and your poverty (but you are rich)" (Rev 2:9).

(18) The remedy: **to buy from Me gold refined by fire so that you may become rich, and white garments.** In a city known for its great commerce and wealth, Christ declared to the church, "Buy from Me." Jesus is the source of imperishable wealth. He is the gold refined in the fire, which speaks of His purity and holiness having passed through the furnace of affliction and even the pangs of death. "It is the blessing of the LORD that makes rich, and He adds no sorrow to it" (Prov 10:22). Wealth often exposes who people really are. It uncovers all the pride, lust, and *avarice** that the wealthy shamelessly parade before people while drowning in their own corruption. "White garments" is another poke at Laodicea because much of its wealth was derived from producing garments made from black wool. To be clothed in white is also significant because it means the righteousness that Christ gives by faith. Only the righteousness of Christ is of eternal value; it cannot be purchased but must be spiritually imputed by faith. Our righteousness is compared to putrid, filthy rags (Isa 64:6).

(a) *clothe yourself, and that the shame of your nakedness will not be revealed:* Putting on Christ and submitting to His lordship and love will cover up a multitude of sins of the spiritually naked. Once again, this is a poke at those who were proud about Laodicea being a center where fine clothing was produced.

(b) *and eye salve to anoint your eyes so that you may see:* Jesus rebuked them for their lack of spiritual sight because their materialism had caused them to go blind. Ironically, Laodicea was known for its medical school and for a famous *eye salve** produced there. But such remedies could not open the eyes of those who were spiritually blinded by greed. Only the Lord can give sight to those whose vision is obscured by the deceitfulness of riches.

(19) *Those whom I love, I reprove and discipline; therefore be zealous and repent:* This is something most of us receive from our parents: discipline (chastisement) out of love and concern for our growth and proper development. Jesus loves us enough to correct us and not let us run headlong into destruction—not without warning anyway (cf. Heb 12:6).

(20) *Behold, I stand at the door and knock; if anyone hears My voice and opens the door, I will come in to him and will dine with him, and he with Me:* The wretched condition of the Laodiceans had closed the door to a close relationship with the Lord. He stood at the door and knocked for entry. What a terrible reality. This was a church with capital but without Christ; it was materially vibrant but spiritually dead. Unfortunately, many churches with lavish edifices and sanctuaries are in this condition today. They have beautiful, sprawling landscaped campuses with all the latest amenities but are void of God's glory. Yet there was still hope for the Laodiceans. Christ stood at their door and knocked. But woe to those churches where Christ is no longer knocking. They cannot buy their way out of their condition with silver and gold. The only way out is through Christ, the gold tried in the fire.

(21) *I will grant to him to sit down with Me on My throne:* The reward of the overcomer will be realized in glory as we share in Christ's rulership. Paul also encouraged the church that we will reign with Him (2 Tim 2:12) and be seated with Him in heavenly places in the ages to come (Eph 2:6–7).

EXCURSUS—WHAT HAPPENED TO THE CHURCH?

Dispensational scholars and authors (those who hold to a Pretrib rapture) overwhelmingly comment on the fact that the word "churches" in Revelation 3:22 is not found in the book again until 22:16. Then they take a quantum leap and suggest that the word *church* not being mentioned in the text means that the actual church, the body of Christ, is not on earth in these chapters. This concept is based, first, on 1:19, where "the things which are" is interpreted to be the entire church age from Pentecost to the rapture, and second, on 3:10, where it states, "Because you have kept the word of My perseverance, I also will keep you from the hour of testing, that hour which is about to come upon the whole world, to test those who dwell on the earth." (See the further discussion on this issue in "3:10: The Hour of Testing Dilemma.") However, to contend that the word *church* not being mentioned in the text means that the true church, the body of Christ, is no longer on the earth is unwarranted and not supported by a plain reading of the text. Unfortunately, this incorrect concept is taught as dispensational truth.

If it is true that the word *church* not being mentioned in the text is the same as the church not being on earth, then consider that the word *church* is not found in 2 Timothy, Titus, 2 Peter, 1 John, 2 John, and Jude. Should we conclude that because these epistles do not use the word *church*, they have nothing to do with the church or that the church was not present at the time they were written? Of course not. The word *church* is also missing from the original text of 1 Peter 5:13, and while many modern Bible versions do not include it, it is found in italic in 1 Peter 5:13 (KJV), meaning that it was added by the translators. In Galatians, the word "church" is found once in 1:13. In its plural form, it is found twice, in 1:2 and 1:22, but the word does not appear again throughout the rest of the book. Because of this, do we conclude that the following five chapters of Galatians do not apply to the church since the word *church(es)* is not there? Of course not. In Romans, the word *church(es)* is mentioned five times in chapter 16 only. Should we then conclude that the church was not on earth for the first fifteen chapters? God forbid.

Two primary terms used to describe a group of Christians are *church* (Gk. *ekklēsia*, "an assembly") and *saints* (Gk. *hagios*, "the holy ones"). In the Pauline epistles, the apostle used both words interchangeably. For example, Romans 8:27 says, "And He who searches the hearts knows what the mind of the Spirit is, because He intercedes for the saints according to the will of God." Here Paul used the word "saints" when he could have used *church* for the body of believers. In Galatians 1:13, Paul stated that he "used to persecute the church." He was referring not to church buildings but to *saints*, God's *holy ones*.

Paul's corporate use of the word *church*, as in "the universal church" or "the body of Christ," was unique to him and different from the other apostles' writings. Outside of the book of Hebrews, all the "church" terminology representing the body of Christ is exclusively contained in the Pauline epistles. Through Paul, God gave us multifaceted doctrines concerning the church, from it being the vehicle for "the manifold wisdom of God [to] be made known" (Eph 3:10) all the way to it being changed in a moment at the rapture (1 Cor 15:51–52). No other apostle taught the doctrines Paul taught, particularly concerning the specifics of the church, possibly because Paul received more revelations than any other apostle, which caused the Lord to give Paul "a thorn in the flesh, a messenger of Satan" to keep him from exalting himself (2 Cor 12:7). Paul declared, "For I would have you know, brethren, that the gospel which was preached by me is not according to man. For I neither received it from man, nor was I taught it, but I received it through a revelation of Jesus Christ" (Gal 1:11–12). Paul was explicit here when he declared the gospel he taught was not of human origin or the result of being taught by another, even the other apostles (vv. 16–19). Therefore, Paul owned what he taught as "[his] gospel" (Rom 2:16; 16:25; 2 Tim 2:8).

Outside of Paul's epistles, with the exception of the book of Hebrews,[111] other apostles used the word *church* in a local congregational sense. For example, James 5:14 speaks of "the elders of the church" praying for the sick among them, 1 Peter 5:13 (KJV only) speaks of "the church . . . at Babylon," and in 3 John the three uses of "church" are all about the local church (vv. 6, 9, 10). This is significant because John is also the author of Revelation. Therefore, we cannot expect John to refer to

---

[111] Hebrews 12:23 speaks of the "church of the firstborn," which is a universal usage. However, the author of Hebrews is unknown, though some attribute it to Paul.

the universal body of Christians as "the church." John did not use the term that way in any of his writings. Neither is it recorded in Scripture that John received the revelation of the universal church as Paul did.

However, the word that John used as an alternative to the word *church*, which Paul also used, is "saints." An explicit example of this is when John wrote of the bride in the passage below.

> "Let us rejoice and be glad and give the glory to Him, for the marriage of the Lamb has come and His bride has made herself ready." It was given to her to clothe herself in fine linen, bright and clean; for the fine linen is the righteous acts of the saints. (Rev 19:7–8)

The "bride" here is the church. However, in the next sentence referencing the bride (v. 8), John did not use the word *church*; he used "saints." The reason John would not have written of the church as being the body of Christ or the universal church is because those revelations were not given to him. They were given exclusively to Paul. It is notable, however, that when Paul wrote of the bride, he used the word "church," which would have been typical of him.

> Husbands, love your wives, just as Christ also loved *the church* and gave Himself up *for her*, so that He might *sanctify her*, having *cleansed her* by the washing of water with the word, that He might present to Himself *the church in all her glory*, having no spot or wrinkle or any such thing; but that she would be holy and blameless. (Eph 5:25–27, emphasis added)

Here in Ephesians, Paul wrote of Christ's presenting "the church" to Himself. In Revelation, John's vision of the bride in heaven at the marriage supper of the Lamb refers to her fine linen as "the righteous acts of *the saints*" (Rev 19:8, emphasis added). There is no doubt that the same group is being referred to in both instances, which is the church in glory. Paul used the word "church," while John used "saints."

Finally, each message to the seven churches of Asia Minor concludes with "He who has an ear, let him hear what the Spirit says to the churches." However, in Revelation 13, when speaking of Christians, John wrote, "If anyone has an ear, let him hear" (v. 9). Many point to the fact that the phrase "to the churches" is missing from the verse and determine that the church is already gone from the earth, indicating that the so-called tribulation saints are a different group of believers. However, this omission is easily understood in other ways when all the circumstances are considered.

To begin, the messages to the seven churches were just that: announcements to seven congregations with different characteristics, circumstances, issues, strengths, and weaknesses. All these churches were in a localized region in Asia Minor during the first century. However, the situation with the Revelation 13 scenario gives a striking difference because it occurs at least twenty centuries later, considering that we are now well into the twenty-first century and the rapture has not yet occurred. Also, in Revelation 13, specific congregations are not being addressed as they are in chapters 2 and 3. In addition, there are no pastoral messages being delivered on a congregational basis. During the time of chapter 13, the church is a worldwide phenomenon, so churches in specific cities are not the focus. The message in chapter 13 concerns Christians (the saints) worldwide who face imprisonment or martyrdom, not individual churches as mentioned in chapters 2 and 3. Since individual churches are not being addressed, the call goes out, "If anyone has an ear, let him hear," which speaks to the urgency to take heed. The Lord commonly used this plea in the Gospel narratives (Matt 13:9, 43; Mark 4:23; Luke 14:35). The fact that the words "what the Spirit says to the churches" are not included in chapter 13 as they are in chapters 2 and 3 is not an indication to embrace the idea that the church is not present at this time. Remember, John never used the word *church* in a universal sense anyway.

The next two verses give more clarity, particularly from the NIV: "If anyone is to go into captivity, into captivity they will go. If anyone is to be killed with the sword, with the sword they will be killed. This calls for patient endurance and faithfulness on the part of God's people ["the saints," NASB]" (Rev 13:9–10). Jesus gives a similar warning in Matthew 24:9–10: "Then you will be handed over to be persecuted and put to death, and you will be hated by all nations because of me. At that time many will turn away from the faith and will betray and hate each other" (NIV). The "saints" addressed in Revelation 13:9–10 are Christians, but without warrant, dispensationalists insist that this is another group of Christians that are not the church. A primary reason for their belief is the word *church* is not found in these verses. (The other reasons dispensationalists have to exclude the church from parts of Revelation will be addressed later.)

In conclusion, many look for the church through the lens of Pauline theology as they study Revelation, thus creating a categorical error. The "universal church" references cannot be found in any of John's or any other apostle's writings. Those looking for the church as such in Revelation are looking for the wrong thing. The universal church language is Pauline. However, in Revelation, "the saints," "His bond-servants," and "your brother and fellow partaker in the tribulation and kingdom" (1:9) are all Johannine expressions for the same body of believers that Paul often interchangeably called "the church" or "the saints." An interesting fact about the Pauline epistles is that Paul's favorite word to use to represent believers was "saints," which he used seventy-eight times. He used "church" sixty-two times. Therefore, it is a mistake to claim that the church—the universal body of believers—is not included in parts of Revelation based on the word *church* not being used after chapter 3. In fact, the word "saints" is used in Revelation to represent the universal body of believers—the same word that Paul also used to describe the body of Christ more often than the word *church* itself.

REVELATION 4:1–4

Come Up Here

[1] After these things I looked, and behold, a door standing open in heaven, and the first voice which I had heard, like the sound of a trumpet speaking with me, said, "Come up here, and I will show you what must take place after these things." [2] Immediately I was in the Spirit; and behold, a throne was standing in heaven, and One sitting on the throne. [3] And He who was sitting was like a jasper stone and a sardius in appearance; and there was a rainbow around the throne, like an emerald in appearance. [4] Around the throne were twenty-four thrones; and upon the thrones I saw twenty-four elders sitting, clothed in white garments, and golden crowns on their heads.

(1) **After these things:** is seen by those holding to a Pretrib rapture as a transition point from the period after the church has been raptured. They insist that the seven churches of Asia Minor addressed in chapters 2 and 3 are representative of the entire church age, which has spanned now into the twenty-first century. Therefore, they conclude that the events in chapters 6–19 occur during Daniel's Seventieth Week, the final seven-year period after the church has already been raptured. They further assert that the word *church* not being found in Revelation again until 22:16 is evidence to support a Pretrib rapture. However, this is no more than Pretrib theory imposed onto this text. None of the aforestated tenets are explicit in the text, and there is no justification to treat the seven churches of Asia Minor, which were active congregations during the first century, as being comprehensive representation of the entire church age, with the

Philadelphian church representing the church at the time of the rapture. The seven churches are not seven templates on which the Lord bases all churches. Certainly, similar characteristics of these ancient churches can be found in churches today. That is primarily because human nature, weakness, proclivity to sin and rebellion, and satanic activity have not changed through the passage of time (see also 1:19).

(a) *Come up here, and I will show you what must take place after these things:* The *Scofield Reference Bible* states, "This call seems clearly to indicate the fulfillment of 1 Thes. 4:14–17. The word 'church' does not again occur in the Revelation till all is fulfilled."[112] Though all who hold to a Pretrib rapture do not see this as a fulfillment of 1 Thessalonians 4:14–17, where the rapture is taught, there are many who do. Scofield was one of them, and countless millions have embraced this teaching from his reference Bible. Though Scofield says, "This call seems clearly to indicate the fulfillment of 1 Thes. 4:14–17," the text is clear that it was John, not the church, who entered heaven. It is close to folly to claim that the body of John is representative of the body of Christ. John recorded the events in Revelation, not the body of Christ.

(2) *Immediately I was in the Spirit; and behold, a throne was standing in heaven, and One sitting on the throne:* According to 1 Corinthians 15:50, Paul declared, "Now I say this, brethren, that flesh and blood cannot inherit the kingdom of God." As the next verse of this text reveals, we must in fact be "changed" to enter heaven (v. 51). Flesh and blood cannot be in God's presence in the heavenly realms. It would be fatal for a mere human being to be in God's direct presence (see Exod 33:20). Our bodies are made for earth, not Heaven, which necessitated John's being "in the Spirit" to be in heaven. In the rapture we will be changed and given an incorruptible, immortal body like Christ's glorious body, suitable for heaven (see Phil 3:21). John's entering heaven cannot be considered a

---

[112] C. I. Scofield, *The Scofield Reference Bible*, Rev 4:1.

rapture because the text does not say that he was *changed* (see 1 Cor 15:51–52). John was "in the Spirit"; he was not given a glorified body. This was probably like what we might call an out-of-body experience, but it was initiated by God. Paul referred to his own heavenly encounter in his letter to the Corinthians (see 2 Cor 12:1–2). The "One sitting on the throne" is God.

(3) *And He who was sitting was like a jasper stone and a sardius in appearance; and there was a rainbow around the throne, like an emerald in appearance*: For John, heaven's appearance was beyond earthly words. He used phenomenological (how things appear to the eyes) language here. God's appearance *was like* a jasper stone and a sardius stone. It is interesting that John also saw what he called "a rainbow." On earth, certain atmospheric conditions must exist before a rainbow is visible—namely, clouds, rain or water particles, and sunlight. It is doubtful that it rains in heaven, but these are the only words John had to describe what had the appearance of a rainbow as he understood it.

(4) *Around the throne were twenty-four thrones; and upon the thrones I saw twenty-four elders sitting, clothed in white garments, and golden crowns on their heads*: Much discussion and debate have occurred concerning the identity of these twenty-four heavenly individuals. Dispensationalists claim these elders represent the redeemed of the church already raptured into heaven. However, no one on earth knows with any certainty who these individuals really are because none of us have been to heaven and interacted with these individuals. The truth is, the word John used to describe them is *presbyteros*, or in English, "elders." BDAG states, "The elders have been understood as glorified human beings of some kind or astral deities (or angels). . . . The number 24 has been referred to the following: the 24 priestly classes of the Jews."[113] We must be mindful that human terminology can be used to describe things in heaven but not to define or determine them. The term "elders" is an

---

[113] Bauer, *Greek-English Lexicon*, s.v. *presbyteros*, "elders."

adjective. John was describing heavenly entities with a limited, earthly vocabulary. So, nothing conclusive can be derived from his descriptive terminology. Certainly, there would be no geriatrics, in the earthly sense of an elder, in heaven. Pretrib goes out on a limb here concluding these are representatives of the raptured church. However, the text doesn't state such.

EXCURSUS—WHO ARE THE TWENTY-FOUR ELDERS?

Probing the controversy of the twenty-four elders further, who then in church history could possibly qualify as candidates for these exalted positions? The twelve apostles were handpicked by Jesus and were the foundation of the church (Eph 2:20). Their names will be enshrined on the twelve foundations of New Jerusalem for all eternity (Rev 21:14). The apostles will also have a throne in heaven, including John (Matt 19:28). But if the twelve apostles hold these spots, that would only account for half the thrones. If the elders are humans, another possibility is that they could have come to heaven after Christ's resurrection, as described in Matthew's obscure account: "The tombs were opened, and many bodies of the saints who had fallen asleep were raised; and coming out of the tombs after His resurrection they entered the holy city and appeared to many" (Matt 27:52–53). From the many saints mentioned in these verses, twenty-four of them could be seated on these thrones described in Revelation. Obviously, these would be OT saints who, after being raised, went into Jerusalem. If they rose after Christ's resurrection, that would imply they were glorified and went to heaven afterward, because remaining on earth in a glorified state would not be tenable.

Another possibility is found in Ephesians: "So that the manifold wisdom of God might now be made known through the church to the rulers and the authorities in the heavenly places" (3:10). Who exactly are these "rulers" and "authorities in the heavenly places"? We are not sure, but since they are "rulers," certainly they could have thrones and wear crowns. Or could the elders be among the host of heaven that Peter alludes to in

1 Peter 1:12? No one is sure. Another option is that the twenty-four are those who make up the heavenly "court" mentioned in Daniel 7:9–10. In 1 Kings 22:19–22, we have this account:

> Micaiah said, "Therefore, hear the word of the LORD. I saw the LORD sitting on His throne, and all the host of heaven standing by Him on His right and on His left. The LORD said, 'Who will entice Ahab to go up and fall at Ramoth-gilead?' And one said this while another said that. Then a spirit came forward and stood before the LORD and said, 'I will entice him.' The LORD said to him, 'How?' And he said, 'I will go out and be a deceiving spirit in the mouth of all his prophets.' Then He said, 'You are to entice him and also prevail. Go and do so.'"

Who are these to whom God queried? Were they angels? Principalities and powers? Or some other order that we know nothing about? No one knows for sure. From our perspective on earth, which is extremely limited, we only know of God and angels in the heavenly realms. No one on earth is qualified to say with any certainty who the twenty-four elders of Revelation are. We certainly do not know enough to make any definitive doctrinal statements. The best we can do is offer conjecture.

REVELATION 4:5–11

THE FOUR LIVING CREATURES

[5] Out from the throne come flashes of lightning and sounds and peals of thunder. And there were seven lamps of fire burning before the throne, which are the seven Spirits of God; [6] and before the throne there was something like a sea of glass, like crystal; and in the center and around the throne, four living creatures full of eyes in front and behind. [7] The first creature was like a lion, and the second creature like a calf, and the third creature had a face like that of a man, and the fourth creature was like a flying eagle. [8] And the four living creatures, each one of them having six wings, are full of eyes around and within; and day and night they do not cease to say, "Holy, holy, holy is the Lord God, the Almighty, who was and who is and who is to come." [9] And when the living creatures give glory and honor and thanks to Him who sits on the throne, to Him who lives forever and ever, [10] the twenty-four elders will fall down before Him who sits on the throne, and will worship Him who lives forever and ever, and will cast their crowns before the throne, saying, [11] "Worthy are You, our Lord and our God, to receive glory and honor and power; for You created all things, and because of Your will they existed, and were created."

(5) *Out from the throne come flashes of lightning and sounds and peals of thunder. And there were seven lamps of fire burning before the throne, which are the seven Spirits of God:* From God's throne proceed lightning, sounds (voices, KJV; rumblings, NIV), and peals of thunder. These phenomena also occur in 8:5, 11:19, and 16:18, but in this case, they emit from God's throne. They typically precede some divine action relating to the temple or the altar, or precede a divine event. In the OT, sights and sounds like these accompanied God's awesome presence when He came down to Mount Sinai (Exod 19:16). When the Father responded to Jesus' "Father, glorify Your name," some of those who heard God's response said, "that it had thundered" (John 12:28–29). Whether it is sight or sound, God's awesomeness is profound, even affecting atmospheric conditions. *And there were seven lamps of fire burning before the throne, which are the seven Spirits of God.* The seven lamps here are similar, but not identical, to Zechariah's vision in Zechariah 4:2. However, in this text, the lamps are identified as the seven Spirits of God. The seven Spirits of God are found in Revelation 1:4, 3:1, 4:5, and 5:6, and it is a reference to the Holy Spirit (see 1:4a) and could be a reference that builds upon Isaiah 11:2's *the Spirit of the Lord*, and of *wisdom, understanding, counsel, might, knowledge* and *fear*. However, some interpret this to be a reference to seven angels (e.g., Mounce).[114]

(6) *and before the throne there was something like a sea of glass, like crystal; and in the center and around the throne, four living creatures full of eyes in front and behind:* John depicted the majesty of heaven with the throne being surrounded by a sea of what he described as being "like crystal." "In the center and around the throne" were the "living creatures full of eyes in front and behind." John had no idea what these heavenly beings were. The best words John could muster up were "living creatures." Certainly, God has an actual designation for what they are, along with a personal name for each. It is not likely that God would refer to them as John did. But remember, John recorded what he saw, and he could only describe, not define.

(7–8) *The first creature was like a lion, and the second creature like a calf, and the third creature had a face like that of a man, and the fourth creature*

---

114 Robert H. Mounce, *The Book of Revelation: The New International Commentary on the New Testament* (Grand Rapids, MI: Wm. B. Eerdmans Publishing Co., 1997), 122.

was like a flying eagle. And the four living creatures, each one of them having six wings, are full of eyes around and within; and day and night they do not cease to say, "Holy, holy, holy is the Lord God, the Almighty, who was and who is and who is to come": These creatures seem to be related to what Ezekiel saw in his "visions of God" (Ezek 1:1). Ezekiel referred to them as "four living beings" (v. 5). Evidently, this is not a formal name but a description. The following are some of the differences between Ezekiel's and John's accounts. In Ezekiel, each creature has a "human form" but with four faces each and four wings (vv. 5–6). (Note: These creatures are the only heavenly beings that are said to have wings, though traditionally wings are attributed to all angels.) In Revelation, the four creatures only have one face each, but the faces are similar to Ezekiel's report, with them being the face of a man, lion, ox or bull, and eagle. Ezekiel's beings had four wings, whereas John's creatures had six wings. Ezekiel called them *cherubim** (Ezek 10:1–20; 11:22).

Isaiah had a similar encounter, except the term he used for the beings is "seraphim" (Isa 6:2–3). He said the seraphim had six wings each and gave no further description. However, in both John's and Isaiah's accounts, the creatures declare God's glory to the superlative degree. However, their declarations are different. Isaiah recorded, "Holy, Holy, Holy, is the Lord of hosts, the whole earth is full of His glory." John recorded "Holy, holy, holy is the Lord God, the Almighty, who was and who is and who is to come."

(11) *Worthy are You, our Lord and our God, to receive glory and honor and power; for You created all things, and because of Your will they existed, and were created:* The great adoration given to the Lord is "glory," "honor," and "power." The reason for such heavenly admiration from the heavenly host is because by His "will they existed, and were created." All created beings, whether in heaven, earth, under the earth, or the entire universe, both seen and unseen, are contingent and finite beings. *Contingent,* meaning they are totally dependent upon God for their very existence. God creates all things according to the working of His own purpose. Paul affirmed this when he declared,

For by Him all things were created, both in the heavens and on earth, visible and invisible, whether thrones or dominions or rulers or authorities—all things have been created through Him and for Him. He is before all things, and in Him all things hold together. (Col 1:16–17)

All contingent beings are *finite*, meaning they had a beginning, a point in which they were created, and they depend on God for their very existence. Because they were created, they are creaturely. They are not omniscient (i.e., all-knowing), omnipotent (i.e., all-powerful), or omnipresent (i.e., all-present, filling all time and space), which are characteristics belonging only to God, who only is self-existent and eternal (i.e., no beginning and no end). Here the heavenly host bestows such honor due to the Lord for all His glory and magnificence. Therefore, when the living creatures begin to give glory to God, the twenty-four elders cast down their crowns before the throne in humility and honor, along with all the host of heaven, and worship the Lord, "who lives forever and ever" (Rev 4:10). The words "forever and ever" emphasize God's awesome eternality.

REVELATION 5:1–10

THE SEVEN-SEALED BOOK

[1] I saw in the right hand of Him who sat on the throne a book written inside and on the back, sealed up with seven seals. [2] And I saw a strong angel proclaiming with a loud voice, "Who is worthy to open the book and to break its seals?" [3] And no one in heaven or on the earth or under the earth was able to open the book or to look into it. [4] Then I began to weep greatly because no one was found worthy to open the book or to look into it; [5] and one of the elders said to me, "Stop weeping; behold, the Lion that is from the tribe of Judah, the Root of David, has overcome so as to open the book and its seven seals."

[6] And I saw between the throne (with the four living creatures) and the elders a Lamb standing, as if slain, having seven horns and seven eyes, which are the seven Spirits of God, sent out into all the earth. [7] And He came and took the book out of the right hand of Him who sat on the throne. [8] When He had taken the book, the four living creatures and the twenty-four elders fell down before the Lamb, each one holding a harp and golden bowls full of incense, which are the prayers of the saints. [9] And they sang a new song, saying,

"Worthy are You to take the book and to break its seals; for You were slain, and purchased for God with Your blood men from every tribe and tongue and people and nation. [10] You have made them to be a kingdom and priests to our God; and they will reign upon the earth."

(1) *I saw in the right hand of Him who sat on the throne a book written inside and on the back, sealed up with seven seals:* There are several books that are in the heavenlies. David wrote about a book where the number of his days were recorded (see Ps 139:16). In Daniel, Gabriel spoke of the "writing of truth" (10:21), "the book in which God has designated beforehand, according to truth, the history of the world as it shall certainly be unfolded."[115] Malachi wrote of a "book of remembrance" as being a record of those who revere and think about the Lord's name (Mal 3:16). And the book of Revelation mentions books of works and the book of life (see Rev 20:12). Books in the ancient world were not like the books we have today. The book in this case is a scroll, written on both sides, rolled up, and sealed with seven seals. To read this book, one would have to break each seal to unroll the scroll.

(2) *I saw a strong angel proclaiming with a loud voice, "Who is worthy to open the book and to break its seals?"* The book is in the hand of God Himself (see v. 1). Now it is the center of attention of the heavenly host. "A strong ["mighty," NIV] angel" is present. Compared with humans, all angels are strong, but this one must have been unusually mighty. The mention of his strength is significant because being "strong" did not qualify him to "open the book." He was looking for someone "worthy" to unroll the scroll and "break its seals." Here, being "worthy" means "having won or obtained the right and therefore being deserving" of opening the scroll. "Seals" were used to secure important documents and, in this case, restrict access to the book's contents.

(3) *And no one in heaven or on the earth or under the earth was able to open the book or to look into it:* This conveys no creature, principality, or power in any realm ("heaven," "earth," or "under the earth") was deserving of opening the book. And without the right or privilege, no one qualified for the task.

---

[115] Carl F. Keil and Franz Delitzsch, *Commentary on the Old Testament*, vol. 9: *Ezekiel, Daniel* (Grand Rapids, MI: Eerdmans, 1986), 775.

(4) John is caught up in the moment and has internalized the pervasive anxiety and therefore has *began* **to** *weep greatly because no one was found worthy to open the book or to look into it*: This exposes a two-part problem. Even if someone was able to break the seals, they would also have to be deserving enough to examine the book's contents.

(5) *and one of the elders said to me, "Stop weeping; behold, the Lion that is from the tribe of Judah, the Root of David":* The dilemma was only supposed because there was a solution to the problem. One of the elders comforted John by saying, "The Lion that is from the tribe of Judah, the Root of David, has overcome ["prevailed," KJV] so as to open the book and its seven seals." The resurrected God-man is the only one found worthy and, by extension, qualified to "open the book." Genesis 49:9 states, "Judah is a lion's whelp; from the prey, my son, you have gone up. He couches, he lies down as a lion, and as a lion, who dares rouse him up?" Symbolically, a lion represents courageous authority and rulership as "a lawgiver" (Gen 49:10 KJV). Lions also represent a ferocious ruler who is to be not roused but reverenced. "The Root of David" is another connection to the Lord's humanity, royal lineage, and rulership. The prophet Isaiah informs us,

> Then a shoot will spring from the stem of Jesse, and a branch from his roots will bear fruit. The Spirit of the LORD will rest on Him, the spirit of wisdom and understanding, the spirit of counsel and strength, the spirit of knowledge and the fear of the LORD.... Then in that day the nations will resort to the root of Jesse, who will stand as a signal for the peoples; and His resting place will be glorious. (Isa 11:1–2, 10)

(a) *has overcome so as to open the book and its seven seals:* Hebrews 2:9 declares, "But we do see Him who was made for a little while lower than the angels, namely, Jesus, because of the suffering of death crowned with glory and honor, so that by the grace of God He might taste death for everyone."

Jesus has prevailed, passing through the womb to the tomb and raising from the dead. Christ has even overcome the pangs of death. Because

He is righteous, death has no claim on Him. The author of Hebrews went further:

> Therefore it was necessary for the copies of the things in the heavens to be cleansed with these, but the heavenly things themselves with better sacrifices than these. For Christ did not enter a holy place made with hands, a mere copy of the true one, but into heaven itself, now to appear in the presence of God for us. (9:23–24)

Though there appeared to be a dilemma in heaven, it quickly turned celebratory as Christ, the Lion from the tribe of Judah, the Root of David, prevailed to open the book!

(6) *a Lamb standing, as if slain*: Revelation, with all its horrific symbols, also reveals beautiful yet mysterious imagery. John beholds the Lamb of God "as if slain." Even in glory, Jesus' earthly sacrifice has impacted heaven and earth for all eternity. Isaiah prophesied, "But the LORD was pleased to crush Him, putting Him to grief; if He would render Himself as a guilt offering, He will see His offspring, He will prolong His days, and the good pleasure of the LORD will prosper in His hand" (Isa 53:10). Therefore, it is essential for the Lamb to take the book from the Father's right hand (Rev 5:7), the hand of authority. Because the Lamb was obedient unto death, "God highly exalted Him, and bestowed on Him the name which is above every name, so that at the name of Jesus every knee will bow … in heaven and on earth and under the earth" (Phil 2:9–10). Since it is the Lamb that has prevailed to open the book, the Lamb becomes the most frequently used title for Jesus in Revelation, as it celebrates, commemorates, and memorializes Christ's efficacious sacrifice on Calvary's cross.

(a) *having seven horns and seven eyes, which are the seven Spirits of God, sent out into all the earth*: The horns are powerful earthly kingdoms (see Dan 7:20–25; 8:1–21). The seven horns are combined with seven eyes and symbolize "the seven Spirits [or "sevenfold Spirit"] of God, sent out into all the earth." In this text, these "eyes" and "Spirits" are symbols of the

Lord's omnipresence, omniscience, and omnipotence and are reminiscent of Zechariah's visions: "For behold the stone that I have laid before
Joshua; upon one stone shall be seven eyes.... They are the eyes of the
LORD, which run to and fro through the whole earth" (Zech 3:9; 4:10 KJV).
Zechariah and Revelation agree—absolutely nothing escapes the gaze
and sagacity of the Lord as He watches throughout the earth. From the
very beginning, the Spirit was in motion: "The earth was formless and
void, and darkness was over the surface of the deep, and the Spirit of God
was moving over the surface of the waters" (Gen 1:2).

(7) *And He came and took the book out of the right hand of Him who sat
on the throne*: The Lamb, whose atoning sacrifice is memorialized in
heaven through all eternity, approached Him who sits upon the throne
and "took the book" from the Father's "right hand," which represents
His power and authority.

(8) *the four living creatures and the twenty-four elders fell down before the
Lamb, each one holding a harp and golden bowls full of incense, which are
the prayers of the saints*: After the Lamb received the book, adoration and
worship followed. The living creatures and the twenty-four elders each
had a harp and golden bowls of incense, which represent "the prayers of
the saints." The psalmist declared, "May my prayer be set before you like
incense; may the lifting up of my hands be like the evening sacrifice"
(Ps 141:2 NIV). The prayers of the saints are a sweet aroma like incense.
Heaven's throne room is now filled with the sweet aroma of the fervent
and effectual prayers of the righteous (see Jas 5:16), which are perfected
by the Holy Spirit (see Rom 8:26). In this scene, they were presented by
the living creatures and the elders, which set forth an atmosphere of
praise before the throne.

(9) They used the *harps** as **they sang a new song**, which had a simple but
powerful lyric, **saying, "Worthy are You to take the book and to break its
seals; for You were slain, and purchased for God with Your blood men from
every tribe and tongue and people and nation"**: Indeed, the testimony of

the Lord was the inspiration for the "new song." Therefore, all who have been redeemed, spanning all humanity, from every tribe, tongue, people, and nation, have a testimony of redemption and a reason for why they sing unto the Lord "a new song" (Ps 149:1–5).

(10) *You have made them to be a kingdom and priests to our God; and they will reign upon the earth:* "A kingdom and priests" also implies a kingdom of priests who will reign on the earth during the millennial kingdom and in the new heaven and new earth in the world without end. However, in vv. 9–10, *textual variant**issues exist. In the KJV and NKJV, the translations read, "and have redeemed *us*," and v. 10, "and have made *us* kings . . . and *we* shall reign on the earth." However, newer translations are different. Verse 9 says, "and purchased for God with Your blood *men*" and v. 10: "you have made *them* . . . and *they* will reign." The NIV v. 9: "you purchased for God *persons*"; v. 10: "You have made *them* . . . and *they*." Those who base their interpretation on the KJV make the argument that the twenty-four elders are the raptured church because the textual variant "us" implies the twenty-four elders include themselves among the redeemed. However, newer translations do not translate the variant as "us" but in an impersonal way. This could mean that the elders were not including themselves as being among the redeemed and therefore opening the possibility to being angelic.[116]

---

[116] John F. Walvoord, "Revelation," in *The Bible Knowledge Commentary: An Exposition of the Scriptures*, eds. J. F. Walvoord and R. B. Zuck, vol. 2 (Wheaton, IL: Victor Books, 1985), 946.

REVELATION 5:11–13

Worthy Is the Lamb

[11] Then I looked, and I heard the voice of many angels around the throne and the living creatures and the elders; and the number of them was myriads of myriads, and thousands of thousands, [12] saying with a loud voice,

> "Worthy is the Lamb that was slain to receive power and riches and wisdom and might and honor and glory and blessing."

[13] And every created thing which is in heaven and on the earth and under the earth and on the sea, and all things in them, I heard saying,

> "To Him who sits on the throne, and to the Lamb, be blessing and honor and glory and dominion forever and ever."

(11–12) John *heard the voice of many angels around the throne* and the number of them was myriads *of myriads, and thousands of thousands, saying with a loud voice, "Worthy is the Lamb that was slain to receive power and riches and wisdom and might and honor and glory and blessing"*: Here the text indicates "the number of them" ("numbering," NIV) is beyond counting and therefore is generalized as "myriads [a very large number, not precisely defined[117]] of myriads, and thousands

---

[117] Bauer, *Greek-English Lexicon*, "myriads."

of thousands." This implies countless millions. Though the holy angels are not *redeemed* (a term that applies to redeemed humanity), they, too, joined in on the corporate praise to the Lord because He *is* worthy to receive power, riches, wisdom, might, honor, glory, and blessing.

(13) *And every created thing which is in heaven and on the earth and under the earth and on the sea, and all things in them, I heard saying, "To Him who sits on the throne, and to the Lamb, be blessing and honor and glory and dominion forever and ever":* This statement is powerful because whatever God created can give Him praise. Whether in heaven, earth, under the earth, or in the sea, all created things must give God the glory! Hence, the psalmist said, "Let every thing that hath breath praise the Lᴏʀᴅ" (Ps 150:6 KJV). However, when the Lamb broke the seven seals, the celebration in heaven gave way to judgment for those who dwelled upon the earth (see chaps. 6–18).

Introduction to the Seven Seals

In the previous chapter we were introduced to the book, or scroll, that was secured with seven seals. No one in heaven, on the earth, or under the earth was able to open or even gaze upon it. However, heaven rejoiced because the Lamb prevailed to open the book, which contains God's plan for the eschaton. Grant R. Osborne observes, "It is also important to realize that the scroll is not opened up until all seven seals are opened. Therefore, these are preliminary, and the contents of the scroll are concerned more with the trumpets, bowls, and ensuing events of chaps 17–20."[118] Another difficulty is the timing of the opening of these seals in relation to Daniel's Seventieth Week timeline. Some place the seals before Daniel's Seventieth Week, and some place the seals in the first half of the week. Still others disperse them in both halves of the week. Because of the varying views, these seals have been the source of much debate among scholars and students alike. "The Sixth Seal Problem" essay gives an alternative view on the placement of the seals regarding Daniel's Seventieth Week.

---

[118] Grant R. Osborne, *Baker Exegetical Commentary on the New Testament: Revelation* (Grand Rapids, MI: Baker Academic, 2002), 269.

✝

REVELATION 6:1–8

[1] Then I saw when the Lamb broke one of the seven seals, and I heard one of the four living creatures saying as with a voice of thunder, "Come." [2] I looked, and behold, a white horse, and he who sat on it had a bow; and a crown was given to him, and he went out conquering and to conquer. [3] When He broke the second seal, I heard the second living creature saying, "Come." [4] And another, a red horse, went out; and to him who sat on it, it was granted to take peace from the earth, and that men would slay one another; and a great sword was given to him.

[5] When He broke the third seal, I heard the third living creature saying, "Come." I looked, and behold, a black horse; and he who sat on it had a pair of scales in his hand. [6] And I heard something like a voice in the center of the four living creatures saying, "A quart of wheat for a denarius, and three quarts of barley for a denarius; and do not damage the oil and the wine."

[7] When the Lamb broke the fourth seal, I heard the voice of the fourth living creature saying, "Come." [8] I looked, and behold, an ashen horse; and he who sat on it had the name Death; and Hades was following with him. Authority was given to them over a fourth of the earth, to kill with sword and with famine and with pestilence and by the wild beasts of the earth.

(1) *Then I saw when the Lamb broke one of the seven seals, and I heard one of the four living creatures saying as with a voice of thunder, "Come":* Here the thunderous voice commanded the first rider to "come." In the KJV, it's "come and see," as if the living creature was speaking to John to *come look.* However, this is not how other versions translate it. The order to "come" is from the living creature to the rider on the white horse (see v. 2). Therefore, newer translations eliminate "and see." This living creature is probably the one that looked like the lion, which is the first living creature mentioned of the four. The second through the fourth seals were opened by the second through the fourth living creatures.

(2) *I looked, and behold, a white horse, and he who sat on it had a bow; and a crown was given to him, and he went out conquering and to conquer.* There are many interpretations of this passage, which is about the first seal being opened and the white horse and its rider being released. Some have said the person on the white horse is Christ. However, this is not tenable because Christ would not open the seal with the purpose of revealing Himself. Unmistakably, 19:11 shows Christ's second coming. Here in 6:2, Christ is not featured. Some see this as the victorious progress of the gospel. Others try to give the rider a precise historical identification, such as the Parthian king Vologases, who won a notable victory over the Romans in AD 62.[119] However, the most popular interpretation that most futurists agree on is that this is the Antichrist coming on the scene in his role as the peace advocate who signs the seven-year covenant at the beginning of Daniel's Seventieth Week.

EXCURSUS—THE RIDER ON THE WHITE HORSE

This author tentatively agrees with the rider on the white horse being related to the Antichrist but with the following reservations. The person who confirms the covenant at the beginning of the Seventieth

---

[119] Leon L. Morris, ed., *Tyndale New Testament Commentaries: Revelation* (Wheaton, IL: Tyndale House Publishers, 2018), , "the first seal."

Week (Dan 9:27) is widely accepted as being the Antichrist or the beast. However, if this is the emergence of the beast on the world stage, this presents a problem because there are two different arrivals, with two different symbolic descriptions. In Revelation 6:2 after the first seal is broken, he rides in on a white horse, wearing a single crown, wielding a bow. However, in 13:1–2, he rises from the sea and is described as a beast, with seven heads and ten horns wearing ten crowns, resembling a lion, a bear, and a leopard. This presents a significant contrast that must be reconciled. If his time starts at the beginning of the Seventieth Week, it will require him to have eighty-four months to rule, which is the number of months in seven years. However, this is untenable because the beast is only given forty-two months to reign (Dan 7:25; Rev 13:5). The Antichrist cannot assume his role before the appointed time (2 Thess 2:6 "In his time he will be revealed"). The starting point of the Antichrist's time as "the beast" (Rev 13), "the man of lawlessness" (2 Thess 2:3), and "the son of destruction" (2 Thess 2:3) is after he commits the "abomination of desolation" (Matt 24:15; 2 Thess 2:4), a middle-of-the-week event.

The Antichrist will undoubtedly be a charismatic, powerful leader who will have Satan's wickedly inspired wisdom to solve humanity's geopolitical problems. He will come in like a savior, fulfilling the meaning of his name ("antichrist" means "instead of Christ"). However, he is actually a pseudo-savior who will eventually turn on Israel, forsake the covenant, and demand to be worshiped as God. The thirteenth chapter describes him as the beast rising from the sea, by extension the abyss (Rev 11:7; 17:8), as opposed to riding in on a white horse. If 6:2 is about the Antichrist or the beast, it creates a reigning duration problem (eighty-four months as opposed to forty-two). Finally, what is the reason for the stark contrast in symbols and how he arrives onto the scene? The answer to these questions will be taken up in *The Beast from the Abyss Excursus*.

(3–4) *When He broke the second seal, I heard the second living creature saying, "Come." And another, a red horse, went out; and to him who sat on it, it was granted to take peace from the earth, and that men would* *slay one another; and a great sword was given to him:* After the Lamb opened the second seal, it was "the second living creature" ("the calf," or "the ox" [NIV], 4:7) who called forth the red horse and its rider. This red horse and rider were given permission "to take peace from the earth." Though the rider possessed "a great sword," he himself was not the one doing the killing. Verse 4 says, "Men [will] slay one another." Elsewhere, Scripture says people will be devoid of natural affection, "unloving" (2 Tim 3:3), and that "because lawlessness [will be] increased, most people's love will grow cold" (Matt 24:12) and people will resort to mercilessly killing each other. Though wars are inherently violent and deadly, something worse than war is meant here in Revelation. When peace is taken from the earth, every sphere of human involvement will be affected. There will be murder, social unrest, lawlessness, bigotry and hatred, crime, and corruption—all circumstances in which people kill each other. Families, communities, cities, states, countries, and ethnicities in all social economic strata will be affected. Today in the United States, there are over three hundred million guns owned by the citizenry, murder is a daily occurrence, and mass shootings occur too frequently. Imagine what it will be like when peace is taken from the earth.

(5–6) *When He broke the third seal, I heard the third living creature saying, "Come." I looked, and behold, a black horse; and he who sat on it had a pair of scales in his hand. And I heard something like a voice in the center of the four living creatures saying, "A quart of wheat for a denarius, and three quarts of barley for a denarius; and do not damage the oil and the wine":* The Lord broke the third seal, and then the third living creature (with "a face like that of a man," 4:7) called forth the "black horse; and he who sat on it had a pair of scales in his hand." This horse and rider represent famine and inflation. The color black emphasizes the dire situation, and the scales represent rationing of food. A quart of wheat, a more nutritious grain (approx. 1–2 pints), and barley, a less nutritious grain, could feed a small family. The denarius was "a Roman silver coin that was a worker's average daily wage."[120] The phrase "do not damage the oil and the wine" implies that the production of crops such as wheat and barley has been affected. The oil and wine "may mean that the necessities of life for the poor will be in short supply while the luxuries of the rich will not cease."[121] In other words, one substance group may be affected while the other is not. For example, during the Great Depression in the United States, many people were in food lines while others were not.

(7–8) *When the Lamb broke the fourth seal, I heard the voice of the fourth living creature saying, "Come." I looked, and behold, an ashen horse; and he who sat on it had the name Death; and Hades was following with him. Authority was given to them over a fourth of the earth, to kill with sword and with famine and with pestilence:* The Lamb broke the fourth seal, and the fourth living creature (which was "like a flying eagle," 4:7) said, "Come." This time the horse was an ashen color, which is "a greenish gray color of the color of a person in sickness"[122] or the color of a corpse. He who sat on this horse was named Death, and Hades (i.e., the abode of the dead) followed him. Unlike the other riders, Death had no instrument in hand (e.g., a bow, sword, or scales), but he had Hades, or hell, following him. Here, Death needed not an instrument but a repository for all the dead—a quarter of the earth's population. Death was responsible for killing with the sword, which primarily means war, but murder and deadly violence are applicable as well. Famines occur after war and also because of severe weather that produces floods and droughts. Pestilences, or diseases, could mean the resurgence of known diseases or completely new ones like COVID-19, which devastated the world from 2019 to 2022.

(a) *and by the wild beasts of the earth:* A source of human death could be *zoonotic diseases,** which come from animals and transfer to humans.

---

[120] Bauer, *Greek-English Lexicon*, s.v. "denarius."

[121] Morris, *Tyndale New Testament Commentaries*, "oil and wine."

[122] Bauer, *Greek-English Lexicon*, s.v. "ashen."

But this would be passive compared to what is described here. If the animal population turns on humankind, this would result in catastrophic death as implied here. Though there are some animals that have no fear of humans, most do. However, if God pulls back the animals' fear of humans, the most passive animals, let alone the ferocious types, will become deadly and cause many deaths, both on land and water.

The Transition

With the breaking of four seals accomplished, the remaining three seals mark a transition, as the last three are different. To review John's vision, the first seal brings the person believed to become the Antichrist, someone covered in a peaceful agenda. Seals two through four will release judgments on the earth. After the Lamb opens each seal, one of four living creatures, coinciding with the number of their seal, will call to the rider and the horse to "come." Next, in seals five, six, and seven, no living creature will order direct action, and there will be not judgments per se but visions in heaven and of the wrath of God under the bowl judgments. Ed Knorr observes,

> Woods puts forth the case that the fifth, sixth, and seventh seals are visionary statements that describe what will take place in the rest of the book of Revelation, that is, before Christ's Second Coming.... In other words, the fifth, sixth, and seventh seals are *not* point-in-time events that can be placed on a timeline since they more broadly describe what is going to take place in the second half of the Tribulation. Thus, we can think of them as being a big picture preview of what is to come.[123]

---

[123] Ed Knorr, *Revelation and Bible Prophecy—A Comparison of Eschatological Views: Dispensationalism and Preterism* (self-pub., updated October 4, 2024), 698–99, accessed September 8, 2024, https://www.cs.ubc.ca/~knorr/public/comparison_of_eschat_models.pdf

REVELATION 6:9–17

How Long O Lord?

[9] When the Lamb broke the fifth seal, I saw underneath the altar the souls of those who had been slain because of the word of God, and because of the testimony which they had maintained; [10] and they cried out with a loud voice, saying, "How long, O Lord, holy and true, will You refrain from judging and avenging our blood on those who dwell on the earth?" [11] And there was given to each of them a white robe; and they were told that they should rest for a little while longer, until the number of their fellow servants and their brethren who were to be killed even as they had been, would be completed also.

[12] I looked when He broke the sixth seal, and there was a great earthquake; and the sun became black as sackcloth made of hair, and the whole moon became like blood; [13] and the stars of the sky fell to the earth, as a fig tree casts its unripe figs when shaken by a great wind. [14] The sky was split apart like a scroll when it is rolled up, and every mountain and island were moved out of their places. [15] Then the kings of the earth and the great men and the commanders and the rich and the strong and every slave and free man hid themselves in the caves and among the rocks of the mountains; [16] and they said to the mountains and to the rocks, "Fall on us and hide us from the presence of Him who sits on the throne, and from the wrath of the Lamb; [17] for the great day of their wrath has come, and who is able to stand?"

(9) When the Lamb broke the fifth seal, I saw underneath the altar the souls of those who had been slain because of the word of God, and because of the testimony which they had maintained: This is a tremendous vision. Here there are no apocalyptic horsemen but the souls of the righteous who were martyred "because of the word of God, and because of the testimony which they had maintained." In 1:9, John identified himself as being "on the island called Patmos *because of the word of God and the testimony of Jesus*" (emphasis added). He didn't identify himself as being part of the body of Christ, the church, or as being in Christ, which are all Pauline terms. He identified himself as being a "partaker in the tribulation" (1:9), which is the universal struggle that all Christians face in one way or another as we live in a world where Satan is the "prince of the power of the air" (Eph 2:2). These souls in John's vision are in the place of sacrifice in heaven; however, they are not *on* the altar but *under* it because the Lamb of God is the ultimate sacrifice, not them. The souls "underneath the altar" belong to people who died on behalf of the Lord and whose service and sacrifice are held in great esteem because they fulfilled their divine appointments. They were so faithful that they loved God more than their own lives and were willing to die to give God the glory (see Rev 12:11; 13:7–10). Those who give their lives on behalf of the Lord are never forsaken in heaven. This has always been true of the faithful in this world. The psalmist said, "Precious in the sight of the Lord is the death of his saints" (Ps 116:15 KJV).

(10–11) and they cried out with a loud voice, saying, "How long, O Lord, holy and true, will You refrain from judging and avenging our blood on those who dwell on the earth?" And there was given to each of them a white robe; and they were told that they should rest for a little while longer, until the number of their fellow servants and their brethren who were to be killed even as they had been, would be completed also: The martyred saints made a key observation. They cried out to the Lord, "How long ... will You refrain from judging?" They were fully aware that God was holding back from unleashing His vengeance. The first four seals had already been opened, and they brought consequences on the earth, yet God was still holding back His personal wrath. The martyred saints wanted vengeance, and rightly so. However, "the day of vengeance of our God" (Isa 61:2) had not come yet. Therefore, each of the martyred saints was given a white robe to wear while they rested longer. White robes are part of the rewards the church receives in heaven (see Rev 3:4–5). Notice, the saints were not told that they were wrong for wanting vengeance, but they were told to wait until the complete number of those to be martyred, as they had been, was reached.

EXCURSUS—HOLDING BACK HIS VENGEANCE

God is holding back His vengeance (i.e., the wrath of God) because of His decision to wait until the full number of martyrs under the Antichrist is complete. There are several important things to understand that support His reason for doing this. (1) The dead in Christ will rise first (see 1 Cor 15:52; 1 Thess 4:16). Therefore, the complete number of dead has to be reached before the resurrection can occur. (2) Since the church is not appointed to wrath (see 1 Thess 5:9), the resurrection/rapture must occur before the day of God's vengeance comes, as depicted in Revelation 16. (3) Once the full number of the Revelation 13 saints are martyred, then the resurrection/rapture can occur. And, after the saints are off the earth, God's wrath can commence. This theme is demonstrated throughout Revelation. God's undiluted wrath is poured out in chapters 16–18 and culminates with the return of the Lord with His saints in 19:11–21. Since the Lord returns with the church, the full number of dead and the last living saint of the church age must be reached before all can be translated in the rapture.

(12–14) *I looked when He broke the sixth seal, and there was a great earthquake; and the sun became black as sackcloth made of hair, and the whole moon became like blood; and the stars of the sky fell to the earth, as a fig tree casts its unripe figs when shaken by a great wind. The sky was split apart like a scroll when it is rolled up, and every mountain and island were moved out of their places:* When the Lamb breaks the sixth seal, we notice some very significant events: "There was a great earthquake ... the sun became black as sackcloth made of hair ... the whole moon became like blood ... the stars of the sky fell to the earth.... The sky was split apart ... and every mountain and island were moved out of their places." Unfortunately, dispensational scholars and commentators have steered in the wrong direction in understanding these events. The fifth, sixth, and seventh seals are visions, not point-of-action judgments, and therefore should not be on the Seventieth Week timeline. The "great earthquake" and cosmic disturbances are key to understanding this because these events actually occur during the sixth and seventh bowl judgments (see 16:13–21) and are not point-in-time actions fulfilled here. (See "The Sixth Seal Problem" essay.)

Starting with the cosmic disturbances, these signs occur before the day of the Lord comes. Joel records:

> It will come about after this that I will pour out My Spirit on all mankind; and your sons and daughters will prophesy, your old men will dream dreams, your young men will see visions. Even on the male and female servants I will pour out My Spirit in those days. I will display wonders in the sky and on the earth, blood, fire and columns of smoke. *The sun will be turned into darkness and the moon into blood before the great and awesome day of the* LORD *comes.* (Joel 2:28–31, emphasis added)

During Peter's sermon on the day of Pentecost, he repeated Joel's prophecy:

> And I will grant wonders in the sky above and signs on the earth below, blood, and fire, and vapor of smoke. *The sun will be turned into darkness and the moon into blood, before the great and glorious day of the Lord shall come.* (Acts 2:19–20, emphasis added)

Isaiah records:

> Behold, *the day of the* LORD *is coming*, cruel, with fury and
> burning anger, to make the land a desolation; and He will
> exterminate its sinners from it. *For the stars of heaven and their*
> *constellations will not flash forth their light; the sun will be dark*
> *when it rises and the moon will not shed its light.* (Isa 13:9–10,
> emphasis added)

Also see Zephaniah 1:14–18 and Zechariah 14:1–7. Matthew records:

> But immediately after the tribulation of those days *the sun*
> *will be darkened, and the moon will not give its light, and the stars*
> *will fall from the sky*, and the powers of the heavens will be
> shaken. (Matt 24:29, emphasis added)

EXCURSUS—THE COSMIC DISTURBANCES

These cosmic disturbances occur after the abomination of desolation is
in place but before the day of the Lord comes. Matthew lists these events:
"the abomination of desolation" (24:15), followed by "a great tribulation"
(24:21), followed by the cosmic disturbances (see 24:29), then "the sign
of the Son of Man will appear" (24:30), "all the tribes of the earth will
mourn" (24:30), and the Son of Man will come "with power and great
glory" (see 24:30).

The day of the Lord should be understood in two ways. First, it's the time
period of God's divine wrath poured out on the world. Exactly how long
this period will last is unknown, but it must occur near the end of the
second half of Daniel's Seventieth Week. Some point to Isaiah 34:8 and
63:4 to argue that it is a year of vengeance and retribution. Second, the
day of the Lord is the climactic day when the Lord returns to the earth
with His invading army (see Rev 19:14). The OT says, "And the LORD my
God shall come, and all the saints ["holy ones," NASB] with thee" (Zech
14:5c KJV). So, the day of the Lord is a period that concludes on a specific

day. The day of the Lord concepts encapsulate the wrath of God. (Also see Zeph 1:14–18 and Zech 14:1–7.)

The Stars Fell from the Sky

Matthew records in 24:29,

> But immediately after the tribulation of those days *the sun will be darkened, and the moon will not give its light,* **and the stars will fall from the sky,** and the powers of the heavens will be shaken. (emphasis added)

The reference to the stars falling from the sky, also found in Revelation 6:13, may not be hyperbolic but phenomenological (how things appear to the eye). Stars like our sun could not fall to the earth because they are so much more massive than the earth. Over one million earths could fit inside our sun. Therefore, it is not possible that the sun, only an average size star, could fall to the earth. However, in the twenty-first century, we have advancements in military weaponry and technology that the OT prophets and John in the first century could not have comprehended or explained. For example, on April 14, 2024, in an unprecedented retaliatory attack, Iran launched hundreds of drones, rockets, and missiles at Israel. International news agencies captured the images of these incoming missiles that appeared as shooting stars falling to the earth from the night sky. It must be considered that the possibility of future battles deploying high-tech weaponry could account for what the prophets could only explain figuratively. In the twenty-first century and forward, high-tech weaponry is a fact of life and will certainly be used on a greater scale in battles like Armageddon than they were on Israel.

The Sky Rolled Away

The sky was split apart like a scroll when it is rolled up . . . (6:14). John's description could be that of nuclear explosions. When a nuclear or hydrogen bomb explodes, it releases massive amounts of energy. The hotter air in the fireball and the shock wave create tremendous atmospheric pressure that pushes away the clouds in a rolling-back manner. This *could be* what John describes as "the sky was split apart like a scroll when it is rolled up." Only since the twentieth century has humankind possessed the weaponry to create this phenomenon.

The prophet Joel gives additional information concerning the day of the Lord, but he describes "fire and columns of smoke" (Joel 2:30). The KJV states, "Fire and pillars of smoke." This description is interesting because smoke rising in a column or pillar occurs during massive explosions, particularly nuclear. On the Day of Pentecost, when Peter quotes Joel's prophecy, he also refers to "fire and vapor of smoke" (Acts 2:19, NASB; "vapour," KJV). Regarding "fire," one of the main features of an atomic explosion is the intense flash that is hotter than the sun and the massive radioactive fireball. Depending on the yield of the bomb, everything for miles would be incinerated. After the flash and fireball, a tremendous shock wave interacts with moist air in the atmosphere, creating a vapor-like dome called the Wilson Cloud. This shock wave flattens everything standing including buildings, towers, and houses. A firestorm immediately ensues from the blast's effects and secondary explosions. The mushroom cloud rises three to five miles, creating a great vacuum that pulls smoke upward, forming the ominous "column or pillar of smoke."

In conclusion, it cannot be ruled out that these events are exclusively divine (see Zech 14:12). Or it could be a combination of the divine and events caused by humans as alluded to in Revelation 11:18: "Destroy those who destroy the earth." Though speculative, the suggestions offered here at least account for technology and weaponry used in the twentieth century and forward that did not exist in the first century, but more than likely will be used in wars in the future.

(15–16) *Then the kings of the earth and the great men and the commanders and the rich and the strong and every slave and free man hid themselves in the caves and among the rocks of the mountains; and they said to the mountains and to the rocks, "Fall on us and hide us from the presence of*

Him who sits on the throne: The inhabitants of the earth—rich, poor, influential, famous, and everyday people—will all be terrified as waves of the wrath of God are poured out on the world. They will cry out to the mountains and the rocks, "Fall on us and hide us from the presence of Him who sits on the throne, and from the wrath of the Lamb." This is exactly what the Lord prophesied when He was led away to be crucified (see Luke 23:30). This is also reminiscent of what was declared in Hosea 10:8, but the most interesting account is found in Isaiah:

> Men will go into caves of the rocks and into holes of the ground before the terror of the Lord and the splendor of His majesty, when He arises to make the earth tremble. In that day men will cast away to the moles and the bats their idols of silver and their idols of gold, which they made for themselves to worship. (2:19–20)

This is an example of how pitiful people will be. They are forced to come to grips with how worthless their false gods and religions are. So, they cast their idols to the moles and bats, in the very caves and holes they attempt to hide from the Lord.

But like the psalmist declared,

> Why are the nations in an uproar and the peoples devising a vain thing? The kings of the earth take their stand and the rulers take counsel together against the Lord and against His Anointed, saying, "Let us tear their fetters apart and cast away their cords from us!" He who sits in the heavens laughs, the Lord scoffs at them. (Ps 2:1–4)

The fact that the mighty and the arrogant think they can hide from the Lord, who made the earth, is absolutely ridiculous! Caves can be natural rock formations or they can be excavated by governments and militaries of the world, who dig deep bunkers into the mountains so they can survive a nuclear attack. But these places will be no match for the Lord, who will send an earthquake so great that it will knock down the very mountains where people hide. Remember, the events under this seal are visions of events that will occur under the bowl judgments of Revelation 16, specifically the battle of Armageddon and the great earthquake (see 16:13–20).

(16–17) *and from the wrath of the Lamb; for the great day of their wrath has come, and who is able to stand?* The wrath of "Him who sits on the throne" (v. 16) and "the wrath of the Lamb" confirms duality to wrath. It is the Lamb who "treads the wine press of the fierce wrath of God" (19:15). It is the Lamb of God who was brutally disfigured after being scourged and spit on and who had a crown of thorns pressed into His head. He was paraded through the city and mocked by Gentiles and the Jews while being forced to bear His cross on the way to Golgotha. He was shamefully disrobed and nailed to a cross by having His hands and feet pierced. The cross was then raised and dropped into a narrow hole so it could stand vertically. The Lord was left to die in agony for hours. When considering these brutalities and all the suffering borne by the people of God throughout history, it is fitting that judgment comes from "the wrath of the Lamb" (v. 16) on the day of vengeance. The verse-by-verse commentary continues on page 147.

ESSAY:
THE SIXTH SEAL PROBLEM

The fifth, sixth, and seventh seals are different from the first four seals because they are not point-in-time judgments but are of a visionary nature. Regarding the sixth seal, many commentators and students of eschatology see this seal as an explicit marker for the wrath of God. As stated in 6:17, "For the great day of their wrath has come, and who is able to stand?" Yes, the sixth seal shows the wrath of the Lamb, but there is more to consider than what meets the eye. Is this where the wrath of God begins? Or is this a vision of wrath that is executed later during the bowl judgments? In this essay, we will answer this question and identify the problem with placing the fifth, sixth, and seventh seals on the Seventieth Week timeline.

> I looked when He broke the sixth seal, and *there was a great earthquake; and the sun became black as sackcloth made of hair, and the whole moon became like blood*; and the stars of the sky fell to the earth, as a fig tree casts its unripe figs when shaken by a great wind. The sky was split apart like a scroll when it is rolled up, and *every mountain and island were moved out of their places.* Then the kings of the earth and the great men and the commanders and the rich and the strong and every slave and free man hid themselves in the caves and among the rocks of the mountains; and they said to the mountains and to the rocks, "Fall on us and hide us from the presence of Him who sits on the throne, and from the wrath of the

Lamb; for the great day of their wrath has come, and who is able to stand?" (Rev 6:12–17, emphasis added)

Concerning the sixth seal, MacArthur observes:

> Unlike the first five seals, each of which involved humans in one way or another (the four horsemen and the saints under the altar), in *the sixth seal* God acts alone. *By the time this seal is opened, the midpoint of the Tribulation has passed* and the world is in the final three-and-one-half-year period known as the "great tribulation." By then the final Antichrist has desecrated the temple in Jerusalem (the "abomination of desolation"), the world worships him, and a massive persecution of Jews and Christians has broken out.[124] (emphasis added)

MacArthur states that the sixth seal is past the midpoint and the world is in the final half of the Seventieth Week, after the abomination of desolation is in place and persecution of Jews and Christians has broken out.

	Sixth Seal
The 70th Week 1st half (3.5 years)	

Walvoord asserts,

> Because the events of chapter 6 and afterward seem to coincide with the Great Tribulation rather than with the time of peace in the first half of the seven years (1 Thes. 5:3), there are good reasons for concluding that these great events are compacted in the last three and one-half years before Christ's return to the earth. Certainly at least by the fourth seal.[125]

---

[124]   *The MacArthur New Testament Commentary: Revelation 1–11*, 203.
[125]   Walvoord and Zuck, *The Bible Knowledge Commentary*, 947.

135

Walvoord states that the seals, trumpets, and bowls are all "compacted in the last three and one-half years" as shown below:

Time of peace	the seals, trumpets, and bowls
First half (3.5 years)	Last half (3.5 years) the 70th Week,

Wiersbe breaks these events into three sections, with the first three and a half years containing the events in chapters 6–9.

> By referring to John's outline (Rev. 1), you will see that his description is in three parts: the first three and a half years (Rev. 6–9), the events at the middle of the period (Rev. 10–14), and the last three and a half years (Rev. 15–19).[126]

The Seals, Trumpets 1–6 (chaps. 6–9),	7th trumpet (chaps. 10–14)	The Bowls and Return (chaps. 15–19)
The 70th Week 1st Half (3.5 years)		Last half (3.5 years)

Finally, Knorr states that James Kaddis and Don Stewart think the first four seal judgments (the four horsemen of the Apocalypse) take place *before* the tribulation starts.[127]

Seals 1–4		
	70th Week 1st half (3.5 years)	2nd half (3.5 years)

Once again, in this small sampling of commentators there are varying opinions. As is the case with most of Revelation, *there is no consensus.*

---

[126] Warren W. Wiersbe, *The Bible Exposition Commentary*, vol. 2 (Wheaton, IL: Victor Books, 1996), 587.

[127] Knorr, *Revelation and Bible Prophecy*, 702.

The Cosmic Disturbances

According to MacArthur's position, the sixth seal is in the last half of the Seventieth Week. I agree with MacArthur. If the sixth seal is on the Seventieth Week timeline, this is where it must go. Why? Because at the opening of this seal we observe the cosmic disturbances of "the sun [becoming] black as sackcloth made of hair, and the whole moon [becoming] like blood" (6:12). To give us perspective on where these cosmic disturbances must be placed in relation to the Seventieth Week, the prophet Joel declared,

> I will display wonders in the sky and on the earth, blood, fire and columns of smoke. *The sun will be turned into darkness and the moon into blood before* the great and awesome day of the LORD comes. (Joel 2:30–31, emphasis added; see also Acts 2:19–20)

It is important to understand that these cosmic disturbances occur *before* the day of the Lord comes. The prophet Isaiah also associated the cosmic disturbances with the time period of God's wrath, not just the actual day the Lord returns:

> See, the day of the LORD is coming—a cruel day, with wrath and fierce anger— to make the land desolate and destroy the sinners within it. *The stars of heaven and their constellations will not show their light. The rising sun will be darkened and the moon will not give its light.* I will punish the world for its evil, the wicked for their sins. I will put an end to the arrogance of the haughty and will humble the pride of the ruthless.... *Therefore I will make the heavens tremble; and the earth will shake from its place at the wrath of the LORD Almighty, in the day of his burning anger.* (Isa 13:9–11, 13 NIV, emphasis added)

Isaiah 13:11 states, "I will punish the world for its evil, the wicked for their sins. I will put an end to the arrogance of the haughty and will humble the pride of the ruthless" (NIV). These events occur during the bowl judgments of Revelation 16. By this time, the Antichrist will have already committed the abomination of desolation and the persecution of the Jews and Christians, events that are detailed in Revelation 13–15. At some point after the persecution but before the bowl judgments commence, "the sun [will become] black as sackcloth made of hair, and the whole moon [will become] like blood" (6:12). These cosmic signs occur "*before* the great and awesome day of the LORD comes" (Joel 2:31, emphasis added; see also Acts 2:20).

THE MOUNT OLIVET DISCOURSE

Jesus described the events that will occur after the abomination of desolation is in place:

> Therefore when you see the abomination of desolation which was spoken of through Daniel the prophet, standing in the holy place (let the reader understand), then those who are in Judea must flee to the mountains. Whoever is on the housetop must not go down to get the things out that are in his house. Whoever is in the field must not turn back to get his cloak. But woe to those who are pregnant and to those who are nursing babies in those days! But pray that your flight will not be in the winter, or on a Sabbath. For then there will be a great tribulation, such as has not occurred since the beginning of the world until now, nor ever will. (Matt 24:15–21)

Verses 15–21 describe the events that usher in the great tribulation—the time "such as has not occurred since the beginning of the world until now, nor ever will." This is the same period (i.e., the great tribulation) that the "great multitude" comes out of (Rev 7:9, 14). The Lord commented on this time in Matthew 24:22–28. However, in verse 29, the Lord declared:

But immediately after the tribulation of those days *the sun will be darkened, and the moon will not give its light,* and the stars will fall from the sky, and the powers of the heavens will be shaken. (emphasis added)

Jesus identified the cosmic disturbances as occurring after the abomination of desolation is in place, the persecution and fleeing from Jerusalem have happened, and all the calamities that will follow have occurred. Many, particularly Posttribulationists, interpret the phrase "immediately after the tribulation of those days" (v. 29) to mean after the end of Daniel's Seventieth Week. However, Jesus is pointing to immediately after the persecution that occurs once the beast (i.e., the Antichrist) comes to power, which is described in verses 16–28, as being the time when God will pour out His wrath in response to all the wickedness. This is when the cosmic disturbances will appear, right before the day of the Lord (i.e., the day of wrath) comes (see Acts 2:20).

Since we have identified where the cosmic disturbances will occur, we can better understand the sixth seal. It is under this seal that we see these cosmic signs. MacArthur and many others, including those in the Prewrath camp, place the sixth seal in the second half of the Seventieth Week because the cosmic disturbances occur after the abomination of desolation is in place.

The Two Witnesses

The two witnesses mentioned in Revelation 11 help solve the sixth-seal problem. As we explain in "The Two Witnesses Must Be in the First Half of the Seventieth Week" excursus, the first half of Daniel's Seventieth Week is where the two witnesses should be placed, for several reasons. After they are killed, raised from the dead, and ascend into heaven, something important occurs, and what the next verse states is critical.

THE SIXTH SEAL PROBLEM

> And they heard a loud voice from heaven saying to them, "Come up here." Then they went up into heaven in the cloud, and their enemies watched them.... *The second woe is past; behold, the third woe is coming quickly.* (11:12, 14, emphasis added)

After the two witnesses are raised, we are informed that "the second woe is past." The second woe is the sixth trumpet. Therefore, wherever on the timeline you place the resurrection of the two witnesses, the sixth trumpet has already sounded and the seventh trumpet follows. Since the two witnesses are in the first half of the Seventieth Week, the preceding five trumpets and the seals have already occurred before the middle of the week.

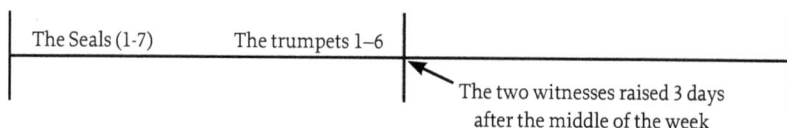

The Seals (1-7)	The trumpets 1–6	

The two witnesses raised 3 days
after the middle of the week

An alternate scenario exists. If the two witnesses are in the second half, then they will be raised three days into the millennium, because their 1,260-day ministry (three and a half years) would span the entire last half of the Seventieth Week. Armageddon is the last conflict of the Seventieth Week when the Lord returns to defeat the Antichrist and his army. After the Lord returns, His millennial reign begins. However, if the two witnesses are inserted into the second half, they would have to be killed at the very end of the Seventieth Week and then raised three days later. Those three days put their resurrection and ascension three days after the end of the Seventieth Week and three days into the Lord's millennial reign because the millennium starts after the Seventieth Week is completed.

After the two witnesses are raised, the second woe (the sixth trumpet) has already passed and the seventh trumpet follows. This causes a bigger problem because the seventh trumpet and the seven bowl judgments would have to occur after the Seventieth Week has concluded because the two witnesses' time lasts for the entire second half of the Seventieth Week. If the bowl judgments are extended beyond the Seventieth Week, the beast's time must also be extended because he is still in power during the bowl judgments. This would necessitate that the beast remain in power beyond the Seventieth Week and beyond his allotted forty-two months (13:5). This makes the placement of the two witnesses in the last half of the Seventieth Week untenable. They must be in the first half. By the time the witnesses are raised, we are between the sixth and seventh trumpet, which means all the preceding seals have already been opened.

The events that are revealed in the sixth seal—the sun turning to darkness and the moon turning into blood—will occur right before the day of the Lord comes (Joel 2:31; Acts 2:20). The day of the Lord cannot come before the abomination of desolation is in place, which doesn't occur until the middle of the week (Dan 9:27). Paul explicitly declared,

> Let no one in any way deceive you, for it [i.e., the day of the Lord] will not come unless the apostasy comes first, and the man of lawlessness is revealed, the son of destruction, who opposes and exalts himself above every so-called god or object of worship, so that he takes his seat in the temple of God, displaying himself as being God. (2 Thess 2:3–4)

Here Scripture teaches that the day of the Lord cannot come until the Antichrist (i.e., the beast) is revealed. To further amplify what is meant by his revealing, Paul described the abomination of desolation, which is when the Antichrist will walk into the temple and declare himself to be God. This will occur in the middle of the Seventieth Week. The "revealing" (Gk. *apkalupto*), which is "a verb . . . with the exclusive meaning 'reveal' in the sense of 'uncovering, or laying open what has previously been hidden,'"[128] cannot be in connection with the signing of the covenant (Dan 9:27) because the Antichrist is not the beast of Revelation at that point. Since the beast only has forty-two months and not eighty-four months, he cannot be revealed at the beginning of the Seventieth Week.

The beast can only be revealed (or uncovered) "in his time" (2 Thess 2:6). The beast is seen rising from the sea, by extension the abyss, in Revelation 13:1 and 17:8 (see "The Threefold Reality of the Beast"). Paul was explicitly teaching that the day of the Lord cannot happen until the man of lawlessness walks into the temple of God and declares himself to be God. The man who eventually becomes the beast does not commit the abomination of desolation at the beginning of the Seventieth Week. He cannot be uncovered (or revealed) until the point that the abomination occurs.

Another important point to consider is that Jesus did not refer to any pre-abomination-of-desolation events, such as the signing of the covenant or temple construction, as the defining event for the day of the Lord to occur. He didn't say, "When the covenant is signed," or "When you see the temple being built," or even "When you see the man of peace arrive." Instead, He said the defining sign for the great tribulation and the day of the Lord is "when you see the abomination of desolation … standing in the holy place" (Matt 24:15; see also 2 Thess 2:3–4).

THE SEQUENCE OF EVENTS

(1) The two witnesses are killed at the middle of the week.

(2) After the two witnesses have been raised from the dead (1,263 days after they began prophesying), the second woe (i.e., the sixth trumpet) has already passed (see 11:14), with the seventh trumpet (i.e., the third woe) following quickly.

---

[128] Stephen D. Renn, ed., *Expository Dictionary of Bible Words: Word Studies for Key English Bible Words Based on the Hebrew and Greek Texts* (Peabody, MA: Hendrickson Publishers, 2005), 820.

(3) Since the sixth trumpet happens near the middle of the week, that means all seven seals and five of the trumpets must occur in the first half of Daniel's Seventieth Week. This means the sixth seal cannot be placed after the abomination of desolation, which is where many scholars place it (e.g., MacArthur).

A. The day of the Lord is the wrath of God (see Isa 13:9–13; Zeph 1:14–18).
B. The day of the Lord happens after the abomination of desolation occurs (see Dan 9:27; Matt 24:15; 2 Thess 2:1–4).
C. Before the day of the Lord arrives the cosmic disturbances occur (see Joel 2:28–31; Matt 24:29; Acts 2:17–20).
D. The seven seals occur before the seven trumpets.
E. The sixth trumpet, or the second woe, has already passed by the time the two witnesses are resurrected (see Rev 11:14).
F. The two witnesses cannot be in the second half because the third woe (i.e., the seventh trumpet) would be forced to happen after the end of the Seventieth Week. This would place all the bowl judgments, including the battle of Armageddon, beyond the end of Daniel's Seventieth Week. The Lord returns at the end of the Seventieth Week, and at that point the beast is captured and thrown into the lake of fire at the end of his forty-two months (see 19:20–21). If the bowl judgments and Armageddon occur beyond the Seventieth Week, then this keeps the beast in power past his forty-two-month allotment. Again, this is not tenable.
G. Scripture places the cosmic disturbances in the second half, after the abomination of desolation and right before the day of the Lord comes.
H. The seventy weeks has six program points that will be accomplished in a 490-year time frame: "To finish the transgression, to make an end of sin, to make atonement for iniquity, to bring in everlasting righteousness, to seal up vision and prophecy

and to anoint the most holy place" (Dan 9:24). These six points are to be completed within the seventy weeks, in particular, the last seven years. Christ will usher in everlasting righteousness when He returns at the end of the Seventieth Week. The vision and prophecy will be sealed up, signifying "that these forms of revelation [will] be closed . . . by bringing about [their] complete fulfillment."[129] Placing the sixth seal in the second half of the Seventieth Week forces the bowl judgments, particularly Armageddon, and Christ's return beyond the end of the Seventieth Week, as suggested by some in the Prewrath camp.

I. Therefore, the sixth seal should not be assigned a position on the Seventieth Week timeline because it represents visions of events that happen past the middle point and *are not* being executed when the sixth seal opens. Likewise, the fifth and seventh seals are visions, not points of execution.

---

[129] Stephen R. Miller, *The New American Commentary*, vol. 18, *Daniel* (Nashville: Broadman & Holman Publishers, 1994), 261.

The Lord Returns

Day of the Lord — The Wrath of God — The Bowl Judgments Rev 16:1-21

For representations purpose only, not to scale

Abomination of Desolation — Middle of the 70th Week

Cosmic disturbances: appear before the bowl judgments begin

The cosmic disturbances belong here, but NOT the 6th seal

3rd Woe (7) — The bowl judgments follow

— 42 Months Antichrist Reigns —

1st Woe (5)   2nd Woe (6)

6th seal shows the cosmic disturbances and the Wrath of God occuring in the 2nd half

— Two Witnesses 1260 days (42 Months) are killed here. —

Seals 5-7 are visions NOT timeline events but follow in sequence after seals 1-4

White Horse Red Horse Pale Horse Black Horse

70th week timeline seal events

The two witnesses are key to where the 6th seal is placed on the 70th week timeline. If the witnesses are placed in the 2nd half, they would have to live out their 1260 days which takes up the entire span of the 2nd half, placing their resurrection, the 7th trumpet, the bowls, and the return of the Lord, beyond the end of the 70th week. This is not tenable. However, after their death and resurrection, Rev 11:14 states the 2nd woe or the 6th trumpet has passed (Rev 11:14). Wherever the death of the two witnesses is placed, it's between the 6th and 7th trumpet. If the two witnesses are in the 1st half, their death would be close to the middle of the 70th week, after the 6th trumpet has already passed, and the 7th trumpet and the bowl judgments follow. Therefore, if the 6th trumpet has passed by the mid-point, all the preceding seals have already been opened. For this reason, the 6th seal cannot be in the second half. However, the cosmic disturbances featured in the 6th seal, occur before the day of the Lord / wrath of God comes (Joel 2:33), a second half event. Therefore the 6th seal reveals events fulfilled in the 2nd half under the wrath of the bowl judgments.

-- **Seals 5 through 7** are visions, not events that can be assigned to specific points on the 70th week timeline.

(a) The **5th seal** is a vision showing martyred souls under the altar, in heaven (Rev 6:9-11).

(b) The **6th seal** shows the **cosmic disturbances (Matt 24:29; Rev 6:12-14)** that appear after the middle of the week but **prior** to the coming of the **day of the Lord** (Acts 2:20; Joel 2:31). It also shows events that occur under the **bowl judgments** (i.e.. **the great earthquake, Armageddon** (Rev 16:13, 20).

(c) The **7th seal** reveals action that occurs in heaven introducing the seven trumpets.

By: Dennis James Woods © 2024

Undoubtedly, these events in the sixth seal occur on the day of the Lord after the middle of the Seventieth Week. This is why many place the sixth seal in the last half of the Seventieth Week. However, placing the sixth seal in the last half is exactly what's causing the problem. The problem of the sixth seal is solved by *not* placing it on the Seventieth Week timeline. Yes, the fifth, sixth, and seventh seals are opened sequentially, but scholars should not assign them a position on the Seventieth Week timeline because the fifth through seventh seals are not specific timeline events but visions. Specifically, the sixth seal contains visions of events that occur further along on the Seventieth Week timeline during the bowl judgments.

The Interlude

Before the seventh seal is opened, there is an interlude, or a parenthesis, that takes up chapter 7 in its entirety. As some commentators assert, "These interludes employ the ancient rhetorical model of a 'digression,' presenting material that is set apart from—and even sometimes more urgent than—the body of the narrative."[130] Many hold to the assertion that John was merely inserting a digression here. Whereas this may be possible, it's not probable because John was not in control of the narrative. Revelation is not a result of John's literary discretion, where he inserted interludes as he pleased. At the very beginning of Revelation, John heard a voice that said, "Write in a book what you see" (1:11). Then at the end of Revelation, the Lord warned not to add to the book or take from it (see 22:18–19). Therefore, the digression cited here is divine, not John's, and includes events that transpire not sequentially between the sixth and seventh seals but occur beyond this interlude. For example, *the great multitude* shown in 7:9-17 comes out of *the great tribulation* which occurred during the reign of the beast in chapters 13 through 16.

---

130   Margaret Aymer, Cynthia Briggs Kittredge, and David A. Sánchez, eds., "The First Interlude: The People of God," in *The New Testament Fortress Commentary on the Bible* (Minneapolis: Fortress Press, 2014), 737.

REVELATION 7:1–8

The Sealing of the 144,000

 After this I saw four angels standing at the four corners of the earth, holding back the four winds of the earth, so that no wind would blow on the earth or on the sea or on any tree. [2] And I saw another angel ascending from the rising of the sun, having the seal of the living God; and he cried out with a loud voice to the four angels to whom it was granted to harm the earth and the sea, [3] saying, "Do not harm the earth or the sea or the trees until we have sealed the bond-servants of our God on their foreheads."

[4] And I heard the number of those who were sealed, one hundred and forty-four thousand sealed from every tribe of the sons of Israel:

[5] from the tribe of Judah, twelve thousand *were* sealed, from the tribe of Reuben twelve thousand, from the tribe of Gad twelve thousand, [6] from the tribe of Asher twelve thousand, from the tribe of Naphtali twelve thousand, from the tribe of Manasseh twelve thousand, [7] from the tribe of Simeon twelve thousand, from the tribe of Levi twelve thousand, from the tribe of Issachar twelve thousand, [8] from the tribe of Zebulun twelve thousand, from the tribe of Joseph twelve thousand, from the tribe of Benjamin, twelve thousand were sealed.

(1) *After this I saw four angels standing at the four corners of the earth:*
Today, there are those who hold to a flat earth theory. Some support

this erroneous theory with a literal interpretation of this verse. Others suggest "the four corners" are the four points on the compass.

(a) *holding back the four winds of the earth*: The four angels are "holding back" (Gk. *krateō*). This means "to control in such a way that something does not happen, hold back or restrain from, hinder."[131]

(b) *the four winds of the earth, so that no wind would blow on the earth or on the sea or on any tree*: One of the important tasks that angels perform is being restrainers. An explicit example of this is given here. Some people have suggested that the "four winds," or four spirits, are the same as the four horsemen of chapter 6. They base this on Zechariah's vision of the four horsemen and chariots that go out to the "four winds" (ESV) or "four spirits" (NASB) of heaven (Zech 6:1–8). Whether natural or spiritual wind, the purpose of holding them back is so the wind does not have any adverse effect on "the sea or on any tree." This was an angelic duty.

(2) *And I saw another angel ascending from the rising of the sun, having the seal of the living God; and he cried out with a loud voice to the four angels to whom it was granted to harm the earth and the sea*: The angel ascends "from the rising sun," which could mean "from the east," and has the "seal of the living God." The Greek word used here for "seal" is *sphragis* and is the same word for the seven "seals" of Revelation 6. However, here its meaning is "the instrument used for sealing or stamping, against the power of demons."[132] Seals are symbols of ownership and security. Christians are "sealed for the day of redemption" (Eph 4:30) and "protected by the power of God" (1 Pet 1:5). Paul affirmed this in the following passage: "Nevertheless, the firm foundation of God stands, *having this seal*, 'The Lord knows those who are His'" (2 Tim 2:19, emphasis added). The purposes of a seal are to mark ownership and provide protection.

---

131   Bauer, *Greek-English Lexicon*, s.v. *krateō*.

132   Bauer, s.v. *sphragis*.

(3) *until we have sealed the bond-servants of our God on their foreheads:*
The demons are aware that Christians belong to Christ; therefore, by
Christians being sealed, they will not be harmed (see Rev 9:4). Among
the Christians who are already sealed now will be the one hundred forty-four thousand Jewish converts who will also be sealed. Historically,
there have always been Jewish converts to Christianity. Today they are
referred to as messianic Jews, meaning those Jews who believe that Jesus
is the Messiah.

(4–8) *And I heard the number of those who were sealed, one hundred and
forty-four thousand sealed from every tribe of the sons of Israel:* The "one
hundred and forty-four thousand" have been the subject of debate for
centuries. Some have seen this group as a spiritual representation of
the church, and the number is wholly symbolic. Others have stated that
these are Jews who converted to Christianity. Jehovah's Witnesses have
claimed that only their members will be saved and "only a little flock
of 144,000 [will] go to heaven and rule with Christ."[133] This erroneous
position is refuted by the fact that no one group can claim exclusivity
to salvation. John saw an innumerable multitude from all nations in
heaven (see 7:9) and said they would reign with Christ (see 20:4). The
144,000 are Israelites from their respective twelve tribes.

Another popular narrative is from the dispensational/Pretrib perspective, which claims the 144,000 are Jewish evangelists who preach to the
world during the tribulation.[134] Though this assertion cannot be ruled
out, there are no Scriptures in Revelation that state as such. Nothing is
said about them being evangelists, preaching the gospel, winning souls
to Christ, or conducting any other evangelistic efforts. This is a wholly
speculative narrative that is used to explain how t*he innumerable multitude** (see 7:9) comes to faith in the absence of the church, who by this

---

[133]   Walter Martin, "Jehovah's Witnesses and the Watch Tower Bible and Tract Society," in *The
Kingdom of the Cults*, ed. Ravi Zacharias (Minneapolis: Bethany House Publishers, 2003), 107.

[134]   MacArthur, *The MacArthur New Testament Commentary: Revelation 1–11.*

point has supposedly been raptured. Though we cannot exclude God using them as evangelists, this idea is not explicit in Revelation. Still, it remains a standard Pretrib talking point.

Of the twelve tribes of Israel listed here, Dan and Ephraim are excluded but Joseph is included. It is unknown why this omission has occurred, and the speculations around this issue vary. However, since specific tribes are named, we take these verses literally, particularly since we are now living during the time when Israel is an actual nation where millions of Jews/Israelis currently live. There are several biblical prophecies that concern the nation of Israel, Jerusalem, and Israel's people returning to their homeland that were fulfilled literally. Therefore, we must consider this as a literal sealing of actual individuals from each named tribe. Though we may not be able to trace the bloodline of each tribe, God knows who they are. It is impossible for us to distinguish a member of Israel's tribes by skin color. There are Ashkenazi Jews from Europe who are white as well as Beta Jews from Ethiopia who are black. Because the people of Israel were scattered all over the earth, other racial groups (e.g., Asian, Middle Eastern) have Israeli blood among them. Once the 144,000 are sealed and identified, there will undoubtedly be some surprises.

REVELATION 7:9–12

The Great Multitude

⁹ After these things I looked, and behold, a great multitude which no one could count, from every nation and all tribes and peoples and tongues, standing before the throne and before the Lamb, clothed in white robes, and palm branches were in their hands; ¹⁰ and they cry out with a loud voice, saying,

"Salvation to our God who sits on the throne, and to the Lamb." ¹¹ And all the angels were standing around the throne and around the elders and the four living creatures; and they fell on their faces before the throne and worshiped God, ¹² saying,

"Amen, blessing and glory and wisdom and thanksgiving and honor and power and might, be to our God forever and ever. Amen."

(9–12) *a great multitude which no one could count, from every nation and all tribes and peoples and tongues*: John saw a great throng of people that was beyond numbering. This is in contrast to the specific number of people (144,000) from the twelve tribes of Israel that is given in the previous verses. The multitude is made of Gentiles from every nation, tribe, people, and tongue standing before God's throne—the ultimate place of honor. In our current life on earth, there are celebratory events with pomp, circumstance, and pageantry for various honorees. But these ceremonies are temporal, and their associated adulation and excitement are fleeting. Paul likened the recipients of these earthly awards to those receiving a "corruptible crown" (1 Cor 9:25 KJV), meaning the awards will soon fade away. However, God honors the redeemed in heaven with awards that are incorruptible and imperishable. Those in the multitude are given *white robes*, which symbolize piety, victory, and the status of being overcomers. The people of the multitude are also given *palm branches* for use in celebration. During the ancient Jewish Feast of Booths, palm branches were used in seven days of celebration (Lev 23:40). At the Lord's triumphal entry into Jerusalem, the crowds celebrated Him by carrying palm branches and shouting, "Hosanna to the Son of David; Blessed is He who comes in the name of the Lord; Hosanna in the highest!" (Matt 21:8–9). Shortly after this celebratory day, the fickle people soon changed their response to "Crucify Him" (Mark 15:12–14). But here in this magnificent scene in heaven, in acknowledgment of God's great redemptive acts, the redeemed, in white robes and with palm branches in hand, cry out, *"Salvation to our God who sits on the throne, and to the Lamb."* The *angels*, the *elders*, and the *living creatures* join in on the high praise and worship by extolling *blessing and glory and wisdom and thanksgiving and honor and power and might* to God and the Lamb *forever and ever.* Indeed, the Lamb was slain—not the Father nor the Holy Spirit—but the Son only. Now He is alive forevermore, a point of tremendous celebration for all the host of heaven throughout eternity.

REVELATION 7:13–17

¹³Then one of the elders answered, saying to me, "These who are clothed in the white robes, who are they, and where have they come from?" ¹⁴I said to him, "My lord, you know." And he said to me, "These are the ones who come out of the great tribulation, and they have washed their robes and made them white in the blood of the Lamb. ¹⁵For this reason, they are before the throne of God; and they serve Him day and night in His temple; and He who sits on the throne will spread His tabernacle over them. ¹⁶They will hunger no longer, nor thirst anymore; nor will the sun beat down on them, nor any heat; ¹⁷ for the Lamb in the center of the throne will be their shepherd, and will guide them to springs of the water of life; and God will wipe every tear from their eyes."

Among the themes of Revelation, the plight and victory of the saints is one of the greatest. Unlike those who embrace a Pretrib rapture, who claim the so-called tribulation saints are the "left behinds" who failed to get caught up at the rapture and have to remain on earth to suffer imprisonment, martyrdom, and destitution, this writer does not support that unfortunate characterization. One popular Pretrib pastor characterized it by saying, "They will be slaughtered like flies." To the contrary—this group of believers is the greatest group of Christians the world has ever known.

The Pretrib view claims that the believers present for the great tribulation will be carnal Christians who were not truly saved. Consequently,

they must suffer under the Antichrist. It is unfortunate that Pretribulationists have relegated this group of exceptional believers to the ranks
of a secondary group of Christians who were too carnal to be raptured.
As we will see throughout this commentary, nothing could be further
from the truth. Each time the saints are mentioned in Revelation, they
are associated with heaven, are the subject of divine blessing, and are
self-sacrificing, even to the point of death. They also win the victory
over the beast.

(13) *These who are clothed in the white robes, who are they, and where have
they come from?* Among the great splendor and pageantry of heaven, as the
Lamb is being celebrated by all the heavenly host, is an elder who gives
attention to this innumerable group of Christians that is standing before
the throne of God—the highest place of honor in heaven for humans and
angels alike. The elder asked, "Who are they, and where have they come
from?" John's response is similar to Ezekiel's response in Ezekiel 37:3: "My
lord, you know." Then, the elder makes a great declaration.

(14) *These are the ones who come out of the great tribulation, and they
have washed their robes and made them white in the blood of the Lamb:*
Indeed, these believers will "come out of the great tribulation." This is
the same period that Jesus spoke of in Matthew 24. It comes after the
midpoint of Daniel's Seventieth Week, at the time when the abomination of desolation occurs in the temple, which as of today, is yet to
be built.

EXCURSUS—THE MISCHARACTERIZATION
OF THE TRIBULATION SAINTS

It is noteworthy that the great tribulation is characterized as being a period of "great distress, unequaled from the beginning of the world until
now—and never to be equaled again" (Matt 24:21 NIV). It is during the
great tribulation that the faith of the tribulation saints is forged. There
are no OT saints or Christians of any church age who have lived under
trials and persecution equaling the intensity that will come in the great

tribulation. For this reason, the tribulation saints are a unique group of Christians that stands among all other believers throughout the history of the world. Because of their unique experience, they are featured prominently throughout Revelation but never as rapture rejects.

Even under immense pressure, they will refuse to bow to Satan or the Antichrist and will remain faithful to Jesus even though it costs them their freedom and their lives. They will face the worst circumstances, during the worst conditions, under the worst tyrannical ruler that the world has ever known. Therefore, with great pomp and circumstance, they will receive the greatest honors of humans or angels as they stand before God, having washed their robes in the blood of the Lamb.

Consider the following points about the so-called tribulation saints: (1) Pretrib paints them as the rebellious, backslidden, unrepentant Christians who are left behind during the rapture. However, there is not one disparaging remark made about this group of faithful believers in the book of Revelation. Criticisms are exclusively leveled by Pretribulationists, who must explain away the presence of Christians (i.e., the church) still being on the earth after the rapture was supposed to have occurred (see Rev 3:10). (2) The first time we see these saints in Revelation, their souls are under the altar in heaven (see 6:9–11). This is hardly a place for the souls of backslidden sinners. (3) They are being honored in heaven and are standing before the throne of God (see 7:9–17). (4) They are so faithful to Christ that they do not love their own lives, even unto the death (see 12:11). (5) They are encouraged by the Holy Spirit Himself, who promises them that they shall rest from their labors and that their deeds will follow them to heaven (see 14:13). (6) Their names are written in the Lamb's book of life because they refuse to take the mark of the beast (see 13:8). (7) They are saved and go to heaven and have eternal life (see 7:9–17). (8) They are the priests of God (see 20:6). (9) They reign with Christ (see 20:6). (10) They are in the first resurrection, the resurrection of the righteous (see 20:5). For a more detailed comparison of the so-called tribulation saints versus the church, see "The Tribulation

Saints versus the Church" essay. Overall, there is no basis to characterize these saints as those who were not worthy to be taken up in the rapture.

(15) *For this reason, they are before the throne of God; and they serve Him day and night in His temple; and He who sits on the throne will spread His tabernacle over them:* This verse begins with "For this reason," meaning that because they came through the great tribulation, the saints receive the great honor to serve God directly in His temple day and night. This is the same honor promised to the church at Philadelphia (see 3:12), who also endured persecution and tribulation. However, not even the Philadelphians went through such great depths of persecution as the tribulation saints will face under the tyranny of the beast.

(16–17) *They will hunger no longer, nor thirst anymore; nor will the sun beat down on them, nor any heat; for the Lamb in the center of the throne will be their shepherd, and will guide them to springs of the water of life; and God will wipe every tear from their eyes:* For all eternity, their trials and tribulations are over. The Lord will be their Shepherd who guides them to springs of living waters that will refresh and rejuvenate throughout eternity. In the process, "God will wipe away every tear from their eyes." They will remember their pain no more.

Some in the Prewrath camp see this as the rapture of the church because this scene happens in heaven between the sixth and seventh seals. However, there is no warrant to place the rapture here. The passage does not say, "They suddenly appeared in heaven." In a succession of visions, these saints are being "featured," not making an "appearance," during the interlude, which is not a time-in-space event but how the visions were shown to John. Therefore, the interlude in the book is not the same as an interlude in time and space. Placing the rapture here is problematic because the fifth, sixth, and seventh seals are not point-of-action seals to be opened on the Seventieth Week timeline. Instead, they are visions of events to be fulfilled during the wrath of God, which will be poured out during the bowl judgments. See "The Sixth Seal Problem" essay.

EXCURSUS—THE TWO THEMES OF CHAPTER SEVEN

There are two notable themes in chapter 7: (1) the sealing of the 144,000 from the tribes of Israel and (2) the innumerable multitude of Gentiles seen in heaven before God's throne. Is this coincidental that both themes are featured here together in the same vision sequence? To give insight to these events, Paul's epistle to the Romans could be helpful. In Romans 11:25, Paul connected two important events:

> For I do not want you, brethren, to be uninformed of this mystery—so that you will not be wise in your own estimation—that a partial hardening has happened to Israel until the fullness of the Gentiles has come in. (Rom 11:25)

Paul declared that Israel's "hardening" or "blindness" (KJV) toward Christ (cf. 2 Cor 3:14–16) will continue "until [or conditioned upon] the fullness of the Gentiles has come in" or has come to Christ. Here Paul is speaking indirectly of the church (see also "The Imminent Return Problem" and "The Mystery of Israel's Blindness"). From this passage it is evident that these two things are inextricably connected. The removal of Israel's hardness and the fullness of the Gentiles coming in are two sides of the same coin, because the former is contingent upon the latter.

According to Pretrib teaching, "the fullness of the Gentiles" and the rapture will occur before Daniel's Seventieth Week arrives. It also claims that the innumerable group of Gentiles that comes out of the great tribulation, featured in Revelation 7:9, will be resurrected at the beginning of the millennium. But it also concedes that both groups of Gentiles are in the first resurrection. Inevitably, this would mean that the first resurrection would have to have two distinct phases consisting of two separate groups of Gentiles. According to Pretrib, the church (consisting of Gentiles, hence "the fullness of the Gentiles" in Rom 11:25) is resurrected and raptured before the seven-year period arrives, and a second group of Gentiles that comes out of the great tribulation is resurrected after the seven years. However, this causes Christ not to wait for the full number of the Gentiles to come in as stated in Romans 11:25, because He gets the first group of Gentiles but then comes back seven years later for the second group of Gentiles. The problem is that Jesus only spoke of two resurrections: one for the righteous and the other for the wicked (see John 5:29). Jesus did not mention three general resurrections—that is, two for the righteous and one for the unrighteous. Nor did Paul divide the first resurrection into two phases separated by seven years.

Concerning the order of the resurrection, Paul declared:

> But now Christ has been raised from the dead, the first fruits of those who are asleep. For since by a man came death, by a man also came the resurrection of the dead. For as in Adam all die, so also in Christ all will be made alive. But each in his own order: Christ the first fruits, after that those who are Christ's at His coming. (1 Cor 15:20–23)

Verse 23 is clear. Every man "in his own order." Christ is the first fruits, or the first to be raised from the dead in a glorified body. The b clause of v. 23 begins with "after that" and follows with "those who are Christ's at His coming." The question is, who belongs to Christ? Are the people of the church the only ones that Christ has purchased with His blood? No! In this text Paul referred back to Adam: "For as in Adam *all* die, so also in Christ *all* will be made alive" (v. 22, emphasis added). "All will be made alive" finds its reference point at the fall, when it became necessary for a Savior and the *protevangelium** was given (Gen 3:14–15). Whether OT or NT saints, everyone that will enter eternal life has been redeemed by the blood of the Lamb.

Though many claim the resurrection/rapture of 1 Corinthians 15 is only for the church, this can be challenged on the basis that Paul declared that the rapture fulfills two OT prophecies. First Corinthians 15:54 states, "When this perishable will have put on the imperishable, and this mortal will have put on immortality, then will come about the saying that is written, 'Death is swallowed up in victory.'" This is based on Isaiah 25:8. Then in 1 Corinthians 15:55, Paul stated, "O death, where is your victory? O death, where is your sting?" This is based on Hosea 13:14. When Paul wrote "then will come about the saying that is written," he was saying that Isaiah's and Hosea's prophecies will be fulfilled at the last trumpet. This will include OT saints who also hoped for the resurrection. This is why we see the resurrection at Revelation 11:18 and see Pretrib admitting this is a reference to the resurrection of OT saints.[135] However, the rapture (i.e., being caught up alive) applies only to those who are living at the time of the last trumpet. These believers will certainly belong to the church because the body of Christ continues adding souls until it reaches fullness. Those who are caught up while alive will never taste death.

Jesus is "the Lamb of God who takes away *the sin of the world!*" (John 1:29, emphasis added). He is the Savior of all humanity—the Savior who was anticipated in the OT and realized in the NT. This is not to say all humanity will be saved. That is the tenet of *universalism,** and it should be rejected. However, those whose names are written in the Lamb's book of life from the foundation of the world (see Rev 13:8)—going back to Adam—are saved by the precious blood of the Lamb. Therefore, Acts declares, "There is salvation in no one else; for there is no other name under heaven that has been given among men by which we must be saved" (Acts 4:12). The resurrection/rapture is for those who belong to Christ. In its broadest sense, this refers to everyone who has been redeemed (or purchased) by the blood of the Lamb.

Therefore, when the fullness of the Gentiles comes in, God will be ready to raise all the righteous dead of the OT and NT, because both groups belong to Christ. "Then we who are alive and remain will be caught

---

135   J. Dwight Pentecost, *Things To Come: A Study in Biblical Eschatology* (Grand Rapids, MI: Zondervan, 1965), 191.

up together with them [OT and NT raised saints] in the clouds to meet the Lord in the air" (1 Thess 4:17). God will also send His angel to mark twelve thousand members from each of the twelve tribes of Israel, which will functionally end Israel's blindness because the 144,000 are closely associated with the Lamb (see Rev 14:4). Though depicted here in apocalyptic imagery, the innumerable multitude of Gentiles seen in heaven indicates fullness, and the sealed tribes of Israel no longer being hardened or blinded to Jesus as the messianic Lamb point to the soon-to-follow crowning event when "all Israel will be saved" and when "the deliverer will come from Zion . . . [to] remove ungodliness from Jacob" (Rom 11:26). It is important to understand that chapter 7 is an interlude between the sixth and seventh seals. The interlude does not show these events sequentially in time and space. Those who have come out of the great tribulation in chapter 7 are also those who will have victory over the beast, which will not occur until chapters 13–15.

REVELATION 8:1–6

SILENCE IN HEAVEN

¹ When the Lamb broke the seventh seal, there was silence in heaven for about half an hour. ² And I saw the seven angels who stand before God, and seven trumpets were given to them. ³ Another angel came and stood at the altar, holding a golden censer; and much incense was given to him, so that he might add it to the prayers of all the saints on the golden altar which was before the throne. ⁴ And the smoke of the incense, with the prayers of the saints, went up before God out of the angel's hand. ⁵ Then the angel took the censer and filled it with the fire of the altar, and threw it to the earth; and there followed peals of thunder and sounds and flashes of lightning and an earthquake. ⁶ And the seven angels who had the seven trumpets prepared themselves to sound them.

(1) *When the Lamb broke the seventh seal, there was silence in heaven for about half an hour:* Among all the joyful noise and celebratory clamor of heaven, a transition to "silence" permeated the heavenly atmosphere. Quietness can also be worship when given in reverence to almighty God. Like the silence that occurs between movements of a symphony, no interrupting sounds were permitted. The prophet Zephaniah stated, "Be silent before the Lord God! For the day of the Lord is near, for the Lord has prepared a sacrifice, He has consecrated His guests" (Zeph 1:7). The silence "for about half an hour" anticipated what God was about to do in the next apocalyptic movement. The seventh seal introduces the seven trumpets.

(2) *And I saw the seven angels who stand before God, and seven trumpets were given to them:* "Seven angels . . . stand before God," and each was given a trumpet. It is understood from the text that God Himself issued the "trumpets," as no other intermediary is identified. These trumpets are *the trumpets of God.* Many Pretribulationists believe the "seven trumpets" are the angels' trumpets, which should be distinguished from "the trumpet of God" mentioned in 1 Thessalonians 4:16. However, as we see here, the angels stood before God and received their trumpets from Him, making all these the trumpets of God.

(3–6) *Another angel came and stood at the altar, holding a golden censer; and much incense was given to him, so that he might add it to the prayers of all the saints on the golden altar which was before the throne:* The portrayal of "the prayers of all the saints" in a golden censer (a vessel used for burning incense) being mixed with "incense" is a beautiful apocalyptic image. It illustrates that prayers from all the saints are precious offerings that do reach God. *And the smoke of the incense, with the prayers of the saints, went up before God out of the angel's hand:* Once the angel releases the prayers and incense more actions follow. *Then the angel took the censer and filled it with the fire of the altar, and threw it to the earth; and there followed peals of thunder and sounds and flashes of lightning and an earthquake:* The same censer that contained the incense and prayers of the saints is filled with fire and thrown to the earth. The reaction is swift with sounds of thunder, lightning, and an earthquake. *And the seven angels who had the seven trumpets prepared themselves to sound them:* The concluding action of the seventh seal introduces the seven trumpets. Subsequently, the seventh trumpet will unleash the wrath of God, contained in the seven bowl judgments (chap. 16).

✝

REVELATION 8:7–13

⁷ The first sounded, and there came hail and fire, mixed with blood, and they were thrown to the earth; and a third of the earth was burned up, and a third of the trees were burned up, and all the green grass was burned up. ⁸ The second angel sounded, and *something* like a great mountain burning with fire was thrown into the sea; and a third of the sea became blood, ⁹ and a third of the creatures which were in the sea and had life, died; and a third of the ships were destroyed. ¹⁰ The third angel sounded, and a great star fell from heaven, burning like a torch, and it fell on a third of the rivers and on the springs of waters. ¹¹ The name of the star is called Wormwood; and a third of the waters became wormwood, and many men died from the waters, because they were made bitter. ¹² The fourth angel sounded, and a third of the sun and a third of the moon and a third of the stars were struck, so that a third of them would be darkened and the day would not shine for a third of it, and the night in the same way. ¹³ Then I looked, and I heard an eagle flying in midheaven, saying with a loud voice, "Woe, woe, woe to those who dwell on the earth, because of the remaining blasts of the trumpet of the three angels who are about to sound!"

(7) *The first sounded, and there came hail and fire, mixed with blood, and they were thrown to the earth; and a third of the earth was burned up, and a third of the trees were burned up, and all the green grass was burned up*: In recent years there has been an increasing number of wildfires that have scorched millions of acres around the world in the United States, Australia, Africa, Russia, Europe, Canada, and South America. What we have been experiencing is just a dress rehearsal for the hail, fire, and blood the first trumpet will bring. It should be noted that these judgments occur in thirds and are not total, yet the global air quality will be seriously degraded from the fire. The narrative spouted today when wildfires occur is that they are caused by the effects of *global warming*. This could be a popular perspective when the first trumpet blows too. Daniel's prophecy is correct when it says, "Many will be purged, purified and refined, but the wicked will act wickedly; and none of the wicked will understand, but those who have insight will understand" (Dan 12:10).

(8–9) *The second angel sounded, and something like a great mountain burning with fire was thrown into the sea; and a third of the sea became blood, and a third of the creatures which were in the sea and had life, died; and a third of the ships were destroyed:* In our scientific age we *could* understand this to mean some type of meteoric or volcanic activity. We know that meteors are set ablaze when they encounter friction as they travel at high speeds through earth's atmosphere. One could easily land in the sea. An exploding volcano blasting a mountainside away and spewing hot magma into the sea could also be possible. Mountains could also represent demonic powers as recorded in 1 Enoch 18:13, "I saw there seven stars like great burning mountains."[136] No one is sure what "the sea" refers to, whether it is the Mediterranean or some other body of water. Those living during the first century would have had limited knowledge about the expanse of the earth's great oceans, believing that the earth was flat. However, what was understood as "the sea" back then should today be understood as being inclusive of all the world's oceans and major bodies of water. As a result of this judgment, a third of the water became blood, or contaminated, which is reminiscent of

---

[136] R. H. Charles and W. O. E. Oesterley, *The Book of Enoch* (London: Society for Promoting Christian Knowledge, 1917), Enoch 18:13.

the plagues of Egypt (see Exod 7:19–21). With such a catastrophic event, it's no surprise there was dead sea life. Finally, a third of the ships were also destroyed, which implies the likelihood of a massive tsunami wave.

Luke possibly gives insight on events like the ones that occur during the second trumpet:

> There will be signs in sun and moon and stars, and on the earth dismay among nations, *in perplexity at the roaring of the sea and the waves*, men fainting from fear and the expectation of the things which are coming upon the world; for the powers of the heavens will be shaken. (Luke 21:25–26, emphasis added)

Jesus prophesied about the same period. He identified signs to come in the heavenlies, in the roaring waves (caused by meteor strikes and earthquakes), and in other calamities that will solicit so much fear that people will faint (heart failure, KJV) as they behold the things that are descending from heaven on this world.

(10–11) *The third angel sounded, and a great star fell from heaven, burning like a torch, and it fell on a third of the rivers and on the springs of waters. The name of the star is called Wormwood; and a third of the waters became wormwood, and many men died from the waters, because they were made bitter:* In addition to the burning mountain of the second trumpet, the third trumpet triggered a falling star that brought calamity with its impact on the earth's surface. The word "star" is from the Greek word *aster*, meaning "a luminous body (other than the sun) visible in the sky, star, single star."[137] Whereas the burning mountain hit the sea, this star struck inland, striking the rivers and causing the sources of fresh drinking water to go bad and kill people. One third of water sources were affected.

---

[137] Bauer, *Greek-English Lexicon, aster.*

Scientists are aware of the real dangers to earth from outer space. For the first time in history, in "a successful attempt to alter the orbit of an asteroid, NASA crashed a spacecraft into the asteroid *Dimorphos* on Sept. 26, 2022. The mission, known as the *Double Asteroid Redirection Test*, or DART, took place on an asteroid that posed no threat to our planet."[138] While a mission to divert the outer space calamities that are detailed in Revelation would be fruitless, the fact that NASA has launched a craft to successfully divert an asteroid is evidence that there will be asteroids that pose a threat to the earth. This first-century prophecy in Revelation, a distant prediction, has become a twenty-first-century reality in a global milieu intrigued with space exploration and extraterrestrial life.

The name of the star is "Wormwood." Wormwood is "a plant of the *genus Artemisia*, proverbially bitter to the taste, yielding a dark green oil (the rendering *wormwood* derives from its association with medicinal use to kill intestinal worms)."[139] The word "star" can also refer to demons (see 9:1). Also, this star has a name, which again, *could* imply demonic involvement and explain how a single strike could poison a third of the freshwater rivers that are scattered around the world.

(12) *The fourth angel sounded, and a third of the sun and a third of the moon and a third of the stars were struck, so that a third of them would be darkened and the day would not shine for a third of it, and the night in the same way:* Cosmic disturbances are a major part of the apocalyptic landscape and will impact day and night intervals, as the powers of heaven are shaken (see Mark 13:25).

(13) *Then I looked, and I heard an eagle flying in midheaven, saying with a loud voice, "Woe, woe, woe to those who dwell on the earth, because of the remaining blasts of the trumpet of the three angels who are about to sound!"*

---

[138] Lyle Tavernier, "The Science Behind NASA's First Attempt at Redirecting an Asteroid," NASA. gov, October 20, 2022, https://www.jpl.nasa.gov/edu/news/2022/9/22/the-science-be-hind-nasas-first-attempt-at-redirecting-an-asteroid.

[139] Bauer, *Greek-English Lexicon*, wormwood, 161.

After the first four trumpets, there is a shift to characterizing the following three trumpets as "woes." "Woe" is from the Greek word *ouai*, which means "a state of intense hardship or distress" (BDAG). This eagle is probably an angelic being, perhaps the same "flying eagle" (4:7) that summoned the fourth horseman (6:7). The message from the eagle flying midair will provoke terror from those who dwell on the earth. The first four trumpets attacked the earth: the first burned the trees and green grass, the second attacked the sea, the third attacked the rivers, and the fourth attacked the earth's daylight. However, these first four trumpets affected only one-third of their targets. The following three trumpet woes are much worse. Pronouncing the woe three times also means the coming distress will be to a superlative degree.

REVELATION 9:1–12

[1] Then the fifth angel sounded, and I saw a star from heaven which had fallen to the earth; and the key of the bottomless pit was given to him. [2] He opened the bottomless pit, and smoke went up out of the pit, like the smoke of a great furnace; and the sun and the air were darkened by the smoke of the pit. [3] Then out of the smoke came locusts upon the earth, and power was given them, as the scorpions of the earth have power. [4] They were told not to hurt the grass of the earth, nor any green thing, nor any tree, but only the men who do not have the seal of God on their foreheads. [5] And they were not permitted to kill anyone, but to torment for five months; and their torment was like the torment of a scorpion when it stings a man. [6] And in those days men will seek death and will not find it; they will long to die, and death flees from them. [7] The appearance of the locusts was like horses prepared for battle; and on their heads appeared to be crowns like gold, and their faces were like the faces of men. [8] They had hair like the hair of women, and their teeth were like *the teeth* of lions. [9] They had breastplates like breastplates of iron; and the sound of their wings was like the sound of chariots, of many horses rushing to battle. [10] They have tails like scorpions, and stings; and in their tails is their power to hurt men for five months. [11] They have as king over them, the angel of the abyss; his name in Hebrew is Abaddon, and in the Greek he has the name Apollyon. [12] The first woe is past; behold, two woes are still coming after these things.

(1) *Then the fifth angel sounded, and I saw a star from heaven which had fallen to the earth; and the key of the bottomless pit was given to him:* Once the fifth angel sounded the trumpet, John stated that he saw "a star from heaven which had fallen to the earth." John was saying not that he witnessed the star falling but that it had fallen *from* heaven. The question is what is meant by the term "star"? One immediate clue is that in 8:10, the word "star" is in reference to *an angel.* John referred to the "star" here with the masculine pronoun "him" when he was given "the key of the bottomless pit [abyss]" and tasked with unlocking it (see 9:2). Obviously, this is an angelic being. Though various views on the identity of the angel have been put forth, such as him being the angel Uriel,[140] the text is silent about his identity. So then, we should be silent. The "bottomless pit," or *abyss,* is "a transcendent place associated with the dead and hostile powers, netherworld, abyss, abode of the demons (Luke 8:31); dungeon where the devil is kept (Rev 20:3); abode of the Antichrist."[141] The fact that it has a key to it implies that this is a secured place of detention.

(2–3) *He opened the bottomless pit, and smoke went up out of the pit, like the smoke of a great furnace; and the sun and the air were darkened by the smoke of the pit. Then out of the smoke came locusts upon the earth, and power was given them, as the scorpions of the earth have power:* Once the horrific "bottomless pit" was opened, thick, black smoke billowed out of it to such a degree that the sun was darkened. This implies that the bottomless pit is on earth because it was "to the earth" (v. 1) where the star fell when he was given the key to the pit. Once opened, the rising smoke blocked the sun's light, which offers a perspective of one who is looking up from the earth.

(4–6) *They were told not to hurt the grass of the earth, nor any green thing, nor any tree, but only the men who do not have the seal of God on their*

---

[140]   R. H. Charles, *A Critical and Exegetical Commentary on the Revelation of St. John,* vol. 1 (London: Edinburgh T. & T. Clark, 1920), 293.

[141]   Bauer, *Greek-English Lexicon, bottomless pit, abyss.*

foreheads. And they were not permitted to kill anyone, but to torment for five months; and their torment was like the torment of a scorpion when it stings a man. And in those days men will seek death and will not find it; they will long to die, and death flees from them: This will be an unimaginable circumstance—torment with no possible relief. No pain mitigation, no medicinal intervention, no alleviation. The only desire will be to wish for death, but death will flee from those in pain. Assisted suicide will not work. Not even the rider of the ashen horse of the fourth seal will be able to bring them death. However, these locusts *cannot harm the redeemed,* who will have *the seal of God on their foreheads,* because they will be divinely protected (see 7:3).

(7–10) *The appearance of the locusts was like horses prepared for battle; and on their heads appeared to be crowns like gold, and their faces were like the faces of men. They had hair like the hair of women, and their teeth were like the teeth of lions:* The appearance of these creatures is monstrous. Though apocalyptic literature is filled with foreboding imagery, these locusts will likely be more horrific than their description here. There is also the possibility that these locusts will be invisible and that the description John was reporting is spiritual. For example, regarding the Antichrist, people will see him as a regular human being; he won't have seven heads and ten horns as depicted in Revelation 13. Regardless of whether these locusts are visible, the pain that they inflict upon the wicked will come from their tails, which are likened to a scorpion's tail, and the torment they give will last for five months (v. 5), the length of this trumpet's fulfillment.

(11) *They have as king over them, the angel of the abyss; his name in Hebrew is Abaddon, and in the Greek he has the name Apollyon:* "*Abaddon* transliterates a Heb. word meaning 'destruction' (Job 26:6; 28:22; Ps 88:11; Prov 15:11). The Gr. equivalent is given as *Apollyon,* which means destroyer."[142] Apollyon/Abaddon (though an evil angel) is one of a few

---

[142] Morris, *Tyndale Commentaries: Revelation,* 104, *Apollyon.*

angelic names revealed in the Scriptures. Other noncanonical writings, such as the *Book of Enoch* and Jewish literature, name Raphael and Uriel, along with Michael and Gabriel. Though some relate Apollyon to being Satan, this is not necessary. "Apollyon" is "the angel of the abyss" (v. 11); *Satan* is "the prince of the power of the air" (Eph 2:2) and has no connection to the bottomless pit until he is cast into it for a thousand years during the millennium (Rev 20:1–3, 7).

(12) *The first woe is past; behold, two woes are still coming after these things*: This statement confirms that the fifth trumpet is the same as the first woe. Two woes, the sixth and seventh trumpets, are still to come.

REVELATION 9:13–21

[13] Then the sixth angel sounded, and I heard a voice from the four horns of the golden altar which is before God, [14] one saying to the sixth angel who had the trumpet, "Release the four angels who are bound at the great river Euphrates." [15] And the four angels, who had been prepared for the hour and day and month and year, were released, so that they would kill a third of mankind. [16] The number of the armies of the horsemen was two hundred million; I heard the number of them. [17] And this is how I saw in the vision the horses and those who sat on them: the riders had breastplates the color of fire and of hyacinth and of brimstone; and the heads of the horses are like the heads of lions; and out of their mouths proceed fire and smoke and brimstone. [18] A third of mankind was killed by these three plagues, by the fire and the smoke and the brimstone which proceeded out of their mouths. [19] For the power of the horses is in their mouths and in their tails; for their tails are like serpents and have heads, and with them they do harm. [20] The rest of mankind, who were not killed by these plagues, did not repent of the works of their hands, so as not to worship demons, and the idols of gold and of silver and of brass and of stone and of wood, which can neither see nor hear nor walk; [21] and they did not repent of their murders nor of their sorceries nor of their immorality nor of their thefts.

(13) *Then the sixth angel sounded, and I heard a voice from the four horns of the golden altar which is before God*: The voice that spoke is not identified, but it could have been the Lord's, one of the living creature's, or some other angelic voice. In Revelation, all of these heavenly characters speak.

(14) *one saying to the sixth angel who had the trumpet, "Release the four angels who are bound at the great river Euphrates"*: Once the sixth trumpet sounded, John heard a voice from the four horns of the golden altar that directed the angel with the sixth trumpet to release "the four angels" bound at the Euphrates River. This reaffirms angels as restrainers. Even though angels are incorporeal beings (i.e., not having a physical body), they can be bound in places such as *Tartaros* (i.e., hell), "a Gr. name for the abode of the damned"[143] (see 2 Pet 2:4), or at a geographical location on the earth, in this case "the great river Euphrates." The four angels were inactive until released when the sixth trumpet sounded.

(15) *And the four angels, who had been prepared for the hour and day and month and year, were released, so that they would kill a third of mankind*: The four angels were prepared to be released at the precise time, which was determined by God (the hour and day and month and year total 391 days), to kill one-third of humankind. Some readers see the massive army mentioned in v. 16 as demons; others see it as a military campaign inspired by the four angels. In either case, both options are horrific. Whoever or whatever they are is not important, but what is important is a third of the human population will be killed.

(16–17) *The number of the armies of the horsemen was two hundred million; I heard the number of them*: This is a very large army. The phrase "I heard the number" implies that this may be an exact number. Other versions refer to this number in v. 16 as "two hundred thousand thou-

---

[143] Robert L. Thomas, *New American Standard Exhaustive Concordance of the Bible* (Anaheim, California: Foundation Publications, 1981, 1998), hell *Tartaros*, s.v. Greek #5020.

sand" (KJV) and "twice ten thousand times ten thousand" (NIV). The various renderings equal the same massive number. Some commentators have associated this great army with the kings of the East, beyond the Euphrates River, perhaps being an army of China, who boasts of being able to field a two-hundred-million-man army. The description of this army is horrific. *And this is how I saw in the vision the horses and those who sat on them: the riders had breastplates the color of fire and of hyacinth and of brimstone; and the heads of the horses are like the heads of lions; and out of their mouths proceed fire and smoke and brimstone:* The description of these death riders is beyond anything that we can relate to in our day-to-day experience. Even with the advances made in computer-generated special effects, filmmakers would be hard-pressed to portray something this horrific.

(18–19) *A third of mankind was killed by these three plagues, by the fire and the smoke and the brimstone which proceeded out of their mouths. For the power of the horses is in their mouths and in their tails; for their tails are like serpents and have heads, and with them they do harm:* The passage states that "a third of mankind was killed by these three *plagues,** by the fire and the smoke and the brimstone which proceeded out of their mouths." Even when put in terms of modern day warfare, it is difficult to imagine this to be a mechanized army. However, the possibility still exists.

(20–21) *The rest of mankind, who were not killed by these plagues, did not repent of the works of their hands, . . . and they did not repent of their murders nor of their sorceries nor of their immorality nor of their thefts:* The Scriptures teach that the heart is desperately wicked and ask, "Who can understand it?" (Jer 17:9). The Bible also says there are those who hate God (see Ps 21:8) and that evil men will get worse and worse (see 2 Tim 3:13). These people have reprobate minds and have been turned over by God to destroy themselves by their own devices (see Rom 1:28). Even under the extreme circumstances of apocalyptic judgment, unredeemed, wicked people will still refuse to repent because there is no light in them.

A Prelude to the Seventh Trumpet Commentary

Of the preceding trumpets, the seventh is by far the most consequential. Revelation 10 and 11:15–18 take up the subject of the impact of this tremendous trumpet. It is important to understand that this commentary does not embrace a dispensational/Pretrib view of the seventh trumpet, which typically disconnects the last trumpet of 1 Corinthians 15:52 from the seventh trumpet of Revelation 10 and 11. Rather, this commentary takes the view that these are the same. Ultimately, our fidelity should be to the Scriptures, not to doctrinal traditions that often invalidate the Word of God (see Mark 7:13). Unfortunately, the doctrines of men have excluded the church's presence in much of this prophetic book. However, God, through His divine providence, ensured Revelation's inclusion into the canon of Scripture, which was specifically given to the church as a written witness that, through Christ, the people of God shall overcome the forces of Satan and the beast through faith, their testimony, and the glorious coming of our Lord and Savior Jesus Christ.

REVELATION 10:1–7

The Voice of the Seventh Angel

[1] I saw another strong angel coming down out of heaven, clothed with a cloud; and the rainbow was upon his head, and his face was like the sun, and his feet like pillars of fire; [2] and he had in his hand a little book which was open. He placed his right foot on the sea and his left on the land; [3] and he cried out with a loud voice, as when a lion roars; and when he had cried out, the seven peals of thunder uttered their voices. [4] When the seven peals of thunder had spoken, I was about to write; and I heard a voice from heaven saying, "Seal up the things which the seven peals of thunder have spoken and do not write them." [5] Then the angel whom I saw standing on the sea and on the land lifted up his right hand to heaven, [6] and swore by Him who lives forever and ever, who created heaven and the things in it, and the earth and the things in it, and the sea and the things in it, that there will be delay no longer, [7] but in the days of the voice of the seventh angel, when he is about to sound, then the mystery of God is finished, as He preached to His servants the prophets.

(1–2) *I saw another strong angel coming down out of heaven, clothed with a cloud; and the rainbow was upon his head, and his face was like the sun, and his feet like pillars of fire; and he had in his hand a little book which was open. He placed his right foot on the sea and his left on the land*: John informs us that he sees yet "another strong angel." He could be commenting on the fact that this angel was "clothed with a cloud" with a "rainbow

... upon his head," a "face ... like the sun," and "feet like pillars of fire." If he was "clothed with a cloud," he was probably massive. Some claim this angel is *Christ* or the *angel of Yahweh*.[144] However, the passage does not state that this is Christ, who is not referred to as an angel in Revelation.

(3–4) *and he cried out with a loud voice, as when a lion roars; and when he had cried out, the seven peals of thunder uttered their voices. When the seven peals of thunder had spoken, I was about to write; and I heard a voice from heaven saying, "Seal up the things which the seven peals of thunder have spoken and do not write them":* It is very interesting to read the commentators' various views on what *the seven thunders* could have said and on the reason God told John not to write it down. Suffice it to say, there is no human being on this planet who knows what was said, the reason why it was said, or why God told John not to write it down. It is a waste of time trying to comment on what is unknowable. God also told John to "seal up the things," meaning he was not to write it *nor speak about it.* Paul also made a similar declaration when he said he "was caught up into Paradise and heard inexpressible words, which a man is not permitted to speak" (2 Cor 12:4). God could have completely left out this interaction from Revelation. Then we would not have known about it. But the fact that God included that He told John not to write it down unambiguously communicates that He did not intend to give us a complete picture. No matter how much we think we know, God left out a major piece of the puzzle. Therefore, we must remain humble because no one knows it all. Regarding a complete succession of "sevens," it should have been the seven seals, the seven trumpets, *the seven thunders*, and the seven bowls. Twenty-five percent of the sevens were purposely kept secret. And because of that, none of us can have a complete understanding of exactly how these things will be fulfilled in real time. We can only know what God has determined to reveal—no more, no less. We can know *the what* of prophecy but not know *the when* or *the how* of its fulfillment.

---

[144] Beale, *The Book of Revelation*, 552.

(5–6) *Then the angel whom I saw standing on the sea and on the land lifted up his right hand to heaven, and swore by Him who lives forever and ever, who created heaven and the things in it, and the earth and the things in it, and the sea and the things in it:* Though some insist this angel is Christ, the text does not state this, and in fact, this angel cannot be Christ because the angel swore to "Him who lives forever and ever," who created all things, which is Christ Himself. John wrote, "Through him [Christ] all things were made; without him nothing was made that has been made" (John 1:3 NIV). And Paul wrote, "For in him all things were created: things in heaven and on earth, visible and invisible, whether thrones or powers or rulers or authorities; all things have been created through him and for him" (Col 1:16 NIV). In Hebrews, the writer stated, "But in these last days he has spoken to us by his Son, whom he appointed heir of all things, and through whom also he made the universe" (Heb 1:2 NIV). Christ is identified as the one who created the universe. Christ is not explicitly stated as being or appearing in angelic form in the book of Revelation. As the text states, this was a "strong angel" (Rev 10:1), not the Lamb.

(a) *that there will be delay no longer:* The KJV states, "That there should be time no longer." There are many opinions concerning what this "delay" is, but once again, there is no consensus. MacArthur asserts, "The specific content of the angel's oath was that there will be delay no longer, answering the question of the martyrs, 'How long?'"[145] Leon L. Morris says, "This has been made the basis for a view that in the next life there will be no such thing as time. We will live in a great eternal present."[146] Considering all of v. 6, Walvoord asserts, "The clear reference to God as Creator answers evolutionary speculation as to the origin of the earth, and it also affirms the omnipotence of God in dealing with the world in judgment when the time is ripe."[147] Mounce says, "The announcement

[145] MacArthur, *The MacArthur New Testament Commentary: Revelation 1–11*, 285.
[146] Morris, *Tyndale Commentaries: Revelation*, 137.
[147] Walvoord, *The Bible Knowledge Commentary: Revelation*, 954.

of no further delay would come as welcome news. The martyrs under the altar had been told to rest a while until the full number of their fellow servants and brothers and sisters should be put to death. The seven thunders would have involved yet another delay had they not been canceled."[148] Randell asserts, "*That time no longer shall be.* 'This may be rendered: Time (a finite terminable period, as opposed to eternity) shall no longer exist, but eternity shall be entered upon'" (emphasis added).[149] Beale says, "When God has decided to complete his purposes and to terminate history, there will be no delay in its termination."[150] Here we have six different views of what this phrase in v. 6 means, and there are plenty more. What this indicates is that there is no consensus on how to interpret this passage. To give a detailed explanation of this passage, one must understand its connection to the following verse.

(7) *but in the days of the voice of the seventh angel, when he is about to sound, then the mystery of God is finished, as He preached to His servants the prophets:* The NIV has "just as *he announced* to his servants the prophets" (emphasis added). The KJV has "*he hath declared* to his servants the prophets" (emphasis added). In the day of the sounding of the seventh trumpet, the "mystery of God" will be completed. This is a *mystery** that was *declared* or *announced* to the prophets. However, what God declared *to* His prophets was also declared *by* His prophets. If this is correct, this mystery can be found in the prophetic writings contained in the OT. We must consider all the details of both v. 6 and v. 7. At the blowing of the seventh trumpet, the *delay* will be over and the "mystery of God" *that God declared to the prophets* will be completed. To approach vv. 5–7 from a Pretrib perspective, we would believe that the church has already been raptured, so there would be no reason to link this passage to the church or to any Pauline mysteries concerning the church. We will

---

[148] Mounce, *New International Commentary: Book of Revelation*, 200.

[149] Thomas Randell et al., *Revelation*, vol. 22–25 of *The Pulpit Commentary*, ed. H. D. M. Spence-Jones (New York: Funk & Wagnalls Company, 1909), 274–275.

[150] Beale, *The Book of Revelation*, 539.

gain a greater understanding of these verses if we look from outside the Pretrib view and connect the *delay*, the *mystery of God*, and the *seventh, and last, trumpet*. For further examination of the impact of this passage, see the essay "The Long Delay Mystery of God." The verse-by-verse commentary continues on page 192.

ESSAY:
THE LONG DELAY
MYSTERY OF GOD

What is this delay, and why has it tarried so long? Though not stated as such in v. 7, why has there been a *long* delay? Since the beginning of the church era at Pentecost, approximately two thousand years have passed. Since the fall of Adam, thousands more years have passed. However, at the blowing of the seventh trumpet, there is delay no longer. Another important question is, What is the *mystery* that God declared to the *prophets?* How are these events connected to the blowing of the seventh trumpet? To answer these questions, we must start with what Peter said about the inquiries of the prophets of old.

> As to this salvation, the prophets who prophesied of the grace that would come to you made careful searches and inquiries, seeking to know what person or time the Spirit of Christ within them was indicating as He predicted the sufferings of Christ and the glories to follow. It was revealed to them that they were not serving themselves, but you, in these things which now have been announced to you through those who preached the gospel to you by the Holy Spirit sent from heaven—things into which angels long to look. (1 Pet 1:10–12)

Peter speaks of the salvation the prophets of old made "careful searches" of concerning "the grace to come" in relationship to "the sufferings of

Christ." In regard to this matter, it was revealed to the OT prophets that they were "not serving themselves ... but [a future body of the redeemed, the church]" in the things that are now announced through the preaching of the gospel through the Holy Spirit. Even the angels were curious about these matters. Peter has informed us that the prophets diligently inquired about God's mysterious plan, which was not made plain to them though it piqued their interest.

It was to Peter that Jesus made the following declaration,

> Simon Peter answered, "You are the Christ, the Son of the living God."And Jesus said to him, "Blessed are you, Simon Barjona, because flesh and blood did not reveal *this* to you, but My Father who is in heaven. I also say to you that you are Peter, and upon this rock *I will build My church;* and the gates of Hades will not overpower it." (Matt 16:16–18, emphasis added)

JOEL AND ISAIAH DECLARED IT

The prophets of old made declarations about the sufferings of Christ. For example, Isaiah 53:5 states, "He was wounded for our transgressions, he was bruised for our iniquities: the chastisement of our peace was upon him; and with his stripes we are healed" (KJV). The glories that would follow, which Peter spoke of, occurred soon after Christ's resurrection—particularly on the *day of Pentecost,* the day *the church* began. This tremendous and miraculous event *was declared* by the prophet Joel (Joel 2:28–32), but he himself did not understand it because the church was not revealed to his generation but to a later one (see Eph 3:5). However, prophets like Joel declared a future in which God's Spirit would be available to all. Then, on the *day of Pentecost,* Peter preached a powerful sermon in which he declared that what the Jews at Jerusalem were witnessing should be understood in light of prophetic fulfillment. Under the power of the Holy Spirit, Peter appealed to the naysayers and mockers.

> But Peter, taking his stand with the eleven, raised his voice and declared to them: "Men of Judea and all you who live in Jerusalem, let this be known to you and give heed to my words. For these men are not drunk, as you suppose, for it is only the third hour of the day; but this is what was spoken of through the prophet Joel." (Acts 2:14–16)

The church that Jesus said He would build began on the day of Pentecost with the outpouring of the Holy Spirit, which was prophesied and declared by Joel (see Joel 2:28–29). Though the church was veiled in mysterious form, it was there in Joel's prophecy. As a result of Peter's anointed sermon, three thousand Jews repented and gave their lives to Christ, a most powerful debut of the Spirit's work in believers' lives that inaugurated the birth of the church.

Another key person in building the church was the apostle Paul, who began his ministry to the Gentiles after being rejected by the Jews (see Acts 13:42–46). Paul's justification for focusing on the Gentiles was based on the prophecy of Isaiah. Paul boldly declared, "For so the Lord has commanded us, 'I have placed you as a light for the Gentiles, that you may bring salvation to the end of the earth'" (Acts 13:47). Here, Paul quoted from Isaiah 42:6: "I, the Lord, have called you in righteousness; I will take hold of your hand. I will keep you and will make you to be a covenant for the people and a light for the Gentiles" (NIV). For Isaiah, the fact that God would save the Gentiles was not a mystery, but the fact that they would be included in a new body of believers called the church was. Once Paul set out to minister to the Gentiles, he wrote letters to regional churches over a period of several years, which later became the content for most of the NT.

Amos Declared It

The apostle James made a passionate appeal before the Council at Jerusalem after Peter had finished his address.

> "Simeon has related how God first concerned Himself about taking from among the Gentiles a people for His name. With this the words of the Prophets agree, just as it is written, 'After these things I will return, and I will rebuild the tabernacle of David which has fallen, and I will rebuild its ruins, and I will restore it, so that the rest of mankind may seek the Lord, and all the Gentiles who are called by My name,' says the Lord, who makes these things known from long ago." (Acts 15:14–18)

James was quoting from Amos 9:11–12. Like Isaiah, Amos prophesied about the salvation of the Gentiles, but he had no knowledge at that time of the future church.

The Mystery Hidden since the Foundation of the World

In the book of Romans, concerning "the mystery," Paul declared,

> Now to him that is of power to stablish you according to my gospel, and the preaching of Jesus Christ, according to the revelation of the mystery, which was kept secret since the world began, but now is made manifest, and by the scriptures of the prophets, according to the commandment of the everlasting God, made known to all nations for the obedience of faith: To God only wise, be glory through Jesus Christ for ever. Amen. (Rom 16:25–27 KJV)

Paul declared that this mystery had been "kept secret since the world began," making it one of the oldest, if not *the* oldest, mysteries referenced in the Scriptures. In Ephesians, Paul continued to reveal more about "the mystery."

That by revelation there was made known to me the mystery, as I wrote before in brief. By referring to this, when you read you can understand my insight into the mystery of Christ, which in other generations was not made known to the sons of men, as it has now been revealed to His holy apostles and prophets in the Spirit; *to be specific, that the Gentiles are fellow heirs and fellow members of the body, and fellow partakers of the promise in Christ Jesus through the gospel.* (Eph 3:3–6, emphasis added)

Paul declared that this mystery reveals how the Gentiles (non-Jewish people) are "fellow members of the body" (i.e., the church) and "fellow partakers of the promise in Christ Jesus through the gospel." Paul's emphasis on redemption "through the gospel" is important because that is where the power of salvation lies. Paul declared, "For I am not ashamed of the gospel, *for it is the power of God for salvation* to everyone who believes, to the Jew first and also to the Greek" (Rom 1:16, emphasis added). It is through the preaching of the gospel that Christ builds His church and creates a "new body" consisting of both Jew and Gentile.

The Significance of Christ and the Church to Marital Union

As we continue to uncover the multifaceted realities concerning the *mystery of God*, we see that from the very beginning, the Lord began constructing the foundation of the mystery. In Ephesians 5:31–32 (KJV), Paul declared,

For this cause shall a man leave his father and mother, and shall be joined unto his wife, and they two shall be one flesh. This is a great mystery: but I speak concerning Christ and the church.

Once again, *the mystery* is further demonstrated in the marital union. James Montgomery Boice says, "When God created marriage it was not simply that God considered marriage to be a good idea, though it certainly is that, or even because God thought it would be a good way to have and rear children. God created marriage to illustrate the relationship between Christ and the church."[151] This is exactly why Paul stated it was such a great mystery. From the very beginning, marriage was not the pattern for Christ's union with the church, but the opposite. Christ and the church was the pattern provided for human marriage. "For this reason a man shall leave his father and his mother, and be joined to his wife; and they shall become one flesh" (Gen 2:24). Paul's revelation of the mystery of Christ and the church stated in his letter to the Ephesians looks back to Adam and Eve's marital union. The Genesis narrative is attributed to Moses (who was a prophet). Moses did not have the understanding that later believers do of Christ and the church. This is exactly why Paul stated it was such a great mystery.

Hosea's Prophecy Declared It

Paul applied Hosea's prophecy, which contextually concerned Israel, to the Gentiles as well. Paul declared,

> Even us, whom He also called, not from among Jews only, but also from among Gentiles. As He says also in Hosea, "I will call those who were not My people, 'My people,' and her who was not beloved, 'beloved.' And it shall be that in the place where it was said to them, 'You are not My people,' there they shall be called sons of the living God." (Rom 9:24–26)

Paul emphasized this thematic truth that the prophets declared: God's salvation is for Jews and Gentiles. The prophets declared this truth without understanding the mystery concerning salvation and

---

151 James Montgomery Boice, Ephesians: An Expositional Commentary (Grand Rapids, MI: Ministry Resources Library, 1988), 205.

the church. Paul applied the revelation of the mystery to the church, though Hosea's prophecy was about Israel.

THE LONG DELAY

Why does the Lord tarry? How long must the church wait for His coming? The apostle Peter gave us insight concerning the *long delay* that is based upon his response to naysayers who were mocking the fact that the Lord hadn't returned yet. This promise of Christ's return was exacerbated because many first-century Christians *diligently* but *erroneously* believed that Jesus was going to return in their lifetime, and they were apparently vocal about it. The fact that things did not turn out that way emboldened the mockers to criticize. Peter addressed this issue during his day, but his words are for us today as well. The apostle declared,

> Know this first of all, that in the last days mockers will come with *their* mocking, following after their own lusts, and saying, "Where is the promise of His coming? For ever since the fathers fell asleep, all continues just as it was from the beginning of creation." (2 Pet 3:3–4)

Peter responded,

> But do not let this one fact escape your notice, beloved, that with the Lord one day is like a thousand years, and a thousand years like one day. The Lord is not slow about His promise, as some count slowness, but is patient toward you, not wishing for any to perish but for all to come to repentance. (2 Pet 3:8–9)

Therefore, the long delay, which has been running for two thousand years now, is equivalent to just two of the Lord's days and accommodates the Lord's plans to save souls during the age of the church. What Christians of the twenty-first century have that believers of the first century did not have is twenty centuries of hindsight. The passing of two thousand years gives today's Christians the historic perspective that Peter wrote of concerning the comparison of God's time frame versus ours. Psalm 90:4 offers a similar comparison. Undoubtedly, the passing of time indicates not slackness or dubiousness on the Lord's part but His grace and longsuffering, and it provides people time to repent so none should perish.

It is important to keep at the forefront of our investigation that the delay and the mystery of God that was declared to and by the prophets will conclude at the blowing of the *seventh trumpet*. We must also keep in mind that there are many events that occur after the seventh trumpet, such as *the bowl judgments, the destruction of Babylon, the battle of Armageddon, the return of Christ, the defeat of the Antichrist and false prophet, the binding of Satan, the thousand-year reign of Christ during the millennium, the great white throne judgment, and the revelation of the new heaven and new earth.*

When the *seventh trumpet* (which is the last trumpet) blows, there will be *no more delay*, and *the mystery of God*, which concerns the church and the salvific process that unites the redeemed to Christ in one body called "the church," will be complete.

The Final Mystery: The Last Trumpet

This leads us to the final aspect of the mystery that occurs when the seventh trumpet blows. Paul said, "Behold, *I tell you a mystery;* we will not all sleep, but we will all be changed, in a moment, in the twinkling of an eye, *at the last trumpet;* for the trumpet will sound, and the dead will be raised imperishable, and we will be changed" (1 Cor 15:51–52, emphasis added). Plainly, this aspect of the mystery will end the age of the church, which also means the long delay will be over. The fact that the prophets also declared this part of the mystery gives further clarity to it. Paul said,

> For this perishable must put on the imperishable, and this mortal must put on immortality. But when this perishable

> will have put on the imperishable, and this mortal will have put on immortality, then will come about the saying that is written, "Death is swallowed up in victory. O death, where is your victory? O death, where is your sting?" (1 Cor 15:53–55)

Concerning the fulfillment of the rapture, Paul quoted two OT prophets. Paul explicitly stated that "when this perishable will have put on the imperishable, and this mortal will have put on immortality, *then will come about the saying that is written,* 'Death is swallowed up in victory'" (emphasis added). This is a quote from Isaiah 25:8. And "O death, where is your victory? O death, where is your sting?" is a quote from Hosea 13:14. Both Isaiah and Hosea made veiled prophecies concerning the mystery of the rapture of the church. Every element of Revelation 10 is addressed in the seventh trumpet finale. The *mystery* will be completed when the church is taken to heaven, which will end the long delay. These tremendous fulfillments will occur at the last trumpet, which just so happens to be *the seventh trumpet.* Is this a mere coincidence? No!

Only after the church is inserted into the Revelation 10:5–7 scenario can all of this align perfectly. When we take the church out of Revelation early through a Pretrib perspective, we are left with various scholars opining without consensus and explaining away texts with speculative interpretations. Regarding v. 7, Osborne observes, "At the same time, the message concerns the church's place in the 'mystery of God' soon to be consummated."[152] Paul declared,

> Yet we do speak wisdom among those who are mature; a wisdom, however, not of this age nor of the rulers of this age, who are passing away; *but we speak God's wisdom in a mystery, the hidden wisdom which God predestined before the*

---

[152] Osborne, *Baker Exegetical Commentary: Revelation,* 402.

ages to our glory; the wisdom which none of the rulers of this age has understood; for if they had understood it they would not have crucified the Lord of glory. (1 Cor 2:6–8, emphasis added)

See more in the 11:18 commentary about the relationship between the *seventh trumpet* and *the resurrection.*

REVELATION 10:8–11

THE LITTLE BOOK

⁸ Then the voice which I heard from heaven, I heard again speaking with me, and saying, "Go, take the book which is open in the hand of the angel who stands on the sea and on the land." ⁹ So I went to the angel, telling him to give me the little book. And he said to me, "Take it and eat it; it will make your stomach bitter, but in your mouth it will be sweet as honey." ¹⁰ I took the little book out of the angel's hand and ate it, and in my mouth it was sweet as honey; and when I had eaten it, my stomach was made bitter. ¹¹ And they said to me, "You must prophesy again concerning many peoples and nations and tongues and kings."

(8) *Then the voice which I heard from heaven, I heard again speaking with me, and saying, "Go, take the book which is open in the hand of the angel who stands on the sea and on the land"*: Here John is told to take from the hand of the angel the little "book," which some have concluded to be the same as the seventh sealed scroll of chapter 8. However, there are many books in heaven, and there is no need to make the two books the same. The purpose of the book here in chapter 10 is what's important. Osborne observes,

> What is emphasized here is that this scroll is "open in the hand of the angel," signifying that its message is now "open" to the church. The plan of God for the consummation of this

world has been revealed through the prophetic ministry of John in writing down these visions.[153]

(9–10) *So I went to the angel, telling him to give me the little book. And he said to me, "Take it and eat it; it will make your stomach bitter, but in your mouth it will be sweet as honey." I took the little book out of the angel's hand and ate it, and in my mouth it was sweet as honey; and when I had eaten it, my stomach was made bitter:* This is interesting because Ezekiel had a similar encounter to John's when the Lord told him to eat a scroll, which was also sweet in his mouth (see Ezek 3:1–3). However, with John, the sweetness was the same, but it made him nauseous after swallowing it. Why? Simply put, God's Word is *good* (see Ps 19:9–10; 119:103), *righteous*, and *holy*. However, human beings are fallen and sinful. Though God's Word is good, after ingesting it, it doesn't always sit well. God's Word contains both blessing and judgment. The scroll's contents bring both. Furthermore, by ingesting the book, its message is internalized, as the preacher must first partake of the message he is to give to others. Often, these messages are convicting and burdensome, and some prophets declare the "burden of the Lord" (Jer. 23). Certainly, the prophet declares the word of God that is good and righteous. However, the fulfillment of that which is declared is often bitter. Revelation begins with a blessing for those who read it. This is good. However, the same prophecy later reveals the wrath of God, which is very bitter. The contents of the "little book" brought blessing and judgment.

(11) *And they said to me, "You must prophesy again concerning many peoples and nations and tongues and kings."* Some interpret this as John being commissioned a second time to "prophesy" concerning the events that will occur after the seventh trumpet. They cite that the first commission was in Revelation 1:19, where John was told to "write the things which [he had] seen, and the things which are, and the things which will take place after these things." However, in that passage, John was

---

not told to *prophesy* but to *write*. Throughout the book of Revelation, John wrote down what he saw (see 1:11). He had no opportunity to go prophesy to anyone while he was recording events. However, if John's *writing* and *prophesying* are understood synonymously, this gives way to a probable explanation as to why John was told to "prophesy again." Some interpret this passage as being parallel to Ezekiel 2:9–10, meaning "prophesy against."[154] However, most modern translations render it (Gk. *palin*) as "again," "about," or "concerning."

EXCURSUS—YOU MUST PROPHESY AGAIN

The view that is favored here requires a look beyond the exegetical parameters of Revelation to consider John's evangelistic work as an apostle and NT prophet. Though the authorship of the books bearing the name *John* are contested by some, it is accepted that John wrote his gospel and his three epistles before he wrote Revelation. John is "the disciple whom Jesus loved" (John 21:20), the one whose contributions to the early church are recorded in Acts 3:1 and 8:14, and the one whom Paul considered to be a pillar (see Gal 2:9). In his first epistle, John addressed believers as "my little children" (1 John 2:1), a term of pastoral endearment. John also led the way in standing against the heresies of the Gnostics, who wreaked havoc in the early churches. And in Acts, Luke recorded that Jesus commissioned John and other disciples to be witnesses: "But you will receive power when the Holy Spirit has come upon you; and you shall be My witnesses both in Jerusalem, and in all Judea and Samaria, and even to the remotest part of the earth" (Acts 1:8). Therefore, here, "the voice ... from heaven" (Rev 10:8) also carried with it heaven's perspective of John's previous evangelistic work of fulfilling *the great commission* (see Matt 28:16–20) and of being a witness for Christ to "the remotest part of the earth" (Acts 1:8) when it gave him *a second mission* in his twilight years (around AD 90) of writing the book of Revelation. The reference point

---

154 David E. Aune, *Revelation 6–16*, vol. 52B, *Word Biblical Commentary* (Dallas: Word, Incorporated, 1998), 573–574.

of "again" (Rev 10:11) should not be restricted to what John had already recorded in previous chapters because John had not left heaven at this point. He had not prophesied to anyone about anything that he had seen.

Therefore, John was told to "prophesy again concerning many peoples and nations and tongues and kings" (Rev 10:11). The phrase "peoples and nations and tongues" is sometimes used in Revelation to mean the people of God (see 5:9; 7:9). History is our witness. Indeed, John has been "prophesying again" to everyone (peoples, nations, tongues, and kings) for the past two thousand years through the book of Revelation. John's ministry has never stopped because his words are included in the Bible. In His high priestly prayer, Jesus petitioned for His disciples, and on our behalf as well, when He appealed, "I do not ask on behalf of these alone, but for those also who believe in Me through their word" (John 17:20). This "word" refers to biblical material written by John and others that continues to bring people to believe in Jesus today.

It is understood that other commentators have not explored the interpretation rendered here. For example, David E. Aune asserts, "As soon as John has eaten the scroll he is commissioned to prophesy against many nations and kings; that is, he is commanded to denounce the wickedness of those who have not responded to the Christian gospel."[155] From this commentary's perspective, Aune's interpretation is problematic because it assumes too much. He asserts that John "is commanded to denounce the wickedness of those who have not responded to the Christian gospel." However, John is not commanded to denounce anything in Revelation. Nowhere is John commanded "to cry aloud and spare not" (see Isa 58:1 KJV). His instructions in Revelation 1:11 were to write the things that he had seen and to send them to the seven churches. John was the human agent to whom God revealed the events of the apocalypse, which has had no equal since the beginning of the world.

---

[155] David E. Aune, ed., *Word Biblical Commentary*, vol. 52B, *Revelation 6–16* (Dallas: Word, Incorporated, 1998), 575.

Now that we are well into the twenty-first century, we have the technological capabilities to institute a global economic and commercial system that can be controlled through the issuance of the mark of the beast (see 13:16–17). Only now do we have the satellite technology to allow the whole world to watch in real time the bodies of the two witnesses as they lay dead in the streets of Jerusalem (see 11:9). When this happens, the entire world will celebrate the death of the two witnesses. People will send gifts to one another (see 11:10) through a system of global commerce, something that has only become possible in modern times.

God uses the book of Revelation and other biblical prophecies to enlighten the people of God concerning future events. Indeed, Revelation was given to the church because it reveals God's plan. Daniel is clear, "Many shall purify themselves and make themselves white and be refined, but the wicked shall act wickedly. And none of the wicked shall understand, but those who are wise shall understand" (Dan 12:10 ESV). God gives Revelation to those who are wise, who take to heart the words of this prophecy. But He will turn the wicked over to strong delusion so they will believe the lie (see 2 Thess 2:9–12 ESV). Since the wicked will not understand and will be turned over to destruction, Revelation's purpose is to give the church a sequential account of what will befall the world during this time so that our faith will not fail. "The secret things belong to the Lord our God, but the things revealed belong to us and to our sons forever, that we may observe all the words of this law" (Deut 29:29).

✝

REVELATION 11:1–6

The Temple and the Two Witnesses

[1] Then there was given me a measuring rod like a staff; and someone said, "Get up and measure the temple of God and the altar,
and those who worship in it. [2] Leave out the court which is outside the temple and do not measure it, for it has been given to the
nations; and they will tread under foot the holy city for forty-two
months. [3] And I will grant authority to my two witnesses, and
they will prophesy for twelve hundred and sixty days, clothed
in sackcloth." [4] These are the two olive trees and the two lampstands that stand before the Lord of the earth. [5] And if anyone
wants to harm them, fire flows out of their mouth and devours
their enemies; so if anyone wants to harm them, he must be
killed in this way. [6] These have the power to shut up the sky, so
that rain will not fall during the days of their prophesying; and
they have power over the waters to turn them into blood, and to
strike the earth with every plague, as often as they desire.

Concerning chapter 11, Morris comments, "The chapter is extraordinarily
difficult to interpret and the most diverse solutions have been proposed."[156]
Since the futurist interpretation is taken in this commentary, there is some
agreement with others as to what the first two verses could possibly mean.

(1) *Then there was given me a measuring rod like a staff; and someone said,*
"Get up and measure the temple of God and the altar, and those who worship
in it. There are various reasons put forth by commentators as to why John
was told to measure the temple and the altar, and to count the worshipers.

---

[156]   Morris, *Tyndale Commentaries: Revelation,* 104.

This commentary would agree with others that interpret this to be the temple that Antichrist will defile (Matt 24:15). Many propose that John's defining the parameters of that which was being measured symbolizes God's ownership and protection of these things. John was to measure, or count, the worshipers along with the altar because the worshipers worshiped there and the priests offered sacrifices on the altar. Daniel 9:27 declares that "he" (the Antichrist) will halt the sacrifices and offerings being rendered.

(2) *Leave out the court which is outside the temple and do not measure it, for it has been given to the nations* ["Gentiles," NIV] *and they will tread under foot the holy city for forty-two months:* In the Jewish temple complex, there was a place for Gentiles called *the court of the Gentiles* or the *outer court.* No Gentile was allowed to enter the temple. There was a warning that was posted for all Gentiles not to enter the temple area under pain of death, because the temple would be defiled by their presence. This is the temple that Jesus spoke about during His Mount Olivet Discourse when He prophesied about the "abomination of desolation" standing in the holy place (Matt 24:15; Mark 13:14). Further, Paul gave the most explicit account of the Antichrist's desolating sacrilege when he wrote that the Antichrist will be the one "who opposes and exalts himself above every so-called god or object of worship, so that he [will take] his seat in the temple of God, displaying himself as being God" (2 Thess 2:4). It is this event that will start the Antichrist's/beast's forty-two-month reign (see Rev 13:5). This is the identical forty-two-month period referred to here in 11:2: "And they will tread under foot the holy city for forty-two months." Those who worship in the temple during this period are worshipers of the Antichrist and his image (see 13:11–12).

EXCURSUS —ISRAEL'S TEMPLES

Israel's first temple was **Solomon's Temple** (see 1 Kgs 6), and after four hundred years it was destroyed by the Babylonians under the leadership of King Nebuchadnezzar. The Babylonian Empire came to an end in about 538 BC, some forty-eight years after the Babylonians destroyed Solomon's Temple.

Then the Medes and Persians took over Babylon (see Dan 5). Approximately one year later, King Cyrus made a decree to authorize the rebuilding of the temple and Jerusalem and the return of the Jews to their homeland (see 2 Chron 36:23; Ezra 1:1–4). This occurred under the leadership of Zerubbabel, whom Cyrus, king of Persia, appointed governor of Judah (see Zech 4:6–10). **Zerubbabel's temple** became Israel's second temple.

However, Zerubbabel's temple has a turbulent history. In 168 BC, Antiochus Epiphanes IV, king of Syria, committed *the abomination of desolation* when a pig was sacrificed on the altar and an idol, a statue of Zeus, was erected in the most holy place. This led to the Maccabean revolt, led by Judas Maccabeus (i.e., the Hammer), who defeated the Syrian army and cleansed and rededicated the temple. The annual observance of Hanukkah celebrates this event (see Dan 8:11; 11:31; 1 Macc 1:54–60; 4:52–59).

Herod's Temple was a renovation project of Zerubbabel's Temple. "Built of white marble, covered with heavy plates of gold in front and rising high above its marble-cloistered courts—themselves a succession of terraces— the temple, compared by Josephus to a snow-covered mountain . . . , was a conspicuous and dazzling object from every side."[157] However, as Jesus prophesied, Herod's Temple was destroyed during the fall of Jerusalem in AD 70 by the Roman general Titus (see Matt 24:1–2; Luke 21:24). For over eighteen hundred years, Israel was in dispersion, but the nation of Israel was reestablished on May 14, 1948. After fighting several battles with surrounding enemies during the Six-Day War in 1967, Israel recaptured East Jerusalem. The famous battle cry from the *Israeli defense commander* was broadcast: "The Temple Mount is in our hands!" However, after being back in the land of Israel for over seventy years, Israel still has no temple. Now the *Dome of the Rock* stands on The Temple Mount. It is a shrine of the Islamic faith, not far from the *Western Wall,* or Wailing Wall, which is the only remaining wall of Herod's Temple. The Jews will build a new temple at this site in the future, possibly during the twenty-first century.

---

[157]   Orr and Nuelsen, *The International Standard Bible Encyclopedia,* "The Temple of Herod," 2880.

Once constructed, it will be the temple that the Antichrist desecrates by committing the *abomination of desolation.* In Revelation 11:1–2, John wrote, "But exclude the outer court; do not measure it, because it has been given to the Gentiles. They will trample on the holy city for 42 months" (NIV). This temple prophecy anticipates the tyrannical forty-two-month reign of the beast.

(3) *And I will grant authority to my two witnesses:* "The two witnesses" are two of the most enigmatic individuals in Revelation. There are many theories as to who they could be. *Elijah* and *Enoch* are preferred by many because neither of these men died. Those who support this idea do so on the basis of a passage in Hebrews that states, "It is appointed for men to die once and after this comes judgment" (Heb 9:27). This would mean that since neither *Elijah* nor *Enoch* tasted death, they must come back as the two witnesses to fulfill their *appointment to die.* The other option is *Moses* and *Elijah* because these two appeared in the transfiguration, and God had previously used Moses to bring ten plagues on Egypt. A final consideration is that if there will be one hundred forty-four thousand Jews chosen by the Lord who are holy, virgins, and without a lie in their mouth (Rev 14:4–5), it is plausible that the two prophets could emerge from among them. However, all the proposed candidates for the witnesses are speculation. Since the Scriptures are silent, then we must be silent and admit that no one is sure who these prophets will be.

(a) *and they will prophesy for twelve hundred and sixty days, clothed in sackcloth:* Unlike our calendar today that has four months with thirty days, seven longer months with thirty-one days, and one short month with twenty-eight days (twenty-nine days every fourth year), every month in the Jewish calendar had thirty days. Therefore, "twelve hundred and sixty days" equals three and one-half years. It is interesting that in v. 2 the period "forty-two months" is cited. This period is also three and one-half years. Each case represents one half of Daniel's Seventieth Week—the seven-year period, or "twelve hundred and sixty days," being the first half, and forty-two months being the second. See the excursus "The Two

Witnesses Must Be in the First Half of the Seventieth Week." They will be wearing "sackcloth," which was the garment of mourners, because their message will be of God's indignation and judgment.

(4) *These are the two olive trees and the two lampstands that stand before the Lord of the earth*: These could be the same "two olive trees" that Zechariah saw (Zech 4:3, 11).

(5) *And if anyone wants to harm them, fire flows out of their mouth and devours their enemies; so if anyone wants to harm them, he must be killed in this way*: During the time of their ministry, the witnesses will be indestructible, because they cannot be killed before their appointed time has expired. Whoever attempts to kill them, they themselves will be killed. This means the two prophets will be divinely protected, but they will be severely hated by the world. Why? The following verse offers reasons.

(6) *These have the power to shut up the sky, so that rain will not fall during the days of their prophesying; and they have power over the waters to turn them into blood, and to strike the earth with every plague, as often as they desire*: For three and a half years, no rain will fall. In addition, the two witnesses will turn the fresh drinking water to blood, which will be reminiscent of the plagues of Moses (see Exod 7:14–19). Finally, the two witnesses will have the power to unleash all the plagues "as often as they desire." Here is the reason why the world will hate them. Undoubtedly, many attempts will be made on their lives, but to no avail because they are under divine protection. When natural disasters occur, we are all shaken to the core. But what if these disasters that kill thousands were caused by two individuals who claimed responsibility for them? How hated would they be? The entire planet would align against them as will be the case here. Because the plagues they release are released as often as they desire to unleash them. These are the reasons why the world will hate the two witnesses. Undoubtedly, people will make attempts to take their lives but to no avail because they will be under divine protection.

REVELATION 11:7–14

The First Mention of the Beast—the Death
and Resurrection of the Two Witnesses

[7] When they have finished their testimony, the beast that comes up out of the abyss will make war with them, and overcome them and kill them. [8] And their dead bodies will lie in the street of the great city which mystically is called Sodom and Egypt, where also their Lord was crucified. [9] Those from the peoples and tribes and tongues and nations will look at their dead bodies for three and a half days, and will not permit their dead bodies to be laid in a tomb. [10] And those who dwell on the earth will rejoice over them and celebrate; and they will send gifts to one another, because these two prophets tormented those who dwell on the earth. [11] But after the three and a half days, the breath of life from God came into them, and they stood on their feet; and great fear fell upon those who were watching them. [12] And they heard a loud voice from heaven saying to them, "Come up here." Then they went up into heaven in the cloud, and their enemies watched them. [13] And in that hour there was a great earthquake, and a tenth of the city fell; seven thousand people were killed in the earthquake, and the rest were terrified and gave glory to the God of heaven. [14] The second woe is past; behold, the third woe is coming quickly.

(7) *When they have finished their testimony, the beast that comes up out of the abyss will make war with them, and overcome them and kill them:* When the two witnesses have completed their twelve-hundred-sixty-day ministry, "the beast" begins his forty-two-month reign. There are a few things to note here. John does not use the term *antichrist* in Revelation. Throughout the entire Bible, the term *antichrist* is only found in John's *first* and *second* epistles (see 1 John 2:18, 22; 4:3; 2 John 1:7). Also, there are many other names used for the Antichrist in Scripture. In 2 Thessalonians 2:3, there's the "man of lawlessness," or "man of sin" (KJV), and the "son of destruction," or "son of perdition" (KJV). In 2 Thessalonians 2:8, there's "that lawless one," or "that Wicked" (KJV), and in Daniel 7:8, there's the "little horn" (KJV). However, in Revelation, he is called "the beast," which in Greek is *thêrion,* [158] meaning "a wild animal." Concerning the *first seal,* the *rider on the white horse* in Revelation 6:2 is often attributed to the person of the Antichrist, but even if it is the same person, he is not in the role as "the beast" at this point, which is the beginning of Daniel's Seventieth Week. The beast does not ride in on a *white horse,* which is what occurs with the rider in 6:2, but "he comes up out of the abyss."

EXCURSUS—THE BEAST FROM THE ABYSS

Usually, when we think of the beast, we attribute his debut Bible appearance as being in Revelation 13. However, he is first mentioned as "the beast" in 11:7. In this text, we are given a specific detail of this wicked individual. He is not only the beast but *the beast that comes up out of the abyss.* This is an extremely important *first mention* of this character; it sets the stage for understanding him throughout Revelation and elsewhere in the Scriptures.

We were first introduced to the abyss, or *bottomless pit,* in the study of the fifth trumpet. The *abyss* was defined as "a transcendent place associated with the dead and hostile powers, netherworld, abyss, the abode ... of demons, dungeon where the devil is kept, the abode of the Antichrist."[159] The last three definitions are the most important to unlocking the mystery of the beast.

---

[158] Thomas, *New American Standard Exhaustive Concordance,* "beast."
[159] Bauer, *Greek-English Lexicon,* 2.

In the Gospels, we get an explicit account from the demons who possessed the demoniac at Gerasenes. "And Jesus asked him, 'What is your name?' And he said, 'Legion'; for many demons had entered him. They were imploring Him not to command them to go away into the abyss ["the deep," KJV]" (Luke 8:30–31). Certainly, these demons did not want to go into detention but desired to stay in the region. In Matthew's account, they ask the Lord, "Have You come here to torment us before the time?" (Matt 8:29). Since it wasn't time for them to be banished to the abyss, the Lord permitted them to possess a nearby herd of swine (see Matt 8:30–32).

Now concerning Revelation 11:7, the beast's ascending from the abyss means that he cannot be a human being but must be a *demonic principality*.* Many expositors make no comment about this aspect. They just simply call him *the Antichrist.* However, the Antichrist is equivalent to "the man of lawlessness" or the "son of destruction" (2 Thess 2:3). He's the *human dictator* that will be possessed by *the beast that ascends from the abyss* (see the comments at Rev 13:1; 17:8 and the essay "The Threefold Reality of the Beast").

(8) *And their dead bodies will lie in the street of the great city which mystically is called Sodom and Egypt, where also their Lord was crucified*: The phrase "great city" here is used in reference to Jerusalem because that is where the(ir) Lord was crucified. However, mystically, Jerusalem receives a pejorative description as Sodom and Egypt, representing spiritual harlotry and oppression. This relates to Israel's historic and contemporary hardness and the Antichrist's control of Jerusalem during his reign. Babylon is also referred to as the great city (14:18; 16:19; 17:18; 18:10, 18, 19, 21). During the millennium, Jerusalem is called the "beloved city" (20:9) and New Jerusalem is called "the holy city" (21:10).

(9) *Those from the peoples and tribes and tongues and nations will look at their dead bodies for three and a half days, and will not permit their dead bodies to be laid in a tomb*: This passage could not have been fulfilled

A UNIQUE PREWRATH PERSPECTIVE

in any generation before the twentieth century. The first reason is that the Jewish state was not formed until 1948. The second reason is that before the technological age that we now live in, it was not possible for the entire world to view a single event in real time. Space exploration, satellite technology, telecommunication, and the internet make this possible today. "And will not permit their dead bodies to be laid in a tomb" demonstrates that after all the havoc the two witnesses will wreak on the world, a hateful global population will want the gratification of seeing their dead bodies shamefully lying in the street, refusing them the dignity of burial.

(10) *And those who dwell on the earth will rejoice over them and celebrate; and they will send gifts to one another, because these two prophets tormented those who dwell on the earth:* Imagine joy and glee coming from parties and celebrations all over the world. People will be dancing in the streets, reveling, carousing, and sending gifts to one another in an event like a worldwide *Mardi Gras*. They will be celebrating not only the deaths of the two witnesses but also the one who killed them—the beast. To the world, the villains will be the two witnesses, and the hero will be the beast. No one will have been able to stop the two witnesses from unleashing havoc on the planet because of their divine protection. But as soon as their twelve hundred sixty days are complete, they will become vulnerable to attack and will be killed by the beast. The end of their twelve hundred sixty days is the beginning of the beast's forty-two-months.

(11–12) *But after the three and a half days, the breath of life from God came into them, and they stood on their feet; and great fear fell upon those who were watching them:* Imagine the world's response when they see these two prophets come back to life. The response may be similar to that of King Belshazzar of Babylon when he saw a hand and fingers writing on the palace walls. "Then the king's face grew pale and his thoughts alarmed him, and his hip joints went slack and his knees began knocking together" (Dan 5:6). Certainly, seeing the two witnesses return to life

205

will strike absolute terror in the heart of the people. But the finale is yet to come. *And they heard a loud voice from heaven saying to them, "Come up here." Then they went up into heaven in the cloud, and their enemies watched them:* The witnesses will come back from the dead, stand on their feet, and then go into heaven in a cloud. It's likely that all the major news networks will be covering this event with live broadcasting. People in Israel and all over the world will watch this awesome event in real time.

A *possible counter narrative* to explain away this event *could be* as simple as someone saying that these two witnesses were extraterrestrial beings. This is a plausible deception because news and entertainment media have fed the earth's populace many scenarios of extraterrestrials, alien abductions and invasions, and UFO sightings since Orson Welles's *War of the Worlds* radio drama in 1938. Ironically, truth can be stranger than fiction: The world will actually be invaded by a hostile army. It won't be aliens arriving in intergalactic spacecraft, but it will be the Lord of Glory and heaven's armies riding white horses. They will come to destroy the beast's armies and take the world by force (see 19:11–21).

Once the two witnesses leave the earth and go to heaven, "the lie" could be propagated. We can see in today's political discourse how lies are passionately embraced as truth. An urgency to prepare for a heavenly invasion *could be one of several* reasons why the nations send their armies to the battle of Armageddon. Certainly, the beast's administration *will not* tell the truth about the two witnesses' having the destructive powers that they had or about their rising from the dead and ascending into heaven. He will not encourage people to read the book of Revelation to learn the truth. No, just like Satan, the beast is a liar.

(13) *And in that hour there was a great earthquake, and a tenth of the city fell; seven thousand people were killed in the earthquake:* In the Mount Olivet Discourse, Jesus predicted that earthquakes would occur in different places. However, this "great earthquake" apparently will strike

Jerusalem and kill "seven thousand people." Though no earthquake where the loss of life occurs is insignificant, the earthquake that struck Turkey and Syria in 2023 killed over fifty thousand people.[160]

(a) *and the rest were terrified and gave glory to the God of heaven*: The combination of the witnesses' coming back to life and being taken up in a cloud, plus the earthquake's happening, will drive many to fear and worship God.

(14) *The second woe is past; behold, the third woe is coming quickly*: This is a very important marker that identifies where we are on Daniel's Seventieth Week timeline here at the close of the two witnesses' ministry. The "second woe," which is the *sixth trumpet*, has passed. This presents a serious problem for those who insist that *the two witnesses* are in *the second half* of Daniel's Seventieth Week. For more on this, see the comments in the following essay. The verse-by-verse commentary continues on page 214.

---

[160] "Türkiye (Turkey) and Syria Earthquake 2023: A Year On," British Red Cross, updated September 11, 2024, https://www.redcross.org.uk/stories/disasters-and-emergencies/world/turkey-syria-Earthquake.

ESSAY:
THE TWO WITNESSES IN THE FIRST HALF OF THE SEVENTIETH WEEK

Many scholars place the two witnesses in *the last half* of the Seventieth Week. The primary reason for this lies in the first three verses of Revelation 11. Verses 1–2 reference *the temple* and the Gentiles' trampling the holy city under foot for *forty-two months*, which will occur in the last half of the Seventieth Week. We agree that the first two verses cover the last half of the Seventieth Week. The third verse begins the passage about the two witnesses. Scholars want to place the two witnesses in the last half of the Seventieth Week simply because v. 3 follows the prior two verses. This is a problem. Though it may seem hermeneutically correct to interpret this way, there are several practical reasons why the two witnesses cannot be in the last half of the Seventieth Week. The following points will substantiate the argument for this point of view.

(1) If the two witnesses are in the last half of Daniel's Seventieth Week, that means, according to 11:7–12, that they would be killed at the very end of the Seventieth Week when their twelve hundred sixty days (three and a half years) of ministry ends. At that time, the whole world would view their bodies and refuse to put them in graves for three and a half days. During this time, the entire planet would be celebrating and rejoicing over them and sending gifts to one another. After the three-day celebration, the two witnesses would be resurrected and taken up into heaven while everyone watched them. If they were in the last half of the week, their death would be occurring at the same time the Lord would be returning (see 19:11–21). And their resurrection would occur three days after the Lord had already returned. This is a major conflict. If their Lord had returned, why would they be called to "come up here" (11:12)?

(2) The Scriptures declare that the beast will kill the two witnesses when their twelve-hundred-sixty-day ministry is complete (see 11:7). This conflicts with the beast being captured by the Lord when He returns at the end of the Seventieth Week. At the battle of Armageddon, the beast will be thrown alive into the lake of fire (see 19:20). The beast cannot be killing the two witnesses and be in the lake of fire at the same time. Killing the two witnesses would not be the beast's priority if the world's armies were gathering to fight the Lord in the battle of Armageddon (see 19:19).

(3) If the two witnesses are in the last half of the Seventieth Week, their 1,260-day period would begin at the midpoint and extend to the very end of the seven-year period. That would force their death and resurrection to occur at the same time the seventh bowl and the battle of Armageddon, covered in chapter 16, are occurring. The great worldwide earthquake that will cause the cities of the nations to fall will take place during the seventh bowl (see 16:18–19). Then, following the worst earthquake to occur since the earth has been in existence, one-hundred-pound hailstones will pulverize what's left (see 16:21). How could there possibly be a worldwide celebration with people sending gifts to one another in the aftermath of such devastation? This is not tenable because the world could not recover so quickly from an earthquake and damaging hail to then turn to a global celebration over the death of the two witnesses. In their rage, people will be blaspheming God for the extreme severity of these plagues, not celebrating (16:21).

Additionally, how could the whole world see the two witnesses' bodies lying dead in Jerusalem after this massive worldwide earthquake? Mountain ranges will be knocked down and islands not found (see 16:20). Undoubtedly, electrical and communicational grids and networks will be destroyed. Global real-time reporting will be totally disrupted. Under these conditions, the people of the earth will not be able to be informed by international news to see the witnesses' dead bodies in the street.

According to Zechariah, Jerusalem will be in shambles after fighting the greatest and bloodiest battle the world has ever known. This battle will be fought in the *plain of Megiddo** in Israel when the Lord returns (see Zech 14:1–5). With this going on, when would there be time for the two witnesses' dead bodies to lie in the street while the world gloats over them and forbids them to be put in graves (see Rev 11:8–9)? This could not be the scenario if the Lord is also returning and splitting the Mount of Olives in two (see Zech 14:4). Everyone's attention would be on the Lord. No one would be focusing on the two witnesses when the Lord Himself returns. When He comes, every eye will be upon Him, and the nations will be mourning over Him, not celebrating the death of the witnesses (see Rev 1:7; 11:10). If we place the two witnesses in the last half of the Seventieth Week timeline, their death and resurrection conflict with the Lord's return.

(4) After the death of the two witnesses, *the second woe has passed* (11:14), and the third woe [the seventh] trumpet follows. All three series (seals, trumpets, and bowls) occur in sequence and are contained within Daniel's Seventieth Week, concluding with the bowl judgments (16:1–21). The seventh of each series introduces the next series. For example, in 8:1, the seventh seal introduces the first trumpet and the rest follow. The seventh trumpet unleashes the bowl judgment under the wrath of God (11:18), actually occurring in chapter 16.

(5) If the witnesses are in the last half of Daniel's Seventieth Week, it forces *the third woe, which is the seventh trumpet,* to occur after the end of the Seventieth Week because the two witnesses must fulfill their 1,260 days (3.5 years) before they can be killed (11:3–5). Placing them in the second half synchronizes their 1,260 days with the forty-two months of the last half of the Seventieth Week. Revelation 11:14 also states "the second woe [the sixth trumpet] is past ... [and] the third woe [i.e., the seventh trumpet] is coming quickly." This means the death and resurrection of the two witnesses occur between the sixth and seventh trumpets. However, the seventh trumpet is also the third woe because it releases the seven bowl judgments, the most severe of the sequence of temporary judgments. This is why the bowl judgments are identified as *the last plagues* (15:1). They are not synchronized with the seven trumpets but follow them. (For more on the bowl judgments, see chapter 16). If you place the two witnesses in the last half of the Seventieth Week, the last day of their 1,260 days would coincide with the end of the Seventieth Week. This forces the seventh trumpet to occur after the end of the Seventieth Week, as well as the bowl judgments that follow.

(6) Additionally, in light of v.14, the third woe [seventh trumpet comes quickly] means the seventh trumpet follows the two witnesses' resurrection. The bowl judgments, which are last, would follow beyond the end of the Seventieth Week. Coinciding with this scheme, some suggest that Daniel 12:12—which says, "Blessed is he who keeps waiting and attains to the 1,335 days," an additional forty-five days after the end of the Seventieth Week—is a reason for why the bowl judgments can be extended past the Seventieth Week. However, if we use this passage as a basis to place the bowl judgments after the Seventieth Week, we create a bigger problem.

(7) The Antichrist is still in power during the bowl judgments (see 19:19). He, along with Satan and the false prophet, dispatches demons to gather the kings of the earth to the battle of Armageddon during the sixth bowl (see 16:13–16; 19:19). To place the seventh trumpet, along with all the bowl judgments, beyond the end of the Seventieth Week would also require the beast to remain in power beyond his allotted forty-two months, possibly extending his reign to a forty-third or forty-fourth month. This is untenable. The Scriptures are explicit: the beast only has forty-two months (see 13:5). His reign begins in the middle of the week and must be terminated when the Lord returns at the end of the Seventieth Week and he is thrown alive into the lake of fire (see 19:20).

(8) In accordance with Daniel 9:24–27, the full prophetic agenda that is to be completed within the time frame of Daniel's Seventieth Week is as follows: "To finish the transgression, to make an end of sin, to make atonement for iniquity, to bring in everlasting righteousness, to seal up vision and prophecy and to anoint the most holy place" (v. 24).

This six-point agenda will be completed within the time span of 490 years, and 483 years have already been fulfilled. The Seventieth Week, the final seven years, will bring about the completion of these six items. Therefore, the worldwide celebration, the resurrection of the two witnesses, the seventh trumpet, and all the bowl judgments would also have to occur after the end of the Seventieth Week. Daniel 9:27 states, "Even until a complete destruction, one that is decreed, is poured out on the one who makes desolate." What is poured out on the desolator (i.e., the beast) is the wrath of God, and this will occur at the end of the Seventieth Week, not beyond it.

(9) At the beginning of the millennium, Satan will be thrown into the abyss (see Rev 20:2–3) after the beast and false prophet have been thrown alive into the lake of fire (19:20). Therefore, because Satan—the power source and inspiration behind the beast and false prophet—will be imprisoned, the Scriptures explicitly state that Satan's power to deceive the nations will be cut off (see 20:3). If it were true that the seventh trumpet and all the bowl judgments occur after the Seventieth Week ends, these events would be occurring without Satan's power and deceptive influence. Placing the two witnesses in the second half creates many more problems than it solves.

(10) Some scholars have concluded that the two witnesses could start their 1,260-day clock earlier in the Seventieth Week. For example, they see it could start one year into Daniel's Seventieth Week. In this scenario, the two witnesses' time would end at the four-and-a-half-year mark. Though this is more tenable than the last-half placement, this places their ministry in both halves of the week. If we place the two witnesses on earth at the same time as the reign of the beast, it would put the witnesses and the beast in direct conflict. However, there are no Scriptures in Revelation describing a conflict.

We do know the beast will be concentrating his efforts on destroying Israel (i.e., the woman) and the saints (see 12:17; 13:7). Nothing is said about the beast's warring against the two witnesses. If the two witnesses' time coincides with the beast's time, destroying the two witnesses would be his top priority because they will be directly responsible for the plagues that will be striking the earth, and the world will hate them. Trying to destroy them would be impossible even for the Antichrist, though, because any attempts on their lives would bring harm on their adversary (see 11:4–6).

However, the beast is not contending with the two witnesses because, per this commentary, they are not in the second half. The false prophet will then come on the scene and perform his miracles in response to the supernatural activities of the two witnesses, who will be dead and resurrected by this time. Since the world will see them go into heaven, this will set up a deception along the lines of the two witnesses' being of extraterrestrial origin, and the world will have to prepare for an extraterrestrial invasion. This invasion *per se* will actually occur when the world is invaded from heaven, not space. The Lord will come with the angels and all His saints (see Zech 14:5; Matt 16:27; 2 Thess 1:7–10; Rev 19:11–14). Those nations that participate in the battle headed up by the beast will soon learn it is the Lord Himself whom they will have gathered against.

Based on the arguments put forth in this excursus, the conclusion is that the two witnesses must be in the first half of the Seventieth Week. When their 1,260 days are complete, they will be killed, as God's sovereign plan permits. Their time's ending will be the beginning of the beast's forty-two-month reign of terror. The beast, being empowered by Satan, will be exalted in the world because he will have defeated the two witnesses.

✝

REVELATION 11:15–19

¹⁵ Then the seventh angel sounded; and there were loud voices in heaven, saying, "The kingdom of the world has become the kingdom of our Lord and of His Christ; and He will reign forever and ever." ¹⁶ And the twenty-four elders, who sit on their thrones before God, fell on their faces and worshiped God, ¹⁷ saying, "We give You thanks, O Lord God, the Almighty, who are and who were, because You have taken Your great power and have begun to reign. ¹⁸ And the nations were enraged, and Your wrath came, and the time came for the dead to be judged, and the time to reward Your bond-servants the prophets and the saints and those who fear Your name, the small and the great, and to destroy those who destroy the earth." ¹⁹ And the temple of God which is in heaven was opened; and the ark of His covenant appeared in His temple, and there were flashes of lightning and sounds and peals of thunder and an earthquake and a great hailstorm.

(15) *Then the seventh angel sounded; and there were loud voices in heaven, saying, "The kingdom of the world has become the kingdom of our Lord and of His Christ; and He will reign forever and ever":* The significance of this tremendous announcement cannot be overstated. We discovered in chapter 10 two powerful fulfillments that were to occur under the administration of the seventh trumpet: *in the days of the voice of the seventh trumpet* there would be *no more delay,* and *the mystery of God,* as He *declared to the prophets,* would be completed (see 10:6–7). Here in chapter 11, the angel sounded

the seventh trumpet. Even more fulfillments occurred when a thunderous chorus of "loud voices in heaven" made one of the most consequential statements in Revelation: "The kingdom of the world has become the kingdom of our Lord and of His Christ." When this announcement is made, a cosmic shift with eternal consequences will occur. With the blowing of the seventh trumpet and in the wake of this colossal announcement, the *third woe* will soon be released in the bowl judgments of chapter 16.

John recorded the following when Jesus stood in the Praetorium during Pilate's interrogation.

> Therefore Pilate entered again into the Praetorium, and summoned Jesus and said to Him, "Are You the King of the Jews?" Jesus answered, "Are you saying this on your own initiative, or did others tell you about Me?" Pilate answered, "I am not a Jew, am I? Your own nation and the chief priests delivered You to me; what have You done?" Jesus answered, "My kingdom is not of this world. If My kingdom were of this world, then My servants would be fighting so that I would not be handed over to the Jews; but as it is, My kingdom is not of this realm." (John 18:33–36)

Here, Jesus made a statement of enormous consequence. Kings have kingdoms and armies to protect them. What Jesus was declaring is that if His kingdom were fully present at that time, His armies would have been fighting to protect Him so that He would not be handed over to the Jews or anyone else (see Matt 26:53). Knowing what Jesus declared to Pilate about His kingdom not being of this world gives a dramatic shift to the announcement made in heaven after the seventh trumpet blows (see Rev 11:15). After the seventh trumpet, "the kingdom of the world [will] become the kingdom of our Lord and of His Christ; and He will reign forever and ever." The announcement paves the way for the second coming of Christ, which is depicted in 19:11–21, when He is revealed as King of kings and Lord of lords.

The kingdom of God is an enduring expectation. Jesus spoke of it in the Lord's Prayer when He said, "Thy kingdom come" (Matt 6:10 KJV). In Colossians, the kingdom is referred to as "the kingdom of His beloved Son" (Col 1:13). Though the coming of the kingdom in full manifestation is yet future, in a spiritual sense, it is among us. The kingdom of God comes without observation because it is within the believer (see Luke 17:20–21). In Romans 14:17, Paul stated that "the kingdom of God is not eating and drinking, but righteousness and peace and joy in the Holy Spirit." Paul also wrote of the kingdom as a future reality and expectation: "The unrighteous will not inherit the kingdom of God" (1 Cor 6:9).

(16–17) *And the twenty-four elders, who sit on their thrones before God, fell on their faces and worshiped God, saying, "We give You thanks, O Lord God, the Almighty, who are and who were, because You have taken Your great power and have begun to reign:* The "twenty-four elders" prostrated themselves before the Lord, praising Him because He had taken control over the earth and had "begun to reign." These verses show that once the seventh trumpet blows and the announcement in heaven is made, it will be a done deal—the Lord will rule forever! Jesus will seize His awesome authority over the earth, which until that time will be controlled by "the prince of the power of the air" (Eph 2:2), "the god of this world" (2 Cor 4:4), and "the ruler of the world" (John 14:30), who is none other than Satan. At that time, the focus of the Lord's Prayer, which says, *"Thy kingdom come, Thy will be done in earth, as it is in heaven"* (Matt 6:10 KJV), will come to pass in stunning, glorious manifestation. But before the Lord returns *in person*, the nations must answer for their continuous rebellion against Him who sits on the throne.

(18) *And the nations were enraged, and Your wrath came:* The seventh trumpet accounts for a duration of time. It is not one event but several, as we learned in chapter 10: "But in the days of the voice of the seventh angel, when he is about to sound" (10:7). This gives us the understanding that the seventh trumpet is not a one-day event. It will cover a period of time near the end of Daniel's Seventieth Week. The impact of the seventh trumpet will affect heaven, but it will affect earth more. It will unleash the wrath of God on the earth, which will come to a climax with the bowl judgments of Revelation 16. With the wrath of God at the door, the elders said, "The nations were enraged" because of the wrath of God. Why God sends His wrath is thematic throughout Scripture, going back as far as the Flood, Sodom and Gomorrah, Pharaoh's defeat in the Exodus, and many other examples. God's wrath is a direct response to men's rebellion and wickedness (see Rom 1:18). We get a glimpse of the folly of the nations' anger at God in the words of the psalmist.

> Why are the nations in an uproar and the peoples devising a vain thing? The kings of the earth take their stand and the rulers take counsel together against the LORD and against His Anointed, saying, "Let us tear their fetters apart and cast away their cords from us!" He who sits in the heavens laughs, the Lord scoffs at them. Then He will speak to them in His anger and terrify them in His fury, saying, "But as for Me, I have installed My King Upon Zion, My holy mountain." (Ps 2:1–6)

God responds to the uproar of nations like a parent responds to the tantrums of a two-year-old—He laughs. What's a two-year-old baby going to do about anything? Absolutely nothing!

God considers all of the weaponry of the nations—the nuclear arms, aircraft, bombs, bullets, missiles, warships, submarines, satellites, and all the troops—as *less than nothing*. Indeed, the nations will be angry, but what are they going to do about it? In the end, they'll do nothing but try to run and hide. The awesome day of the Lord will be at the door.

(a) *and the time came for the dead to be judged, and the time to reward Your bond-servants the prophets and the saints and those who fear Your name, the small and the great, and to destroy those who destroy the earth*: Before we tackle what this passage means, let's first bring in the Lord's words to His disciples found in Matthew 16.

> Then Jesus said to His disciples, "If anyone wishes to come after Me, he must deny himself, and take up his cross and follow Me. For whoever wishes to save his life will lose it; but whoever loses his life for My sake will find it. For what will it profit a man if he gains the whole world and forfeits his soul? Or what will a man give in exchange for his soul? For the Son of Man is going to come in the glory of His Father with His angels, and will then repay every man according to his deeds." (Matt 16:24–27)

Verse 27 of this passage is distinctly eschatological. When the Lord returns, it is going to be payday. At the end of Revelation, the Lord stated, "Behold, I am coming quickly, *and My reward is with Me*, to render to every man according to what he has done" (Rev 22:12, emphasis added). So, it is here, when the seventh trumpet blows and the loud voices make the announcement concerning the kingdom of God, which is the precursor to the coming of the Lord, that He will appear and judge the *living and the dead.* Paul agreed and wrote, "I solemnly charge *you* in the presence of God and of Christ Jesus, who is to *judge the living and the dead,* and by *His appearing* and *His kingdom*" (2 Tim 4:1, emphasis added). It is unfortunate that many scholars, though not all, avoid connecting 1 Corinthians 15:51–55 and 1 Thessalonians 4:13–18 with the seventh trumpet narrative of Revelation.

WHO ARE THE DEAD BEING JUDGED?

Who are the dead to be judged here? This question has sparked debate for many years. Some see this as one group: *the righteous dead's being judged for reward.* For example, *Tony Evans* states, "This is not the resurrection of NT believers because that occurs at the rapture. This is the resurrection of OT *saints*—God's *servants the prophets,* who will be given *the reward* they are due along with *those who fear [his] name, both small and great*"(emphasis added).[161] Therefore, Evans does see a resurrection here,

---

161   Evans, *The Tony Evans Bible Commentary,* 1411.

and he does not separate the resurrected from the rewarded. However, his assertion is these are OT saints.

MacArthur states, "The establishing of Christ's kingdom will be a fitting time for the dead to be judged. The Great White Throne judgment (20:11–15) is not in view in this passage, as some argue, since that judgment explicitly involves only unbelievers. . . . The judgment will first of all be the time for God to reward His bond-servants the prophets and the saints and those who fear His name, the small and the great."[162] Once again, the judgment and the dead are linked to those who receive reward. Obviously, the dead cannot be judged and rewarded unless they are resurrected.

Osborne observes, "Several (e.g., Mounce, Krodel) see 'slaves' as inclusive of all and then two basic groups, the prophets and the saints. Others (e.g., Ford, Johnson, Michaels) see three groups: the prophets, the saints, and 'those who fear God.' Finally, some (e.g., Beale 1999:617) see all the terms as descriptive of the church (with 'prophets' referring to the prophetic ministry of the church)."[163] Others, such as Osborne, observe that those named "saints," "prophets," etc. are part of the church, which is the subject of the rewards here.

Wiersbe comments, "'And the time of the dead, that they should be judged' takes us to the very end of God's prophetic program. . . . This judgment is described in Revelation 20:11–15. There will also be a judgment of God's children, known as 'the Judgment Seat of Christ.' God will reward His faithful servants and the sufferings they experienced on earth will be forgotten in the glory of His presence."[164] Wiersbe states that the judgment of the dead finds its fulfillment in the great white throne judgment, where the Lord will judge all the unrighteous dead. However, this cannot be, because the judgment at hand will occur *during*

---

162 MacArthur, *The MacArthur New Testament Commentary: Revelation 1–11*, 319.

163 Osborne, *Baker Exegetical Commentary: Revelation*, 446.

164 Wiersbe, *Bible Exposition Commentary*, 2:601.

the seventh trumpet. The *great white throne judgment* that Wiersbe cites will occur after the millennium (see Rev 20:5–6).

Once again, there is no consensus on interpretation, and time will not permit an examination of all the competing views. Whatever camp a person is in, that's the direction they go. It is this commentary's commitment to stay faithful to the fact that Revelation is about the church. This view should be the basis for interpreting this passage and others. Dispensational Pretrib proponents are committed to the doctrinal position that the church has already been raptured at this point. Therefore, in order to maintain fidelity with dispensationalism, they have no choice but to explain away the seventh trumpet resurrection reward narrative as being applicable to those other than the church. Explaining away the church is not where we should be placing our emphasis. What is depicted here in 11:18 is the resurrection aspect of the resurrection/rapture event depicted in the texts at 1 Corinthians 15 and 1 Thessalonians 4. For a full refutation of the Pretrib argument, see the essay "The Seventh Trumpet of Revelation and Paul's Last Trumpet."

(19) *And the temple of God which is in heaven was opened; and the ark of His covenant appeared in His temple:* Here the temple of God was opened, and John was able to see inside it. What a magnificent scene. John saw the heavenly "ark of [the] covenant." Now, concerning the earthly temple, the writer of Hebrews stated, "Who serve a copy and shadow of the heavenly things, just as Moses was warned by God when he was about to erect the tabernacle; for, 'See,' He says, 'that you make all things according to the pattern which was shown you on the mountain'" (Heb 8:5). Revelation confirms what we learn from this passage in Hebrews. The earthly temple is to some degree a replica or, as Hebrews states, "a copy and shadow of the heavenly things." John said the *heavenly ark* in the *heavenly temple* was opened. In the earthly tabernacle and temple, the ark was placed in the *holy of holies* situated behind the veil. The fact that it is now opened is a testament to Christ's highly priestly ministry, where He consecrated the way into the presence of God by His own blood (see

Matt 27:51; Heb 9:11–14). The earthly ark has been lost for centuries, but the *heavenly ark* and the *covenant* are *eternal*. God's presence and grace to the redeemed is based on an everlasting covenant.

(a) *and there were flashes of lightning and sounds and peals of thunder and an earthquake and a great hailstorm:* Events in heaven are often punctuated with clamor, "flashes of lightning," and "peals of thunder." These are reactions to the awesomeness of God's dictates and decrees. The "great hailstorm" is probably a reference to the seventh bowl judgment where the earth is pulverized by one-hundred-pound hail (see Rev 16:21), which is still to come. The verse-by-verse commentary continues on page 236.

ESSAY:
THE SEVENTH TRUMPET OF REVELATION AND PAUL'S LAST TRUMPET

One of the amazing aspects concerning the inspiration of the Scriptures is how passages from the OT are fulfilled in the NT. Though different authors over thousands of years wrote the Scriptures, it is God who inspired each person (see 2 Tim 3:16). St. Augustine once said, "The New is in the Old concealed; the Old is in the New revealed." Both the OT and NT paint one grand portrait of God's great redemptive plan for humanity. For many centuries, the OT was the only written Word of God. After Christ's death and resurrection, the writings of the apostles and their associates (e.g., Mark, Luke) developed the NT, which offered a continuation of God's revelation. As the OT primarily looked forward to the Messiah's first advent, the NT looks forward to His second advent.

Because dispensationalism has been a dominant teaching in eschatology, people have had some difficulty interpreting Revelation with fresh eyes. Pretrib seems hesitant to link the church and NT to Revelation. However, if one avoids dispensational boundaries, the natural understanding of Scripture would accommodate linking the seventh and last trumpets. Many holding a Pretrib view have opted for maintaining fidelity to *a position* more than let the Scriptures speak for themselves. Some have mounted their defenses to explain away a plain reading of the text.

Chapters 10 and 11 reveal that there are many significant events that will occur at the blowing of the seventh trumpet: *the delay will end* (see 10:6); *the mystery of God, as He declared to the prophets, will be completed* (see 10:7); the great announcement will be made in heaven: *"The kingdom of the world has become the kingdom of our Lord and of His Christ"* (see 11:15); the Lord will seize power over the earth (see 11:17); *the time comes for judging the righteous dead and giving reward to the prophets, the saints, and those who fear God's name, both small and great* (see 11:18); and *the nations will be angry and God's wrath has come* (see 11:18). Considering all these points, is it mere coincidence that both the *seventh trumpet* and the *last trumpet* (see 1 Cor 15:51–52) are "lasts" and contain resurrections?

Is it a mere coincidence that while the righteous are being rewarded, wrath is happening on the Earth? Is it a mere coincidence that *the mystery of the church* and *the mystery of God* are both completed at the blowing of a last trumpet? Is it a mere coincidence that the *long delay ends* with the blowing of the seventh trumpet, and the *long delay* that Peter defends ends when the Lord comes (see 2 Pet 3)? Isn't it prudent to link these concepts rather than trying to find ways to disconnect them?

EXAMINING THE PRETRIB ARGUMENT AGAINST THE SEVENTH TRUMPET

In his book *Things to Come*,[165] J. Dwight Pentecost puts forth nine points to defeat the concept that the seventh trumpet of Revelation and the last trumpet of 1 Corinthians 15:52 and 1 Thessalonians 4:16 *are* the same.

> (1) *The last trumpet of 1 Corinthians and 1 Thessalonians sounds before the wrath of God is poured out. However, the trumpet in Revelation 11:15 occurs at the end of the time of wrath.*

Response: First, insisting that these are different trumpets creates the need for another group of eschatological trumpets. If the last trumpet

---

[165] J. Dwight Pentecost, *Things to Come* (Grand Rapids, MI: Zondervan Publishing House, 1964), 189–92.

associated with the rapture is different from the seventh trumpet of Revelation 11, Pretrib proponents must locate this other group of trumpets that makes the rapture trumpet "the last" one. The Pretrib argument has no real validity unless those other trumpets are located *in the Scriptures*. On this topic, Pretribulationists make a doctrinal argument that has no scriptural backing. Second, in reference to the *seventh trumpet*, MacArthur, an ardent Pretribulationist, asserts,

> Instead of calling for the moment of the Rapture of the church, as the "last trumpet" does, the seventh trumpet calls for prolonged waves of judgment on the ungodly. It does not parallel the trumpet of 1 Corinthians 15:52 but does parallel the trumpet of Joel 2:1–2: "Blow a trumpet in Zion, and sound an alarm on My holy mountain! Let all the inhabitants of the land tremble, for the day of the Lord is coming; surely it is near, a day of darkness and gloom, a day of clouds "and thick darkness."[166]

Arguments like these are shortsighted. First, MacArthur assumes the *last trumpet* only initiates the rapture. However, readers must consider the context of the 1 Corinthians 15 text, which specifically concerns the resurrection and rapture. Paul's subject is not about any preceding trumpets but about events particular to the resurrection. Not mentioning other events cannot be used to exclude them from occurring during the last trumpet. Second, both the *last trumpet* and the *seventh trumpet* have resurrections attached to them, which indicates similarity, not difference.

Third, MacArthur keys in on Joel 2:1, "*Blow a trumpet* in Zion, and sound an alarm on My holy mountain" (emphasis added), as a basis for comparison to the apocalyptic trumpets. However, this is an expression of warning. A similar phrase is found in Judges 7:18 and Jeremiah 6:1;

---

166   MacArthur, *The MacArthur New Testament Commentary: Revelation 1–11,* 124.

51:27. The idiom "sound of the trumpet," as used in Jeremiah 4:19, is found in several OT passages and means "to warn the people." However, Joel was not stating that he witnessed the blowing of the *apocalyptic trumpet* issued by God and blown from "heaven" by the *seventh angel.* "Blow a trumpet in Zion" is quite different from an angel blowing his trumpet from heaven. If the text in Joel stated an angel descended from heaven and blew his trumpet, only then would there be a parallel.

Therefore, until the church is completed at the sounding of the seventh (i.e., the last) trumpet, the resurrection/rapture event that Paul described in 1 Corinthians 15 cannot occur. When this does occur, the church and the OT saints will be raised, fulfilling the prophecies of Isaiah 25:8 and Hosea 13:14. The OT saints cannot be made perfect or *be glorified* until the resurrection/rapture, which did not occur during their time but will occur at the close of the church age. Consider a relay race. Only the anchor runner crosses the finish line. When the preceding runners finish their legs of the race, they rest. However, all rejoice when the anchor runner wins for the entire team. The church is the anchor generation.

Fourth, Pretrib holds that the entire Seventieth Week is the wrath of God and that the church is raptured before the beginning of the week. This commentary does not accept the premise that the wrath of God lasts for seven years. The Apostle Paul indicated that "the coming of our Lord Jesus Christ and *our gathering together to Him*" (2 Thess 2:1, emphasis added), which is the rapture, require the *falling away first* and the *revealing,* or uncovering, of the *son of destruction* (the Antichrist), whose actions are described in 2 Thessalonians 2:4 as being the *abomination of desolation.* Jesus agreed in Matt 24:15–16 that the abomination of desolation comes before the great tribulation. Additionally, cosmic disturbances will occur sometime after the abomination of desolation is set up (see Matt 24:29). This agrees with Joel's prophecy, which is echoed in Peter's sermon on the day of Pentecost. "The sun will be turned into darkness and the moon into blood *before* the great and awesome day of the Lord comes" (Joel 2:28–32; Acts 2:20). The wrath of God cannot commence before the beast begins his role, which is only forty-two months (three and a half years), not eighty-four months (seven years). The beast does not ride in on a white horse but ascends from the abyss (see Rev 11:7; 13:1; 17:8). The man who becomes the beast does back the covenant with many for seven years. That action initiates the Seventieth Week, but his role as the beast does not start until the middle of the Seventieth Week, hence the reason he only reigns for forty-two months as the beast. For these issues, Pretrib throws down the imminence argument, but that is their line in the sand, not ours.

(2) The trumpet *that summons the church is called the trump of God, while the seventh trumpet is the angel's trumpet.*

Response: This argument has no merit. Paul identified this trumpet as "*the trumpet of God*" (1 Thess 4:16, emphasis added); this does not mean that it is *God who blows the trumpet.* For example, Revelation 15:2 speaks of those in heaven having "harps of God." This does not mean that God is also playing the harp. The CSB translates it "with harps from God." Therefore, if they are "from God," they are considered God's, but it doesn't mean He's the one playing the instrument. However, the most damaging aspect to this faulty line of reasoning is uncovered by the following passage. "And I saw the seven angels who stand before God, and seven trumpets were given to them" (Rev 8:2). Certainly, the angels do not have their *own trumpets.* They stand before God and are *given trumpets.* The clear implication is that God is the one who gives them their trumpets. That being the case, the angels' trumpets *are the trumpets of God* because the trumpets came from Him. This is just like the harps in Revelation 15 being *the harps of God* because they came from God.

(3) *The trumpet for the church is singular. No trumpets have preceded it so it cannot be said to be the last of a series. The trumpet that closes the tribulation is clearly last of a series of seven.*

Response: Once again, this semantic argument does not hold water. Just because Paul doesn't mention any trumpet before the last trumpet does not mean there weren't any trumpets that preceded it. If someone says the grass received plenty of water from the rain, but they do not comment on the wet sidewalks and streets, should it then be concluded that the sidewalks and streets didn't get wet? Wouldn't it be a mistake to assume there were no wet sidewalks and streets based solely on the fact that they were not mentioned? Yes, it would be a mistake to make this assumption. Likewise, it cannot be said that no trumpets preceded the last one based on Paul not making a comment on it.

In one sense, it is true that "the last trumpet" of 1 Corinthians 15:52 is singular, because it is the *only* trumpet associated with the resurrection. But it is also "the last." Therefore, we cannot make the argument that it is the only or a stand-alone trumpet. For this trumpet to be *last*, by definition, another trumpet must precede it, whether Paul stated it or not. The fact that it is *singular* does not negate the fact that it is *last*; both can be true at the same time.

In 1 Corinthians 15, the basis for argumentation was not to settle the number of trumpets but to counter people who insisted that there was no resurrection. There would have been no reason for Paul to mention trumpets that were not associated with the resurrection. Paul was not teaching a lesson on the apocalyptic trumpets. There can only be *one* last trumpet, and just as logic would have it, there can only be one *first* trumpet. That is, unless there is another group of apocalyptic trumpets. Those who insist the last trumpet of 1 Corinthians 15 is a different trumpet than the seventh and last trumpet of Revelation would need to produce evidence of those other trumpets in the Scriptures.

> (4) *In 1 Thessalonians 4, the voice associated with the sounding of the trumpet summons the dead and the living and, consequently, is heard before the resurrection. In Revelation, while the resurrection is mentioned in 11:12, the trumpet does*

not sound until after the resurrection, showing us that two different events must be in view.

Response: Apparently, this is a response to a *Mid-tribulation rapture* argument that suggests that the resurrection of *the two witnesses* is the resurrection of the church. This is not a view that this commentary holds or supports. However, the resurrection and reward that this commentary supports is found just six verses later in v. 18 where the trumpet blows first, then the resurrection occurs.

> (5) *The trumpet in 1 Thessalonians 4 issues a blessing in life and glory while the trumpet in Revelation issues judgment upon the enemies of God.*

Response: The *seventh trumpet* does not *only* issue judgment upon the enemies of God. This is a serious mischaracterization of this trumpet. During this trumpet, Jesus will seize control over the earth, which will reverse Satan's control since the fall and initiate celebration in heaven (see 11:15–16). It will also be the time for the righteous (i.e., the saints, the prophets, His servants, and those who fear His name small and great) to receive rewards. This is huge, because this is the anticipation of every righteous person who has lived and died and who is waiting for their final redemption and reward.

George Eldon Ladd observes,

> The day of judgment will include a rewarding of those who have served God, particularly the prophets and saints. "Saints" designates God's people in general of every era.[167]

The only way to reward saints of "every era" is to first raise them from the dead. The rewarding of all—the righteous, prophets, servants, the saints, and those who fear God's name small and great—is a tremen-

---

167 George Eldon Ladd, *A Commentary on the Revelation of John* (Grand Rapids, MI: William B. Eerdmans Publishing Company, 1972), 163.

dous event that could only happen after a resurrection has occurred. This is emphasized by the phrase "the time came for the dead to be judged" (11:18). The Scriptures explicitly declare we must all stand before the "judgment seat of Christ" (2 Cor 5:10) for reward. At the seventh trumpet, this rewarding will be occurring at the same time and in contrast to the wrath of God being poured out "on those who destroy the earth" (Rev 11:18).

Paul declared in 1 Corinthians 15:54–55 that the resurrection hopes of the OT prophets illustrated in the sayings "Death is swallowed up in victory" (see Isa 25:8) and "O death, where is your victory? O death, where is your sting?" (see Hos 13:14) will be fulfilled at the "last trumpet." This agrees with what the author of Hebrews declared, "All these, having gained approval through their faith, did not receive what was promised, because God had provided something better for us, so that apart from us they would not be made perfect" (Heb 11:39–40). The OT saints looked forward to the Messiah but died without receiving the promise. However, *in the last days*, God poured out His Spirit on all flesh (see Acts 2:17–21) and inaugurated the church, which has received the promise. The church is the "us" of Hebrews 11:40. The seventh trumpet embraces all these aspects. Therefore, it cannot be rightly concluded that the seventh trumpet *only* issues judgment from God.

> (6) *In the Thessalonian passage the trumpet sounds "in the moment, in the twinkling of an eye." In Revelation 10:7 the indication is that the seventh trumpet shall sound over a continued period of time, probably the duration of the judgments that fall under it, for John speaks of an angel that shall begin to sound. The duration gives evidence of the distinction in these two.*

Response: First, the author has mischaracterized 1 Thessalonians 4 text by conflating information from the 1 Corinthians 15 text. "In the twinkling of an eye" is not found in the Thessalonian text. It should be noted that the apostle Paul said not that the trumpet will *sound* in the twinkling of an eye but that *we will be changed* in the twinkling of an eye when the trumpet sounds. This text has nothing to do with the duration of the sounding of the trumpet. That is a completely fallacious talking point. The text reads, "Behold, I tell you a mystery; we will not all sleep, but we will all be changed, in a moment, in the twinkling of an eye, at the last trumpet; for the trumpet will sound, and the dead will be raised imperishable, and we will be changed" (1 Cor 15:51–52). "In a moment, in the twinkling of an eye" has to do with the *instantaneous change*, not *the duration* of the trumpet blast. This is a very common defense that has no basis. The Pretrib short-trumpet-blast argument sounds *flat* when the Scriptures are properly examined.

> (7) *The trumpet in 1 Thessalonians 4 is distinctly for the church, since God is dealing with Israel in particular and the Gentiles in general. In the tribulation, the seventh trumpet, which falls in the period of the tribulation, could not have reference to the church without losing the distinctions between the church and Israel.*

Response: In order to make this argument work, you must first accept that the last trumpet for the church and the seventh trumpet of Revelation 11 are different. We do not accept that tenet. The purpose of this commentary is to harmonize the Scriptures, not compartmentalize them along dispensational lines. It is dispensationalism that insists on the need to maintain a distinction here; the Scriptures do not. The Lord is not bound by human doctrinal traditions. Distinctions between the church and Israel cannot be lost just because the trumpets are the same. That would imply that God cannot accomplish two different things at once.

Another argument in *Things to Come* that concerns the meaning of the last trumpet states, "Not with reference to any preceding series but as connected to the close of this aion (age) and the last scene of this world history."[168] In other words, *last* is not because it's the final trumpet in a

---

[168] Pentecost, *Things to Come*, 189.

series or that other trumpets preceded it, but *last* means it blows during the last scene of this age. According to this reasoning, *last* has to do with *when* it happens, not *the order* in which it happens. Another way to make the same argument is to say the trumpet is blown at the close of a *program*. In that regard, there will be a last trumpet for the church and a last trumpet that closes out Israel, maintaining a distinction between the two. However, there is a fundamental problem with this reasoning. Where in the Scriptures are there any trumpets blown from heaven when a program changes? Was there a trumpet blown when the dispensation of Law closed? Was there a trumpet blown when the church started on the day of Pentecost, when a new age (or aion) started during the *dispensation of grace*? If there were a trumpet that sounded to inaugurate the birth of the church, then it would make sense that the trumpet that sounds during the rapture would be the last one. But no such first trumpet exists. Also, what about the prior dispensations? Were there trumpets blown from heaven to signal the end of those? If so, what are the Scriptures to show this? All these defenses are crafted to defend the Pretrib rapture but are not based on what the Bible explicitly states. Pretribulationists are great at stating doctrinal tenets but come up short on proving the same tenets with Scripture.

> (8) *The passage in Revelation depicts a great earthquake in which thousands are slain, and the believing remnant that worships God is stricken with fear. In the Thessalonian passage there is no earthquake mentioned. There will be no believing remnant left behind at the rapture to experience fear of Revelation 11:13. Such a view would only be consistent with a partial rapture position.*

Response: For some reason, the author has shifted his focus to the time after the two witnesses' death and resurrection, where the Scriptures mention an earthquake that will kill seven thousand people. However, it is strange that he would use this text because the two witnesses die and are resurrected before the seventh trumpet is blown. We know this

231

because v. 14 explicitly states the second woe has passed and the third woe is coming quickly. The second woe is the sixth trumpet, and the third woe is the seventh trumpet. Therefore, the author's assertions concerning events surrounding the two witnesses do not apply to any argument about the seventh and last trumpet, because the seventh trumpet has not yet blown. Lastly, this argument states, "*There will be no believing remnant left behind at the rapture to experience fear of Revelation 11:13.*" If this were the case, then where does the innumerable multitude that comes out of the great tribulation (7:9, 14) come from? The author's point is a very bad argument.

> (9) *While the church will be rewarded at the time of the rapture, the reward given to "thy servants the prophets and to the Saints" cannot be that event. The rewarding mentioned in Revelation 11:18 is seen to take place on earth after the second advent of Christ following the judgment on His enemies. Since the church is to be rewarded in the air following the rapture, these must be two distinct events.*

Response: There are several things wrong with this line of argumentation. The first problem is the author states that the reward ceremony mentioned in 11:18 is seen to take place on earth. However, an examination of the text does not support that conclusion. On the contrary, what is taking place on the earth is the wrath of God.

> And the nations were enraged, and Your wrath came, and the time *came* for the dead to be judged, and the time to reward Your bond-servants the prophets and the saints and those who fear Your name, the small and the great, and to destroy those who destroy the earth. (Rev 11:18)

Where in the text does it state that this reward ceremony is happening on the earth? Where does it say in the text that the Lord has already returned in His second advent? What is clear is that *the nations were angry and God's wrath came,* and *it was time to destroy those who destroy the earth.* What is explicit is the seventh trumpet is the time for rewarding the righteous but also the time for *destroying those who destroy the earth.* The implication is that this rewarding is not happening at the same place where God's wrath is engaging those who destroy the Earth. The reward is for "[God's] bond-servants the prophets and the saints and those who fear [His] name, the small and the great." Some of the righteous enumerated here have been dead for centuries. The only way to reward the dead righteous is to first raise them. None of the argumentation put forth negates the seventh trumpet's being connected to the *last trumpet* of 1 Corinthians 15:51–56. As stated earlier, the rapture fulfills OT prophecy; this is why Paul declared that when the resurrection occurs, it will fulfill Isaiah 25:8 and Hosea 13:14. Therefore, the OT saints cannot be ruled out from this 11:18 resurrection event, because they, too, belong to Christ. Jesus is the only Messiah. He is the only Christ. His blood has redeemed all of the righteous, from Adam to the last human born before eternity starts.

The second problem is that the second coming of the Lord does not happen until after the seventh bowl in Revelation 16. The climactic act of the battle of Armageddon is depicted in Revelation 19 when the Lord returns with all His saints. This event in the bowl judgments does not occur at the blowing of the seventh trumpet. By this point, the seventh trumpet has already blown and opened the door for the finale of the seven bowl judgments. Though the seventh trumpet does last for a duration of time, there is no evidence scripturally that the seventh trumpet is still blowing once the bowl judgments commence. Additionally, there is no evidence in this passage that the Lord has already returned and that these rewards are occurring during the millennium. Revelation depicts events in apocalyptic imagery as opposed to didactic specifics found in the Epistles. Every effort should be made to harmonize Scripture with Scripture, not make Scripture conform to doctrinal tenets.

THE "REVELATION WAS WRITTEN MUCH LATER" ARGUMENT

The argument that Paul's last trumpet and John's seventh trumpet cannot be the same because Revelation was written decades later, after Paul was martyred, is not a convincing argument. First Corinthians was written about AD 55, and Revelation was written decades later in approximately AD 96. It is believed that Paul was martyred around AD 67. Therefore, Paul could not have known about any of Revelation's contents, specifically about the trumpets, making any connection between his *last trumpet* of 1 Corinthians 15 and the *seventh trumpet* of Revelation impossible. However, this is not difficult at all because Revelation and 1 Corinthians come from the same source—the Lord. All the Word of God is one consistent, God-breathed revelation. The individual authors need not be aware of one another's writings because the Holy Spirit is the common factor and source of continuity. The years between authorship would be irrelevant. In Revelation, John saw visions and was caught up in heaven where he heard directly from the Lord. Paul, too, received his doctrines directly from the Lord (see Gal 1:11). Paul, like John, was caught up to heaven (see 2 Cor 12:3–4). Paul's revelations were so extensive that they required him to receive a thorn in the flesh to prevent self-exaltation (see 2 Cor 12:7). The Lord, who is the inspiration of both books, simply gave to Paul only what he needed to know.

However, there is a plausible reason why Paul's trumpet reference lacked numerical specificity. When Paul was alive, Revelation did not exist. Neither had the numerical sequence of the seals, trumpets, and bowls been revealed. As far as 1 Corinthians 15 is concerned, the number of the trumpet is not relevant because the concerned trumpet is the last one. If there were fifty trumpets, it would not make a difference because it is the last one where the resurrection occurs. The Lord only revealed what Paul needed to know. Jesus only disclosed to Paul "the last trumpet" because that is the one that deals specifically with the resurrection, rapture, and rewarding of the saints. From Paul's perspective, where the trumpet was to be placed in numeric sequence was not important. The fact that mattered was that the concerned trumpet was the last one.

It cannot be denied that the seventh trumpet of Revelation includes a resurrection and a time of rewarding of the whole corpus of the righteous dead. The seventh trumpet also ends the two-thousand-year (and running) delay, and it completes the *mystery of God that was declared to the prophets* (see 10:6–7). What God declared to the prophets, the prophets declared to us. The prophet Joel declared the beginning of the church in Joel 2:28–30, and Paul described the end of the church on earth in 1 Corinthians 15:51 through the final "mystery," which is the rapture at *the last*, or *seventh*, trumpet. Likewise, the rapture of the church will end the long period of the church age, which has been present on earth for two thousand years and running. This event was also *declared by the prophets*. In 1 Corinthians 15:54–55, Paul declares, "But when this perishable will have put on the imperishable, and this mortal will have put on immortality, then will come about the saying that is written, 'Death is swallowed up in victory [Isa 25:8].' 'O death, where is your victory? O death, where is your sting? [Hosea 14:13].' " Paul declares that the rapture fulfills two OT prophecies. God declared this to the prophets, and the prophets declared this to us without any understanding of the church. This is a powerful example of God concluding the oldest mystery in the Scriptures, the church, hidden from the foundation of the world (Eph 1:5–11; 3:9–11).

REVELATION 12:1–9

The Woman, the Dragon, the Male Child, and Michael

[1] A great sign appeared in heaven: a woman clothed with the sun, and the moon under her feet, and on her head a crown of twelve stars; [2] and she was with child; and she cried out, being in labor and in pain to give birth. [3] Then another sign appeared in heaven: and behold, a great red dragon having seven heads and ten horns, and on his heads were seven diadems. [4] And his tail swept away a third of the stars of heaven and threw them to the earth. And the dragon stood before the woman who was about to give birth, so that when she gave birth he might devour her child. [5] And she gave birth to a son, a male child, who is to rule all the nations with a rod of iron; and her child was caught up to God and to His throne. [6] Then the woman fled into the wilderness where she had a place prepared by God, so that there she would be nourished for one thousand two hundred and sixty days. [7] And there was war in heaven, Michael and his angels waging war with the dragon. The dragon and his angels waged war, [8] and they were not strong enough, and there was no longer a place found for them in heaven. [9] And the great dragon was thrown down, the serpent of old who is called the devil and Satan, who deceives the whole world; he was thrown down to the earth, and his angels were thrown down with him.

(1) *A great sign appeared in heaven: a woman clothed with the sun, and the moon under her feet, and on her head a crown of twelve stars:* As typical with apocalyptic literature, John displayed an amazing pageant of cosmic proportion with Israel as the central focus. He wrote about the sign from heaven's perspective. Historically, many have seen this woman to be Mary, the mother of Jesus. Other historical options are the church, the heavenly bride, Jerusalem, an astrological constellation, i.e., Virgo, and others. However, a better understanding of this woman, both historically and in the future during the great tribulation, would be as *the nation of Israel.* The imagery goes back to Joseph's dream. The Genesis text reads, *"Lo, I have had still another dream; and behold, the sun and the moon and eleven stars were bowing down to me"* (Gen 37:9). Joseph dreamed about eleven stars because he didn't count himself, but he is listed among the twelve tribes in Revelation 7:8.

(a) *and on her head a crown of twelve stars:* This represents the twelve tribes of Israel (See Rev 7:1–8).

(2) *and she was with child; and she cried out, being in labor and in pain to give birth:* The vision depicts Israel as a woman ready to deliver a child (Isa 26:17–18; Mic 4:10; 5:3). Isaiah depicted national Israel coming forth in the following passage.

> Before she travailed, she brought forth; before her pain came, she gave birth to a boy. Who has heard such a thing? Who has seen such things? Can a land be born in one day? Can a nation be brought forth all at once? As soon as Zion travailed, she also brought forth her sons. "Shall I bring to the point of birth and not give delivery?" says the Lord. "Or shall I who gives delivery shut the womb?" says your God. (Isa 66:7–9)

Also, Israel was to produce the Messiah.

> For a child will be born to us, a son will be given to us; and the government will rest on His shoulders; and His name will be called Wonderful Counselor, Mighty God, Eternal Father, Prince of Peace. (Isa 9:6)

(3) *Then another sign appeared in heaven: and behold, a great red dragon having seven heads and ten horns, and on his heads were seven diadems:* In Revelation, the seven heads and ten horns symbolize two individuals: *Satan* and the *beast.* However, in this chapter, the symbols apply to Satan because the word "dragon" is used. The word "dragon" is found thirteen times in Revelation, and each reference is to Satan. In 13:1, the symbols of seven heads and ten horns are also used but here without *the dragon* modifier. They are in reference to the *beast,* who is also the *Antichrist.*

(4) *And his tail swept away a third of the stars of heaven and threw them to the earth:* "Stars of heaven" are a symbolic reference to angelic beings (9:1). Aune comments, "It is possible that the description of the dragon sweeping a third of the stars and casting them down to the earth alludes to the story of the descent of Satan and his angels to earth in the traditional story of the Watchers (1 Enoch 6–11)."[169] Many understand Revelation 12:4 to indicate Satan's led rebellion in heaven when he caused *one third* of the heavenly host to fall with him. (In reference to Satan's fall, cf. Luke 10:18.) Here in Revelation 12:4, "the stars" make up the ranks of the fallen angels, demons, and wicked spirits that do the bidding of Satan. These rule in the earth and the heavenly realms (outer atmosphere, cf. Dan 10) and make up the league of *principalities, powers, and the rulers of the darkness of this world, spiritual wickedness in the heavenlies* (Eph 6:12). However, they are less powerful than godly angels (2 Pet 2:11) and are outnumbered at least by a two to one ratio, because Satan only "swept away a third" of the angels. Additionally, their numbers are further depleted because many of these wicked angels are in detention in *Tartarus,** the deepest abyss of Hades (2 Pet 2:4 HCSB), or in "the abyss" (Luke 8:31). No one knows when this rebellion occurred, but it certainly predates human history.[170] It at least predates the Garden of Eden encounter, where Satan instigated the fall of Adam.

---

[169] Aune, *Word Biblical Commentary,* 52B:686.

[170] Many commentators do not interpret the "third of the stars" of heaven as a reference to an angelic rebellion. Neither do they see Isaiah 14:2–15 and Ezekiel 28:11–17 as references to Satan's fall. However, many others do hold to these interpretations.

(a) *And the dragon stood before the woman who was about to give birth, so that when she gave birth he might devour her child*: This imagery is in reference to Satan's attempt to use Herod to kill Christ after His birth (Matt 2:13, 16–18), just as Pharaoh tried to kill Moses, Israel's deliverer (Exod 1:22).

(5) *And she gave birth to a son, a male child, who is to rule all the nations with a rod of iron*: "She gave birth to a son" speaks of *Israel's delivering her promised Messiah*, specifically in whom this promise was first declared in Genesis (i.e., the protevangelium): "*And between your seed and her seed; He shall bruise you on the head, and you shall bruise him on the heel*" (Gen 3:15). This is the origin of the battle between the "seed" and the serpent. "Who is to rule all the nations with a rod of iron" speaks of Jesus' messianic rule from "the throne of David" during his millennial reign (Isa 9:7).

(a) *and her child was caught up to God and to His throne*: This indicates Christ's ascension into heaven, which is recorded in the first chapter of Acts:

> And after He had said these things, He was lifted up while they were looking on, and a cloud received Him out of their sight. And as they were gazing intently into the sky while He was going, behold, two men in white clothing stood beside them. They also said, "Men of Galilee, why do you stand looking into the sky? This Jesus, who has been taken up from you into heaven, will come in just the same way as you have watched Him go into heaven." (Acts 1:9–11)

The Greek word for "caught up" in Revelation 12:5 is *harpazô*, meaning "to seize, catch up, snatch away." [171] In Acts 1:9–11, we see the actual fulfillment of what Revelation 12:5 symbolically depicts. Of the fourteen uses of *harpazô* in the NT (Matt 11:12; 12:29; 13:19; John 6:15; 10:12, 28, 29; Acts 8:39; 23:10; 2 Cor 12:2, 4; 1 Thess 4:17; Jude 23; Rev 12:5), none of

---

[171] Thomas, *New American Standard Exhaustive Concordance, harpazô,* "caught up."

them can be interpreted as someone's disappearing.[172] However, in Acts 1:9, when Jesus ascended, He was "caught up" (Gk. *harpazô*, Rev 12:5), and He disappeared, but He did not *suddenly* disappear. When He was "lifted up," the disciples watched Him go up into the clouds. The entire event was observable. Likewise, the Scriptures teach not that Christians will *suddenly* disappear "in the twinkling of an eye" but that "in the twinkling of an eye" Christians will "be changed," where the perishable will put on "the imperishable" and the mortal will put on "immortality" (1 Cor 15:52–53).

At the resurrection of the righteous, the dead in Christ will be raised, from wherever they are planted (i.e., buried), in visible, glorified bodies like Christ's glorious body (Phil 3:21). Then those alive at the time will be "changed . . . in the twinkling of an eye" (1 Cor 15:51–52) and "will be caught up . . . to meet the Lord in the air" (1 Thess 4:17) in the same manner as were the resurrected dead. This is patterned after Christ's resurrection. Unfortunately, the Tim LaHaye and Jerry B. Jenkins *Left Behind* book series, and the movies based on it, have forged an impression of the rapture that is popular but not accurate. The main event will be the saints rising from the dead in glorified bodies, many after being dead for thousands of years. This will be an observable event, just as was the resurrection of the dead saints in Matthew 27:51–52. The catching up of the living will be part two of this glorious event.

(6) *Then the woman fled into the wilderness where she had a place prepared by God, so that there she would be nourished for one thousand two hundred and sixty days*: Again, "the woman" is the nation of Israel, or more spe-

---

[172] David G. Peterson, *The Pillar New Testament Commentary: The Acts of the Apostles* (Grand Rapids, MI: Wm. B. Eerdmans Publishing Co., 2009), 294, states, "When Luke says that the Spirit *suddenly took Philip away* (*hērpasen ton Philippon*), the meaning is that the Spirit 'seized' or 'took hold of' Philip and moved him on to a new place (cf. Mt. 11:12; 12:29; 13:19; Jn. 6:15; Acts 23:10). There is no need to conclude that 'the Spirit brings Philip by supernatural means to Azotus.'" C. K. Barrett, *International Critical Commentary: Acts 1–14* (New York: Bloomsbury Publishing, 1994), 435, agrees. He says, "This verb can be used with reference to the rapture of persons to heaven or to God (2 Cor. 12:2, 4; 1 Thes. 4:17; Rev. 12:5), but that is obviously not the meaning in this context."

cifically, the remnant who will escape Jerusalem during the days of the tribulation and who will be protected for *three and a half years* during the second half of Daniel's Seventieth Week. Concerning the Jews who will be forced to flee Jerusalem, Jesus declared,

> Then those who are in Judea must flee to the mountains. Whoever is on the housetop must not go down to get the things out that are in his house. Whoever is in the field must not turn back to get his cloak. But woe to those who are pregnant and to those who are nursing babies in those days! But pray that your flight will not be in the winter, or on a Sabbath. For then there will be a great tribulation, such as has not occurred since the beginning of the world until now, nor ever will. (Matt 24:16–21)

Speaking of the remnant of Israel's fleeing, Zechariah prophesied,

> You will flee by the valley of My mountains, for the valley of the mountains will reach to Azel; yes, you will flee just as you fled before the earthquake in the days of Uzziah king of Judah. Then the Lord, my God, will come, *and* all the holy ones with Him! (Zech 14:5)

These days will be terrible for *those living in Israel and Christians* worldwide. Satan, through the beast, will persecute anyone who follows Jesus, whether they are *Jews or Gentiles*. The popular idea that the tribulation is *only* "the time of Jacob's distress" (Jer 30:7) does not paint a complete picture because Isaiah declared that the wrath of God is God's anger toward the whole world (Isa 13:10–11). The beast will not discriminate but will be an equal opportunity persecutor and destroyer, whether he's destroying national Israel or the church.

(7–8) *And there was war in heaven, Michael and his angels waging war with the dragon. The dragon and his angels waged war, and they were not strong enough, and there was no longer a place found for them in heaven:*

The angelic war recorded here is literally out of this world because it occurred in the heavenlies. In 2 Corinthians 12:2–4, Paul spoke of the "third heaven," which is "Paradise." However, in some Jewish writings as many as *seven levels of heaven* are cited.[173] In the Bible, the three levels are understood to be the *air*, or *the atmosphere, outer space*, and *the abode of God*. It is doubtful that the war between Michael and Satan occurred in the third heaven, and it is more likely to have been in a lower level of heaven. Ephesians 6:12 speaks about "spiritual forces of wickedness in the heavenly places" ("realms," NIV). Daniel 10 explicitly describes an angelic interception when a demonic principality over the kingdom of Persia withstood the angel coming with an answer to Daniel's prayer. This interception occurred somewhere between the third heaven and the earth. While contending with the demonic principality, the angel received assistance from Michael the archangel, one of the chief (angelic) princes (Dan 10:1–21). "They were not strong enough, and there was no longer a place found for them in heaven." Satan and his army were no match for Michael and his army. The end result was that they were cast out of the heavenly realms. Second Peter 2:11 also informs us that the godly angels are stronger than the wicked angels.

(9) *And the great dragon was thrown down*: After being defeated in the heavenly war, Satan was violently "thrown down" to the earth, and all his wicked angels went with him. Now confined to the earth, Satan focuses his wrath on Israel and the church. One instance of his wrath toward Israel came through *Antiochus Epiphanes IV* after he suffered a defeat in Egypt. Antiochus returned to Israel and took out his fury on the Jews, their religion, and their temple, which caused the first *abomination of desolation* to be set up. In the future, Satan will also work through the Antichrist in an unparalleled rash of tribulation to persecute all who follow Christ.

---

[173] Colin G. Kruse, *2 Corinthians: An Introduction and Commentary*, vol. 8, *Tyndale New Testament Commentaries* (Downers Grove, IL: InterVarsity Press, 1987), 195.

(a) *the serpent of old who is called the devil and Satan, who deceives the whole world:* To some degree, the "whole world" is under the sway of Satan's wicked deceptions. Humans have no ability to comprehend the extent of the devil's influence in every sphere of reality, whether in the visible or invisible realms. Isaiah 14:12 declares, "How you have fallen from heaven, O star of the morning, son of the dawn! You have been cut down to the earth, *you who have weakened the nations!*" (emphasis added). John stated, "The whole world lies in the power of the evil one" (1 John 5:19). Though God limits what Satan can do, no one, whether saved or unsaved, has gone unscathed by Satan's influence in this world.

REVELATION 12:10–17

The Accuser Is Thrown Down

¹⁰ Then I heard a loud voice in heaven, saying, "Now the salvation, and the power, and the kingdom of our God and the authority of His Christ have come, for the accuser of our brethren has been thrown down, he who accuses them before our God day and night. ¹¹ And they overcame him because of the blood of the Lamb and because of the word of their testimony, and they did not love their life even when faced with death. ¹² For this reason, rejoice, O heavens and you who dwell in them. Woe to the earth and the sea, because the devil has come down to you, having great wrath, knowing that he has only a short time." ¹³ And when the dragon saw that he was thrown down to the earth, he persecuted the woman who gave birth to the male child. ¹⁴ But the two wings of the great eagle were given to the woman, so that she could fly into the wilderness to her place, where she was nourished for a time and times and half a time, from the presence of the serpent. ¹⁵ And the serpent poured water like a river out of his mouth after the woman, so that he might cause her to be swept away with the flood. ¹⁶ But the earth helped the woman, and the earth opened its mouth and drank up the river which the dragon poured out of his mouth. ¹⁷ So the dragon was enraged with the woman, and went off to make war with the rest of her children, who keep the commandments of God and hold to the testimony of Jesus.

(10) *Then I heard a loud voice in heaven, saying, "Now the salvation, and the power, and the kingdom of our God and the authority of His Christ have come, for the accuser of our brethren has been thrown down, he who accuses them before our God day and night*: Once again, John heard "a loud voice" in "heaven." This voice said, "The accuser of our brethren has been thrown down, he who accuses them before our God day and night." This "accuser" is Satan, and there are many false narratives about him. One is that he rules from hell. The truth is the devil does not rule his kingdom from a throne in hell. He has not been there and does not want to go there. Up to this point, Satan had access to heaven and God's throne. In our present day, he accuses the brethren because he is the tempter who entices people to sin. He knows and exploits our weaknesses. Whenever we fall short, he makes a case against us as he did with Job (Job 1:6–12). Satan is extremely jealous and hateful of humans because we bear God's image. When Adam fell, the entire human race fell with him, and God set a plan of redemption in action for us. But the angels that sinned were doomed to hell without recourse or redemption. Therefore, in jealous indignation, Satan accuses us before God. An explicit example of Satan's accusations is shown with Joshua the high priest in the book of Zechariah.

> Then he showed me Joshua the high priest standing before the angel of the LORD, and Satan standing at his right hand to accuse him. The LORD said to Satan, "The LORD rebuke you, Satan! Indeed, the LORD who has chosen Jerusalem rebuke you! Is this not a brand plucked from the fire?" Now Joshua was clothed with filthy garments and standing before the angel. He spoke and said to those who were standing before him, saying, "Remove the filthy garments from him." Again he said to him, "See, I have taken your iniquity away from you and will clothe you with festal robes." (Zech 3:1–4)

Situations like those of Joshua the high priest play out "day and night" in heaven, where Satan actively accuses the brethren. However, we have an advocate with God. The apostle John stated, "My little children, I am writing these things to you so that you may not sin. And if anyone sins, we have an Advocate with the Father, Jesus Christ the righteous" (1 John 2:1). However, a time will finally come for Satan the dragon to be "thrown down."

(11) *They overcame him because of the blood of the Lamb and because of the word of their testimony, and they did not love their life even when faced with death*: This is one of the most powerful testimonies concerning the fortitude and commitment of the saints who will face Satan's onslaught. Of all the worldly possessions that can be taken, no one can take an individual's testimony. The saints must overcome the beast's tyranny and torture, the false prophet's deception, and the image of the beast's mandate to worship the Antichrist. John saw that as faithful soldiers, these believers refused to bow down, and they loved not their own lives, even to the death. These are no *namby-pamby* Christians who failed to get caught up in the rapture. No, these are the greatest group of Christians that has ever lived. They are willing to lay down their lives for the Lord and refuse to worship the beast or take the mark that will allow them to buy or sell.

(12) *For this reason, rejoice, O heavens and you who dwell in them*: The heavens rejoice because Satan no longer has access to the third heaven. He could no longer appear before God and make his accusations against the saints. However, with the devil no longer having access to heaven there is *woe* for *the earth and the sea, because the devil* will *come down* with *great wrath, knowing that he has only a short time.* By this time, the world is in the second half of Daniel's Seventieth Week, which means the clock is ticking on Satan's last three and a half years before he is imprisoned in the abyss for a thousand years (20:1–3).

(13) *And when the dragon saw that he was thrown down to the earth, he persecuted the woman who gave birth to the male child*: Without a doubt, this woman is the nation and people of Israel, who Satan has hated and persecuted since the very beginning. Even now in the twenty-first century, antisemitism is high. Jews are a hated people all over the world and particularly in the United States. Much hypocrisy has gone forth in the sense that many love the nation (i.e., the state) of Israel while they despise the Jewish people. However, we know the source of Jewish hatred is Satan, as is shown in v. 13. As his time winds down, Satan is intentional in his attempt to destroy the Jews. But just as Satan's other plots to destroy the Jews have failed, this final attempt to destroy them will fail too.

(14) *But the two wings of the great eagle were given to the woman, so that she could fly into the wilderness to her place, where she was nourished for a time and times and half a time, from the presence of the serpent:* Many people claim that this reference to the "wings of the great eagle" represents the United States' coming to Israel's aid. Others claim that this is an airlift rescue operation. Considering modern aeronautical capabilities and political alignments, these ideas are not out of the realm of possibility. However, it is just as likely that this imagery is drawn from the OT: "Thus you shall say to the house of Jacob and tell the sons of Israel: 'You yourselves have seen what I did to the Egyptians, and how I bore you on eagles' wings, and brought you to Myself'" (Exod 19:3–4). Therefore, by whatever means "the wings of the great eagle" may represent how Israel will speedily reach safety in the wilderness. She will be "nourished for a time and times and half a time," which parallels a passage in Daniel 7:25 that has an identical phrase. The word "time" (Gk. *iddān*), of Chaldean origin, means "a year." "Time" (one year) plus "times" (two years) plus "half a time" (one half year) equals three and a half years, which corresponds with the last half of Daniel's Seventieth Week.

(15–16) *And the serpent poured water like a river out of his mouth after the woman, so that he might cause her to be swept away with the flood:* Satan will respond with a deluge of attacks and resources to hurt Israel. But as the text declares, *"the earth helped the woman,"* meaning that Israel might possibly be helped by finding shelter in the wilderness or by receiving aid from others.

(17) *So the dragon was enraged with the woman, and went off to make war with the rest of her children, who keep the commandments of God and hold to the testimony of Jesus:* God divinely protects His covenant people as He thwarts Satan's plans once again. Following this, Satan is enraged and turns his attention to making war with those who call on the name of Jesus. These Christians are the ones who remain faithful to Jesus during the horrendous times of the tribulation. Their victory comes not by avoiding the pain of death but by enduring it for the Lord's sake.

Chapters 13, 14, and 15 are some of the most powerful chapters in Revelation. The magnification of the apocalyptic microscope increases to give greater detail concerning the rise of the beast, the false prophet, the wicked agenda of the image of the beast, the fortitude of the saints, the messages of the three angels, the grace of God in the midst of the tribulation storm, and the heavenly victory of those who refuse to take the mark of the beast.

REVELATION 13:1–6

THE BEAST WITH SEVEN HEADS AND TEN HORNS RISES

¹ And the dragon stood on the sand of the seashore. Then I saw a beast coming up out of the sea, having ten horns and seven heads, and on his horns were ten diadems, and on his heads were blasphemous names. ² And the beast which I saw was like a leopard, and his feet were like those of a bear, and his mouth like the mouth of a lion. And the dragon gave him his power and his throne and great authority. ³ I saw one of his heads as if it had been slain, and his fatal wound was healed. And the whole earth was amazed and followed after the beast; ⁴ they worshiped the dragon because he gave his authority to the beast; and they worshiped the beast, saying, "Who is like the beast, and who is able to wage war with him?" ⁵ There was given to him a mouth speaking arrogant words and blasphemies, and authority to act for forty-two months was given to him. ⁶ And he opened his mouth in blasphemies against God, to blaspheme His name and His tabernacle, that is, those who dwell in heaven.

(1) *And the dragon stood on the sand of the seashore*: Bible versions vary on where they place this opening statement. Some versions, such as the ESV, close chapter 12 by adding this statement to v. 17. Other versions, such as the CSB, NET, and NLT, add it as an eighteenth verse to chapter 12. And other versions (NASB, NIV) add this sentence to the beginning of chapter 13. Finally, the KJV and NKJV do not include the phrase in chapter 12 or chapter 13. They simply start chapter 13 with "I stood upon the sand of the sea," meaning that it is John who witnessed the rise of the beast.

Commentators (e.g., MacArthur) who use versions that include "the dragon stood on the sand of the seashore" then interpret this passage to mean it is Satan who *summons* the beast. However, "the dragon stood on the sand of the seashore" is different from *the dragon calling forth the beast from the sea*. It is better understood that Satan awaits the rise of the beast, whose ascension from the abyss indicates there is a demonic-principality aspect of the beast (see "The Threefold Reality of the Beast" essay).

(a) *Then I saw a beast* [see the comments on 11:7] *coming up out of the sea, having ten horns and seven heads, and on his horns were ten diadems, and on his heads were blasphemous names*: The narrative here builds upon the foundation Daniel 7 lays.

After this I kept looking in the night visions, and behold, a fourth beast, dreadful and terrifying and extremely strong; and it had large iron teeth. It devoured and crushed and trampled down the remainder with its feet; and it was different from all the beasts that were before it, *and it had ten horns.* While I was contemplating the horns, behold, *another horn, a little one, came up among them,* and three of the first horns were pulled out by the roots before it; and behold, *this horn possessed eyes like the eyes of a man and a mouth uttering great boasts.* (Dan 7:7–8, emphasis added)

In Daniel's passage, the little horn that rose from *the ten horns* and had *the eyes of a man* along with *a mouth speaking great things*, is symbolic of the rise of the beast. In Revelation 13:1, John gives more details about the beast. On the ten horns were "diadems" (i.e., royal crowns), which indicate these are kings (cf. 17:12). Also, "blasphemous names" were on its seven heads. "Blasphemous" (Gk. blasphêmia) means "speech that denigrates or defames, reviling, denigration, disrespect, slander."[174] The

---

[174] Bauer, *Greek-English Lexicon*, "Blasphemous (blasphêmia)."

blasphemous names that were written on its seven heads emphasize the beast's wicked, irreverent character.

(2) *And the beast which I saw was like a leopard, and his feet were like those of a bear, and his mouth like the mouth of a lion:* Though some try to assign modern-day countries here (for example, the "bear" could be Russia), there is much agreement that the beasts Daniel described in his narrative represent the great, historic Gentile world powers. Therefore, the beast's kingdom will have characteristics of ancient empires. The animal imagery here in Revelation is like that in Daniel 7, where the *leopard* represents the ancient kingdom of Greece, the *bear* represents ancient Medo-Persia, and the *lion* represents ancient Babylon. The fourth wild, nondescript beast represents the Roman Empire (Dan 7:2–8). In the *last days*, the ten-horn kingdom of the beast will rise from the fourth beast, and this will likely be Europe. However, alternative views exist. In his book *The Islamic Antichrist*, Joel Richardson argues that the Antichrist will be Islamic and makes numerous comparisons between the *Mahdi*, whom Richardson likens to an Islamic antichrist, and the *Islamic Jesus*, whom he equates with the false prophet.[175] Though Richardson draws parallels between these two Islamic personages and the Antichrist and false prophet of Revelation, Islam interprets these individuals not as diabolical but as righteous saviors.

(a) *And the dragon gave him his power and his throne and great authority:* Once the beast rises, Satan gives him power to rule the wicked world system. We must keep in the forefront of our minds that Revelation is the Lord's plan, not Satan's. God sovereignly determined the events that occur in Revelation. It is God, not Satan, who predetermined when the beast would rise. In Revelation 11:7, the beast ascends from the abyss, or the bottomless pit, over which Satan has no control. God will detain him there for a thousand years (Rev 20:1–3, 7).

It is Satan that gives the beast its "power," "throne," and "great authority."

---

[175] Joel Richardson, *The Islamic Antichrist* (Leawood, KS: Winepress Media, 2009), 175–79.

However, the Scriptures do not teach that Satan possesses the beast or that the Antichrist is Satan's son, as horror films sometimes portray him. Satan gives to the Antichrist what he offered to Jesus in the wilderness.

> And he led Him up and showed Him all the kingdoms of the world in a moment of time. And the devil said to Him, *"I will give You all this domain and its glory; for it has been handed over to me, and I give it to whomever I wish.* Therefore if You worship before me, it shall all be Yours." (Luke 4:5–7, emphasis added)

What Satan offered Christ in the wilderness, he gives to the Antichrist at the end of this age. Satan became "the ruler of the world" (John 14:30), "the prince of the power of the air" (Eph 2:2), and "the god of this world" (2 Cor 4:4) when Adam yielded to the devil's temptation in the garden and thereby abdicated his authority and dominion over the earth to Satan. But all the world's glory is not worth selling out to Satan and losing one's soul.

(3) *I saw one of his heads as if it had been slain, and his fatal wound was healed. And the whole earth was amazed and followed after the beast:* This verse has sparked much controversy, primarily among doctrinal lines. Preterists assert that this was fulfilled by one of the Roman emperors (e.g., *Nero** or *Caligula**). Many from the futurist camp see this as a fake resurrection to parody Christ's resurrection. A deceptive miracle of this magnitude *could be* what is meant in 2 Thessalonians 2 when Paul warned:

> The one whose coming is in accord with the activity of Satan, with all power and signs and false wonders, and with all the deception of wickedness for those who perish, because they did not receive the love of the truth so as to be saved. For this reason God will send upon them a deluding influence so that they will believe what is false, in order that they all may be judged who did not believe the truth, but took pleasure in wickedness. (2 Thess 2:9–12)

Though many accept *the fake resurrection scenario,* no one knows exactly how the events associated with this passage will play out in real-time. However, since this commentary supports the two witnesses being in the first half of the Seventieth Week, a plausible explanation follows.

The beast's forty-two months begin when he kills the two witnesses once their 1,260-day ministry ends. A global celebration ensues after their defeat (11:10). It is logical that while the world is celebrating the demise of the two witnesses, the Antichrist/beast will receive global recognition as the savior of the world. The beast that ascends from the abyss is the spiritual force behind his human counterpart and is given credit for the death of the two witnesses (11:7). This implies that he has already possessed his human counterpart (the Antichrist/son of destruction of 2 Thess 2:3). This possession is a plausible reason why the deadly wound is healed and the beast is brought back to life. His resurrection will be in response to the world just seeing the two witnesses rise from the dead and being caught up into heaven (Rev 11:11–12).

If what this commentary is proposing is correct, the healing of the beast's deadly wound follows a consistent pattern of deception displayed by Satan throughout the ages and parodies found in Revelation (e.g., 13:11). Pharaoh's magicians responded to Moses and Aaron by duplicating their first three miracles (Exod 7:11, 22; 8:7). Satan has always attempted to usurp God's authority by counterfeiting His power through deception, seduction, and lying wonders (2 Cor 11:14). For an additional explanation of the restoration of the wounded head, see the comments on 17:11.

(4) *they worshiped the dragon because he gave his authority to the beast; and they worshiped the beast, saying, "Who is like the beast, and who is able to wage war with him?"* In favor of the beast, the world will exclaim, "Who is like the beast?" The world's excitement should be expected because the beast will have just defeated the two witnesses, whom no one will have been able to kill. However, in response to the witnesses' resurrection, the beast will also rise from the dead, giving him power, authority, and divine status, all inspired by Satan. The world will not see the Antichrist/beast as being wicked. But they will see him as the savior and will love and greatly admire him.

(5–6) *There was given to him a mouth speaking arrogant words and blasphemies, and authority to act for forty-two months was given to him. And he opened his mouth in blasphemies against God, to blaspheme His name and His tabernacle, that is, those who dwell in heaven:* Daniel recorded the fact that the beast is arrogant and a blasphemer (Dan 7:8, 20, 25). However, Paul gave more detail when he stated, "He will oppose and will exalt himself over everything that is called God or is worshiped, so that he sets himself up in God's temple, *proclaiming himself to be God*" (2 Thess 2:4 NIV, emphasis added). Proclaiming to be God is inherently blasphemous. The Jews understood that a man's declaring himself to be God is blasphemy (John 10:33).

The beast/Antichrist will only be in this role for "forty-two months," the last three and a half years of Daniel's Seventieth Week. We cannot start the Antichrist's time at the beginning of the week because he has not been given eighty-four months. Under *the first seal*, the man who will become the beast rides in on a white horse (Rev 6:2). However, *the beast* does not ride in on a white horse but ascends from the bottomless pit (i.e., the abyss, 11:7). The clock for Daniel's Seventieth Week starts at the signing of the "covenant with the many" (Dan 9:27). The beast's three-a-half-year term doesn't start until the middle of the week, when he takes away the daily sacrifice and sets up the abomination of desolation.

EXCURSUS—IN HIS TIME, FORTY-TWO MONTHS

The wrath of God that the church is not appointed to cannot start before the beast has started his forty-two-month reign. At the beginning of the Seventieth Week, the man who becomes the beast/Antichrist has not started his role yet. Indeed, the covenant has been signed, and the Seventieth Week has started, but the beast has not begun his time yet because the beast does not have eighty-four months (i.e., seven years), he only has forty-two months (Rev 13:5). This is when the beast that ascends from the abyss (11:7; 17:8) possesses the Antichrist and Satan gives him his power (13:2). Though it may be the same individual who backs the seven-year covenant when Daniel's Seventieth Week begins, technically he is not the beast/Antichrist until the middle of the week when he takes away the daily sacrifice and sets up the abomination of desolation. That's when his forty-two-month clock will start.

Compared to the second half of the week, not much is known about his activities before he signs the covenant. We do not know when or where he will be born, his name, his nationality, his descendancy, or his political affiliations. At this point in history, neither do we know how to decipher his cryptic number, 666. Certainly, we will understand more as we get closer to the enactment of the covenant. What we do know is he is the little horn that uproots three of the ten horns (Dan 7:8). However, we do not know who these ten horns are. We do know that once the beast comes to power, the wrath of God will be poured out on him.

Paul also agreed that the *day of the Lord*, which will contain God's wrath, cannot come until the man of lawlessness is revealed (Gk. *apokalupto*, meaning "uncovered"). Paul gave his version of the abomination of desolation when he wrote that the son of destruction will oppose and exalt "himself above every so-called god or object of worship, so that he [will take] his seat in the temple of God, displaying himself as being God" (2 Thess 2:4). Jesus also stated, "When you see the abomination of desolation which was spoken of through Daniel the prophet, standing in the holy place (let the reader understand). . . . For then there will be a great tribulation, such as has not occurred since the beginning of the world until now, nor ever will" (Matt 24:15, 21).

The beast's revelation (i.e., his uncovering) will not be when he signs the covenant; his revelation will be the abomination of desolation. This is why neither Jesus nor Paul identified *the building of the temple* or *the signing of the covenant* as his revealing. We must use the Scripture's marker of the abomination of desolation to begin his forty-two-month reign (Rev 13:5). If we start his time at the signing of the covenant, his time would be eighty-four months—the entire span of the Seventieth Week. His forty-two months begin with the abomination of desolation. Paul stated, "So that in his time he will be revealed" (2 Thess 2:6). Most importantly, his revelation is directly connected to the removal of his restraint, which occurs when the demonic aspect of the beast/Antichrist ascends from the prison called the abyss (Rev 11:7; 17:8). Once all these elements come together, the beast can start his reign. Near the end of his time the wrath of God will be poured out on him, beginning with the first bowl judgment of 16:2.

REVELATION 13:7–10

THE PERSEVERANCE AND FAITH OF THE SAINTS

⁷ It was also given to him to make war with the saints and to overcome them, and authority over every tribe and people and tongue and nation was given to him. ⁸ All who dwell on the earth will worship him, everyone whose name has not been written from the foundation of the world in the book of life of the Lamb who has been slain. ⁹ If anyone has an ear, let him hear. ¹⁰ If anyone is destined for captivity, to captivity he goes; if anyone kills with the sword, with the sword he must be killed. Here is the perseverance and the faith of the saints.

(7) *It was also given to him to make war with the saints and to overcome them:* One of the unfortunate narratives concerning the so-called tribulation saints is that they must suffer through the tribulation and be martyred because they *are the left behinds* who missed the rapture because of unconfessed sin. However, nothing could be further from the truth. To begin, nothing is said in Scripture about these saints' being less than faithful or left behind. At the opening of the fifth seal, we are introduced to the martyred saints, whose souls are under the altar in God's temple in heaven. This is hardly a place for disobedient and rebellious people who missed the rapture (6:9–11). Then we see them in heaven in the most prestigious place among men and angels—in the presence of God in His temple. There they join the heavenly host in celebrating God (7:9–17). So, here in this chapter, we find out why their final destination is glory.

"It was also given to him to make war with the saints." The CSB translates it this way: "And it *was permitted* to wage war against the saints" (emphasis

257

added). Who is permitting the beast to make war with the saints? The sovereign Lord. It is mysterious why God permits bad things to happen to good people. For example, there was Job, a blameless and upright man. God permitted Satan to destroy Job's possessions and wealth, to give him a terrible disease, and to kill his servants and his ten children (Job 1:6–22). God also fulfills His plans through death and martyrdom. The Revelation martyrs' faith under extreme circumstances will be displayed as a witness against Satan but for the glory of God. These faithful saints will overcome Satan and his Antichrist "because of the blood of the Lamb and because of the word of their testimony, and they [will] not love their life even when faced with death" (Rev 12:11). Jesus also declared,

> "But before all these things, they will lay their hands on you and will persecute you, delivering you to the synagogues and prisons, bringing you before kings and governors for My name's sake. It will lead to an opportunity for your testimony." (Luke 21:12–13)

Jesus said that for those who will be persecuted, the trials they will endure will be an opportunity to give their testimony, even under the pain of death. No other generation in history will have lived under conditions such as those found in the great tribulation. Therefore, the faithfulness under fire of the Revelation martyred saints makes them the greatest group of church saints that has ever lived. They will be the victorious overcomers whose lives will give glory to God. Pretrib paints these saints as those who were left behind during the rapture, a characterization promoted by the *Left Behind* books and movies. However, Pretrib fails to consider how Revelation, not tradition, portrays these glorious Christians. The Scriptures are clear: for the saints, it will be an honor to remain faithful to Jesus rather than to bow and take the mark of the beast.

(8) *All who dwell on the earth will worship him, everyone whose name has not been written from the foundation of the world in the book of life of the Lamb who has been slain:* The Lamb's "book of life" is a book in heaven that contains the names of all those throughout history who have been redeemed. During the *great white throne judgment,* those whose names are not in the book will be thrown into the "lake of fire" forever (Rev 20:15). A similar phrase about names not being in the book of life since "the foundation of the world" is also in 17:8. This is a clear line of demarcation showing that those *who will* and those *who will not* take the mark of the beast are determined by whether their names are in the book. "From the foundation of the world" means that God has known all those who belong to Him since the beginning (Acts 13:48; Eph 1:4–11; 2 Tim 1:9). This includes the saints who are martyred by the beast.

(9) *If anyone has an ear, let him hear:* The urgency of this message is emphasized by this clarion call. This is a variation of what Jesus often said in the Gospel narratives: "He who has ears to hear, let him hear" (Matt 11:15; 13:9, 43; Mark 4:9, 23; 7:16; Luke 8:8; 14:35). In Revelation, the phrase is also in the letters to the churches: "He who has an ear, let him hear what the Spirit says to the churches" (Rev 2:7a). Though slightly different from one another, the statements all mean the same thing. They are spoken to confirm that anyone who has the willingness to hear a message also has the opportunity to heed it. The absence of the phrase "what the Spirit says to the churches" should not be interpreted as an indication that the church is not on earth. This scene with the beast and the saints will occur at least two thousand years after the existence of the seven churches of Asia Minor. We are now in the twenty-first century, and *the church* is still on earth. In Revelation 2–3, the focus is on specific congregational messages from the Lord to local churches. Here, the message is to the saints who live in a hostile world controlled by the beast, not to specific churches or congregations. (For more on this topic, see the excursus "What Happened to the Church?")

(10) *If anyone is destined for captivity, to captivity he goes; if anyone kills with the sword, with the sword he must be killed. Here is the perseverance and the faith of the saints:* This is another clarion call to inspire the saints to persevere through imprisonment and even death. To the church of Smyrna, the Lord gave a similar instruction:

> Do not fear what you are about to suffer. Behold, the devil
> is about to cast some of you into prison, so that you will be
> tested, and you will have tribulation for ten days. Be faithful
> until death, and I will give you the crown of life. (Rev 2:10)

Jesus was forewarning His followers that the devil is out to imprison
and kill them. However, Jesus emphatically declared, "Do not fear what
you are about to suffer." He said remaining faithful unto death would
lead to eternal life. The fellowship of His suffering is something to be
embraced, not feared. Paul did not see his impending martyrdom as mere
death. He said, "For I am already being poured out as a drink offering
["I am now ready to be offered," KJV], and the time of my departure has
come" (2 Tim 4:6). Also, in Philippians, Paul stated,

> That I may know Him and the power of His resurrection
> and the fellowship of His sufferings, being conformed to His
> death; in order that I may attain to the resurrection from the
> dead. (Phil 3:10–11)

Early Christians lived with the threat of death from hostile pagan societies.
Communities often martyred Christians in public. Government officials
had Christians tortured and killed before cheering crowds in Roman colos-
seums. Having faith in God has never been *a path of ease* (see Heb 11:35–38).
Western Christians, however, have embraced a prosperity perspective
on Christianity, where seeking wealth and blessing and disdaining the
fellowship of the sufferings of Christ are the primary interests. This is
due to most Christians, especially in the United States, being taught that
they will not experience the tribulation. Therefore, they believe that those
who die during the beast's reign are unfortunate. However, Scripture gives
insight on how God sees the sacrifice that the saints make. The psalmist
declared, "Precious in the sight of the Lord is the death of his saints" (Ps
116:15 KJV). Finally, the fact is that Christians are called to suffer. Paul
said, "For to you it has been granted for Christ's sake, not only to believe
in Him, but also to suffer for His sake" (Phil 1:29).

REVELATION 13:11–15

¹¹ Then I saw another beast coming up out of the earth; and he had two horns like a lamb and he spoke as a dragon. ¹² He exercises all the authority of the first beast in his presence. And he makes the earth and those who dwell in it to worship the first beast, whose fatal wound was healed. ¹³ He performs great signs, so that he even makes fire come down out of heaven to the earth in the presence of men. ¹⁴ And he deceives those who dwell on the earth because of the signs which it was given him to perform in the presence of the beast, telling those who dwell on the earth to make an image to the beast who had the wound of the sword and has come to life. ¹⁵ And it was given to him to give breath to the image of the beast, so that the image of the beast would even speak and cause as many as do not worship the image of the beast to be killed.

(11) *Then I saw another beast coming up out of the earth; and he had two horns like a lamb and he spoke as a dragon:* Here, the *second* "beast" rises. He is referred to as the "false prophet" in 16:13; 19:20; and 20:10. Unlike the beast who rises from the sea, this one rises from "the earth" and is "like a lamb," but his message is that of Satan. Some interpret his rising out of the earth to mean he comes from Israel and is a Jewish false prophet. However, there is nothing in the text that identifies Israel or a Jewish lineage. It is best to see the lamb's imagery here as a parody for Christ. Just as *antichrist* means "instead of Christ, an imposter," this lamb is also an imposter, a *false prophet*, and a messenger of Satan.

(12) *He exercises all the authority of the first beast:* The false prophet will have the same worldwide authority as the first beast (i.e., the Antichrist), which leads some to think he could possibly be the head of a powerful religious organization or some other international influencer that will rise in the future.

(a) *And he makes the earth and those who dwell in it to worship the first beast:* The false prophet will *cause* the world to worship the beast. How is it that he will be so convincing?

(13) *He performs great signs, so that he even makes fire come down out of heaven to the earth in the presence of men:* This sign is *a lying wonder* the false prophet will perform to mimic the prophet Elijah's miracle. Elijah called down fire from heaven when contending with the prophets of Baal (1 Kgs 18:36–38).

(14) *And he deceives those who dwell on the earth because of the signs which it was given him to perform in the presence of the beast:* In Matthew 24:24, Jesus warned, "For false Christs and false prophets will arise and will show great signs and wonders, so as to mislead, if possible, even the elect." The *second beast* will be the epitome of all previous false prophets. Those who seek after signs and supernatural experiences will easily fall prey to this diabolical prognosticator. Even the very elect (God's people) could be deceived, but it won't be possible because God will shield His people from the false prophet's deceptive influence. Ultimately, those whose names are written in the Lamb's book of life will not worship the beast nor be deceived by the false prophet.

(a) *telling those who dwell on the earth to make an image to the beast:* Just as *Antiochus Epiphanes IV* erected an image of Zeus in the holy place of the temple in 167 BC, the image of the beast will be *set up* in the temple in the future. The Gospels record Jesus' prophecy about this. He said people will "see the abomination of desolation *standing where it should not be*" (Mark 13:14, emphasis added). The *abomination of desolation* is at least two things: the Antichrist's sitting on the throne of God, declaring himself to be God (2 Thess 2:4), and the beast's image being *set up* in the holy place in the temple (Dan 12:11).

(b) *had the wound of the sword and has come to life*: Once again, there is a possible allusion to the beast being raised from the dead. This seems to indicate at least one of the reasons the image is made to honor the beast and why he is worshiped.

(15) *And it was given to him to give breath to the image of the beast, so that the image of the beast would even speak and cause as many as do not worship the image of the beast to be killed*: This could mean one of two things. First, John might have seen an inanimate object that was brought to life in a similar fashion as when the magicians of Pharaoh cast down their staffs before Moses and Aaron, and their staffs became snakes (Exod 7:12). Or, second, John might have seen something like a robot enhanced with *artificial intelligence** (AI) that appeared to have actual life. Once the image was energized, *it could speak* and *seek to kill* everyone who did not receive the mark of the beast. If the second option is true, John would not have had the language in his first-century vocabulary to explain modern-day technology such as computers, artificial intelligence, *machine learning,** or advanced robotics. Since the image went from being inanimate to functioning, speaking, and seeking the deaths of those without the mark, the only word John had available to him to describe the situation was *pneuma* (meaning "breath, spirit"). Therefore, the passage reads, "to give breath to the image of the beast," but it is not necessarily saying the image will have organic life, but it is like it was actually alive because it could *speak*, a function that in John's day required breath (*pneuma*).

REVELATION 13:16–18

THE MARK OF THE BEAST

[16] And he causes all, the small and the great, and the rich and the poor, and the free men and the slaves, to be given a mark on their right hand or on their forehead, [17] and he provides that no one will be able to buy or to sell, except the one who has the mark, either the name of the beast or the number of his name. [18] Here is wisdom. Let him who has understanding calculate the number of the beast, for the number is that of a man; and his number is six hundred and sixty-six.

(16) *And he causes all, the small and the great, and the rich and the poor, and the free men and the slaves, to be given a mark on their right hand or on their forehead*: The word "mark" comes from the Greek word *cháragma*, meaning "a mark that is engraved, etched, branded, cut, imprinted, *mark, stamp*."[176] However, many assert that this will be some type of computer chip planted under the skin. Though this type of technology is in use in some countries today, this is not implied by the text. The word "mark" implies *something that is graven or etched into something else*. In addition, the beast will require his mark to be visible to show open conformity and allegiance to him. For these reasons, it is unlikely the mark will be a computer chip placed under the skin.

(17) *and he provides that no one will be able to buy or to sell, except the one who has the mark, either the name of the beast or the number of his name*:

---

[176] Bauer, *Greek-English Lexicon*, "Mark *cháragma*."

Today, "mark" technology is widely used for financial transactions in the form of *quick response codes*, or QR codes. QR codes are very easily placed on just about any surface and have no need for any technological components to be attached directly to them. This is what makes them versatile and indispensable. The technology is in reading the QR code. However, it's not being suggested that today's QR codes are the mark of the beast. The point being emphasized here is a type of *mark technology* already among us. China uses a technological advancement called *social scoring*, where one's social standing, obedience to the government, banking information, and credit rating are all integrated into a comprehensive score. The government then links this data to facial recognition technology. Consumers in China with good scores can conduct business by simply having their faces scanned. In the United States, some companies use customers' palm prints interfaced with credit cards to complete financial transactions. Shoppers only need to scan their palms to make a purchase. All these technological advancements are moving us closer to the mark of the beast. The technology itself is not the mark of the beast but is its precursor. It's not the mark of the beast unless the Antichrist/beast is here to implement it. Therefore, you cannot have the mark of the beast without the beast.

In the twenty-first century, we have technology that John could not have comprehended. We know that a lifelike AI person (i.e., the image of the beast) could be created to interface with a future global banking system and thereby manage everyone's financial data. Algorithms* could be deployed to search government databases to identify those non-compliant with receiving the mark of the beast. Warrants could be issued for their arrest and execution. Or people's livelihoods could be terminated, prohibiting the ability to buy or sell at the image's discretion. The "image of the beast" will be tasked to make life-or-death decisions for the global population. However, AI functions without any conscience or compassion because technology has no emotions, feelings, or the capacity to be merciful.

Even with all of this, the world will love the beast. He will not appear to be evil. He will have all the answers and will promise prosperity for everyone that conforms. Those who take the mark of the beast will want it because they will believe that the beast is the world's savior.

Regarding the mark of the beast, it cannot be taken by accident. A person will be aware of what they are doing. This will be an individual's willful act of submission to the Antichrist in open rebellion against God. Some evangelicals, such as John MacArthur, have taught that a person can take the mark and still be redeemed.[177] However, this is absolutely false and extremely dangerous. The Bible is clear, despite what certain people assert. Those who take the mark of the beast are the ones whose names *are not written in the Lamb's book of life* (Rev 13:7–8; 17:8). It would be impossible for someone who takes that mark to be redeemed because only those whose names are found in the Lamb's book of life can be saved (20:15). Therefore, repenting afterward cannot reverse the consequences of this sin. Despite the theological wrangling of scholars, anyone who takes that mark is going to the lake of fire forever. For additional information about who will be in the lake of fire, see 21:8.

(18) *Here is wisdom. Let him who has understanding calculate the number of the beast, for the number is that of a man; and his number is six hundred and sixty-six:* The number 666[178] has stirred controversy for centuries. Many of the preterist camp (those who believe Revelation is historic, not futuristic) believe this number is in reference to Nero. However, this does not at all seem to fit the Seventieth Week scenario. No one today is sure what this number means and who it will identify. The words "Here is wisdom. Let him who has understanding" imply that the wisdom needed to understand this cryptic number will be

---

[177] "John MacArthur Outrage: Take the Mark of the Beast, still be saved. False Teaching," YouTube, posted by Niklas Muench, August 15, 2015, https://www.youtube.com/watch?v=DTc8w5h8UTI.

[178] P115 (Papyrus 115), the oldest preserved fragment of Revelation written on papyrus, renders the number as 616.

given as we get closer to the time of the beast. There may be certain circumstances that will have to occur before it is necessary for God to give the wisdom to decipher the meaning of this number and reveal the man attached to it.

The beast and his economic system will utilize the most advanced technology and security of any previous economic system. The problems that currently arise from lost or stolen credit cards and identity theft will be a thing of the past. Paper money and coinage will be obsolete. Black markets where paper dollars are exchanged will be gone. Counterfeiting and money laundering will be wiped out. In short, the mark of the beast will be the most efficient economic system the world has ever known. It will not appear to be evil but will be accepted as the new way of transacting business. The verse-by-verse commentary continues on page 278.

ESSAY:
THE THREEFOLD REALITY
OF THE BEAST

Any careful analysis of the beast will focus on its three aspects: (1) *the kingdom of the beast,* (2) *the human dictator,* and (3) *the demonic principality that ascends from the abyss.* The first aspect to notice is *the kingdom of the beast,* which is represented by the "seven heads" and the "ten horns" symbology seen in 13:1–2. However, the *first mention* of the *ten horns* is found in the prophecies of Daniel, where he described an exceedingly strong, monstrous beast with ten horns (Dan 7:7–8). Historically, this beast represents ancient Rome, and the *ten horns* are to sprout from ancient Rome at the end of the age. Daniel had a sixth-century-BC perspective. The greatness of the Roman Empire came centuries after his life. However, *the ten horns* will rise much further in the future during Daniel's Seventieth Week, when the beast rises. The ten horns are ten kings who will give their kingdoms to the beast to create a ten-nation confederacy from which the beast (i.e., the Antichrist) will rule (Rev 17:12, 17). Revelation 13:1–2 also gives additional symbology to the *kingdom of the beast.* The beast's kingdom resembles a *leopard,* which looks back to *Daniel 7:6* to the *leopard kingdom* that represents ancient Greece. Another beast in Daniel's vision has *the feet of a bear* (Dan 7:5), which represents Medo-Persia, and another is like *a lion,* which represents ancient Babylon (Dan 7:4). The monstrous beast that has iron teeth and ten horns (Dan 7:7–8) represents ancient Rome. Therefore, the Revelation beast's kingdom will possess characteristics of the historic Gentile world powers of *Babylon, Medo-Persia, Greece,* and *Rome.*

Revelation gives more evidence for the *kingdom of the beast* in the passage about the fifth bowl judgment, where it states that the beast's "kingdom became darkened" (Rev 16:10). It is also the beast's kingdom that will control the worldwide financial system that will issue *the mark of the beast* (13:16–17). From this we can see that an aspect of the beast is that it is a *kingdom*, the final one-world government that will rule the world until it is destroyed at the second coming of the Lord.

The second aspect of the beast is that he is a *man* who will become the final world dictator. In Daniel 7:8b, 24–25 he is called the *little horn* that has "the eyes of a man and a mouth uttering great boasts." It is *the man* who will make the firm seven-year covenant with many but break it in the middle (at three and a half years) of the term. He will then set up *the abomination of desolation* (Dan 9:27). He is the man who is called the *man of sin* or *man of lawlessness*, who takes his seat in the temple of God and declares himself to be God (2 Thess 2:3–4). It is *the man* who will speak great blasphemies against God and those who dwell in heaven (Rev 13:5–6) and who will make war with the saints (13:7). It is *the man* who will be captured and thrown alive into the lake of fire when the Lord returns (19:20).

The third aspect of the beast is the *demonic principality that ascends from the abyss*, first mentioned in Revelation 11:7, which states: "When they [the two witnesses] have finished their testimony, *the beast that comes up out of the abyss* will make war with them, and overcome them and kill them" (emphasis added). The typical dispensational commentary does not comment on the demonic implication of this text. The idea typically expressed is that *the Antichrist kills the two witnesses* (e.g., dispensationalists such as John Walvoord, Charles Ryrie, Tony Evans, William MacDonald), and there is no further explanation of what is implied by an ascension from *the abyss*. However, the abyss indicates demonic activity and involvement. Therefore, this passage attributes the death of the two witnesses to "the beast that comes up out of the abyss" (11:7). This is not the *human* or *kingdom* aspect of the beast but the *demonic* aspect. John first learned about this mysterious aspect of the beast from an angel and recorded it in the following passage:

> And the angel said to me, "Why do you wonder? I will tell you the mystery of the woman and of the beast that carries her, which has the seven heads and the ten horns. The beast that you saw was, and is not, and is about to come up out of the abyss and go to destruction. And those who dwell on the earth, whose name has not been written in the book of life from the foundation of the world, will wonder when they see the beast, that he was and is not and will come. (Rev 17:7–8)

This demon/beast was active in history's past; this is when *he was*. In John's day, this beast *is not* because he was inactive due to being imprisoned in the abyss. However, in the future he *will ascend* from the abyss at the beginning of the last half of Daniel's Seventieth Week. This is when the demonic principality starts his forty-two-month reign through his *human counterpart*, also known as *the little horn, the man of lawlessness, the son of destruction, the Antichrist,* and *the beast.*

As for the place called *the abyss, the deep,* or *the bottomless pit,* the following comments are informative.

> In the NT it is a prison for antichrist (Rev. 11:7), demons (Luke 8:31), scorpions (Rev. 9:3ff.), and spirits (Rev. 9:1; 20:1, 3). It is a well-like abyss from which smoke ascends (Rev. 9:1). Satan will be shut up there for a thousand-year period (Rev. 20:3).[179]

> In the NT the abyss is the abode of the imprisoned demons (Rev. 9:1–21).... Myriads of demons will be let loose during

---

[179] Bromiley, *Theological Dictionary of the New Testament,* "Abyss".

the period of Tribulation to energize age-end apostasy and revolt against God and His Christ, but will be shut up again in this prison together with Satan at the second advent of Christ (Rev. 20:1–3). The abyss is therefore to be distinguished from *sheol* (hell) or *hades*.[180]

The abyss is escape-proof. Any demonic entity that is incarcerated in the abyss must be released from its confines, because like any prison, the abyss is secure. Apparently, the abyss is locked from the outside and requires a key that is kept in heaven to open it (9:1; 20:1). Not even Satan can escape from this place. The devil will be accosted by an unnamed angel who will come down from heaven with the key to the abyss and a great chain in his hand. He will restrain the devil with the chain and throw him into the abyss and seal it over him (20:1–3). When Satan's thousand years in the abyss are finished, he must be let loose from his confines (20:3c, 7). The abyss is also found in the Gospel narratives. The demons begged Jesus not to command them to go there:

> For He had commanded the unclean spirit to come out of the man. For it had seized him many times; and he was bound with chains and shackles and kept under guard, and *yet* he would break his bonds and be driven by the demon into the desert. And Jesus asked him, "What is your name?" And he said, "Legion"; for many demons had entered him. They were imploring Him not to command them to go away into the abyss. (Luke 8:29–31)

In Daniel, we find an interesting passage concerning the destruction of the beast. The passage reads,

> Then I kept looking because of the sound of the boastful words which the horn was speaking; I kept looking until

---

[180] Merrill F. Unger, *The New Unger's Bible Dictionary* (Chicago: Moody Press, 1957), 18.

> *the beast was slain,* and *its body was destroyed* and *given to the burning fire.* (Dan 7:11, emphasis added)

In this passage, "the horn" (identified as *the little horn* in Dan 7:8) is the Antichrist, who meets his destruction. However, after the semicolon, the imagery shifts from the horn to the beast. Daniel said, "The *beast was slain,* and *its body was destroyed* and *given to the burning fire*" (emphasis added). Here, Daniel reported what he observed, but he did so without the details provided to John in Revelation.

In regard to the human aspect of the beast, Paul called him "the man of lawlessness" (or "sin") in 2 Thessalonians. However, he is also called "the son of destruction" (or "perdition"), which means he is the human counterpart to the demonic principality that will ascend from the abyss. Revelation 17:8a declares, "The beast that you saw was, and is not, and is about to come up out of the abyss and go to destruction." Undoubtedly, the end of this demon is already determined, because he *goes to his destruction* once his time is fulfilled through his human counterpart, the beast (i.e., the Antichrist). As the demon from the abyss is destined for destruction so is his human counterpart, who is the man of sin and *the son of destruction.* They share the same destiny. Daniel reported, "The beast was slain, and its body was destroyed and given to the burning fire." This will be fulfilled when the Lord returns.

> And the beast was seized, and with him the false prophet who performed the signs in his presence, by which he deceived those who had received the mark of the beast and those who worshiped his image; these two were thrown alive into the lake of fire which burns with brimstone. (Rev 19:20)

When the Lord returns, the first thing on His agenda will be to destroy the beast and false prophet. They will be seized immediately and thrown right into the lake of fire.

IMPLICATIONS FOR A PRETRIBULATION POSITION

The implications of the beast's three-fold reality have a tremendous impact on aspects of the Pretribulation rapture theory. First, dispensationalists insist that the restrainer holding back the revealing of the Antichrist in 2 Thessalonians 2:6–7 is the Holy Spirit and the church, but they do not consider that there is a demonic aspect of the beast that ascends from the abyss, which is a locked prison for demons. Unfortunately, Paul did not identify who the restrainer is. This has caused an interpretive dilemma since AD 51 when the epistle was written.[181] Many suggestions have been put forth to identify the restrainer. Some of the historical options are *the Roman Empire, the Jewish state, human government and law, Satan, the church,* and *the Holy Spirit.*[182] By process of elimination from the list of the historical candidates for the restrainer, dispensationalists opt for *the Holy Spirit,* who *resides in the church.* The problem with this choice is that it is based on scholars' own thinking, not on any explicit Scriptures. Noted scholar F. F. Bruce quotes John Nelson Darby (who introduced dispensational eschatology to the United States) in his attempt to identify the restrainer, when he states:

> An attempt to do justice to both the interpretations mentioned by Chrysostom was made by Darby ("Notes ...," 452): "the thing which restrained then is not that which restrains now. Then it was, in one sense, the Roman Empire, as the fathers thought.... At present the hindrance is still the existence of the governments established by God in the world; and God will maintain them as long as there is here below the gathering of His church. Viewed in this light, the hindrance is, at the bottom, the presence of the church and of the Holy Spirit on the earth." It is strange that the role once filled by

---

[181] Carson, Moo, and Morris, *An Introduction to the New Testament, 1 and 2 Thessalonians,* 347.
[182] Pentecost, *Things to Come,* 259–62.

the Roman Empire should ultimately be filled by the Spirit in the church.[183]

In this quote, Bruce cites Darby's reasoning for his restrainer view, where he references John Chrysostom, a prolific author and early church father who favored the idea of the Roman Empire's being the restrainer. In Calvin's opinion, *Paul would not have referred to the Holy Spirit in such enigmatic terms*.[184] But as Bruce states, Darby admits that at one time the restrainer *was* the Roman Empire and then shifts his view to the restrainer's being the Holy Spirit and the church. This writer agrees with Bruce's sentiment: That's a strange shift and conclusion for Darby to make. What is it based upon?

When Darby brought dispensationalism to the United States, he settled the identity of the restrainer for Pretribulationists. Traditionally, Darby's idea has been the Pretrib interpretation, which is that the restrainer is the Holy Spirit, who resides in the church, the body of Christ. The problem with this point of view is that there aren't any explicit Scriptures stating such.

As the Pretrib rapture theory developed in the United States, scholars made significant contributions to it, and they continue to do so. The scriptural basis to support the Holy Spirit conclusion unfortunately rests upon several Scriptures that have nothing to do with the subject that Paul addressed in 2 Thessalonians 2. The Holy Spirit's being *the restrainer of sin* is a conceptual argument that Pretribulationists attempt to flesh out with early Scriptures like Genesis 6:3 and Isaiah 59:19b. In the NT (John 14:26; 15:26; 16:8, 13, 14; 1 John 4:4), writers referred to the Holy Spirit with masculine pronouns (i.e., He, Him), and Pretribulationists use these Scriptures as proof texts to support their view. However, Paul's focus was not on the historical restraint of sin in

---

[183] F. F. Bruce, *Word Biblical Commentary*, vol. 45, *1 and 2 Thessalonians* (Dallas: Word, Incorporated, 1982), 171.

[184] John Calvin, *Calvin's Commentaries*, 22 vols. (Grand Rapids, MI: Baker Books), 332.

2 Thessalonians 2 but on what would be restraining *the revealing of the Antichrist* during Daniel's Seventieth Week. Pretribulationists grasp for conceptual straws that have no direct or explicit bearing on Paul's subject at hand. In the text proofs cited earlier, none of the passages has any direct connection to the beast or his restraint. In order to rightly divide who and what is restraining the Antichrist, one must go to passages of Scripture that explicitly relate to that subject. Pretribulationists fail to do this. For a fuller refutation of the Holy Spirit restrainer argument, see the excursus on Revelation 20:3.

A passage that is often quoted to support the idea of the church being the restrainer is Matthew 5:13, which says believers "are the salt of the earth." Pretribers immediately assert that *salt is a preservative* that holds back the spread of corruption. This interpretation means that because the church is the salt of the earth, and salt is a preservative, the church prevents the spread of corruption (or decay). By doing so, it restrains evil because of its presence in the world. Of course, this sounds fine, but that's not how Jesus uses "salt" in the stated passage. In the text, Jesus was referring to *salt not as a preservative* but *as a seasoning*. He was speaking of *its flavor and saltiness*. Besides, just as Paul prophesied (2 Tim 3:1, 13), people have become progressively worse, not better, during the church's presence on earth for the past two thousand years.

In this commentary, it is not being suggested that the Holy Spirit does not restrain sin. However, it is being asserted that this is not what Paul meant in 2 Thessalonians 2:6–7. But most importantly, we put forth that it is irresponsible not to consider a restraining angel referred to in the masculine gender as the one who keeps the beast locked in prison until he ascends from the abyss. Speaking of the restrainer of 2 Thessalonians 2, Bromiley concludes,

> The mysterious ungodly force which will be let loose just before the end, the mystery of iniquity (v. 7) takes concrete shape in an ἄνθρωπος [*anthropos*, man of sin] (v.3),

and therefore κατέχω [*katecho* the restrainer] (who does not have to be a historical magnitude and might be an angel) is a concrete manifestation of the principle of restraint.[185]

Regarding 2 Thessalonians 2:6–7, Bromiley forwards the possibility of *katecho** being angelic. Historically, dispensationalists never recognized that option as viable because they identify the restrainer as the Holy Spirit and His removal as the rapture of the church. However, if the Holy Spirit is not the restrainer, the sequence of Pretrib events (e.g., when the Holy Spirit is removed, then the church is raptured) is in peril. Only with the Holy Spirit being the restrainer can it be affirmed that His ministry to baptize believers into the body of Christ (1 Cor 12:13) has discontinued, as asserted by Pentecost,[186] Walvoord, and other dispensationalists. The discontinuing of the Spirit's baptizing believers into the body of Christ would mean there can be no more additions to the church after the Spirit has been removed via the rapture. On this basis, it is held that the *so-called* tribulation saints cannot be part of the church. Dispensationalists must concede that these saints are Christians who are saved, go to heaven, and have eternal life. Yet they insist these saints are not part of the church because they maintain, without any explicit scriptural proof, that the Holy Spirit restrainer and the church have been removed.

However, if the Holy Spirit is not the restrainer and has not been removed, then that assertion cannot be substantiated. Most importantly, if the Holy Spirit is not the restrainer, then there would be no basis to declare that the saints of Revelation 13 are not part of the church because His ministry to baptize believers into the body of Christ would not be at an end.

---

185   Bromiley, *Theological Dictionary of the New Testament*, 2:829–30, κατέχω (katecho) *the restrainer.*

186   Pentecost, *Things to Come*, 262–63. "It is insisted that the particular ministries of the Holy Spirit to the believers in this present age (baptism, 1 Cor. 12:12–13; indwelling, 1 Cor. 6:19, 20; sealing, Eph. 1:13; 4:30; and filling, Eph. 5:18) do terminate."

By insisting the Holy Spirit and the church are the restrainer of 2 Thessalonians 2, without utilizing the information about the beast's ascending from the abyss, which is a locked prison, the Pretrib point of view has reached a false conclusion. This false conclusion insists that (1) all of the historical candidates for the restrainer have been examined and eliminated, (2) the Holy Spirit is the only one capable of rendering restraint to the beast, and (3) the Holy Spirit is the restrainer. This last point impacts the timing for the church's rapture in regard to the supposed removal of the Spirit before the revealing of the Antichrist. There aren't any Scriptures that state *Christ will come back to remove the Spirit.* Instead, Scripture declares that Christ will come back for *the church,* who is referred to as *the bride* and not with the masculine pronoun "he" (see Rev 19:7). The neuter "what" in v. 6, is also appropriate because the abyss (bottomless pit) is a prison not a person.

Closely connected to the Pretrib restrainer argument is the Pretrib focus that after the word "church" is used to address the seven churches in chapters 2 and 3, it is not found again in Revelation, meaning the church is no longer present on the earth. However, this point is ineffective if it cannot be demonstrated with the Scriptures that the restrainer of 2 Thessalonians 2:6–7 is the church and that the church has indeed been removed. For further discussion on the church in Revelation, refer to the excursus "What Happened to the Church?" and the essay "The Angelic Restrainer Versus the Holy Spirit."

$\dagger$

REVELATION 14:1–5

The 144,000 on Mount Zion

¹ Then I looked, and behold, the Lamb *was* standing on Mount Zion, and with Him one hundred and forty-four thousand, having His name and the name of His Father written on their foreheads. ² And I heard a voice from heaven, like the sound of many waters and like the sound of loud thunder, and the voice which I heard was like the sound of harpists playing on their harps. ³ And they sang a new song before the throne and before the four living creatures and the elders; and no one could learn the song except the one hundred and forty-four thousand who had been purchased from the earth. ⁴ These are the ones who have not been defiled with women, for they have kept themselves chaste. These are the ones who follow the Lamb wherever He goes. These have been purchased from among men as first fruits to God and to the Lamb. ⁵ And no lie was found in their mouth; they are blameless.

(1–5) Once again, there is no consensus on the meaning of the gathering of the *one hundred and forty-four thousand* in this passage. They were *standing on Mount Zion* with *the Lamb*, where John heard a voice like *the sound of harpists playing on their harps, and they sang a new song* of redemption. *No one could learn the song except the one hundred and forty-four thousand.* It was said of them that they were *purchased from the earth*, meaning that they are among the redeemed. They were holy and consecrated unto the Lord and had *not been defiled with women,* as v. 4 says they were *chaste,* or "virgins" (NIV). However, the idea of them being virgins probably goes beyond the actions of sexual activity and speaks to moral purity, meaning they had not defiled themselves with the world. They followed *the Lamb wherever He* went, and John called them the *first fruits to God and to the Lamb.*

In terms of a harvest, the first fruits were the best of the crop that were not to be consumed by the harvester but were an offering to God as a way of showing gratitude for His favor. As for the 144,000, they were holy because *no lie was found in their mouth,* and they were *blameless* because they committed no sin. Some commentators see this group as a vision of heaven. Some see it as occurring on earth after the Lord returns during the millennium. In either case, this is the same 144,000 that consists of twelve thousand from each of the twelve tribes of Israel, which is described in chapter 7. They are not mentioned in Revelation again after chapter 14. The writer of Hebrews gave us some insight into the heavenly Mount Zion when he wrote, "But you have come to Mount Zion and to the city of the living God, the heavenly Jerusalem, and to myriads of angels, to the general assembly and church of the firstborn who are enrolled in heaven, and to God, the Judge of all, and to the spirits of the righteous made perfect" (Heb 12:22–23).

REVELATION 14:6–8

The First Angel: The Eternal Gospel—
the Second Angel: The Fall of Babylon

⁶ And I saw another angel flying in midheaven, having an
eternal gospel to preach to those who live on the earth, and
to every nation and tribe and tongue and people; ⁷ and he said
with a loud voice, "Fear God, and give Him glory, because the
hour of His judgment has come; worship Him who made the
heaven and the earth and sea and springs of waters." ⁸ And
another angel, a second one, followed, saying, "Fallen, fallen
is Babylon the great, she who has made all the nations drink
of the wine of the passion of her immorality."

(6) *And I saw another angel flying in midheaven*: This verse begins with
the introductory statement "I saw another angel." We should expect
John to have said as much because he introduced the reader to many
angels throughout the book. This phrase is used a total of nine times
throughout Revelation.[187]

**(a) *having an eternal gospel to preach to those who live on the earth, and
to every nation and tribe and tongue and people*:** This is astonishing. John
saw the angel *fly in midheaven* and preach the gospel in the middle of the
sky for all to hear and see. Imagine what this will look like. At this point
in Revelation, we are approaching the beginning of the bowl judgments
in chapter 16 that contain the wrath of God. However, it's important to

---

[187] The phrase is found in 7:2; 8:3; 10:1; 14:6, 8, 9, 15, 17, 18.

note that *the grace of God is still open and active.* Though many events have occurred on the earth already with the seals and trumpets, the doors of grace are still open. Regarding the timeline, we are between the sixth and seventh trumpets, just past the middle point of the Seventieth Week. God has already resurrected the two witnesses after the beast killed them (11:11–13), and *the second woe* (the sixth trumpet) *has already past* (11:14).

The beast has already come to power and started his attack on the saints (13:7). Evangelistic efforts by humans will be greatly hindered by the beast, who undoubtedly will outlaw any religious activity other than the worship of himself. Therefore, God gives the "eternal gospel" to an angel to preach. This angel cannot be hindered by the beast, false prophet, or Satan's efforts. Neither will this angel be hampered by language or cultural barriers. The heavenly language he preaches with will be understood by all those who hear it, just as it was on the day of Pentecost (Acts 2:7–8). The fact that God's grace is still active means that the aspect of wrath that the church is not appointed to has not occurred yet. In other words, even at this point, there will still be an opportunity for people to give their lives to Christ. The angel will preach the "eternal gospel . . . to every nation and tribe and tongue and people," fulfilling what Jesus prophesied, "This gospel of the kingdom shall be preached in the whole world as a testimony to all the nations, and then the end will come" (Matt 24:14).

Many commentators cite various gospels (e.g., *the gospel of the kingdom, the gospel of Jesus Christ*) as being different from the "eternal gospel" mentioned here. However, each one proclaims the same good news for everyone: *that sins can be forgiven, death can be overcome, eternal punishment can be avoided,* and *eternal life can be gained*—all because of the gospel (good news) about Jesus Christ, the only name given to the human race so that they might be saved (Acts 4:12). The writer of Hebrews said this about God's people in Moses' days: "For unto us was the gospel preached, as well as unto them: but the word preached did not profit them, not being mixed with faith in them that heard it" (Heb 4:2 KJV). Without a doubt, this passage makes no distinction between the gospel that was heard in Moses' day and then in our day. The gospel must be received by faith in the same God. This fact is eternal, and so is this gospel that the angel preaches.

(7) He declared *with a loud voice,* meaning this angel's message will pierce through all the calamity and chaos present in the world. His gospel message is simple: *"Fear God, and give Him glory, because the hour of His judgment has come; worship Him who made the heaven and the earth and sea and springs of waters."* This gospel message will be particularly important, considering that the false prophet will be demanding that the world should worship the beast. And it also will fulfill what Peter declared on the day of Pentecost. He said that "the sun will be turned into darkness and the moon into blood, before the great and glorious day of the Lord [comes]. And it shall be that everyone who calls on the name of the Lord will be saved" (Acts 2:20–21). The eternal gospel preached by the angel will cause many to call on the name of the Lord. Paul's warning about preaching another gospel is important. "But even if we, *or an angel from heaven,* should preach to you a gospel contrary to what we have preached to you, he is to be accursed" (Gal 1:8, emphasis added). Therefore, what this angel preaches is the same gospel as Paul preached, because it announces the good news about the same salvation that only Jesus' name can bring. "There is no other name under heaven that has been given among men by which we must be saved" (Acts 4:12). According to Galatians 1:8, if this were another gospel, this angel should be under a curse.

(8) *And another angel, a second one, followed, saying, "Fallen, fallen is Babylon the great, she who has made all the nations drink of the wine of the passion of her immorality":* There are two aspects of *Babylon** that require examination: (1) it is a wicked system of false religion, hence the reference "mother of harlots and of the abominations of the earth" (17:5), and (2) it is a commercial and financial center of the world (18:15–17). Babylon will be covered in chapter 18.

REVELATION 14:9–11

The Third Angel's Warning Against Taking
the Mark of the Beast

[9] Then another angel, a third one, followed them, saying with a loud voice, "If anyone worships the beast and his image, and receives a mark on his forehead or on his hand, [10] he also will drink of the wine of the wrath of God, which is mixed in full strength in the cup of His anger; and he will be tormented with fire and brimstone in the presence of the holy angels and in the presence of the Lamb. [11] And the smoke of their torment goes up forever and ever; they have no rest day and night, those who worship the beast and his image, and whoever receives the mark of his name."

(9) *If anyone worships the beast and his image, and receives a mark on his forehead or on his hand*: This warning is universal, applying to "anyone"—rich, poor, free, or bond—who "worships the beast and his image, and receives [his] mark." All of this is considered worshiping the beast and is a punishable offense with eternal consequences.

(10) *he also will drink*: The tense of the verb "will drink" (Gk. *pino*, future indicative) indicates the libation that those who take the mark will experience, that being *the wine of the wrath of God*. This indicates that the "wrath of God" has not fallen yet (see "The Sixth Seal Problem" essay) but will be poured out on those who receive the mark in the bowl judgment of chapter 16. The very first bowl specifically targets those who have taken the mark (see 16:2 note). *Which is mixed in full strength in* *the cup of His anger:* God's wrath will not be diluted but poured out in full strength. This anticipates the horror of the bowl judgments, which stands out from the misery of the other lesser plagues. The cup of His anger will be issued in the seven bowls. ***And he will be tormented with fire and brimstone in the presence of the holy angels and in the presence of the Lamb:*** In this phrase the wrath of God has shifted from His temporary wrath poured during the bowl judgments to His eternal wrath experienced in *the lake of fire.* This is the double whammy. Those who receive the mark will experience God's wrath in the bowl judgments and "will be tormented with fire and brimstone."

(11) *the smoke of their torment goes up forever and ever; they have no rest day and night:* The punishments of those who receive the mark of the beast speak for themselves. This is so impactful that God will warn the people of the earth not to take this mark. He will send a special angelic messenger to deliver this awesome message under the unique circumstance of a time that has never occurred in the history of the world.

EXCURSUS—THE ONE-WAY TICKET TO HELL

Once again, we see the grace of God at work. Taking the mark of the beast is a sin that can only be committed one time in human history. It will occur at a time that Jesus stated would *never be repeated* (Matt 24:21), meaning the great tribulation is a one-time-in-history event. The beast will be the worst tyrannical dictator the world has ever seen. He will be directly backed by Satan, with a co-conspirator called the false prophet who will perform miracles that will deceive the whole world. No tyrant has ever been as diabolical as the beast will be. The circumstances of the great tribulation will be unique. It will be the first time an economic system will be employed by the whole world, issued by a one-world government. Therefore, our righteous Father in heaven will respond to these conditions with a distinct commandment and will address this particular sin in a very specific way. He will send an angel from heaven to warn people of the earth not to take the mark of the beast. This warning for the world about the mark of the beast and the consequence of taking it (eternal judgment in hell fire) will be an unprecedented act of mercy on the part of God.

A person cannot get the mark by accident or without their own knowledge because it will involve the intentional act of worshiping the beast as God, which will mean simultaneously worshiping Satan. People will take the mark of the beast with full knowledge that it is required to buy or sell. Jesus warned, "For what will it profit a man if he gains the whole world and forfeits his soul? Or what will a man give in exchange for his soul?" (Matt 16:26). Taking the mark of the beast will mean exactly that, forfeiting your soul. No matter if a scholar, commentator, preacher, or teacher says differently, the Bible declares that taking this mark will result in nonstop, eternal punishment in the lake of fire, which is *the second death.*

The issue at hand is not whether you can repent and be forgiven after receiving the mark of the beast. Neither is the issue whether taking the mark is an unpardonable sin. Raising these arguments distracts from the most salient point on which the Bible is clear: the ones who take the mark of the beast do not have their names *written in the Lamb's book of life* (Rev 13:7–8; 17:8). This presents an insurmountable problem in that it is impossible for people to enter heaven without their names' being written in the Lamb's book of life. It will not matter if they repent later for taking the mark. It won't matter how sorry they are or that they succumbed to weakness because they were afraid to suffer or die. It will not matter if their favorite minister and their most cherished commentaries told them that they could take the mark and still be redeemed. But know for sure that anyone who takes the mark of the beast will be thrown into the lake of fire forever. If this warning were only to be found in the book of Revelation, then those who never read the Bible would be ignorant of this commandment. But this will not be the case. John told us that God will send an angel to shout a warning from the sky for everyone to hear. Therefore, there will be no excuses.

REVELATION 14:12–13

THE PERSEVERANCE AND BLESSEDNESS OF THE SAINTS

¹² Here is the perseverance of the saints who keep the commandments of God and their faith in Jesus. ¹³ And I heard a voice from heaven, saying, "Write, 'Blessed are the dead who die in the Lord from now on!'" "Yes," says the Spirit, "so that they may rest from their labors, for their deeds follow with them."

(12) *Here is the perseverance of the saints who keep the commandments of God and their faith in Jesus:* This statement is to encourage the saints to endure just a little while longer. This is an obvious appeal to Christians (i.e., the church) to remain faithful to Jesus under the intense pressure to compromise during the reign of the beast. These are the same Christians as those in Revelation 12:11 who "did not love their life even when faced with death" and whose souls were seen under the altar in heaven at the breaking of the fifth seal. God is certainly aware of their tribulation and promises not to forget it.

(13) John was told to write *'Blessed are the dead who die in the Lord from now on!'* This is the *second beatitude* in the book, and it is interesting because it dispels the narrative that says *the tribulation saints* have to suffer because they missed the rapture, which is a belief that MacArthur holds. He asserts,

> Another obvious objection to interpreting *tēreō ek* as a promise of preservation in the midst of the Tribulation is that believers in that terrible time will not be preserved. In fact, many

will be martyred (6:9–11; 7:9–14), leading to the conclusion
that promising preservation is meaningless if the believers
face the same fate as sinners during the Tribulation.[188]

MacArthur makes some key statements in the previous quote: (1) "believers in that terrible time will not be preserved," (2) "many will be
martyred," and (3) "believers face the same fate as sinners." Compare
his statements with what the voice from heaven said about these saints:
"Blessed are the dead who die in the Lord from now on!" This message
is not an example of believers facing the same fate as sinners. It is a
special blessing pronounced over them that was seconded by the Holy
Spirit Himself when He exclaimed, *"Yes, . . . so that they may rest from
their labors, for their deeds follow with them."* These are not forsaken,
unfortunate people who were not being preserved. These are people who
willfully shirked compromise and self-preservation *and who did not love
their [lives] even when faced with death* (12:11). This is what makes them
"blessed" rather than *forsaken*. Heaven is declaring a blessing over them
with a promise of being rewarded. And it's affirmed by the Holy Spirit
Himself, who rarely speaks in Revelation. Their faithfulness has been
preserved as a record and basis for eternal reward. Peter commented on
the sufferings encountered by faithful Christians in 1 Peter. "But if anyone suffers as a 'Christian,' he should not be ashamed but should glorify
God in having that name (1 Pet 4:16 HCSB). Finally, the Spirit promised
these faithful saints that they could "rest from their labors, for their
deeds [would] follow with them." The Pretrib mischaracterization of
these saints as those *left behind* during the rapture is inappropriate. These
Christians will remain steadfast under the worst conditions in human
history and will be recognized and rewarded for their unwavering faith.

---

[188]   MacArthur, *The MacArthur New Testament Commentary: Revelation 1–11*, 125.

REVELATION 14:14–16

The Lord's Harvest

¹⁴ Then I looked, and behold, a white cloud, and sitting on the cloud was one like a son of man, having a golden crown on His head and a sharp sickle in His hand. ¹⁵ And another angel came out of the temple, crying out with a loud voice to Him who sat on the cloud, "Put in your sickle and reap, for the hour to reap has come, because the harvest of the earth is ripe." ¹⁶ Then He who sat on the cloud swung His sickle over the earth, and the earth was reaped.

After all the events of chapter 13 and the announcements of the three angels in chapter 14, we now come to one of the most intriguing passages in Revelation: the Son of Man on a cloud. As stated earlier, it is this commentary's purpose to put the church back into the Revelation text. When we look at this passage through the lens of the church's presence on earth, this text bursts forth with meaning that cannot be appreciated if the church is seen as having been removed.

(14) Here, the *son of man* reference is like the one in 1:13, which is undoubtedly the Lord Himself, and it looks back to Daniel 7:13. The *Son of Man* was Jesus' favorite self-designation, which He applied to Himself over eighty times in the Gospels. Though there are some who see the "son of man" as an angelic figure, most agree that this is the Lord. He is wearing *a golden crown* (Gk. *stephanos*, meaning "a victor's crown"), and angels in Revelation do not wear crowns. The Lord has a *sharp sickle in His hand.* Sickles can represent both *harvest of righteousness* (Mark 4:26–29) or *judgment*

(Joel 3:13). Both uses are here and in the following verses. The word "sickle" is only found in chapter 14 in relation to the harvests. In Revelation, Christ's symbolic instrument of judgment is not the "sickle" but the *two-edged sword* that proceeds out of His mouth (Rev 1:16; 2:12; 19:15, 21).

(15) *And another angel came out of the temple, crying out with a loud voice to Him who sat on the cloud:* The angel here is not shouting an order to the Lord but is bringing a message from the Father to the Son of Man (Christ), who apparently is waiting on God to give the command. This is interesting because Christ declared, "But of that day or hour no one knows, not even the angels in heaven, nor the Son, but the Father alone" (Mark 13:32). Christ, though omniscient, exercised His divine prerogative not to know the hour of His return. Here, the Lord waits for the command to come from heaven. Then the angel cries with a loud voice, *"Put in your sickle and reap, for the hour to reap has come, because the harvest of the earth is ripe."* The "hour to reap has come" represents *the grain harvest* of the righteous.

In Matthew, we find this analogy: "Then He said to His disciples, 'The harvest is plentiful, but the workers are few. Therefore beseech the *Lord of the harvest* to send out workers into *His harvest*'" (Matt 9:37–38). There is no doubt here that the harvest is in reference to those who are saved. He is the Lord of the harvest making it "His harvest." Unfortunately, dispensationalists are committed to the proposition that the church is already raptured at the end of Revelation 3. They are forced to interpret this passage in Revelation 14:14–16 as judgment. However, in this harvest, there is no terminology such as *vengeance, wrath, judgment, wickedness,* or *unrighteous,* which supports the fact that this *is not* a judgment harvest. Speaking of the harvests, Ladd observes, "The first pictures the eschatological judgment with special reference to the gathering of the righteous into salvation; the second pictures the judgment of the wicked into condemnation."[189]

---

[189] Ladd, *A Commentary on the Revelation of John,* 198.

(16) *Then He who sat on the cloud swung His sickle over the earth, and the earth was reaped:* Though it is nuanced, it is important the Lord's sickle is swung "over the earth," as translated in the NIV, ESV, CSB, and others. The Lord receives His harvest without His sickle touching the earth, which could imply that His harvest will come up to Him since He stays on the cloud. After the earth is reaped, nothing else is mentioned in this text about the *Son of Man* or *His harvest.*

We can also draw an analogy from Jesus' *parable of the wheat and tares.*

> Allow both to grow together until the harvest; and in the time of the harvest I will say to the reapers, "First gather up the tares and bind them in bundles to burn them up; but gather the wheat into my barn.... And the field is the world; and as for the good seed, these are the sons of the kingdom; and the tares are the sons of the evil one." (Matt 13:30, 38)

The point here is that there are two different harvests—not the order. One is for the wheat (i.e., the righteous), and the other is for the tares (i.e., the unrighteous). Each has a separate reaper, and each is headed for its own destination. We see this played out in the verses to follow.

REVELATION 14:17–20

The Grapes of Wrath

¹⁷ And another angel came out of the temple which is in heaven, and he also had a sharp sickle. ¹⁸ Then another angel, the one who has power over fire, came out from the altar; and he called with a loud voice to him who had the sharp sickle, saying, "Put in your sharp sickle and gather the clusters from the vine of the earth, because her grapes are ripe." ¹⁹ So the angel swung his sickle to the earth and gathered the clusters from the vine of the earth, and threw them into the great wine press of the wrath of God. ²⁰ And the wine press was trodden outside the city, and blood came out from the wine press, up to the horses' bridles, for a distance of two hundred miles.

(17–18) *another angel* (see 7:2 note) *came out of the temple which is in heaven, and he also had a sharp sickle*: The next group of angels represents the *second harvest*. One *angel . . . has power over fire*. It is interesting that there are angelic beings that have "power over" certain elements, in this case "fire." They have no crowns, nor are they on a cloud as the Son of Man was. But they were told, *"Put in your sharp sickle and gather the clusters from the vine of the earth, because her grapes are ripe."* Unlike the Lord's harvest, this one is categorized as "clusters from the vine" and is a harvest of "grapes."

(19) *So the angel swung his sickle to the earth and gathered the clusters from the vine of the earth, and threw them into the great wine press of the wrath of God*: Once again, this harvest is different from the Lord's. The

291

angel swings his sickle "to the earth." The angels "gather" the "clusters" of grapes with the intention of throwing these into the "wine press of the wrath of God." The results of this wrath and vengeance directed at this grape harvest are in v. 20.

(20) *And the wine press was trodden outside the city, and blood came out from the wine press, up to the horses' bridles, for a distance of two hundred miles:* Here we have a picture of the divine wrath that will be poured out at the battle of Armageddon, where the carnage will be unimaginable. The mention of this sea of blood presupposes the countless dead bodies that will be piled up for miles. The carnage will be incomprehensible. People will be taken from all over the world to participate in this final battle of the age. Speaking of His return, the Lord made the following declaration.

> "I tell you, on that night there will be two in one bed; one will be taken and the other will be left. There will be two women grinding at the same place; one will be taken and the other will be left. [Two men will be in the field; one will be taken and the other will be left."] And answering they said to Him, "Where, Lord?" And He said to them, "Where the body is, there also the vultures will be gathered." (Luke 17:34–37)

There is no shortage of the various ways this passage is interpreted. Many have supposed that the reference to "one will be taken and the other will be left" is pointing to the rapture. However, when the disciples asked where the people were being taken, the Lord's answer, "Where the body is, there also the vultures will be gathered," leaves no doubt for the interpretation. The word "body" (Gk. *soma*) means "a dead body, a corpse,"[190] which is the same word used in reference to Jesus' dead body in Matthew 27:58.

---

[190] Bauer, *Greek-English Lexicon*, "soma."

This is a picture of the carnage that will occur during the day of the Lord when the Lord returns, described as the "wine press of the wrath of God" (Rev 14:19–20; 19:15). It will result in a sea of blood covering two hundred miles. As a part of the cleanup, an angel will call for the birds to come and devour all the dead bodies (19:17–18), fulfilling what Jesus prophesied when He said, "Where the body is, there also the vultures will be gathered." In Luke 17, "taken" is in reference to *being taken* to judgment.

Commentators determine their views of the harvests based on whether they hold to a futurist, dispensational (Pretrib) interpretation. Some commentators see an obvious difference between these two harvests. However, others, holding to a Pretrib rapture, force the harvests' meaning to be only judgment and then miss the richness and clarity of the text. Chapter 15 presents even more issues for the dispensational position to overcome.

A summary of the events concerning the saints is necessary before examining chapter 15. In chapter 13, the beast comes to power and begins his forty-two-month reign. He is permitted by God to make war with the saints—the same saints that make up the innumerable multitude celebrated in heaven (7:9–17). In 12:11, these saints are the overcomers who do not waver or bow to Satan but remain faithful unto death. In 14:13, a voice from heaven announces a blessing concerning those who "die in the Lord," in which the Holy Spirit affirms and promises that their deeds will follow them. Then in 14:14, the Son of Man reaps His harvest from His position on a white cloud by swinging His sickle over the earth. This is the last time the saints (i.e., the church) are seen on earth. The question is what happens to the saints that the beast kills and that the Holy Spirit affirms with the blessing that their works would follow them?

The similarities between the rapture narratives in Revelation 14 and 1 Thessalonians 4 should not be ignored.

Revelation 14:14–16	1 Thessalonians 4:16–17
(1) The Son of Man will sit on a cloud in the earth's atmosphere, which means the Lord will have descended from heaven.	(1) The Lord will descend from heaven in the clouds.
(2) The angel will come out of the temple from heaven and *cry out with a loud voice* to Him who is sitting on the cloud.	(2) The Lord will descend from heaven with the voice of the archangel.
(3) Then He who is sitting on the cloud will swing His sickle *over the earth*, and reap His harvest (c.f. Matt 9:37-38). The saints of 12:10-11, 13:7; 9-10; 14:12-13 are no longer seen on earth. In Revelation 15, these saints are now in heaven praising the Lord *before* the angels with the bowls of wrath leave heaven to pour them out on the world in chap 16. This clearly indicates these saints will not be on earth when God's wrath in the bowl judgments occur, thereby they were not appointed to wrath.	(3) We will be caught up in the clouds to meet the Lord in the air. The saints will no longer be on earth and will not be appointed to wrath. However, the wrath of God has been an ongoing process (Rom 1:18) to which the church has been on earth all along. The church is not appointed to the bowl judgments or the second death (2:11).

The chart above shows some striking similarities between the rapture scenario of Revelation 14 and 1 Thessalonians 4 that are beyond coincidental. In the information age in which we now live, we are used to being inundated with specifics and details. When interpreting the details of the Scriptures, we must consider the genre of the literature. Apocalyptic Literature is typically communicated using symbols, figurative language, and cryptic details. For example, John described the beast as having seven heads and ten horns. Revelation also tells us to *calculate the number of the beast.* On the other hand, the Epistles are didactic in nature and are designed to teach. More attention is given to specifics and doctrine in these letters. In Revelation, subjects are often approached thematically. Such is the case in Revelation 14, where the first theme is the 144,000 on Mount Zion. Next comes the messages of the three angels, followed by the two harvests, where the prominent characters are the reapers. The Son of Man's harvest includes aspects of what Paul taught in the Epistles but without all the details. Revelation 14 features both contrasting harvests together; the righteous and wicked are depicted in apocalyptic *symbolism*, not didactic *specifics*.

Those who assert that 14:14-16 is a judgment narrative have some problems. Where in Scriptures is the Lord ever shown sending judgment on the world in such a manner? Where does He launch an aerial attack with a sickle while seated on a cloud? In the following passages, Dan 7:13, Zech 14:3-5, Matt 24:30; 26:64; Mark 13:26; 14:62, Luke 21:27, the Lord is shown coming with the clouds, meaning the heavenly host of angels and saints. However, in 14:14, He is alone and seated on a cloud. There is a difference between sitting on an atmospheric cloud and coming with the clouds, the host of heaven.

Secondly, if 14:14 is a judgment sequence, when does it occur? In 19:11-21 this is the Lord's second coming that coincides with Daniel, Zechariah, and the Gospel narratives. In chap 19, He is seated on a white horse, not a cloud, with many crowns (diadems) on his head, not only a single crown, being a victor's crown 14:14. Therefore, the harvest that is appropriately connected to chap 19 is the grapes harvest, because it is associated with the wine press of the wrath of God (cf. 14:19-20 and 19:15). In 14:14-16 the Lord's instrument is a sharp sickle but in Revelation 19:15, it's a sharp sword. Undoubtedly, the grape harvest is connected to judgment and the wrath of God, but the first harvest belongs to the Lord of the harvest and those not appointed to God's wrath.

REVELATION 15:1–4

The Seven Last Plagues and the Saints Triumphant

¹ Then I saw another sign in heaven, great and marvelous, seven angels who had seven plagues, which are the last, because in them the wrath of God is finished. ² And I saw something like a sea of glass mixed with fire, and those who had been victorious over the beast and his image and the number of his name, standing on the sea of glass, holding harps of God. ³ And they sang the song of Moses, the bond-servant of God, and the song of the Lamb, saying, "Great and marvelous are Your works, O Lord God, the Almighty; righteous and true are Your ways, King of the nations! ⁴ Who will not fear, O Lord, and glorify Your name? For You alone are holy; for all the nations will come and worship before You, for Your righteous acts have been revealed."

(1) *Then I saw another sign in heaven, great and marvelous, seven angels who had seven plagues, which are the last, because in them the wrath of God is finished*: Here another great and magnificent sign is seen in heaven: the seven angels who had the seven "last" plagues. "Plague" (Gk. *plēgē*, "a sudden calamity that causes severe distress"[191]) is used eleven times in Revelation. The phrase "seven plagues" is found four times (15:1, 6, 8; 21:9), and in each case, it is in reference to the *seven last plagues*. Not only are these plagues *last* but they are also distinct. What the seals, trumpets, and bowls have in common is that they are classified as plagues. However, the phrase *seven last plagues* is distinct because these

---

191   Bauer, *Greek-English Lexicon,* "*plēgē* Plagues."

plagues specifically contain "the wrath of God." The bowl judgments are much worse than the plagues that precede them.

(2) *And I saw something like a sea of glass mixed with fire, and those who had been victorious over the beast and his image and the number of his name, standing on the sea of glass, holding harps of God*: The same saints who were on earth, being persecuted and martyred by the beast, are now in heaven. How did they get there? By the *Son of Man* who received *His harvest.* It is important to note that in 14:13, the Holy Spirit focused on those "who die in the Lord" because the dead in Christ *rise first* (1 Thess 4:16). In addition to that, the saints under the altar at the opening of the fifth seal were told to wait until the full number of their fellow servants and brethren, who were to be killed as they were, had been reached. Then the Lord could avenge their blood (Rev 6:9–11). Unambiguously, God stated that the vengeance the martyrs sought could not be fulfilled until the number of martyrs (i.e., the dead) had been reached. At that point, the saints would be transitioned to heaven. Once they reached heaven, then God's vengeance and wrath, through the seven angels who have the bowls of wrath, could be unleashed on those who dwell on the earth. These saints are not seen on earth again during the rest of the tribulation.

The saints who were on earth and refused to take the mark of the beast are now seen in heaven after the Lord received His harvest because they have not been appointed to this wrath. This is notable because the saints are in heaven *before* the angels have received their bowls or have even been commanded to go pour them out on the world. In 11:15–18, the rewarding of the righteous dead is shown under the theme of the seventh trumpet. Both descriptions are complementary and are the same event from different perspectives. The trumpet shows resurrection and reward, and chapter 15 shows bliss in heaven after the Lord reaps His harvest. Both show the experience of the saints, which precedes the wrath of God, from different perspectives.

Once they reach heaven, the saints give God praise while standing on what appeared to be a sea of glass, which was first mentioned in 4:6. This is explicit proof that these saints were not appointed to the wrath of God but were appointed to rejoice in heaven.

(a) *And they sang the song of Moses, the bond-servant of God, and the song of the Lamb*: The song they sing is not arbitrary. The "song of Moses," *the Song of Deliverance*, goes back to Exodus 15:1–20, when Israel gave glory to God for the great deliverance from Pharaoh's army that was drowned in the Red Sea. This is an important precept; the Deliverer does not come to deliver Egypt, Rome, or great powerful nations. Neither does the Deliverer come at a time of ease. He comes at a time of trouble and peril to deliver His people who cry out to Him. The song was also the "song of the Lamb," who laid down His life and tasted death for every man, who was raised victorious never to die again, and who will rule in His kingdom that will have no end. However, this "song of the Lamb" is different than the praise song given by the heavenly host in Revelation 5:9, 12.

(b) *Great and marvelous are Your works, O Lord God, the Almighty; righteous and true are Your ways, King of the nations* ["King of saints," KJV]! This song is sung by those who had gotten the victory over the beast. They have also experienced being harvested from the earth, which was the punctuating rapturous act that ended their suffering. God's awesome displays of power will thwart Satan's pitiful efforts so they will be brought to nothing.

But now these glorious saints appear in heaven before God's majesty and break out into praising Him through song. The long-awaited opportunity for vengeance (6:9–11) will soon follow when the Lord returns in chapter 19.

(4) *Who will not fear, O Lord, and glorify Your name? For You alone are holy; for all the nations will come and worship before You, for Your righteous acts have been revealed*: The psalmist observed: "All nations whom You have made shall come and worship before You, O Lord, and they

shall glorify Your name. For You are great and do wondrous deeds; You alone are God" (Ps 86:9–10). In Philippians, Paul made a similar declaration. "So that at the name of Jesus every knee will bow, of those who are in heaven and on earth and under the earth, and . . . every tongue will confess that Jesus Christ is Lord, to the glory of God the Father" (Phil 2:10–11).

REVELATION 15:5–8

THE SEVEN ANGELS PREPARE

⁵ After these things I looked, and the temple of the tabernacle of testimony in heaven was opened, ⁶ and the seven angels who had the seven plagues came out of the temple, clothed in linen, clean and bright, and girded around their chests with golden sashes. ⁷ Then one of the four living creatures gave to the seven angels seven golden bowls full of the wrath of God, who lives forever and ever. ⁸ And the temple was filled with smoke from the glory of God and from His power; and no one was able to enter the temple until the seven plagues of the seven angels were finished.

(5) *I looked, and the temple of the tabernacle of testimony in heaven was opened:* This is the second mention of the opening of the temple in heaven (see 11:19). The opening of "the temple of the tabernacle of testimony" allows the seven angels to come forth to unleash the bowls "full of the wrath of God" (15:7).

(6) *and the seven angels who had the seven plagues came out of the temple, clothed in linen, clean and bright, and girded around their chests with golden sashes:* The angels proceed out of the temple ready to be sent forth, but before they go, they receive something.

(7) *Then one of the four living creatures gave to the seven angels seven golden bowls full of the wrath of God, who lives forever and ever:* Once again, one of the four living creatures, who also announced *the four horsemen of the apocalypse*, gives to the seven angels their respective "bowls full of the wrath of God." Chapter 14 describes God's wrath being poured out in full strength in v. 10, meaning it will not be given in thirds as it was with some of the trumpets, where God was holding back. God will not be holding back His wrath at all, which will be contained in these bowls. It is also important to consider the purpose of these bowls. They are not to get men to repent, as these bowls are not chastisement. Even if men did repent, which they won't, it wouldn't be effective at this point. God is past appealing to hardened sinners because the dreadful day of His wrath has come. The question is, Who will be able to stand? Repentance is a two-way transaction. It starts with the person repenting but depends on God's granting or accepting the repentance (2 Tim 2:25; Heb 12:17).

(8) *And the temple was filled with smoke from the glory of God and from His power:* The smoke from God's glory and omnipotent power is certainly in view here, but it cannot be overlooked that God is also angry. It's not good to be in the presence of God when He is angry. Moses declared, "For I was afraid of the anger and hot displeasure with which the Lord was wrathful against you in order to destroy you" (Deut 9:19). Also, in Hebrews, the writer observed, "It is a terrifying thing to fall into the hands of the living God" (Heb 10:31). *And no one was able to enter the temple until the seven plagues of the seven angels were finished:* It is a fearful thing to be in the same room with someone who is enraged, let alone for this person to be almighty God. No one—meaning angels, living creatures, elders, or the redeemed—was able (i.e., had the ability) to enter the temple until God's anger and wrath were fulfilled. This is a sobering thought. If those in heaven could not stand in God's presence while His wrath was being unleashed, woe to those who will be on the receiving end of these judgments.

What is important to understand is that before the angels were released to pour out the bowls of wrath on the earth, the saints who were victorious over the beast were already in heaven. These Christians, who make up the church, were not appointed to the wrath of God. This passage indisputably proves this. The entire sequence of events from chapters 13 through 15 can only be seen in its true light when we properly identify the saints as the church.

EXCURSUS—THE WRATH OF GOD

The wrath of God is an expansive subject (see the essays "The Sixth Seal Problem" and "3:10: The Hour of Testing Dilemma"). In one sense, it has been an ongoing process since the beginning of time (e.g., the flood, the destruction of Sodom and Gomorrah, the Egyptian plagues, the defeat of Pharaoh's army, etc.). In Romans 1:18, Paul spoke of the wrath of God as being "revealed" (Gk. *apokalyptō*, "reveal, disclose, bring to light, make fully known"[192]). This word is in the *indicative present active tense*, which means it is active and ongoing. Looking at Romans, Morris observes, "There is considerable agreement that we should understand the wrath in eschatological terms (cf. 2:5–9). That is, of course, true, but we should not overlook the other truth that it is also a present reality, as this passage shows (cf. the present tense, *is being revealed*, and [1:]24, 26, 28)."[193]

God's ongoing wrath is directed toward *all ungodliness and unrighteousness, against men who suppress the truth.* This is what the world is experiencing now. In Romans 1:19–32, Paul gave a litany of wickedness in which God's wrath is manifested. However, God's wrath will come to a climax in the events described in Revelation. God's wrath is revealed in various intensities as described by the progressive nature of the seals, trumpets, and bowls. Concerning the punishment for those receiving the mark of the beast, God's wrath is said to be "mixed in full strength" or "undiluted" (14:10 NET) in the successive bowl judgments. It is important to understand that God's wrath is not only contained in Daniel's Seventieth Week, which holds temporary manifestations of wrath, but

---

[192] Bauer, *Greek-English Lexicon*, "*apokalyptō.*"

[193] Leon Morris, *The Pillar New Testament Commentary: The Epistle to the Romans* (Grand Rapids, MI: Inter-Varsity Press, 1988), 77.

is also eternal, which is the ultimate expression of God's fury and righteous indignation.

In John the Baptist's warning to the Pharisees and Sadducees, he charged, "You brood of vipers, who warned you to flee from the wrath to come?" (Matt 3:7). Obviously, "the wrath to come," of which John spoke here, is eschatological in the final sense. Those living during John's day will have been long gone before the arrival of Daniel's Seventieth Week. However, John the Baptist was speaking of the wrath of God that all the wicked throughout history will face after the *great white throne judgment*. This wrath is called the *second death* and is eternal destruction in the lake of fire (Rev 20:11–15). Paul also declared, "You are storing up wrath for yourself in the day of wrath and revelation of the righteous judgment of God, who will render to each person according to his deeds" (Rom 2:5–6).

It is interesting to note that the book of Revelation is the most expansive book in the Bible that details the wrath of God. However, the word *wrath* is only used eleven times (NASB1995). In Revelation, two Greek words are used for God's wrath: *orgē*, meaning "strong indignation directed at wrongdoing, with focus on retribution, wrath,"[194] is in 6:16–17; 11:18; 16:19; 19:15, and *thymos*, meaning "a state of intense displeasure, anger, wrath, rage, indignation,"[195] is in 14:10, 19; 15:1, 7; 16:1.

Regarding the seals, only the sixth seal includes the word "wrath" (Gk. *orge*, 6:16–17). That seal is a vision of events that will occur during the bowl judgments, when the sun will turn to darkness and the moon to blood (see Isa 13:10; Joel 2:31; Matt 24:29; Acts 2:20). The great earthquake, where "every island fled away, and the mountains were not found," occurs in Revelation 16:18–20 during the seventh bowl. Therefore, these events are not occurring at the opening of the sixth seal but are visions of events to come under the wrath of God, executed under

---

[194] Bauer, *Greek-English Lexicon*, "Wrath *orge*."
[195] Bauer, "Wrath *thymós*."

the seven bowl judgments. For a more in-depth study of the events under the sixth seal, see "The Sixth Seal Problem" essay.

In relation to *the trumpets*, the word *wrath* (Gk. *orgē*) is only used once in conjunction with the seventh trumpet: "And the nations were enraged, and Your wrath came" (11:18), which, again, is a vision of events that will occur during the sixth and seventh bowls. This passage repeats the same theme given under the sixth seal. This is not a different wrath but points to the same climatic event shown in 16:14–16; 19:16, which fulfills Psalm 2:1–6.

$$\dagger$$

REVELATION 16:1–7

THE BOWL JUDGMENTS ONE THROUGH THREE

¹ Then I heard a loud voice from the temple, saying to the seven angels, "Go and pour out on the earth the seven bowls of the wrath of God." ² So the first angel went and poured out his bowl on the earth; and it became a loathsome and malignant sore on the people who had the mark of the beast and who worshiped his image. ³ The second angel poured out his bowl into the sea, and it became blood like that of a dead man; and every living thing in the sea died. ⁴ Then the third angel poured out his bowl into the rivers and the springs of waters; and they became blood. ⁵ And I heard the angel of the waters saying, "Righteous are You, who are and who were, O Holy One, because You judged these things; ⁶ for they poured out the blood of saints and prophets, and You have given them blood to drink. They deserve it." ⁷ And I heard the altar saying, "Yes, O Lord God, the Almighty, true and righteous are Your judgments."

(1) *Then I heard a loud voice from the temple, saying to the seven angels, "Go and pour out on the earth the seven bowls of the wrath of God"*: This commentary supports the position that the wrath of God *that the church is not appointed to* is the bowl judgments of chapter 16. One of the reasons for this position is that in chapter 14, the Lord's harvest is separate from the harvest of the grapes that are thrown into the wine press of the wrath of God. After the Lord receives His grain harvest, the saints, who had gotten the victory over the beast, are then seen in heaven *before* these angels are given the bowls of wrath to pour out on the earth and *before* they left heaven to do so. Many dispensational scholars are surprisingly silent when it comes to explaining how the saints in the Lord's harvest of 14:14–16, which is the same group of saints as in 13:7, transition from being on earth in 14:12–13 to heaven in 15:1–4 before the angels leave heaven to execute God's wrath on the earth. Of these saints, who had the victory over the beast, Beale comments,

> The saints now stand before God's throne in heaven (before which the heavenly analogue to the earthly sea is set according to 4:6). Perhaps their standing includes the idea of resurrection.... That the saints are said to have "come off victorious" further identifies them with the whole people of God, since overcoming is a trait of all who truly belong in the church.[196]

(2) *So the first angel went and poured out his bowl on the earth; and it became a loathsome and malignant sore on the people who had the mark of the beast and who worshiped his image:* It is important to note that the very first target of the wrath of God will be those who have taken the mark of the beast. This will be a pointed attack that strikes directly at the *kingdom of the beast.** These "sores" (Gk. *helkos*, "ulcers") will be terrible and untreatable. These oozing, odorous, and offensive sores will disfigure the faces of people. This plague will impede buying and selling because without observable marks, the beast's economic system will be derailed. Like any untreatable condition, these sores will probably spread to the entire face and other limbs.

(3) *The second angel poured out his bowl into the sea, and it became blood like that of a dead man; and every living thing in the sea died:* Fresh blood has a distinctive odor, but the blood of a dead person is foul. What John meant by "the sea" or which "sea" he meant is unclear, but we

---

[196] Beale, *The Book of Revelation*, 791.

can understand this to mean earth's large bodies of water. The stinking, contaminated water will kill all the marine life in it. This will create an environmental disaster far beyond the nations' ability to respond.

(4) *Then the third angel poured out his bowl into the rivers and the springs of waters; and they became blood*: Next, God will attack the fresh water sources, which will devastate the sources of drinking water.

(5) *Righteous are You, who are and who were, O Holy One, because You judged these things*: Aune has described this as a "judgment doxology."[197] The doxology contains a variation of the three-part repetition of "who was, who is, who is to come" found in 1:4, 8; 4:8 and is shortened to "who are and who were" because *who is to come* will no longer be anticipated but will be a reality with the outpouring of God's wrath.

(6) *For they poured out the blood of saints and prophets, and You have given them blood to drink. They deserve it*: Since the beast and his minions enjoyed spilling the saints' and prophets' blood, God will metaphorically give them blood to drink. Indeed, they will have this judgment coming. As a chiding parent would say to an obstinate child, "No better for you. You got what you deserve!"

(7) *And I heard the altar saying, "Yes, O Lord God, the Almighty, true and righteous are Your judgments"*: This statement is interesting but not so much because of what is said but because of who is saying it. This is the only place in Scripture where "the altar" speaks. Some scholars see the altar as a personification and that it itself is speaking (Mounce). Others support that John heard the martyred souls under the altar who cried out for vengeance (Aune, Beale). Others relate this voice to the horns of the altar (9:13) and, therefore, attribute this voice to an angel rather than the martyrs themselves (Osbourn).[198] This commentary agrees with the interpretation that the voice is coming from the souls under the altar.

---

197   Aune, *Word Biblical Commentary*, 52B:885.

198   Osborne, *Baker Exegetical Commentary: Revelation*, 585.

This is consistent with their appeal for vengeance against those who dwell on the earth (6:9–11). Vengeance will occur in the bowl judgments, and their desire for vengeance will be fulfilled when they return with the Lord, which John depicted in 19:11–21.

This long-awaited time for vengeance and judgment has finally come. Since the very first murder, God has heard the cries for justice. After Cain killed his brother Abel in a jealous rage, Genesis records God's direct inquiry. "He said, 'What have you done? The voice of your brother's blood is crying to Me from the ground'" (Gen 4:10). In the Gospel of Luke, the Lord proclaims, "Now, will not God bring about justice for His elect who cry to Him day and night, and will He delay long over them? I tell you that He will bring about justice for them quickly" (Luke 18:7–8). However, in the current text, now that judgment and justice are being poured out on the wicked earth dwellers, the cry *for* justice gives way to praise to God for *bringing* that justice. God knows about our suffering. He will never forget it, and He will avenge the righteous and judge the unrighteous. Therefore, the praise is, "Yes, O Lord God, the Almighty, true and righteous are Your judgments" (Rev 16:7).

REVELATION 16:8–16

[8] The fourth angel poured out his bowl upon the sun, and it was given to it to scorch men with fire. [9] Men were scorched with fierce heat; and they blasphemed the name of God who has the power over these plagues, and they did not repent so as to give Him glory. [10] Then the fifth angel poured out his bowl on the throne of the beast, and his kingdom became darkened; and they gnawed their tongues because of pain, [11] and they blasphemed the God of heaven because of their pains and their sores; and they did not repent of their deeds. [12] The sixth angel poured out his bowl on the great river, the Euphrates; and its water was dried up, so that the way would be prepared for the kings from the east. [13] And I saw coming out of the mouth of the dragon and out of the mouth of the beast and out of the mouth of the false prophet, three unclean spirits like frogs; [14] for they are spirits of demons, performing signs, which go out to the kings of the whole world, to gather them together for the war of the great day of God, the Almighty. [15] ("Behold, I am coming like a thief. Blessed is the one who stays awake and keeps his clothes, so that he will not walk about naked and men will not see his shame.") [16] And they gathered them together to the place which in Hebrew is called Har-Magedon.

(8) *The fourth angel poured out his bowl upon the sun, and it was given to it to scorch men with fire:* Our sun is only an average-sized star, and it's over 93 million miles from the earth. The sun is so much larger than the earth that it would take 1.3 million earths to fill the volume of the sun. During the bowl judgments, God will send one angel to pour out his bowl on the sun, which will increase its output. Angelic beings have inconceivable power and can do God's bidding anywhere in the universe.

(9) *Men were scorched with fierce heat; and they blasphemed the name of God who has the power over these plagues, and they did not repent so as to give Him glory:* Death Valley, California, is recorded as having the hottest *air temperature* on earth, with temperatures reaching as high as 134°F (56.7°C). However, this plague will send temperatures well above that, to the point men will blaspheme God. Concerning those who refuse to repent, some commentators claim that these plagues will determine what manner of person they are. MacArthur says, "Unbelievers will either pass the test by repenting, or fail it by refusing to repent."[199] However, the bowl judgments are not about getting sinners to repent. These plagues are not chastisement designed to bring correction. These plagues are God's judgment, vengeance, and wrath. But even if these people did repent, they still would not find salvation because they will have worshiped the beast and taken his mark. Those who take the mark of the beast and worship him do not have their names written in the Lamb's book of life.

What is really damning is how recalcitrant and reprobate these people will be—like a guilty man on death row who refuses to the very end to admit his crime. It seems that after being strapped to a gurney and facing lethal injection, his remorse would catch up with him and produce a confession. Not that it would undo his death sentence, but that it might unburden his soul before leaving this world. At least he would be honest before meeting his maker—but to the very end, he lies. So it is with those who blaspheme God because of these plagues. It seems that people under such circumstances would repent. Their refusal to do so bears witness to their desperately wicked hearts and to the condemnation they will receive.

---

[199] MacArthur, *The MacArthur New Testament Commentary: Revelation 1–11*, 124.

(10) *Then the fifth angel poured out his bowl on the throne of the beast, and his kingdom became darkened; and they gnawed their tongues because of pain:* The beast's kingdom will be thrown into darkness. As seen with the other plagues of sores and water turned to blood, the darkness will also be reminiscent of the plagues of Egypt (Exod 7:19; 9:9–11; 10:21–29). However, this darkness will be worse. Physical darkness occurs when there is no physical light. However, there is also spiritual darkness. Jude wrote, "And angels who did not keep their own domain, but abandoned their proper abode, He has kept in eternal bonds *under darkness* for the judgment of the great day" (Jude 1:6, emphasis added). This bowl will bring spiritual darkness and torment. The absence of light is darkness. However, this darkness will bring terror and pain to the point where people will gnaw their tongues. Whatever words we can assign to describe this darkness, it will actually be much worse.

(11) *and they blasphemed the God of heaven because of their pains and their sores; and they did not repent of their deeds:* These judgments will have an accumulating effect. The sores come in the first bowl and will be persisting in the fifth bowl. However, something else will also persist: the people's refusal to repent. Mounce observes, "Punishment does not bring repentance. The decision to persevere in evil has permanently precluded any possibility of a return to righteousness."[200] This author agrees but would add that they already sealed their eternal doom when they took the mark of the beast and ignored the angel that warned against it. The angel was clear: those who take the mark will suffer wrath from the bowl judgments and will suffer eternal wrath in the lake of fire (14:9–11).

(12) *The sixth angel poured out his bowl on the great river, the Euphrates:* The Euphrates River is the focal point of much activity in Revelation. During the sixth trumpet, the four angels (i.e., wicked angels) bound at the river Euphrates will be released, and they will be responsible for the deaths of a third of humankind (9:13–19). However, under the sixth

---

[200] Mounce, *The New International Commentary: The Book of Revelation*, 297.

bowl, the Euphrates River will be dried up to make way for the kings of the East.

The Euphrates River was the eastern boundary of the land God gave to Abraham and his descendants (Gen 15:18). The river was also a boundary between the Roman Empire on the east and the Parthians, who conquered the territory from the Euphrates to the Indus.[201] *And its water was dried up:* In 1990, Turkey completed the building of the *Atatürk Dam,* which is located in Bozova in southeast Turkey on the Euphrates River. This dam has the capability to dry up the Euphrates. Whether the drying up is of human agency or divine, the purpose of drying up the river is *so that the way would be prepared for the kings from the east:* Who are the "kings from the east"? According to one dispensational scholar, fifty interpretations have been rendered to identify these kings.[202] The phrase "kings from the east" considers several nations. Some of the key countries east of the Euphrates are Iran, Pakistan, Afghanistan, India, China, and as far east as North Korea. Both India and China have populations of over a billion people and could employ massive armies. Any of these nations, if not all, and more, could comprise the "kings from the east."

(13–14) *And I saw coming out of the mouth of the dragon and out of the mouth of the beast and out of the mouth of the false prophet, three unclean spirits like frogs; for they are spirits of demons, performing signs, which go out to the kings of the whole world, to gather them together for the war of the great day of God, the Almighty:* Demons have always been an influencing factor in human matters, particularly in geopolitical affairs. There is an explicit case in the Bible where a demon is used to influence the outcome of a battle that kills King Ahab.

The Lord said, 'Who will entice Ahab to go up and fall at Ramoth-gilead?' And one said this while another said that.

---

[201] Mounce, *The New International Commentary: The Book of Revelation,* 298.
[202] Walvoord, *The Bible Knowledge Commentary: Revelation,* 2:968.

> Then a spirit came forward and stood before the Lord and said, "I will entice him." The Lord said to him, "How?" And he said, "I will go out and be a deceiving spirit in the mouth of all his prophets." Then He said, "You are to entice him and also prevail. Go and do so." (1 Kgs 22:20–22)

Just as a demonic spirit, through Ahab's false prophets, got him to go to a battle where he would be killed, so these demons, which come from the beast, the false prophet, and Satan, will get "the kings of the whole world" to send troops to fight in "the war of the great day of God, the Almighty." The book of Revelation is heaven's perspective of these events. However, it is doubtful that these demons will give heaven's perspective concerning who is actually coming to the earth. These demons are liars and will use their wicked power to deceive through signs and wonders to get the kings of the earth to commit to sending troops to this battle. Though countries may have their own political reasons to come to the Middle East during this time (i.e., Gog of Magog, Ezek 38–39), once there, at some point, they will all unite to take a stand against who they *think* is coming to the earth.

Still on their minds will be the *two witnesses*, who, after coming back to life, were taken up into heaven while the world watched. A possible scenario is that the beast will use the resurrection of the two witnesses as the context to promote an alien invasion of the earth. Satan has planted this seed through television, media, and science fiction movies for decades. No one would show up to a battle against God Almighty if they knew that He was coming.

(15) *Behold, I am coming like a thief:* The thief in the night is an analogy. The thief only comes unawares to those who are *not* watching. There is shame attached to not watching, not being prepared, not being alert to the signs and times the Lord has placed in Scripture for the express purpose that believers would not be caught by surprise. ***Blessed is the one who stays awake and keeps his clothes, so that he will not walk about***

naked and men will not see his shame: This is the third beatitude in Revelation. Those who are prepared until the coming of the Lord will not be caught unaware and will not be exposed, as one would be who bears the shame of being a naked person who is publicly disrobed. The placement of this warning here is not to portray the rapture event, as some assert. However, this is an encouragement that is characteristic of the beatitudes found throughout Revelation. This specific beatitude encourages believers to remain vigilant and watchful.

(16) *And they gathered them together to the place which in Hebrew is called Har-Magedon* ("Armageddon," (KJV, NIV, CSB, ESV): This is the only place in the Bible where the word *Armageddon* is found. Other translations, such as the *Complete Jewish Bible*, translate it as *Har Meggiddo*. *Har* means "mountain." While there is no mountain called *Meggiddo*, it probably indicates the hilly terrain around the plain of Megiddo, some sixty miles north of Jerusalem. Since ancient history, many battles have been fought in this plain. The Scriptures document some (Judg 5:19; 2 Kgs 23:29; 2 Chr 35:22), but it will become ground zero for the greatest and bloodiest battle in earth's history.

REVELATION 16:17–21

The Finale—"It Is Done"

¹⁷ Then the seventh angel poured out his bowl upon the air, and a loud voice came out of the temple from the throne, saying, "It is done." ¹⁸ And there were flashes of lightning and sounds and peals of thunder; and there was a great earthquake, such as there had not been since man came to be upon the earth, so great an earthquake was it, and so mighty. ¹⁹ The great city was split into three parts, and the cities of the nations fell. Babylon the great was remembered before God, to give her the cup of the wine of His fierce wrath. ²⁰ And every island fled away, and the mountains were not found. ²¹ And huge hailstones, about one hundred pounds each, came down from heaven upon men; and men blasphemed God because of the plague of the hail, because its plague was extremely severe.

(17) *Then the seventh angel poured out his bowl upon the air, and a loud voice came out of the temple from the throne, saying, "It is done":* Once the seventh angel pours his bowl out into the air, a loud voice utters a divine punctuation that finalizes the bowls of wrath, which were first introduced in 15:1. John said that "in them the wrath of God is finished" (15:1), and here in 16:17 that finality is realized. "It is done" is similar to Jesus' last words on the cross, "It is finished!" (John 19:30). Both were concerning God's judgment. The wrath of God was fully vindicated by the Redeemer who laid down His life on behalf of the redeemed. While Jesus suffered on the cross, the sky was darkened for three hours (noon to three). Jesus paid our sin debt in full with His own precious blood. In Revelation 16, the words

"It is done" concern God's vengeance on all those who have rejected His only begotten Son, who is "the way, and the truth, and the life" (John 14:6).

(18) *And there were flashes of lightning and sounds and peals of thunder; and there was a great earthquake, such as there had not been since man came to be upon the earth, so great an earthquake was it, and so mighty*: Lightning and thunder often follow actions in heaven; however, at this point, "a great earthquake" will also follow the atmospheric disturbances. This passage provides an incredible point of reference: "Since man came to be upon the earth." This allows us to make no mistake about the magnitude of this cataclysmic event. The most powerful earthquake recorded since 1930, when the Richter scale was employed, occurred in Valdivia, Chile, in 1960 and was a magnitude 9.5. The earthquake of the seventh bowl will be far off the Richter scale.

(19) *The great city was split into three parts, and the cities of the nations fell*: Here, we are offered more information about this earthquake. Babylon was devastated and split into three parts. The "cities of the nations" also "fell," implying that this will be a worldwide earthquake. This is why there has never been one like it before. ***Babylon the great was remembered before God, to give her the cup of the wine of His fierce wrath.*** For more on this statement, see the chapter 18 commentary.

(20) *And every island fled away, and the mountains were not found*: The first view of this earthquake was shown under the sixth seal (6:12, 14). The primary characteristic of this earthquake is that it will be unlike any that has ever occurred since humans have inhabited the planet. John said, "Every island fled away, and the mountains were not found." With this, we understand why the cities of the nations will fall. If "every mountain and island [will be] moved out of their places" (6:14), then manmade structures would have no chance to remain standing. There is no way for humans to comprehend the magnitude of an earthquake that knocks down mountains.

(21) *And huge hailstones, about one hundred pounds each, came down from heaven upon men; and men blasphemed God because of the plague of the*

hail, because its plague was extremely severe: After the unprecedented earthquake demolishes cities all over the world, then giant hailstones will pulverize what's left. Imagine the damage a bowling ball would do if dropped from the sky. A bowling ball may only be fifteen pounds. That's light compared to "one hundred pounds." It is difficult to understand why people will not be begging God for mercy by this point. However, they will refuse to repent and will blaspheme Him all the more. Therefore, God will pay them the wages they have earned, which will be the second death.

EXCURSUS—BABYLON

What follows next on the apocalyptic agenda is the destruction of Babylon. Babylon represents pride, wickedness, religious harlotry, and rebellion. *Babylon* derives from the name "Babel" (Gen 11:9), meaning "confusion." Babel's founder and builder was Nimrod, the first builder of great kingdoms, who also built the great city of Nineveh (Gen 10:8–11). Nimrod started down a dangerous road when he declared,

> Come, let us build for ourselves a city, and a tower whose top will reach into heaven, and let us make for ourselves a name, otherwise we will be scattered abroad over the face of the whole earth. (Gen 11:4)

In response, God came down to confuse their language so that they could no longer communicate. So, construction on this ancient skyscraper halted immediately. Since then, Babylon has been forever associated with wickedness and false religion. Much is said about Babylon throughout the Scriptures. Prophets such as Isaiah, Jeremiah, Ezekiel, Daniel, Habakkuk, and some psalmists all made prophecies about Babylon. The Jews were sent into captivity there for seventy years. In Daniel 7, three of the kingdoms portrayed as animals occupied Babylon: the Chaldeans (lion), the Medes and Persians (bear), and the Greeks (leopard). In Zechariah, the prophet saw the vision of an "ephah going forth" (Zech 5:6), which was a basket-like container, but this one had a lead lid on it. Inside was a woman of whom it was said, "This is Wickedness!" (Zech 5:8). The woman attempted to escape from the ephah, but the angel shoved her back down and set the lead cover on it. Then, two other women figures with wings like a stork lifted the ephah up and flew her away. Then Zechariah recorded,

> I said to the angel who was speaking with me, "Where are they taking the ephah?" Then he said to me, "To build a temple for her in the land of Shinar; and when it is prepared, she will be set there on her own pedestal." (Zech 5:10–11)

The plain of *Shinar* is the region where *Babylon* is located, the place where spiritual wickedness that was personified as a woman resides. A temple was to be built for the woman where she would be placed on her own pedestal. Whether literal or figurative, Babylon serves as a place where idols were erected and false religions were practiced and bred. Babylon has deep roots throughout biblical history. In Revelation, the harlotry of Babylon is set in contrast to the glorious bride of Christ, the church, and new Jerusalem.

REVELATION 17:1–8

THE GREAT HARLOT AND THE BEAST FROM THE ABYSS

¹ Then one of the seven angels who had the seven bowls came and spoke with me, saying, "Come here, I will show you the judgment of the great harlot who sits on many waters, ² with whom the kings of the earth committed acts of immorality, and those who dwell on the earth were made drunk with the wine of her immorality." ³ And he carried me away in the Spirit into a wilderness; and I saw a woman sitting on a scarlet beast, full of blasphemous names, having seven heads and ten horns. ⁴ The woman was clothed in purple and scarlet, and adorned with gold and precious stones and pearls, having in her hand a gold cup full of abominations and of the unclean things of her immorality, ⁵ and on her forehead a name was written, a mystery, "Babylon the great, the mother of harlots and of the abominations of the earth." ⁶ And I saw the woman drunk with the blood of the saints, and with the blood of the witnesses of Jesus. When I saw her, I wondered greatly. ⁷ And the angel said to me, "Why do you wonder? I will tell you the mystery of the woman and of the beast that carries her, which has the seven heads and the ten horns. ⁸ The beast that you saw was, and is not, and is about to come up out of the abyss and go to destruction."

(1) *Come here, I will show you the judgment of the great harlot who sits on many waters*: One of the seven angels who had the bowls of God's wrath began speaking with John concerning "the judgment of the great

harlot," or "whore" (KJV, CJB); "prostitute" (ESV, NET). "Harlot" is an explicit term for an unfaithful, unchaste, lewd woman who has many partners. She manipulates her suitors for money through seduction. Here, she represents a false religious and commercial system that has had great influence over those who dwell on the earth. "Who sits on many waters" means that her influence is worldwide (v. 15).

(2) *with whom the kings of the earth committed acts of immorality, and those who dwell on the earth were made drunk with the wine of her immorality*: The "acts of immorality" and the drunkenness are symbolic of religious apostasy, idolatry, and the pursuit of materialism, which are spread by the kings of the earth, who not only practice immorality with the prostitute but also cause others to do so. Her wickedness will be propagated by the kings of the earth who then engage their citizenry with the libation of her wickedness.

(3) *And he carried me away in the Spirit into a wilderness; and I saw a woman sitting on a scarlet beast, full of blasphemous names, having seven heads and ten horns*: John was transported in the Spirit to perceive and receive the information about the harlot. She was seen in "a wilderness," or desert (cf. Isa 21:1–2), which symbolizes a state of being desolate and depraved, though outwardly, she was lavishly decked (see the essay "The Rebuilding of Babylon"). She was "sitting on a scarlet [red] beast, full of blasphemous names." This is the same beast that was seen rising out of the sea in chapter 13. The spiritual representation of the beast is monstrous, yet the symbols are significant. The harlot was sitting on the back of the beast, which indicates she had some control over the direction of the beast. But this is the reason for the tension that developed between them.

(4) *The woman was clothed in purple and scarlet, and adorned with gold and precious stones and pearls, having in her hand a gold cup full of abominations and of the unclean things of her immorality*: Wickedness uses outward beauty to distract from the evil it represents. The woman was clothed in alluring purple and red and decked with gold and precious stones. She was wearing gorgeous things, but she was far from beautiful. She drank from a golden cup, representing status, but it was filled with the unclean things of her immorality. She was desperately wicked, and the seduction of her whoredoms attracted many through her lavish appearance. Some religious institutions are also outwardly lavish and internally corrupt and full of dead men's bones.

(5) *and on her forehead a name was written, a mystery*: Throughout Revelation, we find the forehead as a place of inscription, whether it is the people of God being sealed on their foreheads in 7:3; 9:4; 14:1; 22:4, or the enemies of God being marked with the beast's number or name in 13:16; 14:9; 17:5; 20:4. These forehead statements declare to whom they belong and whom they worship. In the NASB, NRSV, and NLT, the noun "mystery" is not a part of the name. However, in the KJV, it is "Mystery, Babylon The Great." The NLT translates it, "A mysterious name was written on her forehead." Perhaps this mystery is connected to the *mystery of iniquity* or *lawlessness* spoken of in 2 Thessalonians 2:7 as spiritual wickedness that was already at work in Paul's day.

(a) *Babylon the great, the mother of harlots and of the abominations of the earth*: This phrase indicates that false religion throughout history has been a product or offspring of Babylon, the "mother of harlots," the great whore. The harlot fornicated with many pagan religions and birthed illegitimate children (i.e., false religions) through such unions. Truly, she is the mother of harlots. Then, her harlot children committed spiritual fornication and birthed more illegitimate religions. She has brought forth the abominations of the earth, especially the wicked, apostate Christianity, which will engender an ecumenical church that merges all religions into one noxious concoction of apostate worship that will lead to the worship of the beast. The agenda of the *new world order*, which will be carried out through a one-world government, will support a one-world religion. Therefore, Babylon rode the back of the beast, though their relationship is tenuous.

(6) *And I saw the woman drunk with the blood of the saints, and with the blood of the witnesses of Jesus. When I saw her, I wondered greatly:* John was not astonished at the woman's being drunk. A prostitute is expected to exhibit lewd behavior, but she was "drunk with the blood of the saints." Babylon enjoyed the murder, torture, and martyrdom of the saints, whose precious blood cries out to the Lord for justice. Thus, the souls in the scene under the altar, under the fifth seal, cry out to God for vindication. Babylon not only spilled their blood, but metaphorically she drank it, meaning that she is gratified by the bloodletting.

(7–8) *Why do you wonder? I will tell you the mystery of the woman and of the beast that carries her, which has the seven heads and the ten horns:* The angel begins to explain "the mystery" (Gk. *musterion*, "the unmanifested or private counsel of God, God's secret"[203]). The hidden aspects about the beast were a mystery and not available to John. Therefore, the angel interprets what John just saw. *The beast that you saw was, and is not, and is about to come up out of the abyss and go to destruction:* This is probably the most important information about the true nature of the beast. Here, we have another three-part repetition. The beast "was" (past tense), meaning the beast was active at some time in the past; the beast "is not," which illustrates the beast's status from John's present perspective; and the beast "is about to come up out of the abyss," which is the future action of the beast, beyond John's current perspective. From where does he come? The abyss, or bottomless pit. *And those who dwell on the earth, whose name has not been written in the book of life from the foundation of the world, will wonder:* The word "wonder" comes from the Greek word *thaumázō*, which means "to be extraordinarily impressed or disturbed by."[204] This passage indicates that there is a demonic aspect of the beast that will come out of the prison called the abyss. (See the essay "The Threefold Reality of the Beast.")

---

[203] Bauer, *Greek-English Lexicon,* "mystery, mustêrion."
[204] Bauer, "shall wonder, thaumázō."

REVELATION 17:9–18

⁹ Here is the mind which has wisdom. The seven heads are seven mountains on which the woman sits, ¹⁰ and they are seven kings; five have fallen, one is, the other has not yet come; and when he comes, he must remain a little while. ¹¹ The beast which was and is not, is himself also an eighth and is one of the seven, and he goes to destruction. ¹² The ten horns which you saw are ten kings who have not yet received a kingdom, but they receive authority as kings with the beast for one hour. ¹³ These have one purpose, and they give their power and authority to the beast. ¹⁴ These will wage war against the Lamb, and the Lamb will overcome them, because He is Lord of lords and King of kings, and those who are with Him are the called and chosen and faithful." ¹⁵ And he said to me, "The waters which you saw where the harlot sits, are peoples and multitudes and nations and tongues. ¹⁶ And the ten horns which you saw, and the beast, these will hate the harlot and will make her desolate and naked, and will eat her flesh and will burn her up with fire. ¹⁷ For God has put it in their hearts to execute His purpose by having a common purpose, and by giving their kingdom to the beast, until the words of God will be fulfilled. ¹⁸ The woman whom you saw is the great city, which reigns over the kings of the earth."

(9) *Here is the mind which has wisdom*: Like the statement in 13:18 that speaks of wisdom, the angel here said "wisdom" is required to understand these cryptic verses. The angel then gave an outline without giving specifics. It is possible that specificity will not be needed until the time when these prophecies are closer to fulfillment. The angel's primary focus was to give John the wisdom he needed to understand what he was seeing.

(a) *The seven heads are seven mountains on which the woman sits:* Mounce observes, "There is little doubt that a first-century reader would understand this reference in any way other than as a reference to Rome, the city built upon seven hills. Rome began as a network of seven hill settlements on the left bank of the Tiber River."[205] The hills are Aventine, Caelian, Capitoline, Esquiline, Palatine, Quirinal, and Viminal. However, not all agree (e.g., Alan F. Johnson) that this is a representation of Rome.[206] It should be noted that this is not the only place there is disagreement in Revelation. Commentators have varying views on every verse in the book. What this indicates is that there are no experts on future events. No one knows exactly how these mysteries will manifest in real time. We can know "the what" of prophecy, but "the how" and "the when" often defy investigation and stretch far beyond our ability for exegesis. However, Mounce does make a good point. The first-century Christian would have readily understood this description of "seven mountains" to mean Rome. With all the controversy that Revelation stirs up, we can understand why the angel declared that wisdom is required. It should also be noted that the first-century perspective of these things isn't necessarily the best one, because the content of Revelation was too far away from reality for people who lived then. John, who also lived in the first century, didn't understand all these things either.

(10) *and they are seven kings; five have fallen:* Some see these as seven Roman emperors (e.g., Walvoord).[207] However, there have been seven kings/kingdoms that were world powers and that oppressed Israel. The

---

[205] Mounce, *The New International Commentary: The Book of Revelation*, 315.

[206] Alan F. Johnson, *The Expositor's Bible Commentary: Revelation* (Grand Rapids, MI: Zondervan), 558–60.

[207] Walvoord, *The Bible Knowledge Commentary: Revelation*, 2:971.

five kingdoms that had fallen by John's day were Egypt, Assyria, Babylon, Medo-Persia, and Greece. As for the Grecian kingdom, after the death of Alexander the Great, the kingdom was divided among his four generals (Dan 8:22). Of these four, two became the most prominent: Ptolemy went to the south (Egypt) and Seleucid to the north (Syria). Antiochus Epiphanes IV eventually came from the Seleucid line. He was the most treacherous king. Daniel 8 and 11 have much to say about Antiochus, who committed the abomination of desolation in 167 BC (Dan 11:31). He took away the daily sacrifices and offerings, sacrificed a pig on the altar, and erected a statue of Zeus in the most holy place, after killing thousands of Jews (1 Macc 1:10–62). In Matthew 24:15, Jesus referred to the abomination of desolation spoken of by Daniel, which was a reference that looked back to the historic Antiochus but that also has a future fulfillment yet to come when the Antichrist/the beast enters the rebuilt temple of God. He will declare himself to be God, demand worship, and erect his image in the holy place (2 Thess 2:3–4; Rev 13:14). These actions will be those of the final Antichrist yet to come, whom Antiochus' desecrations foreshadow.

(a) one is, the other has not yet come; and when he comes, he must remain a little while: The "one" that "is" was Rome, the kingdom that was in power during John's day. The seventh head had "not yet come." Some say the seventh head to come is the future Antichrist.[208] Others say it was a Roman emperor, but no one knows for sure because the angel did not disclose that detail. However, since there is no consensus, another person should be considered: Adolph Hitler, whose conquest for world dominance and hatred of the Jews was established in history. According to *Encyclopaedia Britannica Online*, the *Third Reich* (*Reich*, meaning "realm or kingdom")[209] was the official Nazi designation for the regime

---

208 John F. MacArthur, *The MacArthur New Testament Commentary: Revelation 12–22* (Chicago: Moody Press, 2000), 170.

209 Merriam-Webster, "Reich (German noun)," accessed March 29, 2023, https://www.merriam-webster.com/dictionary/Reich.

in Germany from January 1933 to May 1945 and is the presumed succes-
sor of the First Reich (i.e., the medieval and early modern Holy Roman
Empire of 800 to 1806) and the Second Reich (i.e., the German Empire of
1871 to 1918).[210] Hitler envisioned world dominance through military
power and with a genetically modified Aryan race, and he focused his
fury toward committing genocide against the Jews, whom he hated.
Hatred of Jews is inspired by Satan. From the beginning, God said, "And
I will put enmity between you and the woman, And between your seed
and her seed; He shall bruise you on the head, And you shall bruise him
on the heel" (Gen 3:15). Therefore, Satan has tried to destroy the seed and
the bloodline ever since (see Rev 12:1–17). However, Hitler's plans ended
when Germany was defeated in World War II. He committed suicide on
April 30, 1945. Many Jews left Europe for Palestine, where Jewish settlements existed. Then three short years later, on May 14, 1948, almost as if
it were a mocking response to Hitler's futile attempt to annihilate a portion of the covenant people, in one day, God reestablished the nation of
Israel, as prophesied in Isaiah 66:6–9. The establishment of modern-day
Israel put a clear stake in the ground that we are in the last days.

Hitler killed millions of others in his wicked conquest of Europe on a
path to dominate the world. Hitler's conquest lasted twelve years, from
1933 to 1945, which in comparison to the historic empires of the other
six heads was only for a short time (Rev 17:10). Hitler also envisioned
the Third Reich to be a thousand-year kingdom, to form an illegitimate
millennial reign. Finally, another interesting aspect concerning Hitler's
regime is that at the Auschwitz camp, the Jews forced into slave labor
were tattooed with numbers on their left arm.

(11) *The beast which was and is not, is himself also an eighth and is one of*
the seven: The "beast which was and is not" is the one who will *ascend*
from the abyss (v. 8). This is the demonic principality. He *was active in*

---

[210]   Encyclopaedia Britannica Online, "Third Reich," accessed March 29, 2023, https://www.
britannica.com/place/Third-Reich.

the earth realm in one of the five heads that had already fallen. That is why he "was," because he was here before John's days. However, during John's time, the "beast" was already locked in the abyss, meaning that he was in the "is not" status because of his incarceration. However, when he is released from the abyss to rule through the "beast" (i.e., the Antichrist), he will *ascend from the abyss* and become *the* "eighth" *head* in his encore appearance. Therefore, this is a possible explanation for what is meant by "I saw one of his heads as if it had been slain, and his fatal wound was healed. And the whole earth was amazed and followed after the beast" (13:3). According to 17:8, the *amazement* the world will have with the beast is triggered when the world *sees the beast that was, is not, and yet is* when he ascends from the abyss. The seven heads represent Satan's historic network of world-dominating powers. Though this one appears twice, becoming *the eighth head*, he is still counted as "one of the seven."

(b) *and he goes to destruction*: In 2 Thessalonians 2:3, the beast is called "the son of destruction" ("perdition," KJV). The beast's end will come when the Lord returns. Daniel 9:27 states, "until the decreed destruction is poured out on the desolator" (Dan 9:27 CSB). The *decreed destruction* to be poured out on the desolator (i.e., the beast) starts with the first bowl judgment that targets those who have the mark of the beast (Rev 16:2) and ends when the Lord returns and throws him and the false prophet alive into the lake of fire (Dan 7:11; 2 Thess 2:8; Rev 19:20).

(12–13) *The ten horns which you saw are ten kings who have not yet received a kingdom, but they receive authority as kings with the beast for one hour. These have one purpose, and they give their power and authority to the beast*: The angel gives further explanation concerning these "ten kings" and nations. They are yet future and will form an alliance under "the beast," to whom "they give their power and authority." They will reign "with the beast for one hour," meaning a relatively short period of time, which coincides with the short three-and-a-half-year reign of the beast. They "have one purpose," which is to "give their power and authority to the beast." These kings are predestined to fulfill the role that God has purposed according to His divine plan.

(14) *These will wage war against the Lamb, and the Lamb will overcome them, because He is Lord of lords and King of kings:* It is mind-boggling that people will be convinced to join a fight against God Almighty. He is "King of kings" and "Lord of lords" not in name only but also in power and authority. The kings of the earth do not have a chance. Isaiah weighed in when he declared,

> Behold, the nations are like a drop from a bucket, and are regarded as a speck of dust on the scales; behold, He lifts up the islands like fine dust. . . . All the nations are as nothing before Him, they are regarded by Him as less than nothing and meaningless. (Isa 40:15, 17)

For further discussion on this awesome battle, see Revelation 19:11–16, "The Heavenly Invasion."

(a) *and those who are with Him are the called and chosen and faithful:* Some of the saints that return with the Lord will be those souls seen under the altar in the fifth seal, who cried out for vengeance (6:9–10), along with those who are "chosen and faithful." Zechariah prophesied, "And the LORD my God shall come, *and* all the saints with thee" (Zech 14:5 KJV, emphasis added).

(15) *The waters which you saw where the harlot sits, are peoples and multitudes and nations and tongues:* Here, the angel gives further clarity to *the waters where the harlot sits.* Certainly the harlot is Babylon, whose wicked influence has seduced the people, multitudes, nations, and tongues, saturating the entire earth with her wickedness.

(16) *And the ten horns which you saw, and the beast, these will hate the harlot and will make her desolate and naked, and will eat her flesh and will burn her up with fire:* Here, John saw the tension and hatred that "the beast" will have toward "the harlot." Wicked powers, though great, usually rot from the inside, with one being mistrusting and suspicious of another. Though she rides the back of the beast, her superior position of control is only imaginary and temporary. There is no way for this seductive harlot to control the ferocious wild beast she rides. The beast will turn on her because he hates the harlot.

(17) *For God has put it in their hearts to execute His purpose by having a common purpose, and by giving their kingdom to the beast, until the words of God will be fulfilled:* This divine book of prophecy is God's plan, not an account of Satan's activity. God is in sovereign control over every aspect covered in this book. The ten kings will do exactly as God has purposed. They will "give their kingdoms" and authority "to the beast" at the time God has appointed. These kings and their role with the beast have been predetermined to such a degree that God has already written it in the Scriptures, which Jesus declared "cannot be broken" (John 10:35). Though God "put it in their hearts" to fulfill His words, they, along with the beast, will still be judged for their actions. God raises up whom He pleases, even if for destruction, as He did with Pharaoh (Rom 9:17–18, 22).

(18) *The woman whom you saw is the great city, which reigns over the kings of the earth:* Some see the "great city" as ancient or modern-day Rome. However, the next chapters describe Babylon as a global commercial center of the earth that will be destroyed in one hour.

REVELATION 18:1–8

THE DESTRUCTION OF COMMERCIAL BABYLON

¹ After these things I saw another angel coming down from heaven, having great authority, and the earth was illumined with his glory. ² And he cried out with a mighty voice, saying, "Fallen, fallen is Babylon the great! She has become a dwelling place of demons and a prison of every unclean spirit, and a prison of every unclean and hateful bird. ³ For all the nations have drunk of the wine of the passion of her immorality, and the kings of the earth have committed acts of immorality with her, and the merchants of the earth have become rich by the wealth of her sensuality." ⁴ I heard another voice from heaven, saying, "Come out of her, my people, so that you will not participate in her sins and receive of her plagues; ⁵ for her sins have piled up as high as heaven, and God has remembered her iniquities. ⁶ Pay her back even as she has paid, and give back to her double according to her deeds; in the cup which she has mixed, mix twice as much for her. ⁷ To the degree that she glorified herself and lived sensuously, to the same degree give her torment and mourning; for she says in her heart, 'I sit as a queen and I am not a widow, and will never see mourning.' ⁸ For this reason in one day her plagues will come, pestilence and mourning and famine, and she will be burned up with fire; for the Lord God who judges her is strong."

Babylon is a principal aspect of the Revelation landscape in each of the six times it is mentioned (14:8; 16:19; 17:5; 18:2, 10, 21).

(1) *After these things I saw another angel coming down from heaven, having great authority, and the earth was illumined with his glory*: Once again, John wrote that he "saw another angel." However, "another" should not be taken to mean "typical." By no means was this a run-of-the-mill angel. This one was so glorious that the entire earth was illuminated by his majesty. Since angels were created and not procreated or bred, they are unique. It is probable there are no two angels alike.

(2) *Fallen, fallen is Babylon the great! She has become a dwelling place of demons and a prison of every unclean spirit, and a prison of every unclean and hateful bird*: Babylon's fall was first announced in 14:8. Here, we are given more specific details about the destruction, beginning with why she is finally being destroyed: "She has become a dwelling place of demons and a prison of every unclean spirit, and a prison of every unclean and hateful bird." Ephesians 6:12 informs us that the wickedness and struggles of this life originate not with humans but with the demonic principalities and powers, rulers of the darkness, and spiritual wickedness in the heavenly realms. Regarding Babylon, she was infested beyond redemption with the wicked demonic host who is behind wicked human activity. The word "prison" in this passage is not a place of detention. Mounce observes, "The structure of the verse suggests that the word is roughly parallel to 'home.' Demons dwell among the ruins of Babylon, as do unclean spirits and animals. It is not a place of detention but a place where they dwell undisturbed."[211]

(3) *For all the nations have drunk of the wine of the passion of her immorality, and the kings of the earth have committed acts of immorality with her, and the merchants of the earth have become rich by the wealth of her sensuality*: The sphere of Babylon's influence cannot be underestimated. No nation will escape her intoxicating wealth and seductive influence. Participation in the abundance of her lavish riches will be equivalent to committing immoral acts, which are symbolized here as fornication or adultery.

---

[211] Mounce, *The New International Commentary: The Book of Revelation*, 325–326.

(4–5) *Come out of her, my people, so that you will not participate in her sins and receive of her plagues; for her sins have piled up as high as heaven, and God has remembered her iniquities:* This call can refer to either *commercial* or *mystical Babylon.** No one righteous should remain in her. Jeremiah's call for the people of Jerusalem to flee ancient Babylon was remarkably similar:

> Flee from Babylon! Run for your lives! Do not be destroyed because of her sins. It is time for the Lord's vengeance; he will repay her what she deserves. ⁷ Babylon was a gold cup in the Lord's hand; she made the whole earth drunk. The nations drank her wine; therefore they have now gone mad. (Jer 51:6–7 NIV)

Things were bad in ancient Babylon, but eschatological Babylon will be worse. Therefore, the call will be "come out of her … so that you will not participate in her sins … for her sins have piled up as high as heaven." This last statement is reminiscent of Genesis 18:21. A society will exist whose sins will be so grievous that heaven can no longer ignore them or extend any more mercy. Their time will be up, and judgment will fall. Just as angels warned Lot and his family, saying, "Up, take your wife and your two daughters who are here, or you will be swept away in the punishment of the city" (Gen 19:15), a warning will be given to people in the future. Since God's people are not appointed to wrath, God will send a warning to flee before destruction comes. In a broader sense, this call to come out of Babylon is a warning to all believers to separate themselves from a seductive, idolatrous, and wicked world system, whether it be a figurative commercial or spiritual (i.e., religious) Babylon. In the Epistle of James, we find this warning,

> What is the source of quarrels and conflicts among you? Is not the source your pleasures that wage war in your members? You lust and do not have; *so* you commit murder. You are envious and cannot obtain; *so* you fight and quarrel.

You do not have because you do not ask. You ask and do not receive, because you ask with wrong motives, so that you may spend *it* on your pleasures. You adulteresses, do you not know that friendship with the world is hostility toward God? Therefore whoever wishes to be a friend of the world makes himself an enemy of God. (James 4:1–4)

This is sobering for those given over to the pursuit of pleasure and the seductive influence of wealth and materialism. Therefore, God warns His people to come out of her before it is too late.

(6) *Pay her back even as she has paid, and give back to her double according to her deeds; in the cup which she has mixed, mix twice as much for her:* Judgment often is measured by the amount of wickedness a person has given out to others. If someone is unmerciful, they receive no mercy. Therefore, Babylon is to be paid back at the full measure of her wickedness—but only double. This is why it was also said that "they poured out the blood of saints and prophets" and were then given blood to drink (See the third bowl judgment in 16:4–6.)

(7) *To the degree that she glorified herself and lived sensuously, to the same degree give her torment and mourning; for she says in her heart, 'I sit as a queen and I am not a widow, and will never see mourning':* Once again, judgment is measured by the degree of wickedness carried out. Babylon will be given to the same extent that she lived sensuously. Certainly, pride goes before destruction. Arrogantly, she declared, "I sit as a queen and I am not a widow." "I sit as a queen" is another way of declaring, "I have risen above suffering and pain." "I am not a widow" means she needs no one's pity. The level of her debauchery and overindulgence has caused madness because she believes she is beyond God's reach to bring judgment. This looks back to Isaiah's prophecy when God judged ancient Babylon:

Sit silently, and go into darkness, O daughter of the Chaldeans [Babylonians], for you will no longer be called the queen of kingdoms. I was angry with My people, I profaned

My heritage and gave them into your hand. You did not show mercy to them, on the aged you made your yoke very heavy. Yet you said, "I will be a queen forever." These things you did not consider nor remember the outcome of them. Now, then, hear this, you sensual one, who dwells securely, who says in your heart, "I am, and there is no one besides me. I will not sit as a widow, nor know loss of children." But these two things will come on you suddenly in one day: Loss of children and widowhood. They will come on you in full measure in spite of your many sorceries, in spite of the great power of your spells. (Isa 47:5–9)

(8) *For this reason in one day her plagues will come, pestilence and mourning and famine, and she will be burned up with fire*: As this prophecy and Isaiah's prophecy declare, all the plagues shall come in one day. The beast, who hates Babylon and on whose back Babylon rides, strikes Babylon (17:16) and destroys her in one hour (see 18:10, 18–19). ***For the Lord God who judges her is strong*:** God's judgment is sure and cannot be stopped or thwarted. The delay in judgment will make Babylon believe she is invincible. Such will be the case of all powerful nations whose arrogance and wickedness will reach up to heaven and who will be under the strong delusion that their money, influence, and military power will save them from God's wrath. They will be demonically deceived and will think themselves to be invincible—but they will not be.

✝

REVELATION 18:9–14

THE LAMENT FOR COMMERCIAL BABYLON

⁹ "And the kings of the earth, who committed acts of immorality and lived sensuously with her, will weep and lament over her when they see the smoke of her burning, ¹⁰ standing at a distance because of the fear of her torment, saying, 'Woe, woe, the great city, Babylon, the strong city! For in one hour your judgment has come.' ¹¹ And the merchants of the earth weep and mourn over her, because no one buys their cargoes any more — ¹² cargoes of gold and silver and precious stones and pearls and fine linen and purple and silk and scarlet, and every kind of citron wood and every article of ivory and every article made from very costly wood and bronze and iron and marble, ¹³ and cinnamon and spice and incense and perfume and frankincense and wine and olive oil and fine flour and wheat and cattle and sheep, and cargoes of horses and chariots and slaves and human lives. ¹⁴ The fruit you long for has gone from you, and all things that were luxurious and splendid have passed away from you and men will no longer find them.

(9) The lament for *commercial Babylon** is featured in these verses. *The kings of the earth, who committed acts of immorality and lived sensuously with her, will weep and lament over her when they see the smoke of her burning*: Babylon's lavish wealth will make the kings of the earth wealthy; therefore, their lament will be great when Babylon is destroyed by fire. The fire could be the result of a preemptive military attack,

335

possibly nuclear. The question is, Who and where is the great city called Babylon? Several possibilities will be examined here.

Mounce asserts: "The great city that is split into three parts *is undoubtedly to be identified as Rome*. This follows from the fact that in the following chapter [chap. 18] Rome is repeatedly referred to as the 'great city' (vv. 10, 16, 18, 19, 21)."[212] Beale asserts that "it is not just Rome or some later great capital of evil that is decimated but all the world's cultural, political, economic, and sociological centers. They fall because they are part of the Babylonian world system." He also says, "Cities of the nations" might define "Babylon the Great" (16:19).[213] Aune asserts that "The great city" should probably be understood *as* Babylon-Rome; however, for the fact that the city was split into three parts by the earthquake does not mean that it had yet been adequately punished. Further, Babylon-Rome is certainly referred to as "the great city."[214] Morris observes, "The name thus stands for the pride of mankind and for the heathen city-empire. For John, Babylon is the great city, the symbol of mankind in community opposed to the things of God."[215] Wiersbe asserts, "Babylon here refers to the apostate religious political system headed up by the Beast in conjunction with the apostate world church."[216] Walvoord asserts, "While this has been debated at length by scholars . . . it is preferable to view 'Babylon' as the rebuilt city of Babylon located on the Euphrates River, which will be the capital of the final world government."[217] This commentary supports the rebuilding of Babylon. See the essay "The Rebuilding of Babylon."

(10) *at a distance because of the fear of her torment, saying, 'Woe, woe, the great city, Babylon, the strong city! For in one hour your judgment has come':* On September 11, 2001, the world was astonished as hijacked

[212] Mounce, *The New International Commentary: The Book of Revelation*, 303.
[213] Beale, *The Book of Revelation*, 843.
[214] Aune, *Word Biblical Commentary*, 52B:900.
[215] Morris, *Tyndale Commentaries: Revelation*, 20:173.
[216] Wiersbe, *Wiersbe's Expository Outlines*, 836.
[217] Walvoord, *The Bible Knowledge Commentary: Revelation*, 2:969

passenger jets slammed into the World Trade Center in New York. The ensuing fire and destruction of the Twin Towers sent shock waves around the world as the entire globe witnessed televised pictures of the thick black smoke that was visible for miles. As people fled for their lives, they wailed and mourned at this unbelievable sight: the two tallest buildings of the international financial world were collapsing. It may be difficult to imagine, but the sudden destruction of Babylon will be even greater. On 9/11, terrorists targeted two New York buildings. In the future, the Lord will destroy the entire city of Babylon.

(11–14) *And the merchants of the earth weep and mourn over her, because no one buys their cargoes any more:* The list of items is identified as "cargoes"[218] (Gk. *gomos*, "a ship's freight") and implies imports, not natural resources of Babylon itself. These are sources of wealth for the kings and nations of the world. The merchandise can be categorized as follows: (1) precious metals and stones, (2) fine linens and fabrics, (3) natural ornamental items made from ivory and expensive wood, (4) spices and perfumes, (5) agricultural and foodstuffs, (6) livestock, and (7) human trafficking, slaves, domestic workers, and probably sex workers. Once again, this list of products, commerce, and commodities punctuates the variety of global commercial interests that will contribute to the immense global wealth and power of Babylon. John described this list of products from his first-century perspective, and it is, therefore, representative. John would not have listed *trains, planes, automobiles,* and other items not comprehensible in the first century. However, since this commentary supports a futuristic aspect of Revelation, we must also expand the ancient list of commodities to include items we would know today. For example, those of the first century could only understand Jerusalem from what was known to them during that period. They could not have understood Jerusalem in a modern-day context of 1948 onward. Neither could Ezekiel have called *Persia* Iran or *Beth-Togarmah* Turkey,

---

[218]   Joseph H. Thayer, *Thayer's Greek Lexicon of the New Testament* (New York: Harper & Brothers, 1889).

because these names did not exist during his time. Even when prophecy is futuristic, it is still written from the author's contemporary reality.

Babylon's commercial influence will be problematic for the beast's global prosperity interests, which will be supported through the mark of the beast. The problem will be that Babylon will attempt to share a spotlight that the beast wants only for himself. This will lead to the beast launching an attack against Babylon. The beast will want no economic or religious competitors. He will want to be the center of all wealth and worship. The verse-by-verse commentary continues on page 346.

ESSAY:
THE REBUILDING OF BABYLON

After examining a small sampling of scholars, we found no consensus on Babylon's identity. However, it is important that we understand the limitations that confront all scholars. The best scholars can do is create an exegesis for a text, study original languages, research etymologies of words, examine historical data, and scrutinize other scholars' opinions. None of us has a time machine with which we can go back into the past or forward into the future. None of us has been to heaven (and returned to tell about it, anyway). The best we can do is attempt to understand a text using every tool of hermeneutics available, but that doesn't get us any closer to knowing *how* or *when* God is going to fulfill prophecies in Revelation. Fulfillment of future prophecies does not avail itself to theological scrutiny.

No matter how passionately we hold to a tradition or position, no human ingenuity can reliably access the mysteries of God pertaining to the future. Hindsight, not our foresight, is twenty-twenty. That's why there are so many *opinions* but few *absolutes* about future prophecies. God has everything in the universe at His disposal to fulfill prophecy, which makes predictability improbable for events that haven't occurred yet. We have no idea of what exact circumstances will occur to bring any prophecy into fulfillment. As of 2025, there is no city called Babylon where the merchants and kings of the earth are made rich and that is the center of international commerce and revelry.

However, this commentary supports the rebuilding of Babylon because Isaiah's and Jeremiah's prophecies concerning the destruction of Babylon were not completely fulfilled by the conquest of the Medes and Persians. For example, Isaiah's prophecy declares,

> And Babylon, the beauty of kingdoms, the glory of the Chaldeans' pride, will be as when God overthrew Sodom and Gomorrah. It will never be inhabited or lived in from generation to generation; nor will the Arab pitch his tent there, nor will shepherds make their flocks lie down there. (Isa 13:19–20)

The prophecy explicitly states Babylon's fall "will be as when God overthrew *Sodom and Gomorrah* [and that it] will *never be inhabited or lived in from generation to generation*" (emphasis added). Jeremiah's prophecy is similar:

> "Therefore the desert creatures will live there along with the jackals; the ostriches also will live in it, and it will never again be inhabited or dwelt in from generation to generation. As when God overthrew Sodom and Gomorrah with its neighbors," declares the LORD, "No man will live there, nor will any son of man reside in it." (Jer 50:39–40)

Both prophecies, in their grammatical historical context, are in reference to the Medes' and Persians' defeat of the Chaldeans. However, both texts also prophesied concerning Babylon's being destroyed like *Sodom and Gomorrah*, which were two cities rained on from heaven with *fire and brimstone* (Gen 19:24). Therefore, a double reference here is plausible because when the Medes and Persians overtook Babylon, the city was not burned out of existence but was occupied by the Medes and Persians. Additionally, Jeremiah says, "Because of the *wrath of the Lord*," Babylon will not be inhabited but will be wholly desolate (50:13 ESV, emphasis mine).

God's providential words indicated that there was yet to be a future destruction of Babylon, and the Mede and Persian invasion only partially fulfilled His words. The Jeremiah passage explicitly declares that the wrath of God will be the reason that Babylon will not be inhabited again and the reason that it will be wholly desolate. Though not all of God's wrath is eschatological, this prophecy couldn't possibly have been fulfilled with the Mede and Persian invasion because they did not destroy Babylon. Therefore, we can expect an eschatological fulfillment.

Jeremiah gives more details about Babylon's judgment:

> "Behold, I am against you, O destroying mountain, who destroys the whole earth," declares the Lord, "And I will stretch out My hand against you, and roll you down from the crags, and I will make you a burnt out mountain. They will not take from you even a stone for a corner nor a stone for foundations, but you will be desolate forever," declares the Lord. (Jer 51:25–26)

According to this passage, the destruction during Babylon's judgment would be so complete that not even a stone would be used elsewhere for building other structures. This is another example of a prophecy that was not fulfilled with Babylon's fall to the Medes and Persians. On November 24, 2018, NPR (National Public Radio) published an online story titled "In Iraq, a Race to Protect the Crumbling Bricks of Ancient Babylon." The author reported, "For centuries, people in the area saw Babylon as a source of solid bricks to take away to build homes in the city of Hilla and surrounding villages."[219] The prophecy concerning Babylon's bricks was a prophecy made but not fulfilled by ancient Babylon. Jeremiah ended his prophecies concerning Babylon with the following warning:

> So Jeremiah wrote in a single scroll all the calamity which would come upon Babylon, that is, all these words which have been written concerning Babylon. Then Jeremiah said

---

[219] Jane Arraf, "In Iraq, a Race to Protect the Crumbling Bricks of Ancient Babylon," NPR (National Public Radio), November 24, 2018, https://www.npr.org/2018/11/24/669272204/in-iraq-a-race-to-protect-the-crumbling-bricks-of-ancient-babylon.

to Seraiah, "As soon as you come to Babylon, then see that you read all these words aloud, and say, 'You, O LORD, have promised concerning this place to cut it off, so that *there will be nothing dwelling in it, whether man or beast,* but it will be a perpetual desolation.' *And as soon as you finish reading this scroll, you will tie a stone to it and throw it into the middle of the Euphrates, and say, 'Just so shall Babylon sink down and not rise again because of the calamity that I am going to bring upon her; and they will become exhausted.'"* Thus far are the words of Jeremiah. (Jer 51:60–64, emphasis added)

Compare Jeremiah's prophecy with the account in Revelation:

And they threw dust on their heads and were crying out, weeping and mourning, saying, "Woe, woe, the great city, in which all who had ships at sea became rich by her wealth, for in one hour she has been laid waste!" . . . *Then a strong angel took up a stone like a great millstone and threw it into the sea, saying, "So will Babylon, the great city, be thrown down with violence, and will not be found any longer."* (Rev 18:19, 21, emphasis added)

The similarity between these two passages is undeniable. Though it is understandable that some see Babylon here as representing modern-day Rome, that interpretation is difficult because it does not account for the overwhelming description of the city being a center for global commerce that has made the kings of the earth very rich. Therefore, it is doubtful that Babylon represents the seat of the papacy.

On April 18, 2006, the *New York Times* released a story that says Iraqi leaders and United Nations officials are not giving up on reviving Babylon. The article says, "They are working assiduously to restore Babylon, home to one of the Seven Wonders of the World, and turn it into a cultural center and possibly even an Iraqi theme park." It goes on to say, "The United Nations Educational, Scientific and Cultural Organization is pumping millions of dollars into protecting and restoring Babylon and a handful of other ancient ruins in Iraq."[220]

In 2022, Joel C. Rosenberg wrote an article about Babylon for the *Jerusalem Post*. In it, he referred to a 2021 NPR article written by Alice Fordham about tourism in Babylon. Rosenberg's piece says, "'Since Babylon reopened in 2009, tourist numbers have fluctuated,' said Alice Fordham. 'The local tourist board says the best recent year for Iraqi tourists was 2017, when more than 35,000 visited. This winter—normally peak season because of the cool weather—the pandemic affected the numbers and about 10,000 came. The year before, many stayed away for fear of being caught up in violence at demonstrations in nearby cities.'"

In addition, Rosenberg's article says, "By July 2019, so much progress had been made that Babylon was named a UNESCO [United Nations Educational, Scientific and Cultural Organization] World Heritage Site. Last fall, the 'Babylon International Festival' was held again for the first time in two decades."

Rosenberg's article also describes restoration work in Babylon. The piece says that during the late Saddam Hussein's Iraqi administration in the 1970s and 80s, archaeologists started excavating and restoring Babylon's ancient ruins. One of the places of restoration was the prominent Ishtar Gate, originally built in honor of the Babylonian fertility goddess, and other places included walls and buildings of the ancient city.[221]

Considering these examples, it can be argued that we should have a wait-and-see approach to the revitalization of Babylon. In the twenty-first century, things happen much quicker than they did during ancient times. Though many may not see a resurgence of Babylon as

---

[220] Jeffrey Gettleman, "Babylon Awaits an Iraq Without Fighting," *New York Times*, April 18, 2006, World, https://www.nytimes.com/2006/04/18/world/middleeast/babylon-awaits-an-iraq-without-fighting.html.

[221] Joel C. Rosenberg, "Is Babylon Once Again Rising from the Ashes?," *Jerusalem Post*, February 16, 2022, Updated February 21, 2022, Christian World, https://www.jpost.com/christianworld/article-696640.

feasible, Christians should consider the possibility because the prophecies concerning her destruction (which describe it to be like that of Sodom and Gomorrah) were not historically fulfilled.

There is another way to view the revitalization of Babylon. The name Babylon could be a spiritualized name in Revelation. One such name is given to Jerusalem in 11:8, where it is called "Sodom and Egypt." Though Babylon is called "Babylon the great" in 14:8; 16:19; 17:5; 18:2, another city, not located in Iraq and that fulfills Babylon's characteristics described in chapter 18, could emerge in the last days. In chapter 17, John saw Babylon as a "great harlot" who was in the "wilderness," or desert. Could Babylon be a city that rises from an arid desert?

In the twenty-first century, cities can emerge much quicker than they ever have before. For example, in 2019, Saudi Arabia started construction on an entertainment city called Qiddiya, which is scheduled to be completed in 2030. That's only eleven years from start to finish. This city, located outside Riyadh, is designed to attract millions of international tourists. According to Philippe Gas, who was quoted in an online article by Bea Mitchell toward the end of 2023, Qiddiya City "is the world's biggest venture when it comes to entertainment, sports, arts, all together and integrated." He said, "This has never been done before. . . . It is almost three times the size of Walt Disney World."[222] This city is being built specifically for pleasure and commerce. In Jeremiah's prophecy Babylon's total destruction was characterized as a stone thrown into the Euphrates because ancient Babylon was on this river (Jer 61:53). However, in Revelation Babylon's demise is identified as a great millstone being thrown into the sea (18:21). Saudia Arabia has several major ports and conducts international commerce on the Red Sea and Persian Gulf. Could an entertainment and pleasure city like Qiddiya be Babylon? Or does the fact that a city is being built specifi-

---

222 Bea Mitchell, "Saudi Arabia's Crown Prince Unveils Qiddiya City Plans," Blooloop, December 8, 2023, https://blooloop.com/theme-park/news/qiddiya-city-plans/.

cally for entertainment purposes serve as a precursor that new Babylon could rise quickly in the future? Though we don't know how or when it will happen, Babylon will emerge and be destroyed, just as it was prophesied in the books of Isaiah, Jeremiah, and Revelation.

REVELATION 18:15–24

Babylon Will Never Rise Again

[15] "The merchants of these things, who became rich from her, will stand at a distance because of the fear of her torment, weeping and mourning, [16] saying, 'Woe, woe, the great city, she who was clothed in fine linen and purple and scarlet, and adorned with gold and precious stones and pearls; [17] for in one hour such great wealth has been laid waste!' And every shipmaster and every passenger and sailor, and as many as make their living by the sea, stood at a distance, [18] and were crying out as they saw the smoke of her burning, saying, 'What city is like the great city?' [19] And they threw dust on their heads and were crying out, weeping and mourning, saying, 'Woe, woe, the great city, in which all who had ships at sea became rich by her wealth, for in one hour she has been laid waste!' [20] Rejoice over her, O heaven, and you saints and apostles and prophets, because God has pronounced judgment for you against her." [21] Then a strong angel took up a stone like a great millstone and threw it into the sea, saying, "So will Babylon, the great city, be thrown down with violence, and will not be found any longer. [22] And the sound of harpists and musicians and flute-players and trumpeters will not be heard in you any longer; and no craftsman of any craft will be found in you any longer; and the sound of a mill will not be heard in you any longer; [23] and the light of a lamp will not shine in you any longer; and the voice of the bridegroom and bride will not be heard in you any longer; for your merchants were the great

men of the earth, because all the nations were deceived by your sorcery. [24] And in her was found the blood of prophets and of saints and of all who have been slain on the earth."

(15–19) *The merchants of these things, who became rich from her, will stand at a distance because of the fear of her torment, weeping and mourning:* These "merchants" will bewail not only the tragedy of Babylon's fall but also the fact that their source of wealth has perished. *For in one hour such great wealth has been laid waste!* The rapid destruction of Babylon will strike awe and fear in the hearts of those who see her burning. The city's ruin will come through the hatred of the kingdom of the beast, as the ten horns will be set poised to launch their deadly attack that is referenced in 17:16, first announced in 14:8, and executed in 16:19. Though the destruction of Babylon will be carried out through *the ten kings,* it will still be God's doing because He will guide their hearts to fulfill His word (17:17). *And they threw dust on their heads and were crying out, weeping and mourning:* This is the ancient method of showing deep grief. Here, the people are also showing their humiliation because their source of wealth has forever perished beyond recovery.

(20–21) *Rejoice over her, O heaven, and you saints and apostles and prophets, because God has pronounced judgment for you against her:* The destruction of Babylon is a reason for mourning for the merchants of the earth, and simultaneously, it is a reason for rejoicing for the heavenly host, among whom are "saints . . . apostles and prophets." This is clear evidence that the church has already been translated. If the saints were still in Babylon while the city was being destroyed, there would be no cause for rejoicing. Mounce observes, "It is the church glorified, not believers on earth, who are invited to rejoice."[223] MacArthur also asserts, "The angel who began speaking in verse 4, then addressed *the redeemed in heaven:* the saints (a general term for all believers) and apostles and

---

223   Mounce, *The New International Commentary: The Book of Revelation,* 336.

347

prophets (the special class of saints given to the church, as indicated in Eph 2:20; 4:11)"[224] (emphasis added). *Then a strong angel took up a stone like a great millstone and threw it into the sea, saying, "So will Babylon, the great city, be thrown down with violence, and will not be found any longer":* The message here is almost identical to that in Jeremiah 51:63–64.

(22–23) And the sound of harpists and musicians and flute-players and trumpeters will not be heard in you any longer; and no craftsman of any craft will be found in you any longer; and the sound of a mill will not be heard in you any longer; and the light of a lamp will not shine in you any longer; and the voice of the bridegroom and bride will not be heard in you any longer: Popular destinations can be known for their entertainment and night life. International stars and famous "musicians" from all over the world who will be featured in Babylon will also be forever silenced. The skilled workers will no longer practice their "crafts." All the "mills" and production lines will cease. Wedding celebrations, with all their festive activities, will perish, never to return. *All the nations were deceived by your sorcery:* The word "sorcery" here comes from the Greek word *pharmakeia*, where the English word *pharmacy* derives. It means "witchcraft, sorcery, participation in demonic activities; the use of drugs or of evil spirits to gain control over the lives of others or over one's own life."[225] From this definition, we see there is more to sorcery than using magical arts for divination; it also includes drug use. Babylon will be the place to act out every wicked proclivity and vice imaginable. Anything will go; nothing will be off the table. Like a seductive, promiscuous woman, Babylon's wicked influence will allure small and great, rich and poor, with irresistible, unbridled passion, pleasure, and wealth. Those who love her will come under her seductive power, similar to one who is under the influence of a drug.

(24) And in her was found the blood of prophets and of saints and of all who have been slain on the earth: The destruction of commercial Babylon is

224 MacArthur, *The MacArthur New Testament Commentary: Revelation 12–22*, 189.
225 Alpha-Omega Ministries, *Practical Word Studies in The New Testament* (Chattanooga, TN: Leadership Ministries Worldwide, 1998), 2:2315, *Sorcery*.

also the destruction of the apostate Babylon, *the mother of harlots* and abominations (i.e., things that are religiously detestable to God) of the earth. Both aspects of Babylon can be viewed together or separately, as either commercial or religious. The call "Come out of her, my people" (18:4) seems to be in reference to evacuating a geographical location. Since there were "people of God" (i.e., saints and prophets) who were warned to leave, this means there will be Christians there who could undergo persecution and martyrdom. Whether commercial or mystical, historic or futuristic, Babylon would be responsible for the "blood ... of saints" and thereby deserving of judgment. John was astonished by the fact the harlot was drunk with the blood of the saints and the witnesses of Jesus (17:6). Persecuting the righteous is the same as persecuting the righteous One, Jesus (Acts 9:4); therefore, the harlot's sins have come up in remembrance before God. Though judgment may tarry long, it is sure to come.

REVELATION 19:1–6

The Hallelujah Chorus

¹ After these things I heard something like a loud voice of a great multitude in heaven, saying, "Hallelujah! Salvation and glory and power belong to our God; ² because His judgments are true and righteous; for He has judged the great harlot who was corrupting the earth with her immorality, and He has avenged the blood of His bond-servants on her." ³ And a second time they said, "Hallelujah! Her smoke rises up forever and ever." ⁴ And the twenty-four elders and the four living creatures fell down and worshiped God who sits on the throne saying, "Amen. Hallelujah!" ⁵ And a voice came from the throne, saying, "Give praise to our God, all you His bond-servants, you who fear Him, the small and the great." ⁶ Then I heard something like the voice of a great multitude and like the sound of many waters and like the sound of mighty peals of thunder, saying, "Hallelujah! For the Lord our God, the Almighty, reigns."

(1) *Hallelujah! Salvation and glory and power belong to our God*: The judgment of Babylon will be a point of great celebration in heaven. She will finally receive her much-deserved punishment, and the multitude will praise God.

(2) *Because His judgments are true and righteous; for He has judged the great harlot who was corrupting the earth with her immorality*: Make no mistake about it, Babylon's influence has a "corrupting" impact on the whole earth, whether through *false religion* or *commercialism*. This is similar to John's description of Satan as being one "who deceives the whole world" (12:9), which means, to some degree, that we have all been deceived and corrupted by Babylon. However, because judgment does not fall immediately, the wicked make the mistake of believing that God approves of or cannot do anything to stop their wickedness. These ideas are contrived.

The corrupting influence of a false religious system inevitably leads to the worship of materialism and wealth. False gods are typically made of the very material that people deem to be precious. People love gold; therefore, their gods are made of gold. Worship of false deities and worship of wealth go together. The outgrowth of Babylon's false system of religion is commercial Babylon, which is the epitome of mammon, or wealth worship. This is what led to Satan's fall, as stated in the lament against Tyre:

> "Son of man, take up a lamentation over the king of Tyre and say to him, 'Thus says the Lord GOD, "You had *the seal of perfection, full of wisdom and perfect in beauty. You were in Eden, the garden of God; every precious stone was your covering:* The ruby, the topaz and the diamond; the beryl, the onyx and the jasper; the lapis lazuli, the turquoise and the emerald; and the gold, the workmanship of your settings and sockets, was in you. On the day that you were created they were prepared. [14] *You were the anointed cherub who covers, and I placed you there. You were on the holy mountain of God; you walked in the midst of the stones of fire. You were blameless in your ways from the day you were created until unrighteousness was found in you. By the abundance of your trade you were internally filled with violence, and you sinned; therefore I have cast you as profane from the mountain of God. And I have destroyed you, O covering cherub,* from the midst of the stones of fire. Your heart was lifted up because of your beauty; You corrupted your wisdom by reason of your splendor. I cast you to the ground; I put you before kings, that they may see you." (Ezek 28:12–17, emphasis added)

Though there are several aspects of this passage that are interesting, v. 16 stands out. It says, "By the abundance of your trade you were internally filled with violence, and you sinned." Earlier in this chapter of Ezekiel, v. 5 states, "By your great wisdom, by your trade you have increased your riches and your heart is lifted up because of your riches." The word "trade" comes from the Hebrew word *rekullâ,*[226] which means "merchandise," or "the abundance of wealth," which was Satan's covering (vv. 13–14). Satan offered Jesus wealth and splendor if He would worship him. Satan essentially said, "All the wealth of this world's system [i.e., Babylon] belongs to me, and I can give it to whomever I want. Worship me, and it's Yours" (see Luke 4:5–7).

Both Babylon *the system of false religion* and *commercial* Babylon are guilty and full of the blood of the saints. Therefore, God has **avenged the blood of His bond-servants on her**: Whether on account of the blood of the martyrs under the altar, the saints of Hebrews 11:36–38, the prophets of old, the NT apostles, prophets, saints, and servants, or the church persecuted in the past, Babylon must now pay back her iniquities, and heaven is glad about it.

(3) *And a second time they said, "Hallelujah! Her smoke rises up forever and ever"*: While heaven is rejoicing, Babylon will be burning. Her smoke will likely be seen for miles, from both the land and the sea.

(4–6) Heaven breaks out into praise from *the twenty-four elders* and *the four living creatures*: A voice from the throne says, *"Give praise to our God, all you His bond-servants, you who fear Him, the small and the great"*: Then *something like the voice of a great multitude . . . many waters and . . . peals of thunder* says, *"Hallelujah! For the Lord our God, the Almighty, reigns"*: Heaven celebrates the judgment of Babylon and the reigning power of the Lord God Almighty. God's acts are righteous whether in judgment and wrath or in His omnipotent reign in heaven and on the earth.

---

[226] Robert L. Thomas, *New American Standard Hebrew-Aramaic and Greek Dictionaries: Updated Edition* (Anaheim: Foundation Publications, Inc., 1998).

REVELATION 19:7–10

THE MARRIAGE SUPPER OF THE LAMB

⁷ "Let us rejoice and be glad and give the glory to Him, for the marriage of the Lamb has come and His bride has made herself ready." ⁸ It was given to her to clothe herself in fine linen, bright and clean; for the fine linen is the righteous acts of the saints. ⁹ Then he said to me, "Write, 'Blessed are those who are invited to the marriage supper of the Lamb.'" And he said to me, "These are true words of God." ¹⁰ Then I fell at his feet to worship him. But he said to me, "Do not do that; I am a fellow servant of yours and your brethren who hold the testimony of Jesus; worship God. For the testimony of Jesus is the spirit of prophecy."

(7–8) *Let us rejoice and be glad and give the glory to Him, for the marriage of the Lamb has come and His bride has made herself ready*: The destruction of the *great harlot, Babylon,* a lewd and abominable woman of debaucheries, intoxicated with the blood of the saints, decked out in purple, red, and precious stones, will give way to the glorious bride who makes herself ready for "the marriage supper of the Lamb." In Ephesians, Paul declared, "For this reason a man shall leave his father and mother and shall be joined to his wife, and the two shall become one flesh. This mystery is great; but I am speaking *with reference to Christ and the church*" (Eph 5:31–32, emphasis added). After the long delay (two thousand years and running) is over, the bride will be ready and glorified, which will be the final phase of the salvific process. The bride will be adorned in *the righteous acts of the saints*: The "bride" and "the righteous acts of the saints" refer to *the church*. However, John did not say the righteous acts of the *church*; he used the word for "saints," which was typical of John because he never used the word *church* in the sense of the *body of Christ* (see the essay "What Happened to the Church?"). The "marriage of the Lamb" is a point for all of heaven to rejoice.

(9) *Then he said to me, "Write, 'Blessed are those who are invited to the marriage supper of the Lamb.'" And he said to me, "These are true words of God"*: The verse contains the fourth beatitude of Revelation. Those "who are invited to the marriage supper of the Lamb" are special guests of the Lord. The word "invite" comes from the Greek word *kaleô*,[227] which means "to request the presence of someone at a social gathering." Evans asserts that the wedding will take place on earth and the feast will last the entire period of the millennium.[228] Osborne observes, "Some (Walvoord, Thomas) theorize that the bride is the saints from the tribulation, and the guests are the saints who lived earlier, while others (Caird, Beale) believe that the bride is the believers considered corporately … and the guests are the believers considered individually."[229] Mounce observes, "The church is pictured both as the bride and as the guests who are invited to the wedding. Far from constituting a contradiction, this sort of freedom is a normal characteristic of apocalyptic writing."[230]

However, on which side of the debate one falls is not important because to attend the event one must be invited. Jesus is not just the Lamb of the church, but He is the Lamb of God who takes away the sin of the world. Evidently, there will be a wide range of humanity invited from the OT and NT. Whoever is there, surely, they are blessed. "These are true words of God" adds emphasis and the certainty of the blessedness of all "those who are invited to the marriage supper of the Lamb."

---

[227] Bauer, *Greek-English Lexicon*, "kaleô."
[228] Evans, *The Tony Evans Bible Commentary*, 1422.
[229] Osborne, *Baker Exegetical Commentary: Revelation*, 694.
[230] Mounce, *The New International Commentary: The Book of Revelation*, 348–49.

(10) *Then I fell at his feet to worship him. But he said to me, "Do not do that;* *I am a fellow servant of yours and your brethren who hold the testimony* *of Jesus; worship God"*: Much of what John had seen in heaven thus far must have been overwhelming for him. For example, earlier John beheld an angel so glorious that "the earth was lit up by his radiance" (18:1 NET). Now he sees this magnificent angel, which is the first of two similar incidents (see 22:8) where John attempts to "worship" an angel. If this is the same angel of 18:1, it is understandable why John, a mere human, would prostrate himself. From John's perspective, this could have been the Lord. We should also consider that John would have certainly known about the *angel of the Lord*,* which is the Lord in angelic form (see Exod 3:2; Zech 3:1–4). We see this in the NT as well when the writer of Hebrews speaks of the Law. He calls it "the word spoken through angels" (Heb 2:2). In Stephen's rebuke of the Jews, he makes a similar reference to "the angel who was speaking to [Moses] on Mount Sinai" (Acts 7:38). However, here, without rebuke, the angel quickly redirects John by saying, "Do not do that; I am a fellow servant of yours and your brethren who hold the testimony of Jesus; worship God."

(a) *For the testimony of Jesus is the spirit of prophecy*: Through the outpouring of the Spirit on the day of Pentecost, the spiritual enablement of "prophecy" became active during the church age.

> 'And it shall be in the last days,' God says, 'that I will pour forth of My Spirit on all mankind; and your sons and your daughters shall prophesy, and your young men shall see visions, and your old men shall dream dreams; even on My bondslaves, both men and women, I will in those days pour forth of My Spirit and they shall prophesy. (Acts 2:17–18)

The gift or spiritual enablement of prophecy is more of a forthtelling (i.e., exhortation) as opposed to a foretelling (i.e., prediction). The "testimony of Jesus" Christ must be the basis for prophetic utterances (i.e., declaring the Word of God through exhortation or preaching). Acts 4:12

355

declares, "There is salvation in no one else; for there is no other name under heaven that has been given among men by which we must be saved." If prophecy is to have any salvific value, it must be based upon the "testimony of Jesus" Christ. What many call prophecy today focuses on materialism and worldly gain and is false prophecy. It amounts to divination and fortune-telling.[231] However, "The testimony of Jesus is the spirit of [*true*] prophecy."

THE STAGE HAS BEEN SET

Several important events have occurred that will lead up to a grand finale. After the two witnesses (see the essay "The Two Witnesses") are killed, and they lay dead in the streets of Jerusalem, they will suddenly come to life. Then they will be caught up into the sky while the global community watches them disappear into the clouds. Imagine all the news networks that will cover this. One of two things could possibly happen in their response to this miraculous event. The networks will either tell the truth or they will lie. Lying is the likely option. It is plausible they will give a convincing false narrative to claim these men were of extraterrestrial origin, which would explain their supernatural powers, how they came back to life after being killed, and how they left the earth going up into the sky. A follow-up narrative could claim that the departure of the two witnesses is a precursor to a coming full-on alien invasion. Though this sounds like a scene from a sci-fi film, a fascination with *unidentified anomalous phenomenon* (UAPs), formerly known as unidentified flying objects (UFOs), continues to solicit great international interest. Many people believe in extraterrestrial life.

As the world moves headlong toward the battle of Armageddon, it will be just over three years since the two witnesses were resurrected. Demonic spirits will be released from *the dragon, the Antichrist,* and *the false*

---

[231] Dennis James Woods, *Counterfeit Charisma: The Age of False Prophets* (Matteson, IL: Life to Legacy, LLC, 2018), 89–103.

prophet to display signs and wonders to the world leaders of the earth to persuade them to send troops to this great battle. Though no one knows exactly how this will play out, these demonically inspired envoys will be convincing. The text declares,

> And I saw coming out of the mouth of the dragon and out of the mouth of the beast and out of the mouth of the false prophet, three unclean spirits like frogs; for they are spirits of demons, performing signs, which go out to the kings of the whole world, to gather them together for the war of the great day of God, the Almighty. (Rev 16:13–14)

Some nations will come at the behest of demons' persuasion while others may have their political reasons. Coalitions of troops will come with *Gog of Magog* (i.e., Russia), *Persia* (i.e., Iran), *Put* (i.e., Libya, possibly Somalia and Yemen), and *Ethiopia* (i.e., Ethiopia and Sudan), along with *Beth-togarmah* (i.e., Turkey), and *Gomer* (i.e., Armenia). Others will see Israel at peace and say, "I will go up against the land of unwalled villages. I will go against those who are at rest, that live securely, all of them living without walls and having no bars or gates" (Ezek 38:11). The kings of the east will mobilize all their troops and will be there. Every militarized nation will participate. Through the prophet Zechariah, God declared, "I will gather all the nations against Jerusalem to battle" (Zech 14:2).

At some point, the world's nations will come together and aim their weapons toward the sky to fight the "invaders from space" headed toward earth. Having been deceived and believing they will be fighting an invading extraterrestrial army, they will not be prepared for who really shows up at this battle. For decades, Satan has planted the seeds for the big lie through movies, television, science fiction novels, magazines, and mass media. Therefore, they will readily accept this lie, especially in the aftermath of the two witnesses leaving the earth in plain sight (cf. 11:11–12).

REVELATION 19:11–16

THE HEAVENLY INVASION

¹¹ And I saw heaven opened, and behold, a white horse, and He who sat on it is called Faithful and True, and in righteousness He judges and wages war. ¹² His eyes are a flame of fire, and on His head are many diadems; and He has a name written on Him which no one knows except Himself. ¹³ He is clothed with a robe dipped in blood, and His name is called The Word of God. ¹⁴ And the armies which are in heaven, clothed in fine linen, white and clean, were following Him on white horses. ¹⁵ From His mouth comes a sharp sword, so that with it He may strike down the nations, and He will rule them with a rod of iron; and He treads the wine press of the fierce wrath of God, the Almighty. ¹⁶ And on His robe and on His thigh He has a name written, "King of Kings, and Lord of Lords."

(11) *And I saw heaven opened, and behold, a white horse, and He who sat on it is called Faithful and True, and in righteousness He judges and wages war:* The Lord is ready for battle. He's no longer the baby in swaddling clothes, the meek, mild, and lowly Jesus. No, He has come to rule the nations with the rod of iron and take the world from the beast by force. The "white horse" is a symbol of triumph and victory over His enemies, but this is no ordinary horse. The Lord has created living creatures for His purposes, so this is not some clunky machinery that humans would produce for travel. He is the Lord of all creation, surrounded by living beings that give Him glory. The armies of heaven follow Him, also riding white horses (19:14). These cannot be horses that we are familiar with on earth. These creatures are able to transport between heavenly and earthly realms and can function in both places.

(12) *His eyes are a flame of fire*: His anger is focused and fierce. *On His head are many diadems*: One crown means He is king, and the many other crowns mean that He rules in every sphere and is over every kingdom. *And He has a name written on Him which no one knows except Himself*: There is much we do not know about our Savior, because we only know Him from our limited, earthly perspective. For example, no human being knows the name that is "written on Him."

(13) *He is clothed with a robe dipped in blood, and His name is called The Word of God*: Though some here refer to the fact that the Lord treads the wine press of the wrath of God; however, He comes wearing a robe dipped in blood. Since He is the Lamb of God who shed His blood, He has the right to execute judgment on the world for which He gave His life. "His name is called The Word of God." It is from John's Gospel that we learn of Jesus' preincarnate existence as the *Word of God*, the *eternal logos* who, in the beginning, was "with God" and "was God," who "became flesh" (John 1:1, 14). However, here we see "The Word of God" is an actual name as well.

(14) *And the armies which are in heaven, clothed in fine linen, white and clean, were following Him on white horses* (see Jude 1:14). This is a full-on invasion from heaven consisting of *angelic warriors* and glorified *saints* on horses, not extraterrestrials but rather God's powerful heavenly army. The description of their garments and horses as being "white and clean" sets them apart from the armies at Armageddon. "White" represents holiness, righteous indignation, and superiority, thus setting the heavenly army high and above those gathered there in the plain of Megiddo (or "Har Megiddo," CJB; also *Armageddon*).

Zechariah also prophesied about this climactic battle.

> Then the LORD will go forth and fight against those nations, as when He fights on a day of battle. In that day His feet will

stand on the Mount of Olives, which is in front of Jerusalem
on the east; and the Mount of Olives will be split in its middle
from east to west by a very large valley, so that half of the
mountain will move toward the north and the other half toward the south. You will flee by the valley of My mountains,
for the valley of the mountains will reach to Azel; yes, you
will flee just as you fled before the earthquake in the days
of Uzziah king of Judah. Then the LORD, my God, will come,
and all the holy ones with Him! (Zech 14:3–5)

(15) *From His mouth comes a sharp sword, so that with it He may strike
down the nations, and He will rule them with a rod of iron:* The two-edged
sword imagery was first seen in 1:16. In 2:16, the sword is an instrument
of judgment where Christ declared, "I am coming to you quickly, and I
will make war against them with the sword of My mouth." In this verse,
the "sharp sword" of His mouth, though not literal, is an instrument of
judgment to "strike down the nations" that "He will rule . . . with a rod
of iron."

(a) *and He treads the wine press of the fierce wrath of God, the Almighty:*
This scene was first revealed under the sixth seal (6:12–17). Many assert
that the timing of the sixth seal is earlier in Daniel's Seventieth Week,
but remember, the sixth seal is not a point-in-time action and is instead
the vision of the wrath of the Lamb that will be executed during the
bowl judgments. A second preview of the wrath of God is in the passage
about the seventh trumpet (11:18), and the third preview, identified as
the "wine press," is in 14:19–20. Here, in 19:15, it is the culminating day
of God's wrath.

(16) *And on His robe and on His thigh He has a name written, "King of
Kings, and Lord of Lords":* His name indicates that Jesus is the supreme
ruler over all principalities, powers, and governments of the earth. At
the blowing of the seventh trumpet, He will seize control over the earth.
Isaiah prophesied about His glorious reign.

> For a child will be born to us, a son will be given to us; and
> the government will rest on His shoulders; and His name
> will be called Wonderful Counselor, Mighty God, Eternal
> Father, Prince of Peace. There will be no end to the increase
> of His government or of peace, on the throne of David and
> over his kingdom, to establish it and to uphold it with justice
> and righteousness from then on and forevermore. The zeal
> of the Lord of hosts will accomplish this. (Isa 9:6–7)

Jesus is King of Kings and Lord of Lords. No man or angel can challenge
His authority.

REVELATION 19:17–21

THE GREAT SUPPER OF GOD AND THE DOOM
OF THE FALSE PROPHET AND THE BEAST

¹⁷ Then I saw an angel standing in the sun, and he cried out with a loud voice, saying to all the birds which fly in midheaven, "Come, assemble for the great supper of God, ¹⁸ so that you may eat the flesh of kings and the flesh of commanders and the flesh of mighty men and the flesh of horses and of those who sit on them and the flesh of all men, both free men and slaves, and small and great." ¹⁹ And I saw the beast and the kings of the earth and their armies assembled to make war against Him who sat on the horse and against His army. ²⁰ And the beast was seized, and with him the false prophet who performed the signs in his presence, by which he deceived those who had received the mark of the beast and those who worshiped his image; these two were thrown alive into the lake of fire which burns with brimstone. ²¹ And the rest were killed with the sword which came from the mouth of Him who sat on the horse, and all the birds were filled with their flesh.

(17) *Then I saw an angel standing in the sun, and he cried out with a loud voice, saying to all the birds which fly in midheaven, "Come, assemble for the great supper of God"*: Once again, the angel is the agent that calls for action. This is not a supper to which anyone would want an invitation. The birds are summoned to this "great supper" to come and eat the bodies of all the dead soldiers slaughtered by the Lord in the battle of Armageddon. This will be a horrific scene. The sky will be darkened with millions of birds as they descend on the plain of Megiddo, where all the carcasses will be laid out as a banquet for the birds to gorge themselves. Jesus spoke of this terrible yet triumphant day when He said, "One will be taken and the other will be left" (Luke 17:36). When the disciples asked Him where they would be taken, His response was chilling. He said, "Where the body is, there also the vultures will be gathered" (Luke 17:37). In the destruction of Gog of Magog, we see the same scenario prophesied by Ezekiel (Ezek 39:4, 17–20).

(18) On the menu for this avian feast will be *the flesh of kings and the flesh of commanders and the flesh of mighty men and the flesh of horses and of those who sit on them and the flesh of all men, both free men and slaves, and small and great*: The birds will gorge themselves on the bodies of fallen human beings—the rich, the powerful, the influential, both "small and great."

(19) *And I saw the beast and the kings of the earth and their armies assembled to make war against Him who sat on the horse and against His army*: What level of insanity must drive a person to believe it is possible to survive in a battle against God Almighty? These people will be deceived and turned over to strong delusion, so they will believe a lie that forever seals their fate (2 Thess 2:9–12; also see 1 Kgs 22:22–23).

(20) *And the beast was seized*: One of the first things on the Lord's agenda at this great battle will be capturing the beast and the false prophet and immediately casting them into the lake of fire (i.e., the final hell). Daniel also alluded to this.

> Then I kept looking because of the sound of the boastful words which the horn was speaking; I kept looking until the beast was slain, and its body was destroyed and given to the burning fire. (Dan 7:11)

Daniel's text is interesting. Remember, there are three aspects of the beast. The *kingdom of the beast*, the *man*, or *human dictator*, and the *demonic principality that ascends from the abyss*. It is *possible* that the language in this text addresses both the human and demonic aspects of the beast (see the essay

"The Threefold Reality of the Beast"). Daniel wrote, "The beast was slain." Revelation 17:8 is also clear: "The beast that you saw was, and is not, and is about to come up out of the abyss and go to destruction." Here in 17:8, the demonic aspect of the beast comes out of the abyss in his encore appearance in the earthly realm, but he will go to destruction ("perdition," KJV) when the Lord returns. After coming out of the abyss, which is a prison, he will operate through the Antichrist (who is the human aspect of the beast) for three and a half years. When the Lord returns, the beast will be captured and then thrown directly into the lake of fire, fulfilling his destruction. One of the names for the human part of the beast is "the son of destruction" (2 Thess 2:3; "perdition," KJV), meaning that he is *the human* ("son of") aspect of the beast. The *human* and *the beast from the abyss* have the same end—to be cast into the lake of fire. As Daniel declared, "Its body was destroyed and given to the burning fire." The demon's body is the Antichrist, the son of perdition, the human being through whom the beast will operate. In this sense, the two are one. However, there is another diabolical character that the Lord will immediately deal with as well.

(a) *and with him the false prophet who performed the signs in his presence, by which he deceived those who had received the mark of the beast and those who worshiped his image; these two were thrown alive into the lake of fire which burns with brimstone*: The judgment of both of these wicked individuals will be without delay. These are the only individuals identified in the Scriptures who are thrown immediately into the lake of fire without a hearing before *the great white throne* judgment of 20:11–15. They will have no trial, no examination, no presentation of evidence, no plea. The beast and false prophet are damned immediately.

(21) *And the rest were killed with the sword which came from the mouth of Him who sat on the horse, and all the birds were filled with their flesh*: Everyone else who was part of this military campaign will also be killed. Additionally, all those who received the mark of the beast are among those who will be slain by the sword that proceeds out of the mouth of the Lord. And all the birds will devour their flesh.

REVELATION 20:1–3

¹ Then I saw an angel coming down from heaven, holding the key of the abyss and a great chain in his hand. ² And he laid hold of the dragon, the serpent of old, who is the devil and Satan, and bound him for a thousand years; ³ and he threw him into the abyss, and shut it and sealed it over him, so that he would not deceive the nations any longer, until the thousand years were completed; after these things he must be released for a short time.

(1) *Then I saw an angel coming down from heaven, holding the key of the abyss and a great chain in his hand:* John saw an unnamed angel coming down from heaven, holding the key to the abyss. The angel is referred to by the masculine pronouns "his" and "he" (see 2 Thess 2:6–7). As discussed before, the "key of the abyss" indicates that the opening and closing of the abyss is restricted. Osborne writes, "'The abyss' is the prison house of demonic spirits where they await their final destiny, and the 'key' is wielded by the eternal 'warden' of the prison."[232] The angel is also holding a "great chain," which is the *instrument of restraint.* Though angels are incorporeal beings (i.e., not having a physical body), they are able to be bound with chains, as in the case of the angels "bound at the ... Euphrates" (9:14), the angels delivered into "chains of darkness" (2 Pet 2:4 KJV), and the angels reserved in "everlasting chains" (Jude 1:6 KJV). Certainly, these chains are not made of iron like those that humans

---

[232] Osborne, *Baker Exegetical Commentary: Revelation,* 700.

make and use, but these chains are effective for spirit beings in the form of demons or fallen angels.

(2) *And he laid hold of the dragon, the serpent of old, who is the devil and Satan, and bound him for a thousand years*: The fact that the angel lays hold of Satan indicates that he is the aggressor who *accosts and apprehends* Satan with the intention of keeping him restrained and incarcerated for one thousand years.

(3) *and he threw him into the abyss, and shut it and sealed it over him*: Satan will not receive any dignitary treatment or be handled with kid gloves. On the contrary, he will be thrown into the abyss *so that he* will *not deceive the nations any longer.* When Satan is thrown into the abyss, it will be sealed over in such a way that completely incapacitates his power and ability to deceive—*until the thousand years* are *completed.* The millennium will be characterized as a time of peace, partly because the devil will be imprisoned and cannot cause any trouble. However, *after these things he must be released for a short time.* After the thousand years are up, Satan will be set free for a short time from his chains and confinement in the abyss. What happens when Satan is released will be covered in 20:7–10. However, what is key in these passages is that the abyss will be locked and impregnable to such a degree that Satan himself cannot escape its confines. Though it is not explicit in this text, it is *possible* that this restraining angel has remained on station insuring that the devil remains secured until the thousand years are complete. Even in this world, prisons are guarded from the inside and outside.

What is also evident is there is an angel who restrains and abyss that detains. Once restrained and incarcerated in the abyss, Satan or any other spirit "must be released" after their incarceration is complete. None of the inmates of the abyss can leave on their own accord. If these protocols are true for Satan, the same is true for the beast who comes from the abyss (11:7, 17:8). However, the beast will not return to the abyss when his three and a half years are up. He (the demon and the man) will be thrown directly into the lake of fire as soon as the Lord returns.

EXCURSUS—THE RESTRAINING MINISTRY OF ANGELS

Angels are tasked with the restraining ministry. In Daniel 10, the angel (Gabriel) contended with the prince of the kingdom of Persia for three weeks until Michael came to assist him. Gabriel emphatically stated, "I will tell you what is inscribed in the writing of truth. Yet there is no one who stands firmly with me against these forces except Michael your prince" (Dan 10:21). Undoubtedly, the Holy Spirit was not involved with restraining the prince of the kingdom of Persia (the demonic ruler over Persia). The angel stated that no one stood firmly against these forces except Michael, another angel. Godly angels bring God's judgment on wicked angels, "yet even angels, although they are stronger and more powerful, do not heap abuse on such beings when bringing judgment on them from the Lord" (2 Pet 2:11 NIV). The beings in this text are the "celestial beings" (NIV), "angelic majesties" (NASB), or "dignities" (KJV)—all designations for wicked angelic principalities and powers. God uses holy angels to deal with them. In Jude 1:9, Michael is presented as the tactical restraining agent that stopped Satan's agenda for the body of Moses.

In Revelation 7:1, the angels hold back the four winds so that they do not hurt the earth. In 12:7–9, Michael and his angels fought against the devil and his angels and cast them out of heaven down to the earth. The Holy Spirit was not involved in any of these angel-on-angel conflicts. When Satan and the beast are released from the abyss, it will be an angel-on-angel contact in which the Holy Spirit will not be participating. Nowhere in Scripture is it found where the Lord comes to the aid of angels. The Bible declares, "He does not give help to angels, but He gives help to the descendant[s] of Abraham" (Heb 2:16). Obviously, the Holy Spirit is involved with the restraint of satanic activity in defense of humans (Job 1:12), but this is never seen in angel-versus-angel conflicts.

Providentially, God restrains evil. Certainly, He limits what Satan can do to people (1 Cor 10:13). However, though God is sovereign over everything, God does not do everything. God gives the order, and his tactical agents carry them out.

MacArthur and Norman Geisler —and undoubtedly others—use Jude 9 as a basis to counter the angelic restrainer argument by eliminating the chief of godly angels, Michael the archangel. However, they employ a fallacious argument. Jude states,

In the very same way, on the strength of their dreams these ungodly people pollute their own bodies, reject authority and heap abuse on celestial beings. But even the archangel Michael, when he was disputing with the devil about the body of Moses, did not himself dare to condemn him for slander but said, "The Lord rebuke you!" Yet these people slander whatever they do not understand, and the very things they do understand by instinct—as irrational animals do—will destroy them. (Jude 1:8–10 NIV)

The context of Jude 1:9 is brought into clarity by the verses before and after it. Jude was emphasizing the fallacy of the false teachers who are "ungodly people [who] pollute their own bodies, reject authority and heap abuse on celestial beings." In the NASB, the phrase "celestial beings" is translated as "angelic majesties." Heaping verbal abuse on angelic majesties, even the evil ones, is something that humans should not do, because not even angels do such. In this context, the false teachers were doing just that. This passage has nothing to do with showing an inability in Michael to restrain Satan. Events in Revelation 12:7–9 explicitly demonstrate that Michael does have this ability.

Further emphasizing the false teachers' arrogance, Jude wrote, "Yet these people slander whatever they do not understand." Jude emphasized his point by borrowing from an ancient pseudepigraphal book called the Assumption of Moses, which also presents the account of Michael and

Satan's disputing about the body of Moses. Jude refers to this text, when he says, "Michael . . . did not dare to condemn him for slander but said, 'The Lord rebuke you!'" (Jude 1:9 NIV). "Slander" and "rebuke" are verbal actions. The point being made here is that Michael was not slanderous toward Satan. This was not because he was weaker or because he couldn't stop Satan from doing what it was that he had in mind to do. This passage has nothing to do with Michael's capability, prowess, or strength concerning his ability to confront and prohibit Satan's actions. MacArthur and Geisler's assertion that Michael does not have the power to restrain Satan is unsubstantiated. The fact is that Satan did not do what he wanted to do with the body of Moses because Michael (as the tactical restrainer)—not the Holy Spirit—was there to stop him.

EXCURSUS—THE ANGELIC RESTRAINER VERSUS THE HOLY SPIRIT

Pretribulationists do not consider any of the passages that inform us explicitly that the *beast* will *ascend out of the abyss*, which is *a literal prison* and *the place* (i.e., the "what" in 2 Thess 2:6) *that is holding him down* (Rev 11:7; 17:8). They also ignore *the angel with the key to the abyss and a chain* and the fact that this angel is *referred to in the masculine gender* (the "he" in 2 Thess 2:7; Rev 20:2). By not considering these clear biblical facts, they have designed a rapture theory based upon the removal of the Holy Spirit, whom they identified as the restrainer, without any direct scriptural evidence to back that assertion. Though they use Scriptures as proof texts to back up their theory, none of those passages has anything to do with the subject at hand, which is the restraint that is holding back the Antichrist's revelation, as identified in 2 Thessalonians 2:6–7.

The weakness of the Pretrib argument concerning the restrainer is detailed below, based on assertions in Pentecost's book *Things to Come*.[233]

---

[233] Pentecost, *Things to Come*, 262.

1. *Pentecost: By mere elimination, the Holy Spirit must be the re-strainer. All other suggestions fall short of meeting the requirements.*

Response: Pentecost begins his argument with a faulty premise that all the restrainer options have been eliminated. He examines the historical restrainer options (Rome, human government, Satan, the church, the Holy Spirit), but he does not consider the most relevant biblical option. The fact that Pretrib theorists do not include the restraining angel of the abyss, the prison from which the beast ascends, as an option, when they say they've considered all options, starts the theory under a false pretense. To maintain a credible theory, one must examine and rule out all relevant possibilities. In this case, that has not been done.

2. *Pentecost: The wicked one is a personality, and his operations include the realm of the supernatural. The restrainer must likewise be a personality and a spiritual being . . . to hold Antichrist in check until the time for his revealing. Mere agencies or impersonal spiritual forces would be inadequate.*

Response: Angels are indeed supernatural, volitional beings and, therefore, are personalities who have names (e.g., Gabriel) and who operate in both physical and spiritual realms. Though their names are largely unknown to humans, they are in fact referred to in the masculine gender, as is the restrainer of 2 Thessalonians 2:6–7. If a single angel himself can restrain Satan, which Revelation 20:1–3 shows is true, then restraining the beast, a satanic subordinate, is of no consequence. Holding the beast in check until the time for his release is not a problem either, because the abyss is a prison where wicked principalities are detained. Unfortunately, none of this is considered by Pretribulationists.

3. *To achieve all that is to be accomplished, the restrainer must be a member of the Godhead. He must be stronger than the Man of Sin and stronger than Satan who energizes him. In order to*

restrain evil down through the course of the age, the restrainer
must be eternal. . . . The theater of sin is the entire world; there-
fore, it is imperative that the restrainer be one who is not limited
by time or space.

Response: Each one of these arguments is incorrect. First, in 20:1–3, the angel alone restrains Satan with the chain, throws him into the abyss, and then seals and locks the abyss. However, this angel *is not* a member of the Godhead. Second, in Revelation 12, Michael and his angels fight against the dragon and his angels. The text explicitly declares that the dragon and his angels "were not strong enough" (NASB, NIV) for Michael and his angelic army. This is a direct contradiction to Pentecost's assertion, because he implies that only a member of the Godhead could be stronger than Satan. As Revelation 12 shows, angels are indeed *strong enough* to restrain Satan because they threw the devil and his angels out of heaven. Third, Pentecost's position necessitates that only an *eternal being* could qualify as the restrainer. Once again, this point is inaccurate because the angels that restrain Satan and secure the abyss in which the beast is incarcerated are not eternal. The angels who opposed Satan only needed to be present since the time of the heavenly rebellion when sin originated. There is no basis to suggest that evil, Satan, or the beast requires an eternal restraining agent. Angels restrain Satan but are not eternal. And Satan is not eternal either. They are finite, or had a beginning. Because they were created, they are contingent beings that depend on God for their existence. Fourth, holy angels have more than sufficient numbers to counter Satan's army. This is at least implied in the Revelation 12:4 text, where Satan drew only a third of the angels with him to earth. Therefore, holy angels outnumber Satan's angels on a two-to-one ratio, and many of the ungodly angels are imprisoned, further reducing their ranks. Theoretically, no matter where in the universe, whether in the physical or spiritual realms, there are enough holy angels to check or literally oppose demonic forces at any time or place. So at least from a tactical, numerical aspect, holy angels can stop any campaign the devil and his angels could attempt.

4. *The church age commenced with the advent of the Spirit at Pentecost and will close with a reversal of Pentecost, the removal of the Spirit. This does not mean that He will no longer be operative—only that He will no longer be resident.*

Response: It is correctly stated that the church began at the advent of Pentecost. Peter affirms this fact by quoting Joel 2:28–32 (see Acts 2:16–21). The pouring out of God's Spirit was an unmistakable supernatural event recorded in Scripture. However, a *reversal of Pentecost* * is cited, but where in Scripture does this reversal event occur? Certainly, such a consequential event would be recorded in the Bible. Second, where is the Scripture that declares that the Lord is coming back to *take or remove* the Spirit? And what about the supernatural phenomenon that accompanied the arrival of the Spirit, "the noise like a violent rushing wind," "tongues of fire," and the ability to "speak with other tongues"? Where in Scripture is this supernatural exit of the Spirit?

Third, if the Spirit is *no longer resident*, how is it that saints who refuse the mark of the beast are saved during the Seventieth Week? The Scriptures declare, "No one can say Jesus is Lord except by the Spirit" (1 Cor 12:3). However, if the Spirit is *no longer resident*, how do they maintain their confession of faith? And what does it mean that the Spirit will be "operative but not resident"? Do not the Scriptures record the voice from heaven declaring, " 'Blessed are the dead who die **in the Lord** from now on!' **'Yes,' says the Spirit**, 'so that they may rest from their labors, for their deeds follow with them' " (Revelation 14:13, my emphasis)? How is it possible that the saints "die in the Lord" if the Spirit isn't still abiding in these precious saints? For several reasons, this argument has no validity, but the glaring problem is that not one Scripture backs up a reversal of Pentecost.

CONCLUSION

Pretribulationists have presented a less-than-convincing argument for the Holy Spirit's being the restrainer of the Antichrist. The passages they put forth as proof texts such as Genesis 6:3; Isaiah 59:19b; John 14:26; 15:26; 16:8, 13–14; and 1 John 4:4, in their contexts, have nothing to do with the beast, the book of Revelation, or the restraint of the Antichrist. Common sense demands that when investigating who or what is restraining the Antichrist, one must refer to the passages of Scripture that explicitly inform about him. The fact that the beast ascends from the abyss, a locked prison, and is restrained by an angel referred to in the masculine gender (e.g., he, his), who has a chain for restraining and who comes from heaven and has the key to the abyss, should be direct evidence to identify the restrainer. Unfortunately, Pretrib used none of this evidence but instead supports a rapture position based on the removal of the Holy Spirit as the restrainer, when there is no explicit basis to do so. Though God may be sovereign over all things, God does not do all things. (Also see the essays "The Threefold Reality of the Beast" and "Implications for a Pretribulation Position.")

REVELATION 20:4–6

REWARD AND RESURRECTION

⁴ Then I saw thrones, and they sat on them, and judgment was given to them. And I saw the souls of those who had been beheaded because of their testimony of Jesus and because of the word of God, and those who had not worshiped the beast or his image, and had not received the mark on their forehead and on their hand; and they came to life and reigned with Christ for a thousand years. ⁵ The rest of the dead did not come to life until the thousand years were completed. This is the first resurrection. ⁶ Blessed and holy is the one who has a part in the first resurrection; over these the second death has no power, but they will be priests of God and of Christ and will reign with Him for a thousand years.

(4) *Then I saw thrones, and they sat on them, and judgment was given to them:* Osborne makes an important observation here when he comments on "Then I saw." "There is narrative sequence, and the events in the vision flow one after the other, but chronological sequence cannot be proven on the basis of "then I saw.""[234] This is important because all that's revealed in these verses is not necessarily chronological. Since this scene follows the Lord's return in chapter 19, it may be assumed that this judgment occurs at the beginning of the millennium. However, this idea will be challenged later. Who are these who sit on thrones? They have authority to judge *the souls* of the saints who were martyred *because of their testimony of Jesus*

---

[234] Osborne, *Baker Exegetical Commentary: Revelation*, 700.

and because of the word of God: which is the same attribution that John ascribed to himself in 1:2, 9. Though there is a desire "to know," we should take our cues from the Scriptures. Since we are not told who is sitting on these thrones, that alone indicates it is a detail that we do not need to know. Though opinions may vary, no one knows for sure.

(a) *and had not received the mark on their forehead and on their hand:* This verse identifies this group with those whose souls will be under the altar during the fifth seal (6:9–11) and with the saints in the narratives in 13–15, of whom it is said that *they loved not their lives unto the death.* These will be the greatest uncompromising Christians that history has ever known because they will face what Jesus called "a great tribulation, such as has not occurred since the beginning of the world until now, nor ever will" (Matt 24:21).

(b) *and they came to life and reigned with Christ for a thousand years:* This is a portion of those who have a part in the first resurrection (Dan 12:2; John 5:25–29; 1 Cor 15:51–56; 1 Thess 4:14–18; Rev 11:18; 15:2–4). Several passages speak of the church's reigning and being glorified with Christ (Rom 8:17; 2 Tim 2:12; Rev 2:11; 3:21; 5:10). The saints will have the high honor of ruling with Him during His millennial kingdom "for a thousand years."

(5) *The rest of the dead did not come to life until the thousand years were completed. This is the first resurrection:* Here we learn that "the first resurrection" of the righteous and the resurrection of judgment ("damnation," KJV, John 5:29) are separated by one thousand years. Jesus referred to both resurrections without mentioning the thousand-year gap between them (John 5:29).

(6) *Blessed and holy is the one who has a part in the first resurrection:* The blessing of those who have "a part in the first resurrection" is the fifth beatitude. The first resurrection is expansive, even though the tribulation saints are the only ones featured here. All who are part of the first resurrection are blessed because their sins have been forgiven. They have been washed in the blood of the Lamb. They have been purchased by Jesus, the Redeemer. The first resurrection will include all the saints from the OT; though they lived and died before the cross, they looked forward to the same Savior. It is the efficacious blood of the Lamb that has given them eternal life as well. They are also blessed because their names have been written in the Lamb's book of life, and they will serve the Lord in His kingdom that shall have no end. However, since much of Revelation focuses on events during Daniel's Seventieth Week and the triumphant Christians of that period, the first resurrection scenario depicted in Revelation 20:4–6 only focuses on these Christians. These are the saints who will go through the great tribulation, a unique period of testing that no other generation of the church or OT has traversed (7:14–15). Therefore, the book of Revelation prominently features the church of the last days.

(a) *over these the second death has no power*: The "second death" was first introduced in Revelation by Jesus in His address to the church of Smyrna (2:11). Without question, it is the most severe judgment in the book of Revelation (see 20:14). However, the second death can have "no power" over the redeemed.

(b) *but they will be priests of God and of Christ and will reign with Him for a thousand years*: The resurrected tribulation saints will have the privilege of reigning with Christ "for a thousand years" as "priests of God," which is similar to Peter's observation of believers in his epistle (1 Pet 2:9, "a royal priesthood") and to Jesus' promise recorded by John to the church of Philadelphia when He said He would make the overcomer "a pillar in the temple of [His] God" (Rev 3:12). Old Testament priests served in the temple, but these priests will also reign with Christ as a royal priesthood during the millennium and for eternity. Once again, Revelation is primarily the story of the church of the eschaton. Therefore, their story is featured in the Revelation narrative but not to the exclusion of other faithful saints throughout the ages.

EXCURSUS—WHEN DOES THIS JUDGMENT OCCUR?

As we noted earlier, the sequence in vision events is not necessarily sequential in time (see v. 4 note). Many claim that the resurrection award event shown in 20:4–6 occurs at the beginning of the millennium and, therefore, is a different resurrection from what the church experiences. However, the position this commentator takes sees the 20:4–6 scenario as a continuation of Revelation 15, where we see the martyrs of the tribulation, who refused to take the mark of the beast, are already in heaven. The reason why Revelation 15 supports a chapter 20 continuation is because of what is stated when chapter 15 begins:

> Then I saw another sign in heaven, great and marvelous, seven angels who had seven plagues, which are the last, because in them the wrath of God is finished.

The angels who will pour out their bowls of wrath on the earth are still in heaven. This is an important reference point. However, there is another group of individuals that is also in heaven with the angels:

> And I saw something like a sea of glass mixed with fire, and those who had been victorious over the beast and his image and the number of his name, standing on the sea of glass, holding harps of God. And they sang the song of Moses, the bond-servant of God, and the song of the Lamb, saying, "Great and marvelous are Your works, O Lord God, the Almighty; righteous and true are Your ways, King of the nations! (Rev 15:2–3)

Without dispute, the saints who refused to take the mark of the beast are in heaven before the wrath of God is poured out in the bowl judgments. The following verses describe what happens next.

> After these things I looked, and the temple of the tabernacle of testimony in heaven was opened, and the seven angels who had the seven plagues came out of the temple, clothed

in linen, clean and bright, and girded around their chests
with golden sashes. Then one of the four living creatures
gave to the seven angels seven golden bowls full of the wrath
of God, who lives forever and ever. And the temple was filled
with smoke from the glory of God and from His power; and
no one was able to enter the temple until the seven plagues
of the seven angels were finished. (Rev 15:5–8)

The angels have received their bowls of wrath. They are ready to unleash
the final plagues. This is an important marker because the saints who
were being martyred (13:7), who patiently endured under persecution
(12:11; 13:10), and of whom the Holy Spirit pronounced blessing and
recognition (14:13) are not seen again on the earth after the Son of Man
receives His harvest from the earth (14:14–16). However, we see them in
heaven before the angels receive the bowls of wrath. The saints' presence
in heaven before the events of chapter 16 is confirmation that they were
not appointed to the wrath of God. Subsequently, they cannot be raised
at the beginning of the millennium. Therefore, Revelation 20:4–6 is a
continuation of what began in Revelation 15.

The Millennium

The millennium will be characterized by the Lord's ruling from Jerusalem (see Zech 14:1–21). It will be a time of peace without rebellion
because Satan will be imprisoned during this time. Infant mortality will
be wiped out (Isa 65:20). Life will be extended greatly. A person who dies
before the age of one hundred will be considered accursed (Isa 65:20). A
man's days will be like the lifespan of a tree—hundreds of years—which
is similar to the antediluvians who lived before the flood (Isa 65:22).
There will be no more social injustice or economic exploitation (Isa
65:22–23). Offspring will no longer be doomed to misfortune, such as
poverty and crime, but will be blessed (Isa 65:23). The nature of animals
will be changed: "the wolf and the lamb will graze together, and the lion
will eat straw like the ox; and dust will be the serpent's food" (Isa 65:25).

The earth will be inhabited by glorified people (i.e., the saints of the first resurrection who will rule and reign with Christ), and natural people who survived the great tribulation will repopulate the earth and come to worship the Lord (Zech 14:9–21). Dangerous animals will not hurt humans, and the knowledge of the Lord will cover the earth like the waters cover the sea (Isa 11:8–9).

REVELATION 20:7–10

Satan Deceives the World Again

⁷ When the thousand years are completed, Satan will be released from his prison, ⁸ and will come out to deceive the nations which are in the four corners of the earth, Gog and Magog, to gather them together for the war; the number of them is like the sand of the seashore. ⁹ And they came up on the broad plain of the earth and surrounded the camp of the saints and the beloved city, and fire came down from heaven and devoured them. ¹⁰ And the devil who deceived them was thrown into the lake of fire and brimstone, where the beast and the false prophet are also; and they will be tormented day and night forever and ever.

(7) *When the thousand years are completed, Satan will be released from his prison*: Satan will be released from the abyss, a "prison," when the thousand years are completed. Who releases him? The angel that restrained him and locked him into the abyss, not the Holy Spirit (v. 3).

(8) *and will come out to deceive the nations which are in the four corners of the earth, Gog and Magog, to gather them together for the war; the number of them is like the sand of the seashore*: It is amazing that even after the Lord's reigning on earth for a thousand years, Satan will be able to find a multitude of willing people to rebel against the Lord and His people. This points to a fundamental issue and proclivity for fallen humans to be susceptible to temptation and deception. Satan will effectively gather a multitude characterized as "Gog and Magog." Ezekiel 38 and 39 are

dedicated to the prophecy concerning Gog of Magog[235] (i.e., modern-day Russia), who will lead a coalition of nations (i.e., Persia, Libya, Ethiopia, Turkey, and others) against Israel and who will be in the contingency of nations that will gather at Armageddon (Ezek 38:22; 39:17–29). However, in this Revelation text, "Gog and Magog" is used symbolically because Satan will once again gather the nations to attack the beloved city (Jerusalem), which will be similar to the Gog of Magog invasion that occurred a thousand years earlier, near the end of Daniel's Seventieth Week at Armageddon.

(9) *and fire came down from heaven and devoured them*: This ill-fated invasion will never get far because the Lord will send fire down from heaven to incinerate the would-be invaders.

(10) *And the devil who deceived them was thrown into the lake of fire and brimstone, where the beast and the false prophet are also; and they will be tormented day and night forever and ever*: This invasion attempt will be Satan's final act because afterward the devil is thrown into the lake of fire, where the beast and false prophet have already been for a thousand years. The fact that the beast and false prophet are still there proves that the lake of fire is not annihilation but conscious, eternal torment.

---

[235]   Unger, *The New Unger's Bible Dictionary*, 490.

REVELATION 20:11–15

^{11} Then I saw a great white throne and Him who sat upon it, from whose presence earth and heaven fled away, and no place was found for them. ^{12} And I saw the dead, the great and the small, standing before the throne, and books were opened; and another book was opened, which is the book of life; and the dead were judged from the things which were written in the books, according to their deeds. ^{13} And the sea gave up the dead which were in it, and death and Hades gave up the dead which were in them; and they were judged, every one of them according to their deeds. ^{14} Then death and Hades were thrown into the lake of fire. This is the second death, the lake of fire. ^{15} And if anyone's name was not found written in the book of life, he was thrown into the lake of fire.

(11) *Then I saw a great white throne and Him who sat upon it*: John saw a "great white throne," great not only because of its magnitude and impact but also because of "Him who sat upon it." Jesus admonished His disciples when He declared, "I say to you, My friends, do not be afraid of those who kill the body and after that have no more that they can do. But I will warn you whom to fear: fear the One who, after He has killed, has authority to cast into hell; yes, I tell you, fear Him!" (Luke 12:4–5). Indeed, the One who sits on the throne is to be feared because He has the authority to cast souls into the lake of fire.

(a) from whose presence earth and heaven fled away, and no place was found for them: During the seals, the trumpets, and the bowls, the heavens and the earth were violently shaken, but they remained in their places. However, for this event, the universe will flee away from God's fierce and awesome power. Like a curtain that is forcefully flung open, so the universe will retreat from God's presence. Some commentators describe this action as *the uncreating of heaven and earth.*[236] Indeed, though there will be a new heaven and a new earth, no one knows for sure where this will be. God will conduct this judicial proceeding in a place that is neither heaven nor earth. Whatever or wherever this is, it will be an appropriate setting for God to judge all the wicked that have ever lived on earth. Exactly what this means is completely beyond any mortal's ability to comprehend or describe. John simply described it as, "[They] fled away, and no place was found for them." This is like the events surrounding *the great earthquake* of 16:20, where he stated, "And every island *fled away*, and the mountains *were not found*" (emphasis added). However, in this passage, John did his best to describe what he saw. We today certainly do not know the fullest extent of what John meant here. Since words are not adequate to describe what is occurring here, the simplest words are the best: "earth and the heaven fled away."

(12) And I saw the dead, the great and the small, standing before the throne, and books were opened; and another book was opened, which is the book of life; and the dead were judged from the things which were written in the books, according to their deeds: All the wicked dead—small and great, rich and poor—will stand before God. This is the *resurrection of damnation* for the unsaved (John 5:29). Wealth, status, influence, and fame will mean nothing, because God is not a respecter of persons. The Bible declares, "For all have sinned and fall short of the glory of God" (Rom 3:23) and "There is none righteous, not even one" (Rom 3:10). Without the shed

---

[236] MacArthur, *The MacArthur New Testament Commentary: Revelation 12–22,* 249.

blood of the Lamb, no flesh would be saved. Those who appear at this trial will have no lawyer, no advocate, no plea, no possibility of appeal. But what will be before the court is every word, thought, and deed that is recorded in the books of heaven. This will be presented as evidence against each defendant. No action, detail, or circumstance will escape God's omniscient scrutiny. The evidence presented before this heavenly tribunal will speak for itself.

(13) *And the sea gave up the dead which were in it, and death and Hades gave up the dead which were in them:* From every sphere, the dead will be raised. Whether they were buried in the earth, drowned in the sea, or set ablaze in flames, the manner of death makes no difference. All will be present for judgment. However, it is interesting that "death and Hades gave up the dead which were in them." Hell, or Hades, is the place of departed souls, but hell was created for the devil and his angels (Matt 25:41). Before the resurrection of Jesus, the righteous dead and the wicked dead were both held in Hades. However, the righteous were in Abraham's bosom, which was also then called Paradise. This was the place Jesus referred to when He told the thief on the cross, "Today you shall be with Me in Paradise (Luke 23:43). The wicked were in the torment section of Hades[237] (Luke 16:19–31). In Revelation, Death is the rider on the pale, or ashen, horse, and Hades follows along after him (6:8). These two work in conjunction with each other because Death needs a depository for all the dead. The personification of death and hell here is notable and could indicate a broader role for each, beyond just having authority to kill and being a place to hold the dead. *They were judged, every one of them according to their deeds:* So often in this life the wicked go unpunished. They seem to get away with their evil deeds without being held accountable. However, as soon as they leave this life, they go to hell and await the final court of the great white throne judgment, when death and hell will deliver up the souls of the dead that are in them.

---

[237] Some see Luke 16:19–31 as a parable and not as something that actually happened.

(14) *Then death and Hades were thrown into the lake of fire*: This would seem to indicate that death is more than an exit from life and hell more than a place where wicked souls are kept. These entities are more than personifications or a temporary place of containment. They are actual spiritual forces that are fit to be judged along with the devil and his angels. Paul stated, "The last enemy to be destroyed is death" (1 Cor 15:26 ESV). Osborne writes, "Death and hades are symbols for demonic forces and so the demonic realm is rendered powerless."[238]

(a) *This is the second death, the lake of fire*: Those who belong to Christ have been born again. They are born twice but die only once. Those who are lost are born once, but they die twice. The second death is the penalty after being found guilty *before the great white throne judgment.*

(15) *And if anyone's name was not found written in the book of life, he was thrown into the lake of fire*: After all the evidence has been examined, which includes the works and deeds recorded in the books, there is yet one more book to consult—the Lamb's book of life. Whichever person whose name is not found in the book of life will be cast into the lake of fire. Revelation 14:10–11 gives a glimpse of the horror of the second death for those who take the mark of the beast: "And he will be tormented with fire and brimstone in the presence of the holy angels and in the presence of the Lamb. And the smoke of their torment [will go] up forever and ever; they [will] have no rest day and night." This is the purest form of the wrath of God— eternal punishment and constant torment in hell, without rest day or night, forever and ever. The second death is by far the worst judgment in Revelation. The seals, the trumpets, and the bowls, which all will occur during Daniel's Seventieth Week (lasting seven years at best)—all of that is nothing in comparison to eternal punishment. The apostle Paul described it as "eternal destruction" (2 Thess 1:9). The verse-by-verse commentary continues on page 390.

---

[238] Osborne, *Baker Exegetical Commentary: Revelation,* 723.

ESSAY:
THE TRIBULATION SAINTS
VS. THE CHURCH

It is this commentary's position that the saints of Revelation are in fact the last generation of church saints. Since the mid-nineteenth century, dispensationalists have controlled much of the eschatology narrative. End times prophecy has been greatly influenced and impacted by the Pretrib rapture theory. One of the main tenets of this theory is that the tribulation saints are saved but are not a part of the church. We have submitted several refutations to show why this is incorrect, and the following points of comparison are difficult to ignore.

The Tribulation Saints (TS)	The Church Saints
1. TS are called "saints" (Rev 13:7).	1. Members of the body of Christ are called saints (Rom 1:7; 8:27; 1 Cor 1:2; Eph 1:1; Phil 1:1; Col 1:2; 1 Thess 3:13; Heb 6:10; Jude 1:3).
2. TS are washed in the blood of the Lamb (Rev 7:14).	2. The church is washed in the blood of the Lamb (Eph 1:7; Col 1:20; 1 John 1:7).
3. TS are dressed in white (Rev 7:9, 13–14).	3. The Lord promised the church of Sardis they would walk with Him "in white" (Rev 3:4).

4. TS will serve God in His temple "day and night," which indicates permanence (Rev 7:15).	4. The Lord promised the church of Philadelphia they would be pillars in the temple of God. He said, "Never again will they leave it" (Rev 3:12 NIV).
5. TS will be martyred for the same reasons that John gave for being persecuted, which are the word of God and the testimony of Jesus Christ (Rev 20:4).	5. John used no Pauline terminology to identify with being part of the church, but he identified himself with Christians universally by saying he was persecuted for the word of God and the testimony of Jesus Christ (Rev 1:9).
6. TS will reign with Christ (Rev 20:4).	6. The church will reign with Christ (2 Tim 2:12; Rev 2:26–27; 5:9–10).
7. TS saints are declared to be blessed by the Holy Spirit Himself (Rev 14:13) and are designated as "blessed and holy" (Rev 20:6).	7. The church saints are blessed by the Lord and are also holy (Eph 1:3; Col 1:22; James 1:12; 1 Pet 1:16; 2:9).
8. TS will be part of the first resurrection (Rev 20:5).	8. The church will be in the first resurrection (John 5:29; 1 Cor 15:23, 51–52; 1 Thess 4:15–17).
9. TS are called "priests of God" (Rev 20:6).	9. The church is called a "royal priesthood" (1 Pet 2:9).
10. TS have their names written in the Lamb's book of life from the foundation of the world (Rev 13:8).	10. Those of the church have their names written in the Lamb's book of life and are chosen from the foundation of the world (Eph 1:4; Phil 4:3; 2 Tim 1:9).

11. TS are delivered from the second death (Rev 20:6).	11. The church is promised to be delivered from the second death (Rev 2:10–11).
12. TS, who are victorious over the mark of the beast, will be in heaven before the wrath of God is poured out (Rev 15:1–8).	12. The church is not appointed to wrath and will be in heaven while wrath is poured out on the world (1 Thess 5:9).
13. TS will have a resurrection and rewards ceremony at the seventh, or last, trumpet while wrath is being poured out on the earth (Rev 11:18; 15:1–2; 20:4).	13. The church will be raised at the last trumpet and will be rewarded while wrath is being poured out on the earth (1 Cor 15:51–53; 1 Thess 4:15–17; 5:2, 9; Rev 22:12).
14. John saw the Lord on a cloud and heard an angel shout from heaven, "Put in your sickle and reap." Then the Lord reaped His harvest. The TS are no longer seen on earth but appear in heaven before the angels leave heaven with the bowl judgments of God's wrath for the earth (Rev 14:14–16; 15:1–8).	14. The Lord will descend from heaven with the voice of the archangel. From the air He will rapture the church to meet Him in the clouds (1 Thess 4:14–17).
15. TS also die in the Lord (Rev 14:13).	15. Church saints die in Christ (1 Thess 4:13).
16. TS consist of the full number of Gentile nations in heaven (Rev 7:9).	16. The church cannot reach completeness until the full number of Gentiles is reached (Rom 11:25).

These similarities punctuate the narrative that is promoted throughout this commentary. These are not coincidental, nor should they be ignored. It is clear the book of Revelation has much to say about the church saints during the Seventieth Week. Just as passages from the OT are linked to the NT, so should the NT be linked to the book of Revelation. The comparison here is made only to illustrate the fact that the tribulation saints are the church.

REVELATION 21:1–4

The New Heaven
and New Earth

¹ Then I saw a new heaven and a new earth; for the first heaven and the first earth passed away, and there is no longer any sea. ² And I saw the holy city, new Jerusalem, coming down out of heaven from God, made ready as a bride adorned for her husband. ³ And I heard a loud voice from the throne, saying, "Behold, the tabernacle of God is among men, and He will dwell among them, and they shall be His people, and God Himself will be among them, ⁴ and He will wipe away every tear from their eyes; and there will no longer be any death; there will no longer be any mourning, or crying, or pain; the first things have passed away."

(1) *Then I saw a new heaven and a new earth*: Once again, John started with "I saw." Therefore, the new heaven and earth are not theoretical or conceptual but actual. John was not the first to express the idea of "a new heaven and a new earth." Isaiah also records God's declaration: "For behold, I create new heavens and a new earth; and the former things will not be remembered or come to mind" (Isa 65:17). There is a debate as to whether the current heaven and earth will be renovated to make them new, or whether the current ones will be destroyed and others made. The next phrase can help us understand.

(a) *for the first heaven and the first earth passed away*: This can be understood in the light of what Peter states in his second epistle:

> But the day of the Lord will come like a thief, in which the heavens will pass away with a roar and the elements will be destroyed with intense heat, and the earth and its works will be burned up. Since all these things are to be destroyed in this way, what sort of people ought you to be in holy conduct and godliness. (2 Pet 3:10–11).

Here, Peter wrote of the heavens that will "pass away." Jesus also declared that "heaven and earth will *pass away*, but [His] words will not *pass away*" (Matt 24:35, emphasis added). However, Peter's account is interesting because he informed us that "the heavens will pass away with a roar and the elements will be destroyed with intense heat, and the earth and its works will be burned up." As we have seen on a number of occasions, there is disagreement between scholars on this passage as well. It is wise to concede that what John and Peter have written leaves many questions. No human being knows exactly how all this will come about. What is important to understand is that there will be a new heaven and new earth. However God brings this to pass is God's business, not ours. What we do know is this current world is travailing in the birth pangs in anticipation of a whole new creation. Paul wrote,

> For the anxious longing of the creation waits eagerly for the revealing of the sons of God. For the creation was subjected to futility, not willingly, but because of Him who subjected it, in hope that the creation itself also will be set free from its slavery to corruption into the freedom of the glory of the children of God. For we know that the whole creation groans and suffers the pains of childbirth together until now. (Rom 8:19–22)

(b) *and there is no longer any sea:* In this current geological order, water is the most plentiful element on this planet, and all life is based upon it. However, it is stated that "there is no longer any sea," meaning no more large bodies of water. Currently, water covers almost three quarters of the earth's surface, yet on the new earth, there will be no need for oceans, which means the entire ecosystem will be completely reordered. The radical reordering of the new earth is consistent with the *new heaven*, or universe.

(2–4) *And I saw the holy city, new Jerusalem, coming down out of heaven from God, made ready as a bride adorned for her husband*: Once the new heaven and earth are settled, "new Jerusalem" will descend from heaven to earth. In Galatians 4:26, Paul referred to the "Jerusalem above." Hebrews is more vivid: "But you have come to Mount Zion and to the city of the living God, the heavenly Jerusalem, and to myriads of angels" (Heb 12:22). In Revelation, "new Jerusalem" is first mentioned in 3:12, but here she arrives in the imagery of a bride being "adorned for her husband." In chapter 19, the bride is the church, but here, "new Jerusalem" is a glorious "city."

JERUSALEM—HISTORIC NOTE

Jerusalem has a well-established history in the Scriptures and is considered a sacred city for the Jews, Christians, and Muslims. "From the time of Joshua to its destruction by Titus—a period of fifteen centuries—is a succession of changes, revolutions, sieges, surrenders, and famines. Each is followed by restoration and rebuilding."[239] Besides the name Jerusalem, which means "foundation of peace,"[240] it is also called Zion and the city of David. In the Gospels, it is called "the city of the great King" (Matt 5:35) and also "the city that kills the prophets and stones those sent to her" (Luke 13:34). Originally, Jerusalem was called Jebus (Judg 19:10–11). The city was captured during Joshua's time, but the Israelites were not able to drive out the Jebusites (Josh 15:63), so the Israelites and the Jebusites lived together in Jebus (Judg 1:21). However, the city was once again captured by David (1 Chr 11:4–9) and renamed Jerusalem.

---

[239] Unger, *The New Unger's Bible Dictionary*, 676.
[240] "Jerusalem," *NASB Greek Dictionary*, 3389.

In ancient times, Jerusalem was the place of Mount Moriah, where Abraham offered Isaac (the Temple Mount) and where Israel's temples were built. Solomon's Temple (2 Chr 3:1–2) was the first of two temples built there (see the excursus "Israel's Temples"). In AD 70, Jerusalem was destroyed by the Roman general Titus, resulting in the Jews' being scattered around the world. For centuries, Jerusalem was inhabited and controlled by both Muslim and Christian people. After WWI, the British controlled the city until May 14, 1948, when Israel was reestablished as a Jewish nation. After this, Jerusalem was divided between Israel and Jordan. During the Six-Day War of 1967, Jerusalem was recaptured by the Jews. This remains a bone of contention between Israelis and Palestinians to this day. The Western Wall, believed by most to be the site of the Second Temple (Zerubbabel's/Herod's), is also the location of the Islamic shrine, The Dome of the Rock. Both are in close proximity in Jerusalem.

The Last Days

In the last days, Jerusalem will come under attack by the Antichrist and Gog of Magog (Ezek 38–39). All the nations of the world will also converge there during the battle of Armageddon, the final global conflict of this age. Then the Lord will return and set up His millennial kingdom headquarters in Jerusalem (Zech 14). Satan will be bound in the abyss for one thousand years. After the millennium, the devil will be released, and he will cause the nations to come against Jerusalem, "the beloved city," once again, but they will be divinely destroyed (Rev 20:9). After God makes the new heaven and earth, "new Jerusalem" will descend from heaven and be God's capital city throughout all eternity.

REVELATION 21:5–9

It Is Done!

⁵ And He who sits on the throne said, "Behold, I am making all things new." And He said, "Write, for these words are faithful and true." ⁶ Then He said to me, "It is done. I am the Alpha and the Omega, the beginning and the end. I will give to the one who thirsts from the spring of the water of life without cost. ⁷ He who overcomes will inherit these things, and I will be his God and he will be My son. ⁸ But for the cowardly and unbelieving and abominable and murderers and immoral persons and sorcerers and idolaters and all liars, their part will be in the lake that burns with fire and brimstone, which is the second death." ⁹ Then one of the seven angels who had the seven bowls full of the seven last plagues came and spoke with me, saying, "Come here, I will show you the bride, the wife of the Lamb."

(5) *And He who sits on the throne said, "Behold, I am making all things new." And He said, "Write, for these words are faithful and true"*: The promise of the new heaven and earth have tarried for thousands of years since the days of Abraham, who looked for a city whose builder was God (Heb 11:10–16). It was a great expectation of the OT saints (Isa 65:17). Truly, God is going to make "all things new." It is interesting that even though these things have not yet manifested in time and space, in a sense, they are already a reality because John "saw" them. Of course, this defies human comprehension, but it is why the following statement is so powerful. "And He said, 'Write, for these words are faithful and true.'" And they are further backed up by the declaration in the following verse.

(6) *It is done. I am the Alpha and the Omega, the beginning and the end. I will give to the one who thirsts from the spring of the water of life without cost*: The assurance of salvation for the redeemed is tremendously glorious, and the inhabitants of new Jerusalem can freely partake in all its splendor "without cost." In our current order of life, precious and splendid things are very costly, and only the rich and privileged can partake. However, this will not be the case in new Jerusalem.

(7) *He who overcomes will inherit these things, and I will be his God and he will be My son*: This glorious kingdom will not be available to those with the most power and influence. The criterion for gaining the inheritance is to be one who "overcomes." How will one overcome? By the blood of the Lamb and the word of their testimony (Rev 12:11). Everyone who is saved has overcome the world, the flesh, and the devil. Everyone has had to repent and overcome in some area of their life. The Bible declares, "There is none righteous, not even one" and "For all have sinned and fall short of the glory of God" (Rom 3:10, 23). Therefore, those who overcome "will inherit these things." "These things" means the indescribable blessings of God that He prepared for His people to experience in the ages to come, for all eternity.

(8) *But for the cowardly*: There are eight categories of sinners mentioned in v. 8. It is not coincidental that the first is the "cowardly." There will be many people during the time of the Antichrist who will fall specifically due to cowardice. Unfortunately, millions of people have bought into the idea that the church will not be on earth during the time of the Antichrist, and consequently, they will not be prepared when persecution comes. Even worse than this belief is the position that suggests that people who take the mark of the beast can still be saved. Those who believe that the church will not be on earth during the time of the Antichrist *could be* greatly impacted if the church is actually still on earth and Christians are faced with impending death, imprisonment, and disenfranchisement from the economic system controlled through the mark of the beast. Believers will compromise and take the mark of the beast because, at least for some, they will believe that the offense is forgivable. When faced with death or financial loss, they will compromise and take the mark of the beast to save their own skins. These people will be *the cowards*.

In the message to the church of Smyrna, the Lord said, "Do not fear what you are about to suffer. Behold, the devil is about to cast some of you into prison, so that you will be tested, and you will have tribulation for ten days. Be faithful until death, and I will give you the crown of life" (Rev 2:10). This command to be faithful unto death leaves no room for cowardice. Jesus explicitly declared, "If anyone wishes to come after Me, he must deny himself, and take up his cross and follow Me. For whoever wishes to save his life will lose it; but whoever loses his life for My sake will find it" (Matt 16:24–25). Jesus was crucified on the cross, most of the apostles were martyred, and millions of believers through the centuries have faced death and not turned coward. Cowards will have their part in the "lake that burns with fire . . . which is the second death" (Rev 21:8).

(a) *unbelieving and abominable*: "Unbelief" comes from a wicked heart (Heb 3:12). At the core of unbelief is rebellion against God. "Abominable," or spiritually vile, describes worshipers of Satan, demons, and the Antichrist, along with those who sacrifice children, worship idols, and carry out spiritually abhorrent practices. Here's what the Scripture declares about *murderers*: "Everyone who hates his brother is a murderer; and you know that no murderer has eternal life abiding in him" (1 John 3:15). People seem to be fascinated with murder in movies, television, and video games. These forms of media have sparked a perverted thirst for murder. The spirit of murder is heavy throughout the world, and people murder one another for the most trivial reasons. In the United States, mass shootings are at an epidemic level. In many cases, murderers commit their crimes because they crave the media attention that committing murder brings. *Immoral persons* refer to the sexually immoral (adulterers, fornicators, homosexuals, pedophiles, pornographers, etc.). *Sorcerers* is an interesting group of sinners to name because the root word, *sorcery*, comes from the Greek word *pharmakon*, which means (1) "one skilled in arcane uses of herbs or drugs" and (2) "one who does extraordinary things through occult means, sorcerer, magician."[241] Our world currently has a major problem with drug abuse, whether over-the-counter or illicit drugs. Addiction is a social plague that affects nearly every nation and every people. Those involved with the occult, false prophecy, and various forbidden forms of divination also fall under "sorcerers." Next, the list includes *idolaters*. "Idolaters" are not only those who worship false gods, like the image of the beast, but they also include those who are greedy to get rich, because covetousness is idolatry (Col 3:5). *All liars* refer to deceivers, demagogues, and those who bear false witness and cause people to believe a lie. Speaking of Satan, the Scriptures declare, "He was a murderer from the beginning, and does not stand in the truth because there is no truth in him. Whenever he speaks a lie, he speaks from his own nature, for he is a liar and the father of lies" (John 8:44). Like Satan, the liars judged here are those to whom lying comes naturally. Liars cannot be tolerated because they cannot be trusted.

(b) *their part will be in the lake that burns with fire and brimstone, which is the second death*: The "second death," which is eternal separation from God, is by far the worst judgment in Revelation. This is the same "eternal destruction" to which Paul referred in 2 Thessalonians 1:9. Jesus also declared that in hell there will be no reprieve or cessation of torment from hell fire (Mark 9:43–48).

(9–10) *Then one of the seven angels who had the seven bowls full of the seven last plagues came and spoke with me, saying, "Come here, I will show you the bride, the wife of the Lamb." And he carried me away in the Spirit to a great and high mountain, and showed me the holy city, Jerusalem, coming down out of heaven from God*: There is a similar introduction given in 17:1, where one of the angels of the bowl judgments shows John the destruction of Babylon. The similarity in language by John and one of the seven angels is perhaps a basis for contrasting the two women who are presented in these passages. The prostitute Babylon is wicked and lewd. The bride is righteous and pure.

---

[241]   Bauer, *Greek-English Lexicon*, "sorcerer, *pharmakon*."

In chapter 19, *the bride is the glorified church*, decked in white linen, which is the *righteous acts of the saints*. The occasion is *the wedding supper of the Lamb* (19:7–10). However, in this text, the old heaven and earth have passed away. The eternal state is where *the new heaven and new earth* will exist. We know that Satan will be imprisoned for one thousand years and then will be freed for a short time to deceive the world again (20:1–3, 7–10). After that, the great white throne judgment will occur (20:11–15). How long Satan's last rebellion, the great white throne judgment, and the creation of the new heaven and earth will take is unknown. Then "the holy city, Jerusalem," will be presented as "the bride" and make her glorious descent from heaven. Jesus alluded to this when He promised, "In My Father's house are many dwelling places; if it were not so, I would have told you; for I go to prepare a place for you. If I go and prepare a place for you, I will come again and receive you to Myself, that where I am, there you may be also" (John 14:2–3). New Jerusalem will be prepared in heaven, the place from where she will descend once the new earth is ready. New Jerusalem will be not the totality of the eternal state but the capital city of the new earth.

There is a debate over who "the bride" represents. Once again, there is no consensus. Some say it is the church. Others say it was never the church but always new Jerusalem. Still others say new Jerusalem is called the bride because her citizens consist of the bride church. However, we mere mortals need not argue because it doesn't make a difference what any of us think. All these things are far beyond our purview. We know what is written, but none of us knows exactly what this means. One thing is sure: those who make it to the eternal state will dwell in and visit new Jerusalem, an eternal city whose builder is God and whose glory and beauty defy human comprehension. Paul commented on the unknown so adequately when he wrote, "But just as it is written, 'Things which eye has not seen and ear has not heard, and which have not entered the heart of man, all that God has prepared for those who love Him'" (1 Cor 2:9).

REVELATION 21:10–18

¹⁰ And he carried me away in the Spirit to a great and high mountain, and showed me the holy city, Jerusalem, coming down out of heaven from God. ¹¹ having the glory of God. Her brilliance was like a very costly stone, as a stone of crystal-clear jasper. ¹² It had a great and high wall, with twelve gates, and at the gates twelve angels; and names were written on them, which are the names of the twelve tribes of the sons of Israel. ¹³ There were three gates on the east and three gates on the north and three gates on the south and three gates on the west. ¹⁴ And the wall of the city had twelve foundation stones, and on them were the twelve names of the twelve apostles of the Lamb. ¹⁵ The one who spoke with me had a gold measuring rod to measure the city, and its gates and its wall. ¹⁶ The city is laid out as a square, and its length is as great as the width; and he measured the city with the rod, fifteen hundred miles; its length and width and height are equal. ¹⁷ And he measured its wall, seventy-two yards, according to human measurements, which are also angelic measurements. ¹⁸ The material of the wall was jasper; and the city was pure gold like clear glass.

(11–14) *having the glory of God. Her brilliance was like a very costly stone, as a stone of crystal-clear jasper. It had a great and high wall, with twelve gates, . . . :* Some of the glorious features of this city are given in these verses. The first characteristic to note is the "brilliance" of the city's gleaming and refracting light, which is like a "costly" jewel in the midday sun. Jewels are so glamorous and elegant and exhibit wealth and prestige. The "wall" that surrounds the city has "twelve gates," three gates on each of the four sides. As we've seen elsewhere in Revelation, angels play a key role in the kingdom of God here too. "Twelve angels" stand at the gates. The names of the "twelve tribes" of Israel are written on the gates. The wall of the city has "twelve foundation stones" that feature the names of the "twelve apostles," though Jews were also foundations of the church (Eph 2:20). Therefore, both Israel and the church, the old and new covenants, are represented in new Jerusalem.

(15–18) *The one who spoke with me had a gold measuring rod to measure the city, and its gates and its wall. The city is laid out as a square, and its length is as great as the width; and he measured the city with the rod, fifteen hundred miles; its length and width and height are equal. And he measured its wall, seventy-two yards. . . . The material of the wall was jasper; and the city was pure gold, like clear glass*: The angel now measures the city, the walls, and the gates with a "golden measuring rod" that indicates the splendor and importance of the city. The city is laid out as a cube where its "length and width and height are equal." However, these dimensions could also describe a pyramid. After the angel measures the city, the dimensions are given. The wall is "seventy-two yards" thick, just twenty-eight yards short of a football field. The city is "fifteen hundred miles" in length, width, and height, which means it has more than 3.3 billion cubic miles within it. That number of cubic miles laid out linearly is equal to eighteen round trips between the earth and the sun. For comparison, the tallest building on earth is the *Burj Khalifa* in Dubai, which is over 2,700 feet high (one half mile). The highest mountain on earth is Mount Everest, which is over twenty-nine thousand feet high (approximately five and a half miles). New Jerusalem is fifteen hundred miles high. It takes a passenger jet approximately three hours to fly fifteen hundred miles, which is the distance between Chicago and Las Vegas.

The walls are made of "jasper," a non-translucent reddish-brown gemstone. The city itself is "pure gold" but as clear as "glass." This is obviously a gold alloy that is not available on earth. Natural gold is too soft and must be mixed with other alloys to give it the strength to make jewelry. However, the fact that it is clear as glass means that the radiance of God's glory can illuminate the entire city as the light refracts through different levels of crystal gold and all the gems in the city's structure. Mere humans have no words to adequately express the surpassing beauty of new Jerusalem.

REVELATION 21:19–27

THE PRECIOUS STONES
OF THE TWELVE FOUNDATIONS

¹⁹ The foundation stones of the city wall were adorned with every kind of precious stone. The first foundation stone was jasper; the second, sapphire; the third, chalcedony; the fourth, emerald; ²⁰ the fifth, sardonyx; the sixth, sardius; the seventh, chrysolite; the eighth, beryl; the ninth, topaz; the tenth, chrysoprase; the eleventh, jacinth; the twelfth, amethyst. ²¹ And the twelve gates were twelve pearls; each one of the gates was a single pearl. And the street of the city was pure gold, like transparent glass. ²² I saw no temple in it, for the Lord God the Almighty and the Lamb are its temple. ²³ And the city has no need of the sun or of the moon to shine on it, for the glory of God has illumined it, and its lamp is the Lamb. ²⁴ The nations will walk by its light, and the kings of the earth will bring their glory into it. ²⁵ In the daytime (for there will be no night there) its gates will never be closed; ²⁶ and they will bring the glory and the honor of the nations into it; ²⁷ and nothing unclean, and no one who practices abomination and lying, shall ever come into it, but only those whose names are written in the Lamb's book of life.

(19–21) *The foundation stones of the city wall were adorned with every kind of precious stone. . . . :* The opulence of new Jerusalem is revealed by all the precious stones listed here. However, it should not be lost that most of these stones were found on the priest's breast plate and represented each of the tribes of Israel (see Exod 28:17–21; 39:10–13). The first foundation stone is "jasper," a beautiful reddish-brown solid-colored stone. The second, "sapphire," is a deep blue crystal gem. The third, "chalcedony," is a light blue, opaque, semi-translucent stone. The fourth is "emerald," a beautiful green crystal stone. The fifth, "sardonyx" (onyx), comes in a variety of colors but is known for its white streaks. Common colors are black and red. The sixth, "sardius," is an orangish to blood-red stone. The seventh, "chrysolite," is a light green crystal. The eighth is "beryl," a crystal gem of various colors, such as green, yellow, blue, and colorless. The ninth, "topaz," is a gorgeous crystal that comes in a variety of colors, such as blue, pink, goldish, and mystic (multicolor). The tenth, "chrysoprase," is an opaque, light green stone. The eleventh, "jacinth," is a yellow-red to red-brown crystal stone. The twelfth is "amethyst," a crystal that is found in purple, violet, and blue. The gates are made from "twelve pearls." One pearl for each gate would require twelve massive pearls. *And the street of the city was pure gold, like transparent glass:* This probably implies the main boulevard of the city is *made of transparent gold that is as clear as glass.*

(22–24) *I saw no temple in it, for the Lord God the Almighty and the Lamb are its temple:* The primary function of the temple was to serve as a place for God's presence to dwell. Since God will dwell among men in new Jerusalem, there will be no need for a temple. There was a temple in heaven in chapter 7 because the new heaven and new earth had not been created. With their creation, no temple is necessary because God's glorified people will be in His direct presence. A functional temple would be obsolete at this point. In the eternal state, "the Lord God the Almighty and the Lamb are [the] temple." And due to His direct presence, *the city has no need of the sun or of the moon to shine on it, for the glory of God has illumined it, and its lamp is the Lamb:* This is clear evidence that the universe will be reordered. It is *possible* that the physical laws of the old universe, which controlled the movement of the celestial bodies, will no longer be active or will be replaced by new laws.

The earth will no longer be required to revolve around a star (i.e., the sun) in a solar system as it did in the former cosmic order. Social order on the new earth will be utopian and God-centered because *the nations will walk by* the Lamb's *light, and the kings of the earth will bring their glory into it*: It should be noted that *new Jerusalem* will be the capital city that is on the new earth. Not everyone will live in new Jerusalem, but they will come to it through the twelve gates. The earth will be populated with redeemed humanity, all in glorified bodies suitable for eternal existence. Procreation and marriage will not be necessary. Jesus declared, "The sons of this age marry and are given in marriage, but those who are considered worthy to attain to that age and the resurrection from the dead, neither marry nor are given in marriage; for they cannot even die anymore, because they are like angels, and are sons of God, being sons of the resurrection" (Luke 20:34–36). Contrary to popular cultural beliefs, people will not become angels when they are in heaven. Instead, they will share in the characteristics of angels (e.g., immortality and no need for procreation).

(25–27) *In the daytime (for there will be no night there)*: Once again, the affirmation of a new earth is evidenced in the fact that there shall be "no night" in this glorious city. What glory it will be to never have night again. This is not possible on a planet that rotates around a sun. Our human bodies undergo atrophy (i.e., waste away) with the passing of time and require sleep to rejuvenate daily. However, with glorified bodies on a new earth, there will be no night nor need for sleep. *Its gates will never be closed* is a statement of blessed assurance. Today, churches and other places of worship close and lock their doors, and access is restricted. This will never be the case in new Jerusalem because *they will bring the glory and the honor of the nations into it* with the eternal promise that *nothing unclean, and no one who practices abomination and lying, shall ever come into it, but only those whose names are written in the Lamb's book of life*: Nothing wicked can enter the city. This won't even be a possibility because all the wicked will be in the lake of fire. This statement is a way of emphasizing the certainty that only the holy, whose names are written in the Lamb's book of life, can ever enter this glorious city. Contrast is often used as emphasis.

Accommodations like these are necessary for humans, who have only known mortality and death. Everything that we experience in this life is temporary. All that is in this world has an end. Since the fall of Adam, we have only known a cursed world that is fallen and filled with wickedness. There is no experiential basis for us to understand what an existence in eternity is like. For mortals, words like *forever* are words we can say but not fully comprehend. Neither is there any basis to understand perfect holiness and total righteousness. We have never known what it is like to live without temptation or exist without a sinful nature or live a life without aging or decay. But old things will pass away, and in a moment, the mortal will put on immortality, and the corruptible will put on incorruption, and we will be changed (see 1 Cor 15:52–53). We will be like Him and see Him as He is. Certainly, no wicked thing will ever be there for all eternity in a glorious world without end.

REVELATION 22:1–9

THE GLORIOUS BLISS OF NEW JERUSALEM

[1] Then he showed me a river of the water of life, clear as crystal, coming from the throne of God and of the Lamb, [2] in the middle of its street. On either side of the river was the tree of life, bearing twelve kinds of fruit, yielding its fruit every month; and the leaves of the tree were for the healing of the nations. [3] There will no longer be any curse; and the throne of God and of the Lamb will be in it, and His bond-servants will serve Him; [4] they will see His face, and His name will be on their foreheads. [5] And there will no longer be any night; and they will not have need of the light of a lamp nor the light of the sun, because the Lord God will illumine them; and they will reign forever and ever. [6] And he said to me, "These words are faithful and true"; and the Lord, the God of the spirits of the prophets, sent His angel to show to His bond-servants the things which must soon take place. [7] "And behold, I am coming quickly. Blessed is he who heeds the words of the prophecy of this book." [8] I, John, am the one who heard and saw these things. And when I heard and saw, I fell down to worship at the feet of the angel who showed me these things. [9] But he said to me, "Do not do that. I am a fellow servant of yours and of your brethren the prophets and of those who heed the words of this book. Worship God."

(1) *Then he showed me a river of the water of life, clear as crystal, coming from the throne of God and of the Lamb*: Since new Jerusalem will be on the new earth, where the old ecological system has passed away, this may not be water (H$_2$O) as we understand it now. This could be the spiritual water that Jesus referred to in John when He stated, "Everyone who drinks of this water will thirst again; but whoever drinks of the water that I will give him shall never thirst; but the water that I will give him will become in him a well of water springing up to eternal life" (John 4:13–14; see also 7:37–39). Ezekiel also prophesied about a temple that has a flowing river (Ezek 47:1–12). Though there are similarities, Ezekiel's temple is probably the millennial temple, because in his vision the river flows into the Dead Sea (Ezek 47:8). This heavenly river could be the source of living water for the new earth, given that there will be no more sea. The *crystal-clear* river proceeds "from the throne of God and of the Lamb." Here, the Father and the Son's throne are one and the same. Jesus declared, "I and the Father are one" (John 10:30). Though there is no temple, God maintains a throne.

(2) *On either side of the river was the tree of life*: The "tree of life" is mentioned in Genesis 2:9; 3:17, 22, 24 and Revelation 2:7; 22:2, 14. It was at the center of *the Garden of Eden* and was the source of eternal life. Adam and Eve had access to it. However, immediately after the fall, God prohibited their access because if they had eaten from it, they would have continued to live forever in a sinful state. Had Adam and Eve continued to have access to the *tree of life* after they fell into sin, they would have been unredeemable because remission of sin and redemption require death and the shedding of blood (Heb 9:22). Fallen angels such as Satan cannot be redeemed because they cannot die. They are forever locked into wickedness and damnation. To ensure man's destiny would not be the same, God took the following action:

> Then the LORD God said, "Behold, the man has become like one of Us, knowing good and evil; and now, he might stretch out his hand, and take also from the tree of life, and eat, and live forever"— therefore the LORD God sent him out from the garden of Eden, to cultivate the ground from which he was taken. So He drove the man out; and at the east of the garden of

Eden He stationed the cherubim and the flaming sword which turned every direction to guard the way to the tree of life. (Gen 3:22–24)

God also told the serpent that the promised *seed of the woman* would bruise him on the head (Gen 3:15, *the protevangelium*). Jesus is that *seed of the woman* and is the Lamb of God that takes away the sin of the world. Due to the Lamb's sacrifice, Jesus will give the redeemed eternal access to the tree of life, which is located in "the Paradise of God" and is a benefit promised to those who overcome: "He who has an ear, let him hear what the Spirit says to the churches. To him who overcomes, I will grant to eat of the tree of life which is in the Paradise of God" (Rev 2:7). The tree will bear **twelve kinds of fruit, yielding its fruit every month; and the leaves of the tree** will be **for the healing of the nations:** The phrase "for the healing of the nations" has stumped many who ask, "If there is no sin, no more death or sorrow, why would there be a need for the healing of the nations [Gk. *ethnos*, meaning "people groups"]?" Statements like John's could simply be an accommodation for human comprehension. Human beings only know life from a mortal's perspective, where there has always been sickness, suffering, and death, which are all symptoms of a fallen humanity. "Healing" indicates the need for recovery and restoration. However, the maladies that require restoration will be done away with at this point. The word "healing" gives greater emphasis to the eternal reality that such things requiring restoration will not be present in heaven. In other words, whatever caused sickness, death, or sorrow in the former world cannot occur in new Jerusalem or heaven, because old things will have passed away. "Healing," here is not a cure for those who get sick in heaven. It is "the enjoyment of life in the new Jerusalem."[242]

(3–4) There will no longer be any curse: Again, John accentuated what is not in heaven by mentioning what is familiar in life on earth. The *divine*

---

[242] Leon Morris, *Tyndale New Testament Commentaries*, vol. 20, *Revelation* (Downers Grove, IL: InterVarsity Press, 1987), 243.

"curse" is the consequence for man's sin and rebellion. For the countless millions, if not billions, of Christians who have read this passage, the knowledge that the curse is done away with is a tremendous source of joy. Our experience with a cursed life on earth and our hope for a new life to come make John's comparison of the two so impactful. The sin and the consequential curse that separates us from God will be replaced with God's direct presence. *The throne of God and of the Lamb will be in it, and His bond-servants will serve Him; they will see His face, and His name will be on their foreheads:* To see God's face was a great expectation even from OT times (Job 33:26; Ps 17:15). In the NT, John writes, "No one has seen God at any time; the only begotten God who is in the bosom of the Father, He has explained *Him*" (John 1:18). However, after the Lord was crucified, raised, and glorified, John again writes in his first epistle, "Beloved, now we are children of God, and it has not appeared as yet what we will be. We know that when He appears, we will be like Him, because we will see Him just as He is" (1 John 3:2). Paul also weighs in when he writes, "For now we see in a mirror dimly, but then face to face; now I know in part, but then I will know fully just as I also have been fully known" (1 Cor 13:12). Whereas no man on earth could see God's face and live (Exod 33:20), this will not be the case in the *new heaven and earth*, which emphasizes the divine intimacy between God and His people throughout eternity. On the old earth, to see God would be lethal. However, on the new earth, this will be a privilege and a blessing, facilitated by a glorified body that is holy and suited for eternity and being in God's direct presence.

(5) *And there will no longer be any night; and they will not have need of the light of a lamp nor the light of the sun, because the Lord God will illumine them:* In the new heaven and new earth, there will be no need for the sun, which means there will be a completely different cosmic order, where galaxies and solar systems will be things of the past. The idea of no more night, again, brings joy, because night is also a metaphor for evil and wickedness. All these things will pass away. And in this no-night eternity, *they will reign forever and ever.*

(6) *And he said to me, "These words are faithful and true":* The words "faithful and true" are somewhat redundant, but the angel uses them here to emphasize the certainty of the revelation given to John. *And the Lord, the God of the spirits of the prophets, sent His angel to show to His bond-servants the things which must soon take place:* Since John's life, two thousand years have passed. However, the events of this passage will occur well beyond our twenty-first century time frame. They will occur after the millennium, after the final defeat of Satan, and after the great white throne judgment. Some, such as MacArthur, see this phrase as relating to the doctrine of imminence.[243] However, the new heaven and new earth are not imminent, overhanging events that could occur at any time, but are future events that will "soon take place" from a divine perspective.

(7–9) *And behold, I am coming quickly:* Here, it is the Lord who is speaking. *Blessed is he who heeds the words of the prophecy of this book:* This phrase is first found in 1:3. However, here at the end of the book the Lord's blessing emphasizes the significance of Revelation, which many ignore or marginalize. The blessing stated here is the *sixth beatitude* in Revelation and gives emphasis that the Lord and His kingdom are sure to come. Those who keep, or take to heart, the prophecies of this book are indeed blessed. Among those who study end times prophecy, many do not believe the church has any involvement in most of this book. However, this statement in 22:7 is like a bookend that confirms all that is written in this book is true and of great importance to the church.

I, John, am the one who heard and saw these things. And when I heard and saw, I fell down to worship at the feet of the angel who showed me these things. But he said to me, "Do not do that. I am a fellow servant of yours and of your brethren the prophets and of those who heed the words of this book. Worship God": Once again, John is overwhelmed and begins to worship the angel, but the angel's response is immediate: "Do not do that" (see 19:10 note).

---

[243] MacArthur, *The MacArthur New Testament Commentary: Revelation 1–11*, 1:20.

✝

REVELATION 22:10–16

The Final Admonition

¹⁰ And he said to me, "Do not seal up the words of the prophecy of this book, for the time is near. ¹¹ Let the one who does wrong, still do wrong; and the one who is filthy, still be filthy; and let the one who is righteous, still practice righteousness; and the one who is holy, still keep himself holy. ¹² Behold, I am coming quickly, and My reward is with Me, to render to every man according to what he has done. ¹³ I am the Alpha and the Omega, the first and the last, the beginning and the end." ¹⁴ Blessed are those who wash their robes, so that they may have the right to the tree of life, and may enter by the gates into the city. ¹⁵ Outside are the dogs and the sorcerers and the immoral persons and the murderers and the idolaters, and everyone who loves and practices lying. ¹⁶ "I, Jesus, have sent My angel to testify to you these things for the churches. I am the root and the descendant of David, the bright morning star."

(10) *Do not seal up the words of the prophecy of this book, for the time is near:* This command is the opposite of what Daniel was told when he was given his prophecy. "But as for you, Daniel, *conceal these words and seal up the book until the end of time*; many will go back and forth, and knowledge will increase" (Dan 12:4, emphasis added). Pentecost writes, "Understandably Daniel and his immediate readers could not have comprehended all the details of the prophecies given in this book. Not until history continued to unfold would many be able to understand these prophetic revelations."[244] Therefore, the command to seal up the vision and prophecy makes sense because Daniel's prophecies were given over 2,500 years ago. However, now we are in the "last days," the period that started at the day of Pentecost (Acts 2:17). Though we have been in *the last days* since the day of Pentecost, now we are in the *end times*. One of the primary markers of being in the end times, also called the *latter years*, is Ezekiel's prophecy about Israel:

> After many days you will be summoned; *in the latter years* you will come into the *land that is restored from the sword*, whose inhabitants *have been gathered from many nations to the mountains of Israel which had been a continual waste; but its people were brought out from the nations*, and they are living securely, all of them. (Ezek 38:8, emphasis added)

This passage states that "in the latter years" Gog of Magog, which is modern-day Russia, will invade the land of Israel. This was not possible until May 14, 1948, when Israel was reborn as a nation. Now that we are in the twenty-first century, Russia has political, economic, and military alignments with Iran, Libya, Ethiopia/Sudan, and Turkey—the nations named in the prophecy (Ezek 38:5–6). The fulfillment of all these things puts us in what Ezekiel called the "*latter years*," or the *end times*. Whereas Daniel was told to seal up a prophecy because of the distance away from its fulfillment, John was commanded, "Do not seal up the words of the prophecy of this book, for the time is near." This is because, since the day of Pentecost, we have been in the last days.

(11) *Let the one who does wrong, still do wrong; and the one who is filthy, still be filthy*: In view of the *closeness* and the *certainty* of the events written in Revelation, how people respond to God's Word will be the final indicator of whom they are, either wicked or righteous. Jesus stated, "A good tree cannot produce bad fruit, nor can a bad tree produce good

---

[244] J. Dwight Pentecost, "Daniel," in *The Bible Knowledge Commentary: An Exposition of the Scriptures*, ed. J. F. Walvoord and R. B. Zuck, vol. 1 (Wheaton, IL: Victor Books, 1985), 1373.

fruit. So then, you will know them by their fruits" (Matt 7:18, 20). In the end, people will receive the wage for the life they have chosen to live. In that regard, the appeal here is not to *change* but to *maintain*. Either way, God's Word is fulfilled as bringing salvation unto eternal life or judgment unto eternal damnation.

In 2 Thessalonians 2:10–12, the Lord said,

> And with all the deception of wickedness for those who perish, because they did not receive the love of the truth so as to be saved. For this reason God will send upon them a deluding influence so that they will believe what is false, in order that they all may be judged who did not believe the truth, but took pleasure in wickedness.

And let the one who is righteous, still practice righteousness; and the one who is holy, still keep himself holy: Those who heed and keep the words of this prophecy are encouraged to stay the course and continue to be "holy" and "righteous." Those who endure to the end shall receive their reward.

(12–13) ***Behold, I am coming quickly, and My reward is with Me, to render to every man according to what he has done:*** The Lord emphasized what He had just stated in v. 7, but here He said, "Behold I am coming quickly, and My reward is with Me" (see the essay "The Imminent Return"). In Matthew, Jesus made a similar statement to His disciples when He stated, "For the Son of Man is going to come in the glory of His Father with His angels, and will then repay every man according to his deeds" (Matt 16:27). Throughout the Scriptures, recompense of reward is a prominent theme (Ps 62:12; Prov 24:12; Rom 2:6; 14:12; 1 Cor 3:13; 2 Cor 5:10; Eph 6:8; Col 3:25; Rev 2:23; 20:12; 22:12). It is sobering to know that God will reward Christians according to their deeds. One would think this would be a point of celebration, and indeed it can be. However, not everything that the saints have done is good. Nevertheless, we will give account for it. Speaking of the judgment seat of Christ, Paul wrote,

> Now if any man builds on the foundation with gold, silver, precious stones, wood, hay, straw, each man's work will become evident; for the day will show it because it is to be revealed with fire, and the fire itself will test the quality of each man's work. If any man's work which he has built on it remains, he will receive a reward. If any man's work is burned up, he will suffer loss; but he himself will be saved, yet so as through fire. (1 Cor 3:12–15)

The reward will be eternal, and the loss will bring temporary sadness for falling short, possibly for having wrong or ulterior motives as we rendered service. However, the bliss of eternal paradise will soon overtake all those in glory, and once and for all, God will wipe away all tears.

(a) *I am the Alpha and the Omega, the first and the last, the beginning and the end.* (See 1:8 note.)

(14) *Blessed are those who wash their robes, so that they may have the right to the tree of life, and may enter by the gates into the city*: This is the last of the seven beatitudes of Revelation and alludes to what has already been stated about this magnificent group of Christians that comes out of the great tribulation (7:14). They have washed their robes in the blood of the Lamb. Keep in mind that all of the redeemed throughout history are ultimately saved by the blood of the Lamb.

(15) *Outside are the dogs and the sorcerers and the immoral persons and the murderers and the idolaters, and everyone who loves and practices lying*: A similar list of the immoral is given in 21:8, with the addition of the word "dogs" here. In ancient times, dogs were nasty animals, not like the domesticated pets we have today. Dogs were scavengers who ate rubbish, rotting food, and dead animals, and they were dangerous. When a person is called a dog, it means they are of poor character, untrustworthy, and deviant. This passage is not teaching that the wicked will be lying in wait right outside the gates of New Jerusalem. By using comparison, the righteous versus the wicked and the redeemed versus the damned, John emphasized the state of the blessed environment that citizens of the new heaven and earth will live in—one that will never again coexist with evil.

(16) *I, Jesus, have sent My angel to testify to you these things for the churches*: Revelation closes with this first-person statement from the Lord Himself, reiterating a point first emphasized in 1:1, which is that the Lord sent His "angel to testify" of these things to "the churches" (i.e., the seven churches of Asia Minor) and, by extension, all churches. This word "churches" has not been used in Revelation since 3:22. Here it is like a bookend, meaning that the entire book of Revelation is for—and much of it is about—the church. This chapter contains five incidents where the Lord speaks in first person (vv. 7, 12, 13, 16, and 20). This has not occurred since chapter 3. Jesus accentuated the gravity and weight of the entire book (also see 1:3). There is no ancient writing in the world that comes close to the wide range of futuristic, prophetic information as is found in this divinely inspired book.

(a) *I am the root and the descendant of David*: Jesus identified Himself as the "root . . . of David" (cf. 5:5), meaning that the human aspect of His sonship comes from the lineage of David, which is also implied in Isaiah 11:1 and Romans 1:3. Jesus is the prophesied *son of David* (Matt 1:1; Luke 1:32), which is a common title for Jesus found nine times in Matthew and three times in both Mark and Luke. It cannot be overlooked, however, that Jesus is not just the "descendant [or "offspring"] of David" but He is also the "root," meaning that Jesus is David's sustainer and Lord. David is not the Lord's root. Jesus makes His relationship to David clear in the following passage:

> Now while the Pharisees were gathered together, Jesus asked them a question: "What do you think about the Christ, whose son is He?" They said to Him, "The son of David." He said to them, "Then how does David in the Spirit call Him 'Lord,' saying, 'The Lord said to my Lord, "Sit at My right

hand, until I put Your enemies beneath Your feet'"? If David then calls Him 'Lord,' how is He his son?" No one was able to answer Him a word, nor did anyone dare from that day on to ask Him another question. (Matt 22:41–46)

The unavoidable answer that the Jews refused to concede was that the Messiah was both David's son by human lineage and David's Lord by divine lineage. Therefore, Jesus is "the root and the descendant of David."

(b) *the bright morning star:* It is possible this is referencing the same thing as in 2:28, and it could look back to a reference to the Messiah in Numbers 24:17, which says, "A star shall come forth from Jacob, a scepter shall rise from Israel." Jesus is the "morning star."

REVELATION 22:17–21

¹⁷ The Spirit and the bride say, "Come." And let the one who hears say, "Come." And let the one who is thirsty come; let the one who wishes take the water of life without cost. ¹⁸ I testify to everyone who hears the words of the prophecy of this book: if anyone adds to them, God will add to him the plagues which are written in this book; ¹⁹ and if anyone takes away from the words of the book of this prophecy, God will take away his part from the tree of life and from the holy city, which are written in this book. ²⁰ He who testifies to these things says, "Yes, I am coming quickly." Amen. Come, Lord Jesus. ²¹ The grace of the Lord Jesus be with all. Amen.

(17) *The Spirit and the bride say, "Come." And let the one who hears say, "Come." And let the one who is thirsty come; let the one who wishes take the water of life without cost*: Many interpret "the Spirit and the Bride" saying, "Come" as the call for the *parousia** (i.e., the coming of the Lord). However, as Mounce states, "It is more likely that the first half of the verse should be interpreted by the second, and that the entire invitation is addressed to the world. . . . It is the testimony of the church empowered by the Holy Spirit that constitutes the great evangelizing force of this age."[245] Therefore, here we have the divine invitation, which is being emphasized with let the one who is thirsty come; let the one who wishes take the water of life without cost," for

---

[245] Mounce, *The New International Commentary: The Book of Revelation*, 409.

all who will heed the words of this prophecy. This invitation echoes Isaiah's words.

> Ho! Every one who thirsts, come to the waters; And you who have no money come, buy and eat. Come, buy wine and milk without money and without cost. (Isa 55:1)

Jesus also declared,

> Now on the last day, the great day of the feast, Jesus stood and cried out, saying, "If anyone is thirsty, let him come to Me and drink. He who believes in Me, as the Scripture said, 'From his innermost being will flow rivers of living water.'" (John 7:37–38)

Isaiah's and the Lord's words coincide with this appeal directed toward those who hunger and thirst for salvation. The emphasis "without cost" underlines the fact that what has already been purchased by the precious blood of the Lamb is free—to those that will accept it.

(18) *I testify to everyone who hears the words of the prophecy of this book: if anyone adds to them, God will add to him the plagues which are written in this book*: This is another unique aspect of the book of Revelation: it opens with a blessing but closes with a severe warning that is identical to Deuteronomy 4:2, "You shall not add to the word which I am commanding you, nor take away from it, that you may keep the commandments of the LORD your God which I command you." So important is the content of this book that it is not to be subtracted from or added to. God's Word does not need human help. Whenever people add to the Word of God, inevitably, they corrupt it. The psalmist declared, "The words of the LORD are pure words; as silver tried in a furnace on the earth, refined seven times" (Ps 12:6). People make the Word of God have no effect through their traditions. Jesus declared,

> "'But in vain do they worship Me, teaching as doctrines the precepts of men.' Neglecting the commandment of God, you hold to the tradition of men." He was also saying to them,

"You are experts at setting aside the commandment of God in order to keep your tradition." (Mark 7:7–9)

Therefore, God warns us in Scripture not to add to or take away from this book, or God's Word in general, as it is a dangerous thing to do.

(19) *and if anyone takes away from the words of the book of this prophecy, God will take away his part from the tree of life and from the holy city, which are written in this book*: This means they will be eternally damned because God taking away their "part from the tree of life and from the holy city" is synonymous with being damned.

(20) *He who testifies to these things says, "Yes, I am coming quickly"*: Jesus makes His final comment by declaring, "Yes I am coming quickly." As stated earlier, "coming quickly" should be understood from God's *eternal now* perspective. "Quickly" to the Lord and "quickly" to us have different meanings. However, it is possible that what is meant here is that once Jesus actually leaves heaven to come, *at that point* He will come quickly. The delay *is not* in His getting here but in His leaving to come. For example, He told the souls under the altar that "they should rest for a little while longer, until the number of their fellow servants and their brethren who were to be killed even as they had been, would be completed also" (6:11). This would be considered a program delay, because the full number of martyrs needed to be reached before the Lord could return to earth with His saints to execute vengeance on those who dwell on the earth. *Amen.* The response to the promise of coming quickly is met with "Amen" (see 3:14 note), then punctuated with *Come, Lord Jesus.* "Come" (Gk. *erchomai*), meaning "of movement from one point to another, with focus on approach from the narrator's perspective,"[246] in this context is reminiscent of "maranatha," found in 1 Cor 16:22 and meaning "our Lord come."[247] This should be the active hope of all the redeemed from all ages.

---

[246] Bauer, *Greek-English Lexicon*, "come."

[247] Bauer, "maranatha."

(21) *The grace of the Lord Jesus be with all. Amen:* Concerning this brief benediction, Morris observes that it "is unusual as an end to an apocalypse, but [it is] the normal close to a first-century Christian letter."[248] It is through God's grace that any are saved, even during the tribulation. Though the apocalypse is primarily wrath, grace is the blessed contrast. Through judgment comes newness. In Revelation, God's grace shines through in many ways. It is by grace the redeemed are standing before the throne of God (7:9–17). It is by grace that the 144,000 are marked on their foreheads (7:1–8). It is by grace that one is named in the Lamb's book of life (13:8; 17:8). It is by grace that God sends an angel to the planet to preach the eternal gospel (14:6–7). It is by grace that God sends another angel to warn people not to take the mark of the beast (14:9–12). However, one of the most profound aspects of God's grace is that He has given the book of Revelation to the church. God has declared future events that read like history, all by His amazing grace. "Be with all" is translated "be with you all" (KJV), "be with God's people" (NIV), "be with everyone" (CSB), and "be with all the saints" (NRSV). No matter how the various versions render these closing words, the meaning is the same. This is a benediction that is for all believers, for all the saints who anticipate the ages to come. "Amen," let it be so, and *Maranatha,* our Lord come! Amen.

CONCLUSION

Without a doubt, the world is drawing closer to fulfilling the events detailed in this awesome prophecy. The very book that has been misunderstood, overlooked, and even marginalized will become critical as these apocalyptic events continue to unfold. Those who know Scripture, especially the book of Revelation, will have insight concerning what's coming next. This will present tremendous opportunities to witness for Jesus during the inevitable confusion and widespread deception that will engulf the entire globe. Daniel declared, "Those who have insight

---

248 Morris, *Tyndale New Testament Commentaries: Revelation,* 20:250.

will shine brightly like the brightness of the expanse of heaven, and those who lead the many to righteousness, like the stars forever and ever.... Many will be purged, purified and refined, but the wicked will act wickedly; and none of the wicked will understand, but those who have insight will understand" (Dan 12:3, 10).

The power of the Holy Spirit is the only source that illumines God's Word to give people understanding and insight. God reveals secret things to those who serve the Lord. Indeed, God's purpose for Revelation is to impart the necessary wisdom and understanding for a time coming that has no equal. Therefore, it is appropriate that we end this commentary with the very blessing found at the beginning of Revelation. "Blessed is he who reads and those who hear the words of the prophecy, and heed the things which are written in it; for the time is near" (Rev 1:3). May the will of the Lord be perfected in the lives of all who believe and who trust in Jesus as the way, the truth, and the life. So, Lord, come. Amen.

BIBLIOGRAPHY

Alpha-Omega Ministries. "L–Z." Vol. 2 of *Practical Word Studies in the New Testament.* Chattanooga, TN: Leadership Ministries Worldwide, 1998.

Arraf, Jane. "In Iraq, a Race to Protect the Crumbling Bricks of Ancient Babylon." National Public Radio, November 24, 2018. World. https://www.npr.org/2018/11/24/669272204/in-iraq-a-race-to-protect-the-crumbling-bricks-of-ancient-babylon.

Ashcraft, W. Michael. "Progressive Millennialism." In *The Oxford Handbook of Millennialism,* edited by Catherine Wessinger, 44–64. Oxford: Oxford University Press, 2011. Quoted in James H. Moorehead. *World Without End: Mainstream American Protestant Visions of the Last Things, 1880–1925.* Bloomington: Indiana University Press, 1999.

Augustine of Hippo. "St. Augustin's City of God." Vol. 2, bk. 18, chap. 52, of *Nicene and Post-Nicene Fathers of the Christian Church,* edited by Philip Schaff. Translated by Marcus Dods. Edinburgh, Scotland, 1886.

Aune, David E. *Revelation 6–16.* Edited by Bruce M. Metzger, David Allen Hubbard, and Glenn W. Barker. Vol. 52B of *Word Biblical Commentary,* edited by John D. W. Watts, James W. Watts, Ralph P. Martin, and Lynn Allan Losie. Dallas: Word, Incorporated, 1998.

Baker, Warren, and Eugene Carpenter, eds. *The Complete Word Study Dictionary: Old Testament.* Chattanooga, TN: AMG Publishers, 2003.

Barrett, C. K. *Acts 1–14.* Vol. 1 of *The International Critical Commentary.* New York: T.T. Clark, 1895–2023.

Barry, John D., David Bomar, Derek R. Brown, Rachel Klippenstein, Douglas Mangum, Elliot Ritzema, Carrie Sinclair Wolcott, Lazarus Wentz, and Wendy Widder, eds. *Lexham Bible Dictionary*. Bellingham, WA: Lexham Press, 2016.

Barton, Bruce B., Philip W. Comfort, Grant R. Osborne, Linda K. Taylor, and Dave Veerman. *Life Application New Testament Commentary*. Wheaton, IL: Tyndale, 2001.

Bauer, Walter. *A Greek-English Lexicon of the New Testament and Other Early Christian Literature*. Edited by Frederick Danker, William Arndt, and Wilbur Gingrich. Chicago: University of Chicago Press, 2000.

Beale, G. K. *The Book of Revelation*. Vol. 13 of *The New International Greek Testament Commentary*. Grand Rapids, MI: W.B. Eerdmans, 1998.

Beasley-Murray, George R. "Revelation." In *New Bible Commentary: 21st Century Edition*, 4th ed., edited by D. A. Carson, R. T. France, Alec Motyer, and Gordon J. Wenham. Downers Grove, IL: InterVarsity Press, 1994.

Benware, Paul N. *Understanding End Times Prophecy: A Comprehensive Approach*. Chicago: Moody Publishers, 2006.

Boice, James Montgomery. *Ephesians: An Expositional Commentary*. Grand Rapids, MI: Ministry Resources Library, 1988.

Boles, John B. *The Great Revival, 1787–1805: The Origins of the Southern Evangelical Mind*. Lexington, KY: University Press of Kentucky, 1972. Referenced in Jack P. Maddex. "Proslavery Millennialism: Social Eschatology in Antebellum Southern Calvinism." Baltimore, MD: John Hopkins University Press, 1979.

Brand, Chad, Charles Draper, and Archie England, eds. *Holman Illustrated Bible Dictionary*. Nashville, TN: Holman Bible Publishers, 2003.

Bromiley, Geoffrey W. *Theological Dictionary of the New Testament*, edited by Gerhard Kittel and Gerhard Friedrich. Grand Rapids, MI: William B. Eerdmans, 2006.

Bruce, F. F. *1 and 2 Thessalonians*, edited by Bruce M. Metzger. Vol. 45 of *Word Biblical Commentary*, edited by John D. W. Watts, James W. Watts, Ralph P. Martin, and Lynn Allan Losie. Dallas: Word, Incorporated, 1982.

Byle, Ann. "LaHaye, Co-Author of *Left Behind* Series, Leaves a Lasting Impact." *Publishers Weekly*, July 27, 2016. https://www.publishersweekly .com/pw/by-topic/industry-news/religion/article/71026-lahaye -co-author-of-left-behind-series-leaves-a-lasting-impact.html.

Calvin, John. *Calvin's Commentaries*. 22 vols. Grand Rapids, MI: Baker Books, 1974.

Carson, D. A., Douglas J. Moo, and Leon Morris. *An Introduction to the New Testament*. Grand Rapids, MI: Zondervan, 1992.

Charles, R. H. Vol. 2 of *A Critical and Exegetical Commentary on the Revelation of St. John*. London: Forgotten Books, 2018.

Cyprian of Carthage. "The Epistles of Cyprian." In *Fathers of the Third Century: Hippolytus, Cyprian, Novatian, Appendix*, edited by Alexander Roberts, James Donaldson, and A. Cleveland Coxe. Translated by Robert Ernest Wallis. Vol. 5 of *Ante-Nicene Fathers: The Writings of the Fathers Down to AD 325*. Buffalo, NY, 1886.

Earle, Ralph. "The Book of Revelation." *Hebrews Through Revelation*. Vol. 10 of *Beacon Bible Commentary*. Kansas City, MO: Beacon Hill Press, 1967.

Elwell, Walter A., and Philip W. Comfort, eds. *Tyndale Bible Dictionary*. Tyndale Reference Library. Wheaton, IL: Tyndale House Publishers, 2001.

Charles, R. H., trans. *The Book of Enoch*. London: Society for Promoting Christian Knowledge, 1917.

Evans, Tony. *The Tony Evans Bible Commentary: Advancing God's Kingdom Agenda.* Nashville, TN: Holman Bible Publishers, 2019.

Gaebelein, Arno C. *Romans to Ephesians.* Vol. 7 of *The Annotated Bible.* Bellingham, WA: Logos Bible Software, 2009.

Geisler, Norman. *Church/Last Things.* Vol. 4 of *Systematic Theology.* Minneapolis, MN: Bethany House, 2005.

Gettleman, Jeffrey. "Babylon Awaits an Iraq Without Fighting." *New York Times,* April 18, 2006. https://www.nytimes.com/2006/04/18/world/middleeast/babylon-awaits-an-iraq-without-fighting.html.

Gundry, Robert H. *Commentary on Revelation.* Vol. 19 of *Commentary on the New Testament.* Grand Rapids, MI: Baker Academic, 2010.

Harrill, J. Albert. "The Use of the New Testament in the American Slave Controversy: A Case History in the Hermeneutical Tension Between Biblical Criticism and Christian Moral Debate." *Religion and American Culture: A Journal of Interpretation* 10, no. 2 (Summer 2000): 149–86. https://doi.org/10.2307/1123945.

Ice, Thomas D. "A Short History of Dispensationalism." Scholars Crossing. The Institutional Repository of Liberty University. May 2009. Article Archives. https://digitalcommons.liberty.edu/pretrib_arch/37.

———. "James Hall Brookes: Early Pretribulational Rapture Pioneer—Tom's Perspectives." Pre-Trib Research Center. https://www.pre-trib.org/pretribfiles/pdfs/Ice-JamesHallBrookes.pdf.

Inglis, James. *Waymarks in the Wilderness.* New York, 1857. https://archive.org/details/waymarksinwilder00ingl/page/2/mode/2up.

Johnson, Alan F. *The Expositor's Bible Commentary.* Grand Rapids, MI: Zondervan, 1996.

Keil, Carl F. and Franz Delitzsch. "Scripture of Truth" in vol. 9 of *Commentary on the Old Testament* Peabody, MA: Henderickson, 1996.

Knorr, Ed. "Revelation and Bible Prophecy A Comparison of Eschatological Views: Dispensationalism and Preterism." Unpublished
manuscript.

Kruse, Colin G. *2 Corinthians: An Introduction and Commentary.* Vol. 8 of *The
Tyndale New Testament Commentaries.* Downers Grove, IL: InterVarsity
Press, 1987.

Ladd, George Eldon. *A Commentary on the Revelation of John.* Grand Rapids, MI: William B. Eerdmans Publishing Company, 1972.

MacArthur, John F. *1 & 2 Thessalonians.* Vol. 23 of *The MacArthur New
Testament Commentary.* Chicago: Moody Press, 2002.

———. *Revelation 12–22.* Vol. 2 of *The MacArthur New Testament Commentary: Revelation.* Chicago: Moody Press, 2000.

MacDonald, William. *Believer's Bible Commentary*, edited by Arthur L.
Farstad. Nashville, TN: Thomas Nelson Publishers, 1995.

Maddex, Jack P. "Proslavery Millennialism: Social Eschatology in
Antebellum Southern Calvinism." *American Quarterly* 31, no. 1
(Spring 1979): 46–62. https://doi.org/10.2307/2712486.

Mangum, Douglas. *The Lexham Glossary of Theology.* Bellingham, WA:
Lexham Press, 2014.

Martin, Walter. "Jehovah's Witnesses and the Watch Tower Bible and
Tract Society." In *The Kingdom of the Cults*, edited by Ravi Zacharias.
Minneapolis, MN: Bethany House Publishers, 2003.

Menzies, Allan, ed. Part 1–3 in *Latin Christianity: Its Founder, Tertullian.*
Vol. 3 of the *Ante-Nicene Fathers: The Writings of the Fathers Down to AD
325.* Edinburgh, Scotland, 1867.

Miller, Stephen R. *Daniel.* Vol. 18 of *The New American Commentary.*
Nashville, TN: Broadman & Holman Publishers, 1994.

Mitchell, Bea. "Saudi Arabia's Crown Prince Unveils Qiddiya City Plans." Blooloop. December 8, 2023. https://blooloop.com/theme -park/news/qiddiya-city-plans.

Morris, Leon. *The Epistle to the Romans*. The Pillar New Testament Commentary. Grand Rapids, MI: Eerdmans, 1988.

———. *Revelation: An Introduction and Commentary*. Vol. 20 of *The Tyndale New Testament Commentaries*. Downers Grove, IL: InterVarsity Press, 1987.

Mounce, Robert H. *The Book of Revelation*. The New International Commentary on the New Testament. Grand Rapids, MI: Wm. B. Eerdmans Publishing Co., 1997.

Muench, Niklas. "John MacArthur Outrage: Take the Mark of the Beast, Still Be Saved. False Teaching." YouTube, August 15, 2015. https:// www.youtube.com/watch?v=DTc8w5h8UTI.

Robert L. Thomas, *New American Standard Hebrew-Aramaic and Greek Dictionaries: Updated Edition*. Anaheim: Foundation Publications, Inc., 1998.

Orr, James, John L. Nuelsen, Edgar Y. Mullins, and Morris O. Evans, eds. *The International Standard Bible Encyclopedia*. Chicago: The Howard-Severance Company, 1915.

Osborne, Grant R. *Revelation*. Baker Exegetical Commentary on the New Testament. Grand Rapids, MI: Baker Academic, 2002.

Pentecost, J. Dwight. "Daniel." In *Old Testament*, edited by J. F. Walvoord and R. B. Zuck. Vol. 1 of *The Bible Knowledge Commentary*. Wheaton, IL: Victor Books, 1985.

———. *Things to Come: A Study in Biblical Eschatology*. Grand Rapids, MI: Zondervan, 1964.

Peterson, David G. *The Acts of the Apostles*. The Pillar New Testament Commentary. Grand Rapids, MI: Eerdmans Publishing Co., 2009.

Randell, T., A. Plummer, A. T. Bott, and C. Clemance. *1 John*. Vol. 22 of *The Pulpit Commentary*, edited by H. D. M. Spence and Joseph S. Excell. London; New York: Funk & Wagnalls Company, 1909.

———. *The Revelation*. Vol. 22 of *The Pulpit Commentary*, edited by H. D. M. Spence and Joseph S. Excell. New York; Toronto: Funk & Wagnalls Company, 1909.

Reid, Daniel G., Robert D. Linder, Bruce L. Shelley, and Harry S. Stout, eds. *Dictionary of Christianity in America*. Downers Grove, IL: Inter-Varsity Press, 1990.

Renn, Stephen D. *Expository Dictionary of Bible Words: Word Studies for Key English Bible Words Based on the Hebrew and Greek Texts*. Peabody, MA: Hendrickson Publishers, 2005.

Richardson, Joel. *The Islamic Antichrist*. 2nd ed. Leawood, KS: Winepress Media, 2015.

Roberts, Alexander, and James Donaldson, eds. "The Martyrdom of Polycarp." Chap. 12 in *The Apostolic Fathers with Justin Martyr and Irenaeus*. Vol. 1 of the *Ante-Nicene Fathers: The Writings of the Fathers Down to AD 325*. Buffalo, NY, 1886.

Rosenberg, Joel C. "Is Babylon Once Agan Rising from the Ashes?" *Jerusalem Post*. Updated February 21, 2022. https://www.jpost.com/christianworld/article-696640.

Rossing, Barbara. "The First Interlude: The People of God." In *Fortress Commentary on the Bible: The New Testament*, edited by Margaret Aymer, Cynthia Briggs Kittredge, and David A. Sánchez. Minneapolis, MN: Fortress Press, 2014.

Rowland, Christopher C. "The Book of Revelation." In vol. 10 of *The New Interpreter's Bible Commentary*. Nashville, TN: Abingdon Press, 2015.

Ryrie, Charles C. *Ryrie Study Bible: New American Standard 1995 Expanded Edition.* Chicago: Moody Press, 1995.

Scofield, C. I. *The Scofield Study Bible.* Oxford University Press, American Branch, 1909, 1917.

Showers, Renald E. *Marantha: Our Lord Come: A Definitive Study of the Rapture of the Church.* Bellmawr, NJ: Friends of Israel Gospel Ministry, 1995.

Spencer, Stephen. "Dispensationalism." In vol. 1 of *The Encyclopedia of Christianity,* edited by Erwin Fahlbusch, Jan Milic Lochman, John Mbiti, Jaroslav Jan Pelikan, Lukas Vischer, and David B. Barrett. Translated by Geoffrey W. Bromiley. Grand Rapids, MI: Wm. B. Eerdmans, 1999.

Sproul, R. C. "The End of All Things." In *1–2 Peter: An Expositional Commentary.* Wheaton, IL: Crossway, 2011.

Strong, James. *Strong's Hebrew Dictionary of the Bible.* Hawthorne, CA: BN Publishing, 2012.

Tavernier, Lyle. "The Science Behind NASA's First Attempt at Redirecting an Asteroid." NASA Jet Propulsion Laboratory, October 20, 2022. https://www.jpl.nasa.gov/edu/news/2022/9/22/the-science -behind-nasas-first-attempt-at-redirecting-an-asteroid/#:~:text= In%20a%20successful%20attempt%20to,no%20threat%20to%20 our%20planet.

Thayer, Joseph H. *Thayer's Greek-English Lexicon of the New Testament.* New York: Harper & Brothers., 1889.

Thomas, Robert L. *New American Standard Exhaustive Concordance of the Bible.* Nashville, TN: Holman Bible Publishers, 1981.

Thornwell, James H. *The Collected Writings of James Henley Thornwell,* edited by John B. Adger and John L. Girardeau. Richmond, VA:

Presbyterian Committee of Publication, 1871–73. Referenced in Jack P. Maddex. "Proslavery Millennialism: Social Eschatology in Antebellum Southern Calvinism." Baltimore, MD: John Hopkins University Press, 1979.

Triantafillidou, Maximina. "Patmos." Grecias Vision. Accessed January 26, 2023. http://greciasvision.com/patmos.

Unger, Merrill. *The New Unger's Bible Dictionary*. Chicago: Moody Press, 1957.

Walvoord, John F. "Revelation." In *New Testament*, edited by J. F. Walvoord and R. B. Zuck. Vol. 2 of *The Bible Knowledge Commentary*. Wheaton, IL: Victor Books, 1985.

Wiersbe, Warren W. *The Bible Exposition Commentary: An Exposition of the New Testament Comprising the Entire "BE" Series*. Wheaton, IL: Victor Books, 1996.

———. *Wiersbe's Expository Outlines on the New Testament*. Wheaton, IL: Victor Books, 1992.

Wingfield, Mark. "What's Wrong with 'Left Behind'?" Baptist News Global. August 12, 2021. Analysis. https://baptistnews.com/article/whats-wrong-with-left-behind.

WorldData.info. "Spread of Christianity." Accessed February 16, 2003. https://www.worlddata.info/religions/christianity.php.

Wright, Louis B., and Marion Tinling, eds. *The Secret Diary of William Byrd of Westover, 1709–12*. Richmond, VA: Dietz Press, 1941. Referenced in Jack P. Maddex. "Proslavery Millennialism: Social Eschatology in Antebellum Southern Calvinism." Baltimore, MD: John Hopkins University Press, 1979.

Yamauchi, Edwin. *The Archaeology of New Testament Cities in Western Asia Minor*, 35–36. Grand Rapids, MI: Baker Book House, 1980.

GLOSSARY

A

Abolitionist / Abolitionist Movement. A person that supports and advocates for the end of a practice or institution. As a movement, it was a social and political initiative aimed at ending slavery and liberating enslaved individuals. This movement was active in the United States from approximately 1830 to 1870.

Abomination of Desolation. Refers to the desecration of the Jewish temple predicted in Daniel 9:27, 11:31, and 12:11. A notable instance of this occurred in 167 BC, in an attempt to Hellenize the Jews, when Antiochus Epiphanes IV, king of Syria, commanded the installation of a pagan idol (Zeus) in the most holy place of the Jewish temple. The Syrians also offered sacrilegious sacrifices (swine) on the altar. Jesus prophesied about a future occurrence of the abomination of desolation in Matthew 24:15 and Mark 13:14. At the end of the age, during Daniel's Seventieth Week, the Antichrist will commit the ultimate abomination by declaring himself to be God after entering the temple in Jerusalem yet to be constructed (2 Thessalonians 2:3). The Antichrist will also set up his image, demanding worship under the threat of death (Revelation 13:14-17).

Abyss, or the bottomless pit. A locked place of detention for demonic powers and principalities. The demonic aspect of the beast rises from the abyss (Revelation 11:7, 17:8). During the millennium, Satan is imprisoned there (Revelation 20:1-3, 7). Demons dreaded being sent there (Luke 8:31). During the fifth trumpet, demonic locusts are released from this place (Revelation 9).

Algorithms. A computer program designed to solve problems. For example, search engines use algorithms to find information. However, they can be programmed to perform very complex, even nefarious functions. With access to global financial data, the image of the beast is likely to utilize algorithms to identify which individuals have received the mark of the beast and those who have not. This will give the image of the beast the information to decide who can buy or sell, live, die, or be incarcerated (Rev 13:14-18).

Alpha and the Omega. The first and last letters of the Greek alphabet, also serving as a divine title declared by the Lord (Revelation 1:8, 21:6, 22:13).

Ancient of Days. A title for God found in the book of Daniel (7:9, 13, 22).

Angel of the Lord. (Angel of Yahweh). Primarily used in the Old Testament to describe God's appearance in angelic form (e.g., Exodus 3:2-5, Zechariah 3:1-6).

Antichrist. This term signifies opposition to, an adversary of, or instead of Christ. It appears only in 1 John 2:18, 22; 4:3, and 2 John 1:7. In the last days, it pertains to the final wicked dictator who will rule the world just prior to the Lord's second coming. While he is known by various names, in Revelation, he is referred to as "the beast" (Revelation 13:1). In 2 Thessalonians 2, he is called *the son of perdition* (or destruction) and *the man of sin* (or lawlessness) (2 Thessalonians 2:3-4). In Daniel, he is identified as the "little horn" (Daniel 7:8).

Antebellum. This refers to the period before the war, particularly before the Civil War, covering the time after the War of 1812 and leading up to the Civil War in 1861.

Apocalyptic. Relating to judgments associated with the end of the world or future judgments described in the book of Revelation. This term is also used to characterize significant calamities, whether natural or human-made (e.g., devastating wildfires or the aftermath of war may be described as apocalyptic).

Apocalyptic Literature. Writings that focus on the apocalypse, such as the books of Daniel and Revelation, contain highly figurative and symbolic language that typically concerns the end of the world. This literature is also found in ancient Jewish writings such as the Book of Enoch.

Armageddon. Mentioned solely in Revelation 16:16. The term means "mount of Megiddo," referring to the plain of Megiddo in Israel, believed to be the location of the final battle where the world's armies will converge as they approach Jerusalem. This will be the site where the beast and his forces will make a futile stand against Christ and His heavenly army (Revelation 19:11-21). After the battle, blood will flow for 200 miles (Rev 14:20), and the Lord will call for the birds to devour the dead from the armies that gathered against the Lord (19:17-18,21).

Artificial Intelligence (AI). Refers to technology that imitates human intelligence using advanced computers. AI significantly surpasses human capabilities in analyzing, creating, problem-solving, and processing information. It can manage millions, if not billions, of data points in mere seconds. The likelihood that the Antichrist will utilize artificial intelligence is quite high. The false prophet will command the creation of the image of the beast that is then "brought to life." This image will likely be powered by AI technology due to its ability to distinguish between individuals who have and those who have not received the mark of the beast worldwide. This task alone far exceeds human capability and would necessitate the integration of hi-tech algorithms and international banking data with AI technology. The image of the beast will have the authority to determine life and death without the ability to show mercy or compassion, as it is a machine, not a human. They create the image of the beast; thus, it is not organic, yet it will operate like a human (Rev 13:11-18). The next step in AI is AGI, (artificial general intelligence), where computers can function in the full spectrum of human cognition (the ability to learn and process information) but far beyond human capability.

Asclepius. The Greek god associated with healing, possibly linked to the city of Pergamum, symbolized by a single snake entwined around a healing staff.

Asia Minor. An ancient region in the first century that corresponds to present-day Türkiye (Turkey), where seven cities and their local churches received messages in chapters two and three of Revelation. The Lord provided specific messages for each church that included critiques, commendations, encouragement, rebukes, and remedies.

Aspringius (of Beja). A sixth-century Latin Church Father who composed a commentary on the Book of Revelation, though only fragments of his work remain.

Avarice. An extreme greed for wealth or material possessions.

B

Babylon, Commercial. The international commercial hub of the end times will serve as a draw for entertainment, trade, indulgence, and revelry, enticing thrill seekers, both great and small, as well as political and business elites and heads of state. Babylon will promote every conceivable form of immortality. This center of wickedness could be a current city or one that could be built in the future. The Lord will use the beast to launch an attack on her and she will be destroyed by fire in one hour (Rev 17:16-18;18:1-24).

Babylon, Mystical. A wicked religious system stemming from Nimrod's ancient city of Babel (Gen 10-11) that promotes and propagates false religion and idolatry throughout the Earth and down through the ages. She is also called the mother of prostitutes because she spreads heresy and false doctrine.

BDAG (Bauer, Danker, Arndt, and Gingrich) a widely used and respected scholarly Greek Lexicon.

Beast (the). See Antichrist

Beatitudes. A beatitude is a divine pronouncement of blessing upon the righteous or faithful consisting of "the blessed are" statements declared during Jesus' sermon on the mount. However, in Revelation, seven beatitudes are also found (1:3; 14:13; 16:15; 19:9; 20:6; 22:7, 14).

Bond-servants. Pertaining to the servants of the Lord, the concept is that those born again are redeemed by the precious blood of the Lamb. The Lord declares, "...you are not your own? For you have been bought with a price..." (1 Cor 6:19-20), and our soul, spirit and body belong to the Lord. Bond-servants live to please the Lord, not themselves.

Bottomless Pit. (see the Abyss)

Bowl (or vial). In the book of Revelation, bowls containing the wrath of God are poured out by seven angels on the kingdom of the beast at the end of the age, just before the return of Christ (Rev 15-16).

Brookes, James Hall (1830–1897). A Presbyterian minister recognized as the father of American Dispensationalism and a mentor to C. I. Scofield. Although he attended Princeton Theological Seminary in 1853–1854, he was unable to complete his studies due to financial constraints. Nonetheless, Brookes' lack of formal seminary education did not impede his achievements. He was ordained by the Miami Presbytery and served congregations in Ohio and St. Louis, Missouri. Brookes was a compelling conference speaker, presiding over the Niagara Bible Conference and participating in the International Bible Conference. Through his connection with John Nelson Darby and his own Bible study, Brookes contributed his insights to Dispensation-alism, which he imparted to his most notable disciple, C. I. Scofield. (Also see Dispensationalism Comes to the United States).

C

Caduceus. A short staff entwined by two snakes, occasionally topped with wings, carried by the mythological figure Hermes, from which the contemporary medical symbol originates.

Caligula. The third Roman emperor who ruled from AD 37 to 41. His complete name was Gaius Julius Caesar Augustus Germanicus, a de-praved and cruel leader who was murdered by the Praetorian guards.

Canon of Scripture (canonical). The sixty-six books (thirty-nine of the Old Testament and twenty-seven of the New Testament) that are considered to be authoritative and inspired. The word *canon* means measuring rod from which a standard can be determined. The list of the books in the authorized Bible, were finalized during several coun-cils such as the council of Rome (382) and the Councils of Carthage (397, 419). The Catholic Bible has seventy-three books because it con-tains the apocrypha, seven books not considered inspired by Protes-tants. The Ethiopian Orthodox Bible contains 88 books.

Chafer, Lewis Sperry. Chafer was a soloist for Arthur T. Reed and Dwight L. Moody, who studied music at Oberlin College for three se-mesters and later worked as an assistant pastor in Ohio and New York. In 1901, he met C.I. Scofield and became closely affiliated with him, serving as an extension teacher at Scofield's correspondence school. Chafer became a significant speaker during the Bible Conference Movement. Although he did not graduate from seminary, he trans-ferred his credentials to the Presbyterian Church in 1907. While pas-toring at Scofield's previous church and overseeing a mission found-ed by Scofield in 1924, Chafer established the Evangelical Theological College, which was renamed Dallas Theological Seminary (DTS) in

1936. Chafer became one of the leading advocates of Dispensationalism in the twentieth century. He authored several books and held
the position of president and professor of systematic theology of DTS
until his death in 1952. (See Introduction: Dispensationalism Comes
to the United States.)

Cherubim. Angelic beings, first mentioned in Genesis 3:24 and frequently referred to in the Old Testament, are typically associated with
God's direct presence. Symbolically, they were fixtures on the ark of
the covenant whose wings covered the mercy seat (Exod 25:20). They
are also described as multi-winged, possessing the body of a lion, the
wings of a bird, and the face of a human. They are likely similar to the
beings that John referred to as "living creatures." Ezekiel gives a similar description but calls them Cherubim (Ezek 10:14-15).

Church (the). The ekklesia, an assembly, the called-out ones. All individuals who have been born again since the Day of Pentecost up to
the rapture. The church also referred to as the body of Christ, is not an
organization but a living organism of people saved during the church
age rather than edifices, buildings, and institutions.

Contingent being. A contingent being is reliant on God, the supreme
being, for its very existence. Every created being, and everything else in
all creation, is contingent or dependent on God for their existence and
sustenance.

Council of Carthage of 397 AD. The council where the New Testament canon was confirmed. Carthage was located in Tunisia, North
Africa. It is no longer a city today but a suburb of Tunis, where the
ruins of Carthage serve as a tourist attraction.

Cyprian Thascius Caecilius. Cyprianus, Bishop of Carthage (210-
258), is an early Christian church leader and author whose writing
helps us understand issues pertinent to early Christian thought and
theology on subjects such as the antichrist.

D

Dallas Theological Seminary (DTS). An institution established by Lewis Sperry Chafer in 1924, originally named the Evangelical Theology College and renamed Dallas Theological Seminary in 1936. DTS has emerged as the leading institution for dispensational eschatology and continues to be a highly respected Evangelical seminary, producing many well-known pastors, church leaders, scholars, and authors who advocate for and uphold dispensationalism.

Daniel's Seventieth Week. Refers to a week of years recorded in Dan 9:27. It marks the last seven-year period of the current age. At the start of this week, a covenant will be established by the person who becomes the Antichrist, likely a peace agreement between Israel and its neighboring countries. This covenant may ensure the safety and peace of all parties involved. However, three and a half years into the seven-year time frame, the Antichrist will violate the covenant, halt the daily sacrifices made in the temple, commit the abomination of desolation, and proclaim himself as God. This action initiates the great tribulation, which will lead to the Lord's return and the Antichrist's defeat at the end of the seven years.

Darby, John Nelson (1800-1882). An Anglican minister born in London, England, to affluent parents John Darby and Anne Vaughn, being the youngest of six sons. His father accumulated wealth by supplying goods to the Royal Navy, while his mother's family, the Vaughns, had a considerable interest in slaveholding in the Caribbean. The Vaughn family also maintained close ties with Benjamin Franklin and other founding fathers (Dr. Crawford Gribben, J.N. Darby, and the Roots of Dispensationalism). In 1819, after graduating from Trinity College in Dublin, Darby briefly pursued a career in law. He then became a priest in the Church of Ireland but grew disillusioned with the institutional church. In 1831, he departed from the Church of England and joined a group of like-minded individuals who rejected the formalism of the institutional church and clerical hierarchy, later known as "The Plymouth Brethren." One of the Brethren's areas of study was eschatology, where Darby formulated what would eventually be recognized as dispensationalism. Between 1859 and 1874, Darby made several trips to the United States and Canada. His dispensational ideas gained traction as he spoke at churches and Bible conferences, supported by his connections with influential figures such as Dwight L. Moody, James Hall Brookes, and others. While Darby introduced a version of Dispensationalism to America, it was individuals like Brookes and C.I. Scofield who significantly expanded upon Darby's concepts. Additionally, Darby was a proficient linguist and created his translation of the Bible called the Darby Translation. His influence on fundamentalist and Evangelical Christians is immense, having a profound effect on American eschatology and the interpretation of the book of Revelation.

Day of Christ. The day of reward for the church associated with the rapture and resurrection. This judgment is only for the righteous to determine the level of reward in eternity. Though this judgment is not to determine one's eternal destination, Christians will answer for the good and the bad done while alive on Earth. On this day the believers' works shall be tried in the fire. The works that are not burned up will receive a reward. Those works that are burned up that believer will suffer the loss, but themselves will be saved (1 Cor 3:12-15).

Day of Pentecost. The term Pentecost means fiftieth and refers to an annual Jewish festival that takes place 50 days after Passover. However, in Acts 2, on the "Day of Pentecost," the Lord bestowed the Holy Spirit in accordance with Joel's prophecy (Joel 2:28-32), marking the birth of the Church.

Demonic principality. Demonic principalities refer to orders or hierarchies of evil angels. In Ephesians 6:12, they are identified as principalities, powers, the rulers of the darkness of this world, and spiritual wickedness in high places (or heavenly realms). (See also Eph 3:10.) A clear instance of an evil angelic principality is found in Daniel, where a godly angel was obstructed from reaching Daniel. This hindrance was caused by the prince of Persia, the demonic ruler over the Persian kingdom. The godly angel was aided by Michael the archangel, referred to as "one of the chief princes," which enabled the angel to proceed to Daniel. The godly angel informed Daniel that he had been delayed for three weeks by the prince of Persia—the demonic principality. Also refer to 2 Pet 2:10-11 for "angelic majesties."

Dispensational(ism). A method of biblical interpretation that emerged as a movement in the late nineteenth century credited to Anglican minister John Nelson Darby, although some concepts of Dispensationalism predated him. While Dispensationalism is now a well-established doctrinal framework, it arose from personal study and the individual interpretations of several key figures, including John Nelson Darby, James Hall Brookes, Dwight L. Moody, C. I. Scofield, and Lewis Sperry Chafer, none of whom completed formal seminary training. As Dispensationalism gained traction in America, others significantly contributed to its development, including James Hall Brookes, who is regarded as the father of American Dispensationalism. Brookes mentored C. I. Scofield and imparted this doctrinal system to him. Later, Scofield promoted Dispensationalism in the Scofield Reference Bible, where he described a dispensation as "a period during which man is tested in respect of obedience to some specific revelation of the will of God." "At the core of dispensationalism is the division of all time into distinct administrations (or dispensations), viewed as different phases in God's progressive revelation" (Weber). Scofield identified seven dispensations: Innocence, Conscience, Human Government, Promise, Law, Grace, and Kingdom. Thus, the American interpretation of Dispensationalism extends Darby's views. The first edition of the Scofield Reference Bible was released by Oxford Press in 1909 and sold millions of copies, thereby spreading this teaching around the world. Other key beliefs of Dispensationalism include a clear separation between the church and Israel, an imminent return of Christ, and a pretribulation rapture. Ironically, the term "dispensationalism" was coined in the twentieth century after Darby's passing in 1882. Modifications to Dispensationalism are still ongoing. (See Introduction, Dispensationalism Comes to the United States).

Doctrine of Imminence. This doctrine maintains that there are no signs or prophetic events that must occur before the rapture of the church. The concept of imminence implies that the rapture could happen unexpectedly at any moment. In the first century, Christians believed that Christ would return within their lifetime. However, this represented a misinterpretation of God's intentions for the church's extensive future, which has continued into the twenty-first century. Among the key advocates of imminence in the 19th century were John Nelson Darby and, even more prominently, James Hall Brookes, a Presbyterian pastor from St. Louis, Missouri, who is regarded as the father of American dispensationalism. The doctrine of imminence was a compelling feature of dispensationalism that was readily adopted by those who held postmillennial views until the Civil War and the collapse of the Confederacy. The belief in an imminent return of Christ was much more appealing than the distant return suggested by postmillennial optimism. Another reason for the preference for imminence was that it circumvented the issues associated with attempting to predict the exact day of Christ's return, which always resulted in disappointment and embarrassment. Many southern Christians were discontented with the political and social climate that followed emancipation and Reconstruction. Nevertheless, the doctrine of imminence provided hope that Christ would return at any moment to deliver judgment on what many Southerners viewed as an irredeemable world that emerged after the Civil War. Former Confederate soldier C.I. Scofield championed the doctrine of imminence in his widely popular Scofield Reference Bible, which contributed to the widespread acceptance of dispensationalism, pretribulationism, and the doctrine of imminence throughout the world.

Domitian. Also known as Emperor Titus Flavius Caesar Domitianus Augustus, lived AD 51–96; Roman emperor from AD 81 to 96. The son of Vespasian, the third (and last) emperor of the Flavian Dynasty. It was Domitian who banished John to the Island of Patmos, where the book of Revelation was written.

E

Eschatology/Eschaton. The theological subject that focuses on "the last things" and subjects related to the end times, such as the apocalypse, the return of Christ, the great tribulation, the Antichrist, the mark of the beast, the final judgments, the millennium, the New Heaven and Earth, the eternal age to follow and all other subjects related to the end of the age and beyond.

Esoteric. Knowledge or information that is understood by select individuals who share in a secretive special interest, especially mystics, the occult, or secretive societies or groups.

Eusebius of Caesarea (260-340 AD). A Greek, Syro-Palestinian historian regarded as the father of Christian history, who chronicled many events during the early Christian era. In his promotion and defense of Christianity, he was quite prolific, though he is best known for his work titled Ecclesiastical History.

Eye salve. A type of unknown ointment applied to the eye to alleviate eye conditions. The city of Laodicea was renowned for its medical school and the production of this eye salve, which some associate with the hot springs found there, which some believed to have medicinal properties.

F

False Prophet (the). The "second beast" mentioned in Rev. 13:11-18, a religious figure endowed with miraculous powers who will govern alongside the beast. He will cause the world to worship the beast as God and will command that an image of the beast be created for worship purposes. He, alongside the beast, will also compel the world to accept the mark of the beast. At the battle of Armageddon, the false prophet and the beast will be cast alive into the lake of fire upon the Lord's return (Rev 19:20).

First and Last. (See Alpha and Omega.)

First Resurrection. Refers to the resurrection of the righteous, encompassing all those whose names are recorded in the Lamb's book of life. This first resurrection takes place at least a thousand years prior to the second resurrection, which occurs during the great white throne judgment of the wicked.

Firstborn of the dead. A designation that not only highlights Jesus' supremacy in the resurrection but also indicates that he is the first of a kind to be glorified or resurrected from the dead. Those redeemed by the Lamb's blood will also partake in this glorification, with Christ being the first of this kind to rise from the dead. Also see Col 1:18.

G

Gabriel. The name signifies "strong man of God." Gabriel is the divine messenger (angel) who explained Daniel's visions and is likely the angel who faced the demonic authority known as the "prince of Persia" in Daniel 10. He also appears in the New Testament to proclaim the births of John the Baptist (Luke 1:8–20) and Jesus (Luke 1:26–38).

Gentile(s). Refers to any ethnic or people group that does not belong to the twelve tribes of Israel.

Gigantomachy. This term describes the battle between the gods of

Olympus and the rebelling giants, depicted on the altar of Zeus located in the city of Pergamum, one of the seven churches mentioned in Revelation.

Great Embarrassment. In the nineteenth century, Baptist minister William Miller convinced many followers that Jesus would return between 1843 and 1844. The significant embarrassment arose when Christ's return did not occur as he had predicted.

Great Tribulation. (See the Tribulation.)

H

Hanukkah. The Jewish *Feast of Dedication* was established in 164 BC following the vile desecrations of the Jewish Temple in Jerusalem by the Syrian king Antiochus Epiphanes IV three years prior in 167 BC. A revolt led by Judas Maccabeus ensued, which successfully defeated and expelled the Syrians. After this victory, the temple required cleansing and rededication. To mark this new beginning, an eight-day celebration was instituted, which has since become the annual celebration of Hanukkah. The treachery of Antiochus Epiphanes foreshadows the ultimate abomination of desolation to come, when the Antichrist desecrates the rebuilt temple during Daniel's Seventieth Week. Similar to Antiochus, the Antichrist will set up his image in the temple but also proclaim himself to be God (2 Thess 2:3-4, Rev 13:14-17).

Harps. Stringed instruments used for worship and praise not only on Earth but also in heaven. In 5:8, the twenty-four elders played harps during their worship. In 14:2, heavenly harpers played their harps, and in 15:2, those who triumphed over the beast and his image played harps and sang praises to the Lord after reaching heaven.

Hidden Manna. (See 2:17 note.)

Hypostatic Union. The theological concept that Christ was fully human and fully God at the same time. Debates about Christ's divine and human nature began in the early centuries and was discussed extensively during the councils of Nicaea, Chalcedon and others.

I

Imminent Return of Christ. A concept essential to the Pretrib rapture theory. It means that Christ can return at any time without any prophetic sign that must occur first. Additionally, no end times prophecy signs recorded in Scripture can be used as a sign for the rapture. The doctrine of imminence insists the rapture is a signless event. Without the doctrine of imminence, a Pretrib rapture is not feasible or defensible. Therefore, the Pretrib rapture position relies heavily on the concept. If one prophecy must occur before the rapture, then the rapture cannot be imminent.

Inerrancy. The concept that the Bible is without errors in its original writings (the autographs). Inerrancy is based on the doctrine of God. If God cannot lie or make mistakes, then whatever He says is true. The Bible declares, "All Scripture is inspired by God and profitable for teaching, for reproof, for correction, for training in righteousness; so that the man of God may be adequate, equipped for every good work" (2 Tim 3:16-17). Jesus declared, "Sanctify them through thy truth: thy word is truth" (John 17:17). Jesus also declared, "...the scriptures cannot be broken" (John 10:35). Since Scripture is God breathed (exhaled) it is inerrant and trustworthy.

Innumerable Multitude. Refers to those who came out from the "great tribulation," depicted in triumphant glory standing before the throne of God, a place of prestige and honor. These redeemed individuals are not the "left behinds," as dispensationalists claim. This group of Christians is the final generation of church saints who have come through the great tribulation—a unique period—of which no other believers on Earth during any age, either Old or New Testaments, have experienced. These saints have the honor to serve God in His temple. There is no greater honor in heaven than to serve God because nothing in heaven is better than Him.

Irenaeus. A second-century church father and bishop of Lyons in Gaul. One of the foremost early Christian theologians, who defended the orthodoxy of Christian doctrine. His writings also give confirmation that the apostle John is the author of Revelation.

Island of Patmos. A small island located in the Aegean Sea, off the southwestern coast of Asia Minor. This small rocky island was used for the exile of criminals who labored in the mines. It is on this isolated island that John was exiled, where he later received and wrote the book of Revelation. (Also see Rev 1:9a note).

Israel (modern day). A small yet influential nation with a population of 9.5 million, situated in the Middle East, where Tel Aviv serves as its capital, although many regard Jerusalem as the true capital. The nation and its people have a rich historical background. It is through Israel that God chose to reveal Himself to the world via numerous saints, servants, and prophets as recorded in the Scriptures. The ancestry of the people of Israel can be traced back to Abraham, Isaac, and Jacob. God changed Jacob's name to Israel (Gen 32:28). Israel had twelve sons: Reuben, Simeon, Levi, Judah, Zebulun, Issachar, Dan, Gad, Asher, Naphtali, Joseph, and Benjamin. These sons became the twelve tribes of Israel. Jacob's fourth son, Judah (the Jews), is the tribe from which Jesus is descended. The entire Bible, whether directly or indirectly, chronicles God's interactions with the world through the nation of Israel. Both Israel and Jerusalem hold significant importance in key events anticipated to occur at the end of the age. After the fall of Jerusalem in 70 AD, the Jewish people were scattered worldwide. However, on May 14th, 1948, the Jews returned to their homeland, reestablishing the state of Israel. Since their return, Israel has been in a continuous state of alertness and conflict due to the hostile actions of neighboring nations. In Revelation 7, 144,000 (twelve thousand individuals from each tribe of Israel) will be marked by God. Jerusalem is the city where the Antichrist will defile the rebuilt temple, where global forces will assemble to confront the Lord during the battle of Armageddon, and where the Lord will return to establish His kingdom on Earth, ruling the world from Jerusalem during the millennium.

J

Jerusalem. The name means "habitation of peace," is an ancient city that holds sacred significance for Jews, Christians, and Muslims. It is also known as the *City of God* and the *City of David*. The city has an extensive history that is recorded in the Bible and has a crucial role in end times prophecies. All nations will gather against it, but the Lord will return to save Israel, the Jews, and Jerusalem. This is the city where Jesus made His triumphant entry (Matt 21:1-11) and where He mourned over Jerusalem for being the city that killed its prophets (Matt 23:37-39). It is also the location of His crucifixion and resurrection. In eternity, the New Jerusalem will be the capital city of the New Heaven and New Earth.

Jezebel. The false prophetess at the church of Thyatira who seduced the church to commit acts of immorality through her teaching. Whether Jezebel was her actual name is unknown. However, her sins are reminiscent of the wicked Queen Jezebel of 1 Kings 16:31 and 21:25, who promoted witchcraft and whoredoms (2 Kings 9:22) that brought judgment on herself and her husband King Ahab.

K

Katecho. The Greek term meaning "restrainer" is crucial for understanding what is preventing the revelation (uncovering) of the Antichrist. Pretribulationists argue that the Holy Spirit and the church are responsible for this restraint. This traditional viewpoint lacks explicit scriptural support. However, Revelation 11:7 and 17:8 indicate that the beast rises from the abyss, which serves as a prison for demonic powers. Pretribulationists have not factored in this detail while formulating their theory regarding the force that restrains the Antichrist's revelation. The scriptures clearly state that the demonic nature of the beast is confined in the abyss. This is significant because an unnamed angel referred to as "he" and "his" possesses the key to the abyss and has a chain to actively restrain those imprisoned there (Rev 20:1-3,7). (See also the excursuses on the Restraining Ministry of Angels and the Angelic Restrainer Versus the Holy Spirit.)

Key(s). Keys symbolize divine or spiritual authority, granting the right or privilege to open, close, or manage something. This power was bestowed upon Peter, referred to as the keys of the Kingdom of heaven (Matt 16:19). In the book of Revelation, keys are mentioned in four verses: 1:18 speaks of the keys of death and hades (hell), 3:7 refers to the key of David, and there are two mentions concerning the abyss, the sealed prison for demons, in 9:1 and 20:1.

Kingdom of the beast. The global domain of the beast's political, economic, and military influence, empowered by Satan. This empire consists of a confederation of ten nations led by ten kings who grant their power to the beast, enabling him to govern the world (Rev 17:12-14).

L

Lampstands. Lampstands were sacred ornamental items that played an important role in the worship of God in the ancient tabernacle and temple, as well as in heaven. The lampstand was made up of a base and shaft crafted from pure gold, which held oil vessels that burned to provide light or held candlesticks. In the book of Revelation, lampstands are referenced in two contexts: (1) the seven golden lampstands symbolize the seven churches of Asia Minor. Additionally, lampstands refer to the two witnesses whose prophetic ministry of 1260 days will cause significant disruption worldwide.

Laodicea. (Refer to Laodicea "History Note.")

Late Great Planet Earth. A bestselling nonfiction book authored by Hal Lindsey in 1970 that probed end-time prophecy events. Lindsey emphasized current news events, geopolitical alignments, and the rising frequency and severity of natural disasters, which are described as "birth pangs" in the Mt. Olivet discourse (Matt. 24). Lindsey, a graduate of DTS, was a strong advocate of the Pretrib rapture position. His writings generated substantial interest, introducing a new generation to eschatological and apocalyptic topics. Lindsey authored over 50 books and was a well-known conference speaker, television host, and Bible teacher.

Left Behind. A fictional book series authored by Tim LaHaye and Jerry Jenkins, released in 1995. It focuses on the events of the end times that take place during Daniel's seventieth week, including the rapture and the emergence of the Antichrist. While the narratives in the books and films are fictional, they strongly advocated for the dispensational belief in a pretribulation rapture. The series has sold over 80 million copies, and the original movie starring Kirk Cameron was well-received by evangelical audiences.

The Lord's day. A term mentioned in Revelation 1:10, which most interpret as referring to Sunday, the first day of the week. (See 1:10 note).

Luther, Martin. A German Catholic priest and theologian of the sixteenth century, he was recognized as the father of the Protestant Reformation. Luther's protest was in response to the Catholic church practice that encouraged the sale of indulgences as a means of salvation. Luther saw this method of fundraising as reprehensible and unbiblical, insisting that Scripture taught salvation cannot be earned by good works but through grace and faith alone. The protest that Luther began eventually led to the emergence of the Lutheran church and Protestant denominations. Luther also held anti-Semitic sentiments and had a strong dislike for the book of Revelation, seeing it as neither apostolic nor prophetic. However, Luther did believe that the pope fulfilled the role of the beast of Revelation.

<h2 style="text-align:center">M</h2>

Maccabean Revolt. This uprising is named after the Maccabean family, who successfully revolted against Antiochus Epiphanes IV, the king of Syria, in 167 BC, following the siege of Jerusalem and the desecration of the Jewish temple. Furious about the actions of the Syrians, Judas Maccabeus led the uprising that resulted in the defeat of Antiochus and his forces. Once the Syrians were conquered, Jerusalem was restored, and the temple needed to be purified. In honor of the dedication of the temple, an eight-day celebration was initiated, which became the Jewish festival of Hanukkah.

Machine learning. This refers to a form of autonomous intelligence that enables systems to learn and enhance their performance based on data without needing explicit programming.

Man of sin. This is another term for the Antichrist (2 Thess 2:3).

Maranatha. This phrase translates to "our Lord come."

Merism. This is a rhetorical device where two contrasting parts of a whole are combined to refer to the entire entity. An example of a merism would be "I looked high and low..." (See 1:8 note.)

Michael the Archangel. He is the most notable angel mentioned in the Scriptures. In Revelation, Michael leads an army of holy angels to defeat the devil and his angels, casting them out of Heaven to the Earth (Rev 12:7-10). His first mention occurs in Daniel 10:13 and again in Daniel 12:1, where he is described as the prince who defends Israel. In Daniel 10:4-21, Michael assists another angel engaged in battle with the prince of Persia, the demonic force controlling Persia. Jude 9 references the apocryphal text known as *The Assumption of Moses,* which recounts Michael contending with Satan over Moses' body.

Midtrib. This is an abbreviation for the midtribulation rapture position, which asserts that the rapture takes place at or near the midpoint of Daniel's Seventieth Week. (See Rapture position chart p. lxii)

Millennium. A broad eschatological topic that varies based on one's eschatological perspective. For futurists, the millennium is a literal thousand-year period during which Christ returns to reign from Jerusalem, characterized by justice, peace, prosperity, and significantly extended life spans, with fierce animals becoming gentle (Isa 65:20-25). For Amillennialists and Postmillennialists, the millennium represents a non-specific period that has been ongoing since Christ's first advent and continues today. (See Introduction, Millennial views.)

Millerites. These were individuals who followed William Miller in the nineteenth century. Miller and his followers, who numbered in the tens of thousands, believed that Christ would return around 1843-44. Miller's followers eventually became the Seventh Day Adventists. (See Introduction, Dispensationalism Comes to the United States.)

Morning Star. An award given in glory. In Revelation 2:28, Jesus grants the morning star to those "who keep his deeds to the end." However, in 22:16, Jesus is referred to as *the bright and morning star.* (Refer to notes on 2:28 and 22:16.)

Mount Olivet Discourse. This refers to the discussion Jesus had with his disciples on the Mount of Olives in Jerusalem, where he foretold the destruction of the temple that took place in 70 AD and provided signs of his second coming at the end of the age. This discourse can be found in Matthew 24:1-25:46, Mark 13:1-37, and Luke 21:5-36.

Mystery. God's secret or concealed plans that He reveals to His servants, which are otherwise unknown or unknowable.

N

Nero. A wicked emperor of Rome, the sixth in the line of Caesars who governed the Roman Empire from 54 to 68 AD. Following a fire that erupted at the Circus Maximus in Rome, it rapidly spread and devastated a significant portion of the city. In response, Nero blamed the Christians, leading to severe persecution and martyrdom of the saints. Preterists believe that the beast mentioned in Revelation 13 refers to Nero and that 666 is the numerical representation of Nero's name.

New Apostolic Reformation (NAR). It is a contemporary movement that asserts modern apostles and prophets have the divine authority and revelation from God to bring about change in society through strong Spirit-filled leadership. Church growth and missiologist Professor C. Peter Wagner (2016) coined the phrase "New Apostolic Reformation" after evaluating super churches in Africa and China and their remarkable growth under the leadership of charismatic and Pentecostal pastors. These churches were sensitive to the Spirit and were growing while denominational churches were in decline. This movement has attracted both denominational and nondenominational churches, comprising evangelical, charismatic, and Pentecostal Christians. It is one of the fastest-growing global church movements, but it is not a specific denomination or organization.

Niagara Bible Conferences. Well attended conferences that took place in Canada and the United States during the summer months from 1883 to 1897, where premillennial, dispensational, Pretrib eschatology was promoted and popularized. These conferences attracted many notable ministers including Dwight L. Moody and James Hall Brookes that featured various prominent dispensational speakers. These conferences were the platform for the acceptance of dispensationalism across the United States and Canada. Such meetings were prevalent during a period known as the Bible Conference Movement that emerged after the 1870s. (See Dispensationalism Comes to the United States.)

The Nicolaitans. A group of ancient heretics responsible for spreading false teachings in the churches of Ephesus and Pergamum. (See 2:6 note)

O

Oceumenius. A theologian from the sixth or seventh century who wrote a commentary on the book of Revelation. His writings help us understand some of the beliefs concerning eschatology during the early centuries.

Origen. A respected church father and teacher in Alexandria Egypt that lived from 185 to 254 AD. Among his many contributions his writings affirmed John's authorship of the book of Revelation.

P

Parousia. A Greek term meaning "presence" or "coming" is typically used in an eschatological context to refer to the second coming of Christ at the end of the age. The concept of the Parousia delay arises from the belief held by first-century Christians that the Lord would return during their lifetime. However, as this did not occur, their understanding of the timing of His return had to be revised. Some believe that Peter addressed this issue in 2 Peter 3:1-9, where he responds to mockers who question, "Where is the promise of his coming?" However, Peter's response was that the Lord is not slow in fulfilling His promises but that a day with the Lord is like a thousand years, and a thousand years is like a day. Instead, time was being provided for people to come to the Lord for salvation.

Peace Covenant. In an end-times context, the peace covenant refers to "the covenant with many" foretold in Daniel 9:27, which will be supported or guaranteed by the individual who becomes the Antichrist. It is thought that this covenant will ensure Israel's safety and peace with its neighboring countries. Many believe that nations such as Russia, Iran, Turkey, Libya, Ethiopia, and others mentioned in Ezekiel 38 will observe Israel living in security, having become a nation without walls or gates (38:1-11). Currently, Israel has constructed hundreds of miles of walls since the early 2000s. However, once the seven-year peace covenant is established, the Antichrist will break it three and a half years later by stopping the daily sacrifices and grain offerings. He will enter the rebuilt temple and proclaim himself as God, thereby committing the abomination of desolation, which will trigger the great tribulation (Matthew 24:15,21).

Plagues. Throughout the Scriptures, any disastrous visitation or judgment. In the book of Revelation, whether from the seals, trumpets, or bowls, it is considered a plague and part of God's judgment events.

Plain of Megiddo. The location in Israel where the world's armies will assemble for the battle of Armageddon the final battle of this age. Some equate Megiddo with the valley of Jezreel. Meggido is approximately seventy miles north of Jerusalem.

Plymouth Brethren. A nondenominational evangelical fellowship that originated in Plymouth, England, and Dublin, Ireland, formed by individuals dissatisfied with the formalism of the denominational churches in England. They began gathering for Bible study and prayer, focusing on missions and evangelism. John Nelson Darby, one of their most prominent leaders, advocated for eschatology and developed a form of dispensationalism during his time with the Brethren, which he introduced to the United States during his visits between 1859 and 1874. Today, there are approximately 1,600 "Open Brethren" assemblies in the United States and Canada.

Polycarp. A respected and beloved bishop of the church of Smyrna who was burnt at the stake for refusing to declare that Caesar is lord, around 155 AD. Tradition holds that Polycarp was a disciple of the apostle John.

Postbellum. Refers to the period following the Civil War, such as the Reconstruction era.

Postmillennialism. (See Millennial views.)

Posttrib. The abbreviation for the post tribulation rapture position. This teaching asserts that the rapture will occur at the end of Daniel's seventieth week. (See the rapture position chart.)

Preeminence. The preeminence of Christ signifies that Jesus Christ is the highest and supreme above all. Colossians 1:18 states, "that in everything he might be preeminent." In Revelation 1:5, Christ is referred to as *the firstborn from the dead,* indicating that He is also preeminent among those who will be glorified and will follow in the likeness of His resurrection.

Premillennialism. (See Introduction/Millennial views.)

Preterist Interpretation. This position asserts that Revelation is primarily historic (See Introduction/Historic Methods of Interpretation.)

Pretribulation Rapture Theory (Pretrib). This rapture position asserts that the rapture will take place before the beginning of Daniel's seventieth week (the seven-year tribulation period). This view also teaches the rapture is imminent with no signs that must occur prior to it. This theory also insists that the entire church age is represented in Rev chapters 2-3, and that the church is not on earth during the events of chapter 6-19. (See rapture position chart.)

Prewrath. This rapture position argues that the church remains on Earth during the reign of the beast, with the rapture occurring between the middle and end of Daniel's Seventieth Week.

Progressive Dispensationalism. Progressive dispensationalism is a modification of traditional dispensationalism. Though, in most cases the differences are not major, Progressive dispensationalists view the dispensations as progressive stages in salvific history hence the term progressive. However, a key distinction would be that some Progressive dispensationalists do not assert the necessity of a pretribulation rapture and lean closer to the posttribulation rapture position. Another difference is progressives assert that Christ is already sitting and ruling on David's throne although it has yet to be manifested. This concept is known as "already but not yet." Progressive dispensationalist also allows for more flexibility between the dispensations and loosen the distinctions between Israel and the church.

Proslavery Millennialism. A term used to describe the belief held by many southern Christians in the Antebellum South that slavery was divinely ordained, supported by the Bible, and would persist up to and after Christ's return and throughout the millennium. See Dispensationalism Comes to the United States.

Protevangelium. It is the first prophetic allusion to the Gospel message that the Messiah was to come to destroy the works of the devil through His sacrificial death on the cross. "...I will put enmity between you and the woman, And between your seed and her seed; He shall bruise you on the head, and you shall bruise him on the heel" Gen 3:15.

Pseudo-Ephraem. This text is attributed to Ephrem the Syrian (306–373 AD) under a pseudonym, whose writings are cited to support a Pretrib rapture of the church. However, a more thorough examination of his texts suggests otherwise. See Introduction/Dispensationalism Comes to the United States.

R

Rebellion. The Greek term associated with rebellion is apostasia, which signifies opposition to established authority. It often pertains to disobedience towards God. Additionally, it indicates a departure or falling away from the faith. For instance, in 2 Thess 2:3, the KJV translates it as "falling away," while the NIV uses "rebellion," and the NASB refers to it as "apostasy." The antichrist, or the beast, will instigate a global rebellion against Christ, marked by the persecution of the saints, imprisonment, martyrdom, blasphemy against God and those in heaven, and by compelling individuals to accept the mark of the beast. The final rebellion will occur when Satan deceives the world once more after being released from the abyss following the Millennium. However, this rebellion will be annihilated by God with fire from heaven (Rev. 20:7-10).

Restrainer (the). Concerning 2 Thess 2:6-7, dispensationalist/Pretribulationists assert that the restrainer is the Holy Spirit and the church, despite lacking direct textual evidence to support this claim. Darby promoted this interpretation. However, dispensationalists overlook the demonic nature of the beast that emerges from the abyss, which is a secured prison for demonic powers. The agent that restrains in association with the abyss is an unnamed angel, referred to in the masculine gender (he, his), who restrains with a chain, including Satan, the chief of all wicked principalities (Rev 20:1-3,7). The place of detention is the abyss (the what). (See the Threefold Reality of the Beast Essay/Implications for a Pretrib Position, The Restraining Ministry of Angels, and The Angelic Restrainer Versus the Holy Spirit Excursus.)

Reversal of Pentecost. This concept pertains to the removal of the Holy Spirit and the church at the rapture, which reverses the arrival of the Holy Spirit at the church's inception. However, such an event is not found in any Scripture. (See The Angelic Restrainer Versus the Holy Spirit Excursus, point 4.)

S

Sagacity. Possessing acute discernment and understanding. Having the ability to make sound judgment.

Saints. This term refers to the redeemed individuals, also known as holy ones, mentioned throughout the Scriptures in both the Old and New Testaments. However, in Revelation, the beast engages in conflict with the saints. Pretribulationists argue that these saints are those left behind due to being backslidden Christians and are not part of the church, as the Holy Spirit, who is the restrainer of sin, has been taken away, and the church has already been raptured. However, this commentary asserts that the saints in Revelation 13 are indeed the church, representing the most significant group of church saints the world has ever known because they remain faithful during the most challenging period in human history. (See the Mischaracterization of the Tribulation Saints Excursus and The Tribulation Saints vs. the Church Essay.)

Scofield, C. I. An influential pastor and editor of the Scofield Reference Bible, through which Dispensationalism and the Pretrib rapture spread throughout the world. C.I. Scofield was a former Confederate infantryman, lawyer, and legislator who was also a disciple of James H. Brookes, considered the father of Dispensationalism in America. Scofield was also a highly regarded pastor who, through the Scofield Reference Bible, had a profound impact on fundamentalism, evangelicalism, and the interpretation of the Book of Revelation. Scofield's most notable disciple was Lewis Sperry Chafer, the founder of Dallas Theological Seminary. (Also see Dispensationalism Comes to America.)

Scofield Reference Bible. This reference bible was first published in 1909 by Oxford Press, edited by C. I. Scofield. It featured the Dispensational/Pretribulation position of John Nelson Darby and James Hall Brookes, making it widely recognized. This groundbreaking and immensely popular reference Bible has sold several million copies. The Scofield Bible made a complex eschatological doctrine accessible to ordinary Christians and ministers. Successive revisions came in 1917 and 1967 (Scofield Study Bible). Although other study Bibles adopt a dispensational approach, the influence of the Scofield Bible on Evangelicals and Fundamentalists is immeasurable. C.I. Scofield mentored Lewis Sperry Chafer, who founded Dallas Theological Seminary, the leading institution for teaching dispensationalism.

Second death. This refers to eternal destruction in the lake of fire, designated for those whose names are not recorded in the Lamb's Book of Life. It is first mentioned in the Bible when Jesus speaks of it in His message to Smyrna. Due to the level of torment associated with it and its eternal nature, this judgment is the most severe in Revelation, far exceeding any temporary seal, trumpet, or bowl judgments. Both wicked humans and angels will ultimately face this sentence and penalty as a result of the proceedings at the great white throne judgment.

Seven Mountain Mandate (SMM). This mandate advocates that spirit-filled Christians, under the guidance of contemporary apostles and prophets, should exert influence over seven spheres of influence: education, religion, family, business, government, entertainment, and media. This global initiative aims to convert society to Christianity, creating a golden age that eventually paves the way for Christ to return. Many conservative, evangelical, and Pentecostal Christians aligned with this ideology galvanized their political power and predominantly voted Republican. Many Republican politicians, judges, and legislators align with the SMM. The SMM proceeded out from the NAR movement and is linked to Lance Wallnau and Bill Cunningham. The eschatology would be more aligned with postmillennialism rather than dispensationalism. (See Introduction, Millennial Views/Postmillennialism.)

Seventy Weeks (of Daniel). This prophetic timeframe is found in Dan. 9:24, where the weeks are interpreted as years rather than days, totaling 490 years. Sixty-nine of these weeks (483 years) have already been fulfilled with the crucifixion, resurrection of Jesus, and the fall of Jerusalem in 70 AD. The final week (7 years) remains unfulfilled and is the central focus of much of Revelation and eschatology.

Son of perdition. Also known as the son of destruction in eschatological contexts, this term refers to the Antichrist. However, Jesus' disciple Judas was also referred to as the son of perdition in John 17:12.

T

Temple Institute. This organization, based in Jerusalem, aims to rebuild the Third Temple. According to their website, "The Temple Institute is dedicated to all aspects of the Divine commandment for Israel to build a house for G[o]d's presence, the Holy Temple, on Mount Moriah in Jerusalem. The range of the Institute's involvement with this concept includes education, research, activism, and actual preparation." The future temple is believed to be the site where the Antichrist will perform the abomination of desolation and proclaim himself as God, demanding worship as such.

Tertullian. A theologian and apologist from North Africa, he was a significant figure in the Carthaginian church and the first to use the term Trinity. He is also credited with the phrase, "The blood of the saints was the seed of the church." Tertullian lived from the late second to the early third century, producing most of his writings between 195 and 220 in Carthage, which was a central intellectual and cultural hub in North Africa. He also affirms the authorship of Revelation by the apostle John.

Textual variant. When two or more Greek or Hebrew manuscripts differ in wording from a critically prepared Old Testament or New Testament text, these differences are referred to as "variants." Since early manuscripts were copied by hand, errors in copying occurred, leading to some textual variations. Nevertheless, none of these variants affect any fundamental or essential Christian doctrine.

Theological Liberalism. A theological system that seeks to reform historic Christianity by incorporating more contemporary ideas of liberal culture. Developments in science, history, psychology, sociology, and biblical interpretation have inspired a move away from traditional views of God, the orthodoxy of Scripture, to a greater acceptance of concepts considered culturally relevant. A significant effect of liberalism is the understanding and acceptance of sin, including how it is defined and what is considered sinful. Human experience is prioritized over Scripture, and truth is seen as relative. There is also an acceptance of other belief systems as equally valid, which leads to a rejection of Jesus being the only path to salvation. Other doctrinal aspects of liberalism include the rejection of Christ's virgin birth, His divinity, His sacrificial death on the cross, and His bodily resurrection.

Tribulation Period. This seven-year timeframe corresponds to Daniel's Seventieth Week, marking the final seven years of this age. Much of the book of Revelation addresses this period, which aligns with the seven-year covenant mentioned in Daniel 9:27. It is also divided into two halves, with the latter half referred to by Jesus as "the great tribulation," a time of distress that has never been and will never be repeated (Matt 24:21). It is during the last half of Daniel's seventieth week that the beast (Antichrist) begins his forty-two-month reign, and when most of the judgments of Revelation occur.

Tribulation Saints. According to dispensationalists and those who believe in a Pretrib rapture, the tribulation saints are seen as a separate group of believers who are left behind after the rapture and come to faith during the tribulation. However, this view mischaracterizes these saints, who are actually some of the most courageous Church saints in history, as they remain loyal to Jesus under the most challenging circumstances. Revelation never depicts this group in any compromised moral light but as faithful, unwavering, connected to heaven, and favored by God. All adverse comments about the so-called tribulation saints are narratives that come from the dispensational camp, who, through their doctrinal tenets, are forced to explain away these valiant saints as being other than the church. Refer to What Happened to the Church and The Mischaracterization of the Tribulation Saints Excursuses.

Tartarus. Translated "hell" is the term that refers to the place of eternal punishment designated for the fallen angels who were cast into hell waiting for judgment day. Jude 6 also speaks about the "angels that did not keep their own domain but abandoned their proper abode" they are bound in chains of darkness in (hell) Tartarus.

U

Universalism (Christian). The belief that all individuals will eventually receive salvation through Christ's atoning sacrifice. Universalism teaches that God is a God of love and that there is no eternal hell punishment. All humans, Satan and fallen angels will be saved and reconciled to God.

V

Victorinus. A bishop and martyr from the third century. Victorinus is recognized for his early commentary on the Book of Revelation and his defense of Christian doctrine during the Roman persecutions.

Z

Zoonotic diseases. Infectious diseases that can be transmitted between animals and humans (e.g., rabies, bird flu). These diseases could play a role in the plagues unleashed during the judgment events specifically of the fourth seal where a source of death will include contact with animals.

ABOUT THE AUTHOR

Dennis James Woods has studied eschatology for over 50 years. His fascination with end times prophecy began in 1976 while serving in the Navy aboard the U.S.S. England, after reading Hal Lindsey's The Late Great Planet Earth. In 1982, after being honorably discharged, he continued to pursue his eschatological interests studying the work of many dispensational authors and teachers.

In 1994, while on staff at the Milwaukee Rescue Mission, Dr. Woods' first book Unlocking the Door: A Key to Biblical Prophecy was published, giving him national exposure. In 1995, he further sharpened his eschatological skills by taking a Revelation course taught by the renowned New Testament scholar Dr. D.A. Carson, at Trinity Evangelical Divinity School, Elmbrook Church, in Brookfield Wisconsin. The specific reason for taking Carson's course was to have his theories that challenged dispensationalism, evaluated by a renowned scholar. Alongside the (A) he received on his final paper, Dr. Carson wrote "very gifted work." In 1996-97, he then corresponded with Dallas Theological Seminary giants Dr. John Walvoord and J. Dwight Pentecost with the expressed intent of challenging their work in support of the pretribulation rapture theory. Dr. Woods' book Revelation Revolution: The Antichrist, Angels, and the Abyss, highlights aspects of these exchanges with Walvoord and Pentecost.

As a minister, Woods has impacted the lives of several members of the clergy by mentoring and advising ministers and pastors. He has also been an advisor and context associate for two doctoral candidates. Dr. Woods has written eight books and has advised, contributed, and edited over fifty books. Today, Dr. Woods is President of Life To Legacy, a thriving independent book publisher having published several titles for various authors nationwide.

Dr. Woods was ordained in 1990, and in 2004, received his Doctor of Biblical Studies from Midwest Theological Institute of Indiana. He is also the pastor of Power of the Holy Ghost Deliverance Ministries, where until 2021, he and his wife Chantia, conducted nursing home ministry for 20 years. For the last 24 years he has taught the PHD radio bible class on WBGX radio Chicago, and since 2018, has hosted the Revelation Revolution Podcast reaching national and international audiences.

Woods has appeared in national magazines such as Ebony, Gospel Today, Today's Christian, and a number of local newspapers through-out the country and television networks such as TBN and the Word Network. He currently serves as the President of Couples Mentoring Youth and Family Services, an innovative social services agency that for the past 22 years has serviced thousands of youths and their families throughout the greater Chicagoland and Northwestern Indiana areas.

For the past 27 years, Dr. Woods has been happily married to his lovely wife Chantia Woods who faithfully serves God and has supported her husband throughout all their ministry and business endeavors. Through their marriage, God has used them to spread faith, hope, and love to countless individuals, through preaching and teaching the Gospel, all for the glory of God.

Send inquiries or engagement requests to:

Revelationcommentary@gmail.com

or

20650 S. Cicero Ave, P.O. Box 1239,
Matteson IL 60443